Published by Leisure Press
A division of Human Kinetics Publishers, Inc.
Box 5076
Champaign, IL 61820

Library of Congress Cataloging in Publication Data

Riess, Steven A.
   The American sporting experience.

   1. Sports—United States—History—Addresses, essays,
lectures. I. Title.
GV583.R53   1984   796′.0973   84-7188
ISBN 0-88011-210-7

THE AMERICAN
SPORTING EXPERIENCE:

A Historical Anthology of Sport in America

Steven A. Riess, Ph.D.

LEISURE PRESS

CHAMPAIGN, ILLINOIS

Table of Contents

Preface

This book has been designed for the general reader interested in the history of American sport, and particularly for college courses focusing on the history of American sport and popular culture. I have taught courses on sport history since 1974, and like many of my colleagues, have been disturbed by the inaccessibility of suitable supplementary readings to assign to my classes. This key problem in the teaching of sport history courses has usually been a major subject of discussion at various meetings of the North American Society for Sport History and other conferences of learned societies which have held sessions focusing on the teaching of American sport. I myself have addressed some of these issues in a brief essay "Sport History in the Classroom," *AHA Perspectives* 20 (Sept. 1982): 29-30. I believe this anthology can be a useful supplement in the classroom when read in conjunction with the principle sport history textbooks, notably, John R. Betts, *American Sporting Heritage: 1850-1950* (Reading, Mass.: Addison-Wesley, 1974); Betty Spears and Richard A. Swanson, *History of Sport and Physical Activity in the United States* (Dubuque: Wm. C. Brown, 1978); John A. Lucas and Ronald A. Smith, *Saga of American Sport* (Philadelphia: Lea & Febiger, 1978); and Benjamin G. Rader, *American Sports: From the Age of Folk Games to the Age of the Spectators* (Englewood Cliffs, N.J.: Prentice Hall, 1983).

The purpose of this anthology is to provide students of American sport history a convenient opportunity to read many of the finest monographs written on the subject as well as to read a variety of primary sources that illustrate significant developments in our sporting heritage. The scholarly study of sport history is still a relatively new field and there have been very few book-length monographs written. Most of the academic research in sport history has appeared as short monographs (learned treatises on one aspect of history). These essays deal in much greater depth with the topic they are covering than can be found in sport history textbooks. The articles in this anthology sweep over the entire span of American history, from the colonial era up through the 1970s. They cover a wide spectrum of subjects, including amateur sport, ethnicity, professional sport, sporting fads, and women in sport. Among the essays are some broad interpretative studies and others which are more narrowly conceived narratives. Reading these essays will hopefully introduce students to the sundry methodologies sport historians have utilized to explain various historical problems. In addition, each of the five sections of the anthology has at least one primary source included among the readings. These are the types of resources that scholars depend upon for their evidence when trying to explain some historical development. By reading these documents, each student has an opportunity to become his own historian, drawing upon the raw materials out of which history is fabricated, to generate explanations to account for certain historical phenomena. A wide variety of primary sources are included in this anthology, including an autobiographical account, a congressional hearing, and a newspaper report. Finally, for students interested in further reading, a bibliography of selected articles and books is appended to each section.

I have been the grateful beneficiary of wise counsel while working on this project. I wish to thank my sport history colleagues Melvin Adelman, Jack Berryman, Lawrence Fielding, Thomas Jable, Alan M. Kraut, Donald Mrozek, Eugene Murdock, Benjamin Rader, Ronald Smith, Nancy L. Struna, and others. They have all made important suggestions which have improved this anthology from my original conception. Special thanks are due my dear wife Tobi for her editorial assistance. I would also like to thank Mary Hamilton, Florence Levy, and Nell Musolf for typing.

Dedication

*To the Community of Scholars
of the North American Society
for Sport History*

The Colonial Experience

Introduction

The culture developed in the American colonies was shaped in part by the new environment, but it was mostly influenced by the cultural baggage the new settlers brought with them from England. Sporting life in the American colonies was a reflection of English attitudes to sport and leisure. In sixteenth century England much of the sporting life was restricted to the nobility who had the discretionary time and money to spend on such activities as hunting and hawking. However the rural masses also had a lot of free time during those seasons of the year when their work load was lightest, as well as on Sundays and the many holidays and festivals dispersed throughout the year. They participated in a variety of traditional sports, including some like football and wrestling, which were rowdy and dangerous.

The matter of leisure became an important social issue in the early seventeenth century because of the growing political power of middle class Puritans, who sought to restrict many forms of traditional recreation. The Puritans were religious reformers who wanted to restore the Church to a pure state, undefiled by either pagan or Roman Catholic influences. They stressed the importance of work and warned about the dangers of idleness. The Puritans were not opposed to all leisure activities, but did expect them to be useful and moral. These reformers criticized gambling and blood sports as sinful and opposed sport on the Sabbath because that day was reserved for the Lord. King James I (1603-1625) opposed the Puritan reforms and feared their increasing power. He sought to maintain his popularity with the English people by supporting their traditional recreations. In response to Lancaster petitioners who were complaining that the local Puritan magistrates were stopping their Sunday recreation, James issued *The Book of Sports* in 1618. In this document he supported many forms of Sunday recreation, with the exception of bowling and animal baiting, sanctioning traditional village pastimes and parish feasts. The document was a political ploy against Puritan clerics and magistrates and helped James curry favor with his subjects. The edict remained in force (amended by his son Charles I in 1633) until 1641, when the Puritan dominated Parliament imposed a rigid Sabbath on the country.

Massachusetts Bay, founded in 1630 as a model community, was the colony most directly influenced by the Puritan philosophy. The colony was run by the "Visible Saints," those members of the Church who were predestined for eternal salvation. Historians used to regard these people as very dour detesters of pleasure. They decried idleness, proscribed Sabbath entertainment, and placed severe constraints on recreation. However, the Puritans in Massachusetts Bay were not opposed to useful and moral sports when played in moderation, such as marksmanship, which improved hunting and defensive capabilities.

The issue of Puritan participation in sport is carefully examined in "Puritans and Sport: The Irretrievable Tide of Change," by Nancy Struna. Professor Struna indicates that there always was a proper time and place for sport in Puritan New England. In this essay, the attitudes and behavior of the Puritans towards sport are examined over a period of three generations. Struna relates the changing pattern of recreation to the developments that occurred in Puritan society. A confident first-generation of colonists gave way to a second-generation of defensive doubters, and by the third generation, leadership in the community had passed from the ministers to the merchants. As this society became increasingly secularized and heterogeneous, interest and participation in sports grew apace.

In the southern colonies, social life and sporting practices differed markedly from Puritan New England. The southern colonists had not come to establish an ideal community, but to obtain wealth. They established a plantation economy based on tobacco. The great planters became the leaders of a highly stratified social order, and they looked to the English gentry as a role model. The southern aristocrats emulated the social behavior of the landed English, and that meant participation in sport, particularly the elite sport of horse racing. The mechanisms by which horse racing became and sustained itself as the preeminent sport of the Virginia elite is described by Timothy Breen in his imaginative essay, "Horses and Gentlemen: The Cultural Significance of Gambling Among the Gentry of Virginia." Anglican southerners enjoyed gambling, which was strictly forbidden in Puritan New England. Breen's main purpose is to analyze the social values of the elite class, and he employs the methods of cultural anthropology, which consist of studying a culture's artifacts to gain an understanding of that society's principal values. He argues that gambling among the Virginia elite reflected their individualism, sense of honor, and materialism. Breen suggests that horse racing was an excellent means for colonial leaders to certify their superior social status (by excluding the lesser sorts) and also deflect potential social conflict through agreements and conventions that were made to facilitate the contests.

'The Kinges' Majesties Declaration Concerning Lawfull Sports.

by the King, James I

"Whereas upon our returne the last yere out of Scotland, we did publish our Pleasure touching the recreations of Our people in those parts under Our hand. For some causes Us thereunto mooving, Wee have thought good to command these Our Directions then given in Lancashire with a few words thereunto added, and most appliable to these parts of Our Realmes, to bee published to all Our Subjects.

'Whereas wee did justly in Our Progresse through Lancashire, rebuke some Puritanes and precise people, and tooke order that the like unlawfull carridge should not bee used by any of them hereafter, in the prohibiting and unlawfull punishing of Our good people for using their lawful recreations, and honest exercises, after the afternoon Sermon or Service: Wee now finde that two sorts of people, wherewith that countrey is much infected (Wee meane Papists and Puritanes), have maliciously traduced and calumniated those Our just and honourable proceedings. And, therefore, lest Our reputation might, upon the one side (though innocently), have some aspersion layd upon it, and that, upon the other part, Our good people in that Countrey be misled by the mistaking and misinterpretation of Our meaning: We have, therefore, thought good hereby to cleare and make Our pleasure to be manifested to all Our good People in those parts.

'It is true that at Our first entry to this Crowne, and Kingdome, We were informed, and that too truely, that Our County of Lancashire abounded more in Popish Recusants than any County of England, and thus hath still continued since, to Our great regreet, with little amendment, save that now of late, in Our last riding through Our said County, Wee find both by the report of the Judges, that there is some amendment now daily beginning, which is no small contentment to Us.

'The report of this growing amendment amongst them, made Us the more sorry, when with Our own eares We heard the general complaint of Our people, that they were debarred from all lawful Recreation, and exercise upon the Sundayes afternoone, after the ending of all Divine Service, which cannot but produce two evils: The one, the hindering of the conversion of many, whom their Priests will take occasion hereby to vexe, persuading that no honest mirth or recreation is lawful or tolerable in Our Religion, which cannot but breed a great discontentment in Our people's hearts, especially of such as are, peradventure, upon the point of turning; The other inconvenience is, that this prohibition barreth the common and meaner sort of people from using such exercises as may make their bodies more able for warre, when Wee, or Our Successors, shall have occasion to use them. And, in place thereof, sets up filthy tiplings and drunkennesse, and breeds a number of idle and discontented speeches in their Ale houses, For when shall the common people have leave to exercise, if not upon the Sundays and holy daies, seeing they must apply their labour, and win their living in all working daies?

'Our expresse pleasure therefore is, that the lawes of Our Kingdome, and Canons of Our Church be as well observed in that Countie, as in all other places of this Our Kingdome. And on the other part, that no lawfull Recreation shall bee barred to Our good People, which shall not tend to the breach of our aforesayd Lawes, and Canons of our Church: which, to expresse more particularly, Our pleasure is, That the Bishop, and all other inferiour Churchmen, and Churchwardens, shall, for their parts, bee carefull and diligent, both to instruct the ignorant, and convince and reforme them that are misled in Religion, presenting them that will not conform themselves, but obstinately stand out, to our Judges and Justices, Whom We likewise command to put the Law in due execution against them.

'Our pleasure therefore is, That the Bishop of that Diocesse take the like straight order with all the Puritanes and Precisians within the same, either constraining them to conform themselves, or to leave the County according to the Lawes of Our Kingdome, and Canons of our Church, and so to strike equally on both hands, against the contemners of our Authority, and adversaries of Our Church. And as for Our good people's lawfull Recreation, Our pleasure likewise is, Our good people be not disturbed, letted, or discouraged from any lawfull recreation, Such as dancing, either of men or women, Archery for men, leaping, vaulting, or any other such harmlesse Recreation, nor from having of May Games, Whitson Ales, and Morris-dances, and the setting up of Maypoles, and other sports therewith used, so as the same be had in due and convenient time, without impediment or neglect of Divine Service: And that women shall have leave to carry rushes to the Church for the decoring of it, according to their old custome. But withall we doe here account still as prohibited all unlawfull games to bee used upon Sundayes onely, as Beare and Bullbaitings, Interludes, and at all times, in the meaner sort of people, by Law prohibited, Bowling: And likewise we barre from this benefite and liberty, all such knowne Recusants, either men or women, as will abstaine from comming to Church or Divine Service, that will not first come to the Church and serve God: Prohibiting, in like sort, the said Recreations to any that, though conform in Religion, are not present in the Church at the Service of God, before their going to the said Recreations.

'Our pleasure likewise is That they to whom it belongeth in Office, shall present and sharpely punish all such as in abuse of this Our liberty, will use these exercises before the ends of all Divine Services for that day. And we likewise straightly command, that every person shall resort to his owne Parish Church to hear Divine Service, and each Parish by itselfe to use the said Recreation after Divine Service.

'Prohibiting likewise any offensive weapons to bee carried or used in the said times of Recreations, And Our pleasure is That this, Our Declaration, shall bee published by order from the Bishop of the Diocesse, through all the Parish Churches, and that both Our Judges of Our Circuit, and Our Judges of Our Peace be informed thereof.

'Given at Our Mannour of Greenwich, the foure and twentieth day of May, in the sixteenth yeere of Our Raigne of England, France and Ireland, and of Scotland the one and fiftieth."

Puritans and Sport: The Irretrievable Tide of Change

by Nancy Struna

Year after year the historical, or hysterical, battle has raged over the New England Puritans and their sport. Did they, or did they not sport? Did they forbid others within society to sport? Upon what bases did they accept or reject sport? To answer such questions, historians have frequently relied upon evidence provided by certain individuals who lived at distinct times within the colonial period. Newspapers, legal sources, and sermons, as well, have rendered valuable, if limited, information.

Too often, however, these historians have insufficiently considered the perspective of the sources. They have ignored or underrated the importance of chronology and the role in which his society had cast that individual. Thus, historians may have ascertained the scope of participation of selected individuals within Puritan society, and they may have isolated the attitudes toward sport of discrete portions of the population. They have not, however, produced a comprehensive analysis of sport reflecting the dynamic totality of Puritan society. In fact, the failure to acknowledge the perspective of the evidence has frequently obscured the changes evident in the course of Puritan society, particularly in light of the vast research of the last two decades detailing the transformation of that society in America.

A developmental examination of sport within the first century of Puritan society in Massachusetts Bay can perhaps more adequately provide the necessary societal perspective. In Massachusetts Bay, the initial Puritan enterprise in the new world, three generations appeared in the course of the first one hundred years, 1630-1730.

Nancy Struna is Assistant Professor, Department of Physical Education, University of Maryland.

From Nancy Struna, "Puritans and Sports: The Irretrievable Tide of Change," Journal of Sport History 4 (Spring 1977): 1-21. Copyright © 1977 by the North American Society for Sport History. Reprinted with permission.

During this century a transformation occurred within the value system as structured and interpreted by those Puritans. Initiated as a Puritan attempt to preserve the visible church, the colonial enterprise coalesced as a mercantile outpost of the British empire.[1]

As a behavioral form defined in terms of the seventeenth century,[2] *sport becomes a vehicle for the observation of changes in societal attitudes and institutions.* Thus, the habits of participation and attitudes in Massachusetts Bay achieve greater clarity as these emerge within the context of that dynamic society, and as they represent similarities and differences among three generations.

The Plan for Society, 1630-1730

The initial generation of Puritans who settled in Massachusetts Bay resolved to establish a society dedicated to the preservation of the visible church and bound by a philosophy which clearly defined man's role and niche in the world. As descendants of Adam, the Puritans recognized themselves as corrupt men who had been given a second chance to achieve salvation. To escape the experiences of the disorderly, ungodly world, the Puritans established a "city upon a hill" in Massachusetts Bay.[3] John Winthrop, the first governor of the Massachusetts Bay Company in the new world, identified for his colonists the values which God had ordained for all his creations. Heirarchy, inequality, mutability, variety, and order were all observable in nature.[4] Conformity to the rest of God's works demanded the implanting of these values in society. Only through self-consciousness of one's emotions and attitudes toward behavior could a Puritan hope to entertain a godly mind.[5]

A few years before the journey to New England, John Downame advised his congregation of the lifetime service required by God and, though possibly inadvertently, of the place that sport might hold in the Puritan value system:

> Wee must constantly and continually, in everything, and at everytime, perform service unto God in all our actions and throughout our whole course and conversation...in the meanest duties of the basest calling, yea even in our eating and drinking, lawful sports and recreations, when as wee doe them in faith.[6]

Sport might thus be as mutually beneficial to man as eating and drinking, especially if pursued in lawful forms and attentive to order. In a later publication Downame emphasized the necessity of "due recreation." He acknowledged the fatigue and dissatisfaction bred by dull constance in one's calling and encouraged moderate participation in ". . . allowable Sports as best fit with mens severall dispositions for their comfort and refreshing."[7] Downame suggested, as well, that sport was a dichotomous concept, implying both conformance and nonconformance to the Puritan value system.

About the same time in Massachusetts Bay, Winthrop struggled with the occurrence of sport in his life:

When I had some tyme abstained from suche worldly delights as my heart most desired, I grewe melancholick and uncomfortable, for I had been more careful to refraine from an outward conversation in the world, than to keepe the love of the world out of my heart, or to uphold my conversation in heaven... I grewe unto a great dullnesse and discontent: which being at last perceived, I examined my heart, and findinge it needfull to recreate my minde with some outward recreation, I yielded unto it, and by a moderate exercise herein was much refreshed...[8]

Abstention had created disorder in Winthrop's life; melancholy and discomfort had 'detracted from his attention to God. Yet to ensnare his "heart so farre in worldly delights" forced him to cool "the graces of the spirit by them."[9]

Moderation, Downame had called the key to order in one's life. Winthrop discovered a similar sense of sobriety when "outward recreation" was necessary. The mind dominated God's gifts to man, but activities of the body might refresh an overworked mind. The maintenance of order necessitated mutual operations between mind and body. Moderation in sport, in its recreative sense, provided a balancing factor ordained by God.

Unfortunately for the reputation of sport, not all of the Puritan immigrants shared Winthrop's conceptions of values. Even as the earliest settlers embarked from English shores, the Reverend John White of Dorchester noted a diversity present among the voyagers:

As it were absurd to conceive they have all one minde, so were it ridiculous to imagine they have all one scope. Necessitie may presse some; Noveltie draw on others, hopes of gaine in time to come may prevaile with a third sort; but the most and most sincere and godly part have advancement of the Gospel for their maine scope I am confident...[10]

Members of the Company realized that men were corrupt and that few, if any, could adhere to the strict behavioral code every moment of his life. To this end the Puritans employed the civil government, wherein elected magistrates covenanted with freeholding church members to govern according to "God's laws and man's."[11] The people had the liberty to do what was good, just and honest, as exemplified by right thinking men.

As the epitome of right thinking men and guardians of the churches, the magistrates had to insure the sanctity of the Sabbath. The Court of Assistants in 1630 ordered that John Baker "...shalbe whipped for shooteing att fowle on the Sabbath day."[12] The implication is that the Court punished Baker for his inattention to the Sabbath, rather than for his fowling. Within five years all person absent from church meetings faced fines or imprisonment.[13] The records indicate that church absentees engaged in sport less frequently than they drank, labored unnecessarily, or traveled. Sport apparently maintained its position in the delicate hierarchy on the Sabbath.

Magistrates similarly restricted sport, or more precisely the occasion for sport, when this detracted from the economic success of the colony and social order. Perhaps the underlying theme of the first generation was the promotion of the public good. Thomas Hooker warned against the designs and devices of individuals whose selfish activities would precipitate "the distraction and desolation of the whole" and "prejudice the publike good."[14] In a society without institutions to care for the poor, the criminals, and other societal malcontents, the magistrates had to prevent such unstabilizing germs, rather than wait to treat the products.

Initially the magistrates assumed that the family, the cornerstone of society since Biblical times, would establish and maintain social order. To the master reverted the responsibilities of maintaining a financially successful calling and insuring proper behavior.

When heads of families failed in their duties, the General Court enacted legislation providing for the disposition of the poor, and for constables to "search after all manner of gaming, singing and dancing" and "disordered meetings" in private residences.[15] Magistrates regulated occasions for vast expense of money and time and those conducive to disorderly conduct. They apparently perceived that gaming with cards, dice, or tables threatened the financial security of both individuals and colony, and they placed the burden of responsibility predominantly upon the family head.[16]

In many respects the inns and common houses of entertainment disrupted the orderly arrangement of society. Though necessary for the housing of travelers, these houses encountered rigid surveillance of visitor tenure, volume and price of liquors and tobacco, and activities permitted on the premises. The General Court scrutinized the taverns primarily because:

...it hath appeared unto this court, upon many sad complaints, that much drunkenness, wast of the good creatures of God, mispence of precious time, & other disorders have frequently fallen out in the inns...whereby God is much dishonored, the profession of religion repoched, & the welfare of this comonwealth greatly impaired, & the true use of such houses (being the necessary releefe of travellers) subverted...[17]

Owners who disregarded these laws lost their licenses, while offenders faced fines and corporal punishment.

Since people could not legally enjoy gaming in their own residences, apparently some traveled to the inns for that opportunity. Not until 1647 did the General Court outlaw shovelboard, and shortly after bowling and gaming in general, "...whereby much precious time is spent unfruitfully, & much wast of wine & beare occasioned thereby..."[18]   The delay in banning these games, as well as the emphasis on unprofitability and drunkenness, suggest that the magistrates did not intend to denounce the nature of the game, but rather to attack overspending and inebriation.

Aside from the desire, in varying degrees, for economic stability and order in society, sport reflected other values and habits of Puritan life. In 1639 the first military company organized and depended upon physical exercise, marksmanship and athletic contests, and mock battles as the core of the training day.[19] Competitive matches emerged as tests of skill.

Military leaders sometimes restricted other occasions for sport. Near Salem in 1636, three men vacated their posts to go fowling. Instead of being happily diverted by birds, they fell prey to lurking Indians. Only one man returned to face the wrath of the lieutenant whose orders had been countered.[20]

Sport provided a means by which some men could support both the hierarchical composition of society and the public welfare. On the *Arbella* Winthrop had announced that "...in all times some must be rich, some poor; some high and eminent in power and dignity; others mean and in subjection."[21] In the first decade alone two men seemingly tried to replicate the English game preserve. In 1632 John Perkins reserved two areas in which he could "...take Fowle with netts."[22] From the town of Salem in 1639, Emmanuell Downing received five hundred acres for the ". . . takeing wild foule by way of duck coy." The General Court, ". . . being desiros to encourage . . . such designs as to tend to publike good . . .," forbade all others to shoot within a half mile of the pond.[23]

The experience of Downing and Perkins suggest that sport provided some occasions for society to focus upon the individual, especially when the needs of the individual and the community coincided. By 1641 the rights of freemen appeared printed as the Body of Liberties. One of the articles insured householders of their rights to fish and fowl for sport or livelihood within the limits of their towns.[24] Six years later concerns for horses as property and the rights of their owners instigated a law against "...a very evill practice of some disordered persons . . .who do use to take other mens horses . . .& ride them at their pleasure. . ."[25] This did not ban horseracing, and was only intended to protect the rights of horseowners.

Thus, in the first two decades of Puritan life in Massachusetts Bay, the occurrence of sport was very real, reflecting both values and diversity within that society. Frequently the occasions for sport detracted from societal values, at least as conceived of by magistrates. Magistrates sought to limit these occasions and, in effect, may have restricted participation. Yet, when Samuel Maverick described Boston, he noted that its streets were lined with "...good shopps well furnished with all kinds of merchandize..." and "...full of Girles and Boys sporting up and down, with a continued concourse of people."[26]

Imposed Homogeneity, 1650-1690

Maverick's approving comments on the progress of society do not in any way predict the crisis which befell the Puritans after mid century. As members of the second generation came of age, fewer of them joined the congregations. In their failure either to experience or relate conversion experiences and thus become baptized members, they threatened the original mission of the colony to preserve the church. Ministers and magistrates reacting to the decline in membership, which reached a record low in the 1650's and continued through the 1680's, transformed their mission into one of preserving an entire people.[27] They isolated groups within society and attacked heterogeneous attitudes. In a miscalculated effort to resurrect the supposedly homogeneous society of the first generation, they succeeded only in arousing hostility, some guilt, and greater diversity.

Ministers believed that the key to the survival of the pure church lay within the grasp of the children. If the children failed in their demonstrations of conversion, God would vent his wrath upon the entire plantation. Magistrates, by virtue of their guardianship of the churches, ordered all family masters and town officials to prevent:

> ... soundry abuses and misdemeanors, comitted by soundry persons of the Lords day, not only by children playing in the streetes and other places, but by youths, majds and other persons, both straungers and others, uncivily walking the streets and feilds, travailing from toune to toune, goinjg on shipboard, frequenting common howses and other places to drincke, sport and otherwise mispend that pretjous tyme ... [28]

Youths over the age of fourteen and strangers, " ... the reputed great provokers of the high displeasure of Almighty God," apparently seized upon sport and other socializing activities as alternatives to Sabbath solitude.

The General Court decried the youths who took the " ... liberty to walke & sporte themselves in the streets or feilds ... ", disturbed the religious preparations of others, and " ... too frequently repajre to publique houses of entertainment & there sitt drincking; ... [29] Apparently the Court sought to enforce a rigid homogeneity within a society which had already become diverse. In an effort to preserve the efficacy of the congregations, the Court legislated against religious disturbances and excessive drinking. Many people did not carefully discriminate places or times for their participation, at a time when the colony's leaders had chosen to preserve the plantation from the fire and brimstone of God.

One must realize, however, that within society a common acceptable focus on sport must have existed. Without a sporting vernacular and some recognized values, there would have been no basis for the apparent divisions which arose. John Cotton and Increase Mather concurred that one's perspective determined the efficacy of the activity.[30] In nearly the same breath in which he denounced gaming, the second generation Mather admitted that "For a Christian to use Recreation is very lawful, and in some cases a great Duty . . . "[31]

Ministers generally applied to sport the dictates of service to God. Some Puritans observed that sport provided desirable opportunities for socialization, for military preparedness, or for recreation and catharsis. Whether in London or Boston, Samuel Sewall swam, fished, and recognized bowling greens.[32] In 1679 John Richardson exhorted the militia men to attain greater skill:

Victory is the Mark that skill aims at; Skill of hand, Strength of body, & Courage of mind do make a compleat Champion.[33]

Harvard College officials even allotted a minimum two and one-half hours for sport among their students after 1655.[34]

A man relaxed and refreshed through sport could function more efficiently in his calling. If this calling fulfilled the needs of the community, the benefit to all was obvious. Puritans continued to respond to the communal idea so obvious during the first twenty years in Massachusetts Bay. However, the degree of commitment to that response varied. Whereas once Winthrop had to judge only for himself and record in his own diary how much sport he might enjoy, now Cotton defined and printed for others similar limitations.[35] Ministers at training days seemingly cajolled, or at least challenged, recruits to strive for skills and to distinguish the play of boys from that of men.[36] Yet, no longer did they act and speak simply to vindicate their own actions. They could not stamp out the heterogeneous attitudes toward sport. Even the Reverend Peter Thatcher of Milton purchased "a pack of ninepins and bowle'."[38] Soldiers on active duty during King Philip's War in 1675 lost their arms while gaming.[39]

Those who attempted to dictate the acceptable values of sport probably did not fear that men would sport, but rather certain occasions for sport and the aftermath of some of these. The laws and sermons of the second generation anticipated God's wrath, for the most part, because of the largely misunderstood decline in church membership. By instilling order, a sense of conforming order ascertained by more and more artificial officers and institutions, these leaders hoped to return their people to the path of God. The gradual increase in population, Indian threats to a more distant frontier, and vacillating periods of economic expansion and contraction presented new problems to second generation leaders.

In an attempt to enforce uniformity, Harvard College had actually reacted in a positive sense by permitting sport on campus and not allowing students to venture off campus.[40] Magistrates, however, did not so readily solve the problems of filling the churches and preserving the communities. Taverns continually irritated those who tried to order society. Leaders among the second generation became ever more concerned about the opportunities these taverns provided. Shuffleboard and bowling had already become forbidden, at least partly because of the gaming element. In 1651 the General Court forbade dancing at weddings in taverns because " . . . there are many abuses and disorders by dancing in ordinaryes . . ."[41]

It is quite possible that dancing itself was not the target of the Court. John Cotton and, later, Increase Mather, accepted dance, although Cotton favored its mixed form, while Mather, unmixed.[42] The abuses and disorders may, in fact, have arisen not from dancing but from the assemblage of a crowd, the containment of which posed great problems for the few constables and selectmen. Dancing and drinking, when enjoyed together, enabled people to perpetrate actions which threatened the lives around them and elicited God's wrath.

The Essex County Court arrested Thomas Wheeler in 1653 for " . . . profane and foolish dancing; singing and wanton speeches, probably being drunk . . . "[43] Wheeler's crime actually lay in his "speakinge sinfull and reprochfull speeches" against Reverend Corbett of Lynn. His imbibing had probably supplied the impetus for "profane dancing." The court records are replete with cases involving drunkenness, fornication, and lewd behaviors, not with dancing.

On other occasions as well, sport constituted a threat to the safety of the colonists and to the order of society in general. In Boston the selectmen and the council reacted to the dangers of foot-ball:

Forasmuch as sundry complaints are made that several persons have received hurt by boys and young men playing at football in the streets, these are therefore to enjoin that none be found at that game in any of the streets, lanes, or enclosures of this town, under penalty of twenty shillings for every such offense.[44]

By 1662 cases of "violent rideing in the streets" of Boston occurred so frequently that the General Court railed against the effect of " . . . indaingering the bodies and lives of many persons . . ."[45] Apparently, by 1672, the danger had not abated. Coupled with the economic disasters attendant upon horse racing for money, the Court of Assistants cited the "Hazard of their limbs and lives" as reasons for refusing to permit this sport within four miles of any town.[46]

Men carrying cocks offered an exciting pastime for some Bostonians. Samuel Sewall described one such incident:

Jos. Maylem carries a Cock at his back, with a Bell in 's hand, in the Main Street; several follow him blindfolded, underpretence of striking him or 's cock, with great cartships strike passengers, and make great disturbance.[47]

Judge Sewall ordered the constables to " ... take effectual care to suppress and dissipate all unlawful Assemblies or tumultuous gatherings ... " arising from " ... Shailing or throwing at Cocks and such like Disorders, tending to the disturbance of their Magesties liege People, and breach of the peace."[48] Governor Bradford himself signed the order. Though the magistrates uttered not a word against cock scaling itself, they condemned the dangers to the community inherent in the situation.

Perhaps the concept of gaming most adequately represents the diversity in attitude present within Puritan culture. During the first twenty years of settlement, gaming emerged as an illegal activity, primarily as a result of economic necessity. After 1650 gaming seemingly attracted more numerous proponents and opponents.

Concurrent with the unfavorable decline in church membership, John Cotton pictured the enmity of religion to card games. Since the distribution of cards lay in the hands of God, he argued " ... to appeal to him and his providence for dispensing these ludicra, seemeth ... a taking of God's name in vain."[49] Nearly thirty years later, Increase Mather deplored the lottery even more adamantly:

Now a Lot is a serious thing not to be trifled with; the Scripture saith not only (as some would have it) of Extraordinary Lots, but of a Lot in general, that the whole Disposing (or Judgement) thereof is of the Lord ... He that makes use of a Lot, wholly commits his affair to a Superior Cause than either nature or art, therefore unto God. But this ought not to be done in a Sportful Lusory way.[50]

Mather's son, Cotton, while deploring the further fallen state of young people, even more viciously attacked the "Scandalous Games of Lottery."[51]

The ministers' outcries must have fallen on many deaf ears. In 1662 the Pynchon Court heard testimony from John Henryson who, along with five others, played cards because " ... I was willing to have recreation for my wife to drive away melancholy." He admitted that " ... he was willing to do anything when his wife was ill to make her merry."[52] Paul Parker, a two time gamester, was finally convicted for " ... being a very ill example to the youth..."[53]

By 1670 the General Court noted the great increase in gaming and issued yet another law on the basis that:

Whereas the great sin of gaming increaseth with in this jurisdiction to the great dishonour of God, corrupting of youth & expending of much pretjous time & estate ... [54]

Into the preamble of this law, the Court bound all the major concerns of the colony's leaders: sin, wayward or less than ideal youth, and economy, both of time and money.

It is quite possible that gaming was more popular and widespread than the General Court would have liked to have believed. Both civil and military personnel continued to play cards. Masters, innkeepers, and servants alike played cards and used dice.[55] Nor did the Court succeed in halting the importation and sale of devices for gaming. In a single court session in Suffolk County, five ships inventoried packs of cards sold for three shillings apiece.[56]

Two primary factors appeared to negate, or at least limit, the effectiveness of the laws and the desired conformity to first generation values. The first of these was the declining ability of the family to instill discipline and thus preserve social order. To offset this decline, magistrates had to instill more artificial institutions and officers to carry out what were once family responsibilities. By 1655 the General Court had established houses of correction.[57] It empowered constables and selectmen to " . . . take notice of common coasters, unprofitable fowlers, and other idle persons . . .", as well as to restrain the "Unreverent carriage and behavior of divers young persons."[58] Within the next twenty years tithingmen replaced the heads of families as executors of Sabbath discipline and, shortly thereafter, could interfere in all family disorders.[59] The poor, the unbridled, and the indolent faced rehabilitation within the militia, jails, homes of esteemed families, and minor alms houses.[60]

The second emanated from inconsistencies within the calling doctrine and stewardship of wealth concept. Some Puritans envisioned financial gain to be derived from sporting ventures. Yet the speculation involved in gaming or providing dancing lessons was not recognized by the authorities as a legitimate and fruitful economic venture. As long as men with economic success sat in judgment of the colony, they ruled against the elements of chance in sport, its apparent unprofitability, and disorder. At least two dancing masters left Boston in a state of financial insolvency, while a tavern owner was prevented from renting a room to a man "to shew tricks in."[61]

The second generation society, at least the Puritan leaders among them, did not preserve a Christian utopia in Massachusetts Bay, nor did they succeed in impressing a homogeneous character upon the ruled. By singling out distinct groups, the ministers marked an actual fragmentation in society. Laws involving sport illustrate the merging of concerns for sin, economy, and order.

For many members of society, sport retained much of its original essence. Sport provided diversion, recreation, competitive skill training, and healthful exercise. Henryson even rationalized that an illegal sporting activity might indeed provide the same essential benefits. Others began to envision economic opportunities.

The Fracturing of Society, 1690-1730

As the second generation merged with the third, this fragmenting process continued. A new English administration and interference with Massachusetts introduced several variables into the predominantly Puritan culture of Massachusetts. More direct colonial contact with England and greater proximity to British society at home and abroad helped to diversify colonial society.[62] As a result of both external and internal factors, Massachusetts society generated a greater degree of attitudinal and role change than it ever had previously. Sport was both affected by and reflected this transformation. Opportunities for the recreational and economic functions of sport increased, while positive and negative attitudes solidified. Newspaper advertisements of sporting events appeared and laws regulating sport as a behavior declined in frequency.

After 1690 external factors enhanced the religious fluctuations within Massachusetts. In the aftermath of the Glorious Revolution, the English parliament had passed the Act of Toleration. To the Anglican population and other sects in Massachusetts, coupled with a franchise based on financial qualifications, this meant greater freedom from Puritan religious restraint. Ministers reacted intensely to their loss of domination and to the failures of their own congregation members to exhibit conversion experiences. The treatment of sport by the ministers illustrates their confused and frequently reactionary opinions and attitudes.

At militia trainings, always a natural forum with an isolated audience, ministers frequently used metaphors of sport to praise, inspire, and harangue the men. The Christian soldier, who vigilantly protected his god and his society, warranted great praise. "Indeed men of Martial Spirits and Skill ought to be Encouraged. These Trainings and Exercises are very commendable . . ." , emphasized Peter Thatcher.[63] Benjamin Wadsworth cited biblical injunctions and maneuvers for artillery men and grenadiers. More importantly, however, Boone differentiated between classes in society. He warned the private soldier to avoid drunkenness and gaming, but to gentlemen and commanders he spoke in terms of "healthful Exercise," so becoming to their stations in life.[65]

Joseph Belcher reminded his listeners of the spiritual purpose of one's calling. He urged his comrades to battle effectively, to win the prize, and to obtain victory, and he portrayed the Apostle Paul as the epitome of the ultimate victor in heaven. Possibly Belcher believed that the utilization of talent and training for success in one's particular calling had finally superseded the societal goal of unity and the attainment of heaven. "You are not called to quit your pleasures, only change the objects of them," Belcher advised the militia.[66]

The militia sermons and attitudes toward training days represent a mingling of concerns. At times the ministers appeared as a conservative force trying to revitalize the essence of community with God as the focus. Sport was useful to them as a medium for instilling discipline, cooperation, and the will to struggle. Almost simultaneously however, they recognized other, more personal interpretations of the same elements which could and did exist. The ministers helped to consummate a class society by speaking to gentlemen in a different tone than to others. They advocated rational thought and efficiency of body, mind, and spirit.[67]

The minister's treatment of the family and children is similarly reflective of the struggle to accommodate the style of a fluctuating society to the values of their fathers and grandfathers. For some, such as Cotton Mather and Benjamin Wadsworth, sport provided a medium through which they could regulate and educate their children. Mather even translated sporting phrases into Latin for his son Sam to study.[68]

The society did recognize that childhood represented a stage in maturity distinct from that of youth or adulthood. Benjamin Wadsworth urged parents to distinguish between the play of children and that of youth.[69] Henry Gibbs, by 1727, noted that too many parents cared more for the worldly circumstances of their children than for their spiritual fulfillment, just as the former did for themselves.[70]

In 1709 Increase Mather authored a simmering "Advice to a Young Man" distinguishing between lawful, moderate sporting and the indulgence in "sinful sports and pastimes."[71] William Cooper published an entire sermon dedicated to "How and Why Young People Should Cleanse Their Way," while Thomas Foxcroft admonished impenitent youth to ". . . abandon evil Company, Forsake the foolish, and live."[72] Daniel Lewes vigorously condemned the "waste" among the young and ministered to youth as an impersonal state of being, an "it."[73]

The impersonality and harsh tones present within Lewes' sermon seem to indicate a more complete ministerial isolation from society. Rather than to comply with the values of a changing society, many of these ministers chose to follow the paths established by predecessors. They could not meet the needs of the society by developing constructive sermons, so they splintered the flock into distinct groups and criticized those. Azariah Mather attacked travelers and sailors who, he believed, refused to observe the sanctity of the Sabbath when absent from Massachusetts.[74] Cotton Mather, as well, viewed returning seamen as being detrimental to the moral code which the ministers advocated.[75]

As had been the practice of their fathers and grandfathers, the ministers after 1690 turned to magistrates for legitimate support of their position on behavior. The General Court retained its duty to protect the churches throughout the seventeenth century and well into the eighteenth. "An Act for the better Observation and Keeping the Lords-Day," published a minimum of four times between 1692 and 1727, prohibited people from engaging in any unnecessary aspects of their ordinary callings, to travel, or to ". . . use any Game, Sport, Play or Recreation."[76]

The frequency with which this law appeared, the appearance of penalties for second offenders in 1716, and the additions of proscribed activities suggest, among other ideas, that the laws were disobeyed, ignored, or unknown. These factors may help to explain the continuous appearance of lotteries, sport, and drinking at taverns.

By 1719 the General Court concluded that the popularity of private lotteries, "Mischievous and Unlawful Games," had increased among those who would least afford these diversions. The Court illegalized all private lotteries because:

. . . the Children and Servants of Several Gentlemen, Merchants, and Traders and other unwary People have been drawn into a vain and foolish Expence of Money, which tends to the utter Ruin and Impoverishment of many Families, and is to the Raproach of this Government, and against the Common Good, Trade, Welfare and Peace of the Province.[77]

While public lotteries may have promoted the public welfare, private lotteries did not. Yet, continue they did. Three months after the law's passage, Samuel Sewall entered in his diary confirmation of four newspaper advertisements for private lotteries.[78]

Inns and taverns continued to be closely scrutinized by the General Court. To limit incentives for people to misspend or misuse time and money, the magistrates prohibited ". . . Dice, Cards, Tables, Bowles, Shuffleboard, Billiards, Coyts, Cales, Logats, or any implements used in Gaming."[79] Unfortunately for the gamesters, who now bore the brunt of fines and punishment, many could not bear the expense of paupers. Magistrates legislated against the root causes of poverty and indolence and assured the colonists that if they did not make the proper choices, the choices would be made for them.

This idea of proper choices permeated society and became a very personal consideration when one's safety became endangered. Citizens of Boston, in reacting to the bodily harm inflicted by young boys sporting in the streets, restricted opportunities for throwing footballs, squibs, snowballs, and long bullets. Throwing the long bullet, made of iron, lead, brass, wood, or stone, resulted in ". . . divers Inconveniencies and may be of the Pernicious Consequence . . ."[80]

The disapproval of foot-ball seems to relate directly to the site of its occurrence. Away from the confines of town streets and yards, players presumably did not endanger spectators or passersby. John Dunton, an English traveler, described the circumstances of such a game in Rowley:

> . . . there was that day a great game of Foot-ball to be play'd with
> their feet, which I thought was very odd; but it was upon a broad
> Sandy Shoar, free from stones, which made it more easy. Neither
> were they so apt to trip up one anothers heels and quarrel, as I
> have seen 'em in England.[81]

The players maintained a sense of fair, competitive play and
apparently had chosen to disallow any raucous behavior.

Apparently public recalcitrance to other sport forms diminished
as some patrons of horse racing, bear baiting, and billiards removed
these from the streets and taverns.[82] Particularly after 1715,
newspapers advertised rules, weights, wagers, and prizes, often to
"gentlemen and others." The designs of racing competition became
increasingly complex, as exemplified by this notice in the *Boston
Gazette* in 1725:

> This is to give notice to all gentlemen and others that there is to be
> Thirty Pounds in Money run for . . . by Six Horses, Mares or
> Geldings, Two miles . . . to carry 9 stone Weight, the Standard to
> be 14 hands high . . . Each one that Runs to have their Number
> from 1 to 6, to be drawn, and to run by 2 . . . , the 3 first Horses to
> run a second Heat . . .[83]

The colonists who wrote and read this and other notices
apparently knew how to organize sporting events and understood a
concept of competition. Horses of fairly equal stature frequently ran
for symbols of wealth and esteem, not merely for money purses. The
prize signified the achievement of status for a single winner, an
individual who relied upon his own talents to his own benefit rather
than always for that of the community.

Some members of the third generation seized the opportunities
provided by sport among the people to achieve financial gain in
legitimate business ventures. Merchants in Salem and Boston
stocked children's playthings, at times supplied by privateers.[84]
Dancing masters taught for fees in Boston, where the popularity of
dancing and balls among British officials probably helped to sway
public opinion in their favor.[85] Cabinet makers fashioned card tables
for sale to wealthy colonists, as indicated in estate inventories.[86] A
farmer sold his orchard in 1712 to the Harvard College Corporation,
which designated the land as ". . . a place of recreation and
exercise for the scholars."[67]

A 1714 advertisement in the *Boston Newsletter* of a bowling
green includes several intriguing comments about the society of that
day. Daniel Stevens, the owner of the British Coffee House, invited
men according to their position in society, ". . . all Gentlemen,
Merchants, and others, that have a mind to Recreate themselves,
shall be accomodated . . ."[88] By accommodating these men
Stevens apparently sought to provide a service, in the form of
recreation, to three distinct and recognized social groupings. Further,

as the owner of the British Coffee House, Stevens was not bound by laws regulating sporting activities in inns or taverns. Either the laws did not apply to coffee houses, or they were simply ineffective.

The Stevens' case is only one of many that reveals how far in practice the third generation had strayed from the ideal values established by the first. Economic success and social position, rather than the authority of God, reckoned the hierarchical organization of society. Individual initiative and a worldly competitive spirit replaced the older sense of mutuality, as the welfare of the individual superseded that of the community in many instances. Rational thought, particularly in matters of economic stability and personal safety, not revelation, helped to transform the concept of order. Men relied upon themselves rather than God for the plan of society.

Even the ministers could not stem the tide of change. Verbal vengeance became their weapon against practices which they did not completely understand or for which they assumed primarily negative consequences. To them the contraction of family responsibilities in maintaining order meant only that the family unit ministers realized that this transformation within the family might actually produce a more stable one, with members bound by love rather than fear.

Both Puritans and non-Puritans within the first century in Massachusetts Bay did sport and, undoubtedly, with increasing frequency as the century progressed. Several primary factors have arisen to at least partially explain this phenomenon. Perhaps the most obvious is that the Puritans were human and, as such, they demanded refreshment, relaxation, socialization, and competition, all of which sport provided. Secondly, is the fact that from the onset of the colony the immigrants never formed a uniform society, either in purpose or in action. Consequently, the interpretations of values and social mores varied widely among those possessing authority and those without such. Time and money served both God and men; however, the use of such by men did not always conform to religious dictates or civil enactments. What was idleness to some apparently represented the economic use of time to others.

Throughout this century the initially Puritan-oriented society diversified ever further. Non-Puritan immigrants speeded changes within towns and countryside. Massachusetts gradually turned to the world, especially to that of mercantile Britain. The occasions for sport now fit the needs of the world of Daniel Stevens rather than that of John Winthrop.

Thus, the enigmatic status of sport in Puritan society emerges slightly less puzzling when viewed in the perspective of the first century society in Massachusetts Bay. Diverse sporting habits and attitudes existed because of the demands placed on sport and the roles devised for sport by the Puritans themselves. As a behavioral form, sport mirrored developments within Massachusetts Bay and, in turn, was affected by the transformation and diversification of that society. Individuals sported and groups sported, but only in the context of the entire society do their activities and attitudes begin to fit as pieces of an interlocking puzzle.

Footnotes

[1]Particular treatments of the change in Puritan society to which one should refer include: Paul Conkin, *Puritans and Pragmatists* (New York: Dodd, Mead and Company, 1968); Stephen Foster, *Their Solitary Way: The Puritan Social Ethic in the First Century of Settlement in New England* (New Haven: Yale University Press, 1971); David Hawke, *The Colonial Experience* (New York: The Bobbs-Merrill Company, 1966); Kenneth Lockridge, *A New England Town: The First One Hundred Years* (New York: W.W. Norton and Company, 1970); Robert Middlekauff, *The Mathers: Three Generations of Puritan Intellectuals, 1597-1728* (New York: Oxford University Press, 1971); Darrett B. Rutman, *Winthrop's Boston: Portrait of a Puritan Town* (New York: W.W. Norton and Company, 1972); Gary Warden, *Boston, 1689-1776* (Boston: Little, Brown and Company, 1970); and Larzar Ziff, *Puritanism in America* (New York: Viking Press, 1973).

[2]Sir John Murray *Oxford English Dictionary,* reprint of *New English Dictionary* (Oxford: Clarendon Press, 1933), X, 665-667. Broadly stated in seventeenth century terms, sport connotes: (1) a pleasant pastime; entertainment or amusement; recreation, diversion; (2) to amuse, entertain, or recreate oneself, especially by active exercise in the open air; to take part in some game or play; to frolic or gambol; (3) to deal with in a light or trifling way. Further limitations on the term appear within the literature of the Puritans.

[3]John Winthrop, "Modell of Christian Charity," in *Winthrop Papers* (6 vols. Boston: Massachusetts Historical Society, 1929-1947), II, 295.

[4]*Ibid.,* 282-283.

[5]Robert Middlekauff, *op. cit.,* 6.

[6]John Downame, "Guide to Godlynesse" (London, 1622), 164.

[7]John Downame, "The Christian Warfare," (London, 1634), 969-990. Puritans used the term calling in three senses, in each of which God always called to man. Most broadly, God called man to commit himself in any given right action. Secondly, God called man to be saved; thus the "general" or "effectual" calling. Finally, God summoned man to a worldly occupation, the "particular" calling for one's own subsistence and that of the public good. Edmund Morgan, *The Puritan Family* (New York: Harper and Row, Publishers, 1966), 69-70.

[8]John Winthrop, *op cit.,* I, 201-202.

[9]*Ibid.*

[10]John White, "The Planters Plea: or the Grounds of Plantations Examined and Usuall Objections Answered" (London, 1630), n.p.

[11]John Winthrop, "Remarks on Liberty," in Russell Nye and Norman Grabo, editors, *American Thought and Writing* (Boston: Houghton Mifflin Company, 1965), I, 59-61.

[12]*Records of the Governor and the Company of the Massachusetts Bay,* edited by Nathaniel B. Shurtleff (Boston: William White Press, 5 vols., 1853), I, November 30,

1631, 82. Hereafter cited as *Massachusetts Records.* For the purposes of the paper the colonial practice of double dating the months of January-March has been deleted, and those months are included as the first and third of each new year.

[13]*Massachusetts Records,* I, March 4, 1635, 140.

[14]Thomas Hooker, "A Survey of the Summe of Church Discipline" (London, 1648), 188.

[15]*Massachusetts Records,* II, 70, 180.

[16]*Massachusetts Records,* I, March 22, 1631; November 5, 1639, 280.

[17]*Massachusetts Records,* I, November 30, 1637, 213.

[18]*Massachusetts Records,* II, May 26, 1647, 195; III, June 19, 1650, 201.

[19]*Massachusetts Records,* I, March 13, 1639, 250; John Winthrop, *Journal,* edited by James K. Hosmer (New York: Charles Scribner's Sons, 2 vols., 1908), II, September 15, 1640, 42; Norma Schwendener, *A History of Physical Education in the United States* (New York: A.S. Barnes and Company, 1942), 6.

[20]John Winthrop, *Journal, op. cit.,* I, October 8, 1636, 192.

[21]John Winthrop, *Papers, op. cit.,* II, 282.

[22]*Massachusetts Records,* I, April 3, 1632, 94.

[23]*Massachusetts Records,* I, September 6, 1638, 236; Sidney Perley, *The History of Salem, Massachusetts* (Salem: by the author, 1926), II, 25-27.

[24]"Body of Liberties of 1641," number 16, in Edwin Powers, *Crime and Punishment in Early Massachusetts, 1620-1692* (Boston, Beacon Press, 1966), 535.

[25]*Massachusetts Records,* II, May 26, 1647, 195; "Body of Liberties," number 92, *Op. Cit.,* 544.

[26]Samuel Maverick, "A Briefe Description of New England and the Severall Townes therein," *Massachusetts Historical Society Proceedings,* Second Series, I (1885), 238.

[27]Stephen Foster, *Op. Cit.,* 177, Boston's First Church entered 265 in 1630, 31 in 1650's; 39 in 1680's; Charleston entered 98 in 1630's, 26 in 1650's, and 39 in 1680's; Roxbury entered 112 in 1630's, 21 in 1650's, and 49 in 1680's. Other congregations substantiated similar declines at a time when the population increased fourfold. Further discussions of these facts and the effect on the quantity of the freeman electorate may be found in: Edmund S. Morgan, *Visible Saints: The History of a Puritan Idea* (New York: New York University Press, 1963), 88, 104-105; Richard C. Simmons, "Freemanship in Early Massachusetts: Some Suggestions and a Case Study," *William & Mary Quarterly,* 19 (1962), 422-428; Simmons, "Godliness, Property, and the Franchise in Puritan Massachusetts: an Interpretation," *Journal of American History,* 55, (1968-1969), 495-511; Robert E. Wall, Jr., "The Massachusetts Bay Colony Franchise in 1647," *William and Mary Quarterly, 27 (1970), 136-344.*

[29]*Massachusetts Records,* IV part I, October 19, 1657, 347.

[30]John Cotton, "A Practical Commentary, or An Exposition with Observations, Reasons and Uses upon the First Epistle Generall of John" (London, 1656), 125-128; Increase Mather, "A Testimony Against Several Prophane and Superstitious Customs" (Boston, 1688), 37.

[31]*Ibid.*

[32]Samuel Sewall, *The Diary of Samuel Sewall, 1674-1729,* Massachusetts Historical Society Collections Fifth Series, 1878-1882 (New York, Arno Press, 3 vols., 1972), I, July 8, 1689, 264; July 12, 1687, 182.

[33]John Richardson, "The Necessity of a Well-Experienced Soldiery" (Cambridge, 1679), 10.

[34]*Harvard College Records* (Boston: Publications of the Colonial Society of Massachusetts, 3 vols., 1935), III, 330-333.

[35]John Cotton, *op. cit.*, 125-126.

[36]John Richardson, *op. cit.*, 10, Samuell Nowell, "Abraham in Arms" (Boston, 1678), 19.

[37]Increase Mather, *op. cit.*, 37.

[38]*Alice M. Earle, Customs and Fashions in Old New England* (New York; Charles Scribner's Sons, 1893), 237-238.

[39]*Massachusetts Records*, V, October 13, 1675, 50.

[40]*Harvard College Records, op. cit.*, 330-331.

[41]*Massachusetts Records*, II, May 7, 1651, 224.

[42]John Cotton, "Letter to R. Levett," quoted in E.D. Hansom, editor, *The Heart of the Puritan* (New York: The MacMillan Company, 1917), 177; Samuel Foster Damon, *The History of Square-Dancing* (Worchester, Massachusetts: The Davis Press, Inc., 1952), 64.

[43]*Essex Quarterly Court Records* (Boston: Essex Institute, 8 vols., 1911-1921), I, 286-287.

[44]"Second Report of the Boston Records Commissioners," In *The Memorial History of Boston, 1630-1880,* edited by Justin Windsor (Boston: James R. Osgood, 1880), 229.

[45]*Massachusetts Records*, IV part II, October 8, 1662, 59-60.

[46]*Massachusetts Court of Assistants Records,* 1630-1692 (Boston: published by the County of Suffolk, 3 vols., 1901), II, April 9, 1672.

[47]Samuel Sewall, *Diary*, I, February 15, 1687, 167; February 16, 1686, 122.

[48]*Ibid.*, March 4, 1690, 312-313.

[49]John Cotton, *op. cit.*, 177.

[50]Increase Mather, *op, cit.*, 30.

[51]Cotton Mather, *The Diary of Cotton Mather,* edited by Worthington C. Ford (New York: Frederick Ungar Publishing Company, 2 vols., 1911), I, July 30, 1690, 202.

[52]*Colonial Justice in Western Massachusetts, 1639-1702: Pynchon Court Records,* edited by Joseph H. Smith (Cambridge University Press, 1961), March 20, 1662, 257. Hereafter cited as *Pynchon Court Records.*

[53]*Court of Assistants,* III, March 1, 1669, 201; *Massachusetts Records,* IV part II, May 31, 1670, 453.

[54]*Massachusetts Records*, IV part II, May 11, 1670, 449.

[55]*Pynchon Court Records,* March 20, 1678, 289; *Records of the Suffolk County Court, 1671-1680* (Boston: Published by the Colonial Society of Massachusetts, 2 vols., 1933), I, October 2, 1672, 184; April 29, 1673, 259. 263; II, January 27, 1680, 1162. Hereafter cited as *Suffolk Court Records.*

[56]*Suffolk Court Records,* I, January 30, 1672, 58.

[57]*Massachusetts Records*, IV part 1, May 23, 1655, 222.

[58]*Massachusetts Records*, IV part I, May 17, 1658, 325; IV part I, October 19, 1654, 200.

[59]Larzar Ziff, *op. cit.,* 193.

[60]*Massachusetts Records,* I, June 6, 1639, 264; II, November 4, 1646, 179-180; V, June 1, 1677, 144.

[61]Sewall, *Diary,* I, November 12, 1685, 103-104; December 17, 1685, 112; July 28, 1686, 145; December 4, 1687, 196; *Court of Assistants,* I, 1681, 197.

[62]Gary B. Warden, *op. cit.,* 36; Stephen Foster, *op. cit.,* 92-93; David Hawke, *op. cit.,* 342-244.

[63]Peter Thatcher, "The Saints' Victory" (Boston, 1696), 37.

[64]Benjamin Wadsworth, "Good Soldiers A Great Blessing" (Boston, 1700), 8, 21.

[65]Nicholas Boone, "Military Discipline: The Compleat Soldier" (Boston, 1701), 55, 57.

[66]Joseph Belcher, "A Victory Over Those Habits of Sin Which War Against the Soul" (Boston, 1698), 4-8.

[67]Ebenezer Pemberton, "The Souldier Defended and Directed" (Boston, 1701), 15, 17-18.

[68]Cotton Mather, *Diary,* II, 1712, 144; II, Jan. 29, 1716, 340.

[69]Benjamin Wadsworth, "The Well-Ordered Family" (Boston, 1712), 47.

[70]Henry Gibbs, "Godly Children Their Parents Joy" (Boston, 1727), 26, 28.

[71]Increase Mather, "Advice to a Young Man" (Boston, 1709), 28; "Meditations on the Lords Day" (Boston, 1711), n.p.

[72]William Cooper, "How and Why Young People Should Cleanse Their Way" (Boston, 1716), 11; Thomas Foxcroft, "The Secure and Impenitent Youth: Exhortations and Directions to Young People" (Boston, 1721), 20.

[73]Daniel Lewes, "The Sins of Youth Remembered" (Boston, 1725), 5.

[74]Azariah Mather, "The Sabbath-Day's Rest Asserted" (Boston, 1709), 37-39, 67.

[75]Cotton Mather, "The Sailour's Companion" (Boston, 1709), 37-39.

[76]*Acts and Laws of the Massachusetts General Court, 1684-1730,* June 8, 1692, 17; 1714, 15; 1716, 279-280; November 22, 1727, 380-381. Hereafter cited as *Acts and Laws.*

[77]*Acts and Laws,* May 27, 1719, 319.

[78]Samuel Sewall, "Letter to William Dummer," August 12, 1719, in "Letter-book," Massachusetts Historical Society Collections Sixth Series, II, 102-103.

[79]*Acts and Laws,* June 8, 1692, 16-17; May 25, 1698, 275-276.

[80]*Orders and By-Laws of the Inhabitants of Boston,* 1701, 11; 1719-1724, 27.

[81]Albert Bushnell Hart, *Common Wealth History of Massachusetts* (New York: The States History Company, 5 vols., 1927), II, 280.

[82]*Boston News-Letter,* August 22-29, 1715; May 22-29, 1721; *Boston Gazette,* May 22, 1721, May 23-30, 1726; *New England Courant,* April 30, 1722.

[83]*Boston Gazette,* April 19-26, 1725.

[84]Sidney Perley, *op. cit.,* III, 127; Alice M. Earle, *Child Life in Colonial Days* (New York: The MacMillan Company, 1899), 361.

[85]*Boston News-Letter,* March 1, 1713; Thomas J. Wertenbaker, *The Puritan Oligarchy* (New York: Charles Scribner's Sons, 1947), 176-177; Sewall, *Diary,* III, November 29, 1716, 111, January 7, 1718, 158; September 8, 1718, 193.

[86]George Dow, *Everyday Life in the Massachusetts Bay Colony* (Boston: Published by the Society for the Preservation of New England Antiquities, 1935), 112, 115.

[87]*Harvard College Records, op. cit.,* I, 401.

[88]*Boston News-Letter,* April 26-May 3, 1714.

3

Horses and Gentlemen: The Cultural Significance of Gambling Among the Gentry of Virginia

By T.H. Breen

In the fall of 1686 Durand of Dauphiné, a French Huguenot, visited the capital of colonial Virginia. Durand regularly recorded in a journal what he saw and heard, providing one of the few firsthand accounts of late seventeenth-century Virginia society that has survived to the present day. When he arrived in Jamestown the House of Burgesses was in session. "I saw there fine-looking men," he noted, "sitting in judgment booted and with belted sword." But to Durand's surprise, several of these Virigina gentlemen "started gambling" soon after dinner, and it was not until midnight that one of the players noticed the Frenchman patiently waiting for the contest to end. The Virginian— obviously a veteran of long nights at the gaming table—advised Durand to go to bed. " 'For,' said he, 'it is quite possible that we shall be here all night,' and in truth I found them still playing the next morning."[1]

The event Durand witnessed was not unusual. In late seventeenth- and early eighteenth-century Virginia, gentlemen spent a good deal of time gambling. During this period, in fact, competitive gaming involving high stakes became a distinguishing characteristic of gentry culture. Whenever the great planters congregated, someone inevitably produced a deck of cards, a pair of dice, or a backgammon board; and quarter-horse racing was a regular event throughout the colony. Indeed, these men hazarded money and tobacco on almost any proposition in which there was an element of chance. Robert Beverley, a member of one of Virginia's most prominent families, made a wager "with the gentlemen of the country" that if he could produce seven hundred gallons of wine on his own plantation, they would pay him the handsome sum of one thousand

Timothy Breen is Professor of History, Northwestern University, and author of Puritans and Adventurers: Change & Persistence in Early America *(New York: 1980).*

From Timothy Breen, "Horses and Gentlemen: The Cultural Significance of Gambling Among the Gentry of Virginia," William & Mary Quarterly, 34 (April 1977): 329-47. *Copyright © 1977 by T.H. Breen, Reprinted with permission.*

guineas. Another leading planter offered six-to-one odds that Alexander Spotswood could not procure a commission as the colony's governor. And in 1671 one disgruntled gentleman asked a court of law to award him his winnings from a bet concerning "a Servant Maid."[2] The case of this suspect-sounding wager—unfortunately not described in greater detail—dragged on until the colony's highest court ordered the loser to pay the victor a thousand pounds of tobacco.

The great planters' passion for gambling, especially on quarter-horse racing, coincided with a period of far-reaching social change in Virginia.[3] Before the mid-1680s constant political unrest, servant risings both real and threatened, plant-cutting riots, and even a full-scale civil war had plagued the colony.[4] But by the end of the century Virginia had achieved internal peace.[5] Several elements contributed to the growth of social tranquility. First, by 1700 the ruling gentry were united as they had never been before. The great planters of the seventeenth century had been for the most part aggressive English immigrants. They fought themselves for political and social dominance, and during Bacon's Rebellion in 1676 various factions within the gentry attempted to settle their differences on the battlefield. By the end of the century, however, a sizable percentage of the Virginia gentry, perhaps a majority, had been born in the colony. The members of this native-born elite—one historian calls them a "creole elite"—cooperated more frequently in political affairs than had their immigrant fathers. They found it necessary to unite in resistance against a series of interfering royal governors such as Thomas Lord Culpeper, Francis Nicholson, and Alexander Spotswood. After Bacon's Rebellion the leading planters—the kind of men whom Durand watched gamble the night away—successfully consolidated their control over Virginia's civil, military and ecclesiastical institutions. They monopolized the most important offices; they patented the best lands.[6]

A second and even more far-reaching element in the creation of this remarkable solidarity among the gentry was the shifting racial composition of the plantation labor force.   Before the 1680s the planters had relied on large numbers of white indentured servants to cultivate Virginia's sole export crop, tobacco. These impoverished, often desperate servants disputed their masters' authority and on several occasions resisted colonial rulers with force of arms. In part because of their dissatisfaction with the indenture system, and in part because changes in the international slave trade made it easier and cheaper for Virginians to purchase black laborers, the major planters increasingly turned to Africans. The blacks' cultural disorientation made them less difficult to control than the white servants. Large-scale collective violence such as Bacon's Rebellion and the 1682 plant-cutting riots consequently declined markedly. By the beginning of the eighteenth century Virginia had been transformed into a relatively peaceful, biracial society in which a few planters exercised almost unchallenged hegemony over both their slaves and their poorer white neighbors.[7]

The growth of gambling among the great planters during a period of significant social change raises important questions not only about gentry values but also about the social structure of late seventeenth-century Virginia. Why did gambling, involving high stakes, become so popular among the gentlemen at precisely this time? Did it reflect gentry values or have symbolic connotations for the people living in this society? Did this activity serve a social function, contributing in some manner to the maintenance of group cohesion? Why did quarter-horse racing, in particular, become a gentry sport? And finally, did public displays such as this somehow reinforce the great planters' social and political dominance?

In part, of course, gentlemen laid wagers on women and horses simply because they enjoyed the excitement of competition. Gambling was a recreation, like a good meal among friends or a leisurely hunt in the woods—a pleasant pastime when hard-working planters got together. Another equally acceptable explanation for the gentry's fondness for gambling might be the transplanting of English social mores. Certainly, the upper classes in the mother country loved betting for high stakes, and it is possible that the all-night card games and the frequent horses races were staged attempts by a provincial gentry to transform itself into a genuine landed aristocracy.[8] While both views possess merit, neither is entirely satisfactory. The great planters of Virigina presumably could have favored less risky forms of competion. Morever, even though several planters deliberately emulated English social styles, the widespread popularity of gambling among the gentry indicates that this type of behavior may have had deeper, more complex cultural roots than either of these explanations would suggest.[9]

In many societies competitive gaming is a device by which the participants transform abstract cultural values into observable social behavior. In his now-classic analysis of the Balinese cockfight Clifford Geertz describes contests for extremely high stakes as intense social dramas. These battles not only involve the honor of important villagers and their kin groups but also reflect in symbolic form the entire Balinese social structure, Far from being a simple pastime, betting on cocks turns out to be an expression of the way the Balinese perceive social reality. The rules of the fight, the patterns of wagering, the reactions of winners and losers—all these elements help us to understand more profoundly the totality of Balinese culture.[10]

The Virginia case is analogous to the Balinese. When the great planter staked his money and tobacco on a favorite horse or spurred a sprinter to victory, he displayed some of the central elements of gentry culture—its competitiveness, individualism, and materialism. In fact, competitive gaming was for many gentlemen a means of translating a particular set of values into action, a mechanism for expressing a loose but deeply felt bundle of ideas and assumptions about the nature of society. The quarter-horse races of Virginia were intense contests involving personal honor, elaborate rules, heavy betting, and wide community interest; and just as the cockfight opens up hidden dimensions of Balinese culture, gentry gambling offers an opportunity to improve our understanding of the complex interplay between cultural values and social behavior in Virginia.

Gambling reflected core elements of late seventeenth- and early eighteenth-century gentry values. From diaries, letters, and travel accounts we discover that despite their occasional cooperation in political affairs, Virginia gentlemen placed extreme emphasis upon personal independence. This concern may in part have been the produce of the colony's peculiar settlement patterns, The great planters required immense tracts of fresh land for their tobacco. Often thousands of acres in size, their plantations were scattered over a broad area from the Potomac River to the James. The dispersed planters lived in their "Great Houses" with their families and slaves, and though they saw friends from time to time, they led for the most part isolated, routine lives.[11] An English visitor in 1686 noted with obvious disapproval that "their Plantations run over vast Tracts of Ground . . . whereby the Country is thinly inhabited; the Living solitary and unsociable." Some planters were uncomfortably aware of the problems created by physical isolation.[12] William Fitzhugh, for example, admitted to a correspondent in the mother country, "Society that is good and ingenious is very scarce, and seldom to be come at except in books."[13]

Yet despite such apparent cultural privation, Fitzhugh and his contemporaries refused to alter their life styles in any way that might compromise their freedom of action. They assumed it their right to give commands, and in the ordering of daily plantation affairs they rarely tolerated outside interference.[14] Some of these planters even saw themselves as lawgivers out of the Old Testament. In 1726 William Byrd II explained that "like one of the Patriarchs, I have my Flocks and my Herds, my Bond-men and Bond-women, and every Soart of Trade amongst my own Servants, so that I live in a kind of Independence on every one but Providence."[15] Perhaps Byrd exaggerated for literary effect, but forty years earlier Durand had observed, "There are no lords [in Virginia], but each is sovereign on his own plantation."[16] Whatever the origins of this independent spirit, it bred excessive individualism in a wide range of social activities. While these powerful gentlemen sometimes worked together to achieve specific political and economic ends, they bristled at the least hint of constraint.[17] Andrew Burnaby later noted that "the public or political character of the Virginians corresponds with their private

one: they are haughty and jealous of their liberties, impatient of restraint, and can scarcely bear the thought of being controuled by any
superior power."[18]

The gentry expressed this uncompromising individualism in
aggressive competitiveness, engaging in a constant struggle against
real and imagined rivals to obtain more lands, additional patronage,
and high tobacco prices. Indeed, competition was a major factor
shaping the character of face-to-face relationships among the colony's gentlemen, and when the stakes were high the planters were
not particular about the methods they employed to gain victory.[19] In
large part, the goal of the competition within the gentry group was to
improve social position by increasing wealth.

Some gentlemen believed that personal honor was at stake as
well. Robert "King" Carter, by all accounts the most successful planter of his generation, expressed his anxiety about losing out to
another Virginian in a competitive market situation. "In discourse with
Colonel Byrd, Mr. Armistead, and a great many others," he explained,
"I understand you [an English merchant] had sold their tobaccos in
round parcels and at good rates. I cannot allow myself to come
behind any of these gentlemen in the planter's trade."[20] Carter's pain
arose not so much from the lower price he had received as from the
public knowledge that he had been bested by respected peers. He
believed he had lost face. This kind of intense competition was
sparked, especially among the less affluent members of the gentry,
by a dread of slipping into the ranks of what one eighteenth-century
Virginia historian called the "common Planters."[21] Gov. Francis
Nicholson, an acerbic English placeman, declared that the "ordinary
sort of planters" knew full well "from whence these mighty dons
derive their originals."[22] The governor touched a nerve; the efforts of
"these mighty dons" to outdo one another were almost certainly motivated by a desire to disguise their "originals," to demonstrate anew
through competitive encounters that they could legitimately claim
gentility.

Another facet of Virginia gentry culture was materialism. This
certainly does not mean that the great planters lacked spiritual concerns. Religion played a vital role in the lives of men like Robert Carter
and William Byrd II. Nevertheless, piety was largely a private matter.
In public these men determined social standing not by a man's religi-
osity or philosophic knowledge but by his visible estate—his lands,
slaves, buildings, even by the quality of his garments. When John
Bartram, one of America's first botanists, set off in 1737 to visit two of
Virginia's most influential planters, a London friend advised him to
purchase a new set of clothes, "for though I should not esteem thee
less, to come to me in what dress thou will, —yet these Virginians are
a very gentle, well-dressed people—and look, perhaps, more at a

man's outside than his inside."[23] This perception of gentry values was accurate. Fitzhugh's desire to maintain outward appearances drove him to collect a stock of monogrammed silver plate and to import at great expense a well-crafted, though not very practical, English carriage.[24] One even finds hints that the difficulty of preserving the image of material success weighed heavily upon some planters. When he described local Indian customs in 1705, Robert Beverley noted that native Americans lived an easy, happy existence "without toiling and perplexing their mind for Riches, which other people often trouble themselves to provide for uncertain and ungrateful Heirs."[25]

The gentry were acutely sensitive to the element of chance in human affairs, and this sensitivity influenced their attitudes toward other men and society. Virginians knew from bitter experience that despite the best-laid plans, nothing in their lives was certain. Slaves suddenly sickened and died. English patrons forgot to help their American friends. Tobacco prices fell without warning. Cargo ships sank. Storms and droughts ruined the crops. The list was endless. Fitzhugh warned an English correspondent to think twice before allowing a son to become a Virginia planter, for even "if the best husbandy and the greatest forecast and skill were used, yet ill luck at Sea, a fall of a Market, or twenty other accidents may ruin and overthrow the best Industry."[26] Other planters, even those who had risen to the top of colonial society, longed for greater security. "I could wish," declared William Byrd I in 1685, "wee had Some more certain Commodity [than tobacco] to rely on but see no hopes of itt.'[28] However desirable such certainty may have appeared, the planters always put their labor and money into tobacco, hoping for a run of luck. One simply learned to live with chance. In 1710 William Byrd II confided in his secret diary, "I dreamed last night . . . that I won a tun full of money and might win more if I had ventured."[28]

Gaming relationships reflected these strands of gentry culture. In fact, gambling in Virginia was a ritual activity. It was a form of repetitive, patterned behavior that not only corresponded closely to the gentry's values and assumptions but also symbolized the realities of everyday planter life. This congruence between actions and belief, between form and experience, helps to account for the popularity of betting contests. The wager, whether over cards or horses, brought together in a single, focused act the great planters' competitiveness, independence, and materialism, as well as the element of chance.[29] It represented a social agreement in which each individual was free to determine how he would play, and the gentleman who accepted a challenge risked losing his material possessions as well as his personal honor.[30]

The favorite household or tavern contests during this period included cards, backgammon, billiards, nine-pins, and dice. The great planters preferred card games that demanded skill as well as luck. Put, piquet, and whist provided the necessary challenge, and Virginia gentlemen—Durand's hosts, for example—regularly played these games for small sums of money and tobacco.[31] These activities brought men together, stimulated conversation, and furnished a harmless outlet for aggressive drives. They did not, however, become for the gentry a form of intense, symbolic play such as the cockfight in Bali.[32] William Byrd II once cheated his wife in a game of piquet, something he would never have dared to do among his peers at Williamsburg. By and large, he showed little emotional involvement in these types of household gambling. The exception here proves the rule. After an unusually large loss at the gaming tables of Williamsburg, Byrd drew a pointed finger in the margin of his secret diary and swore a "solemn resolution never at once to lose more than 50 shillings and to spend less time in gaming, and I beg the God Almighty to give me grace to keep so good a resolution. . ." Byrd's reformation was short-lived, for within a few days he dispassionately noted losing another four pounds at piquet.[33]

Horse racing generated far greater interest among the gentry than did the household games.[34] Indeed, for the great planters and the many others who came to watch, these contests were preeminently a social drama. To appreciate the importance of racing in seventeeth-century Virginia, we must understand the cultural significance of horses. By the turn of the century possession of one of these animals had become a social necessity. Without a horse, a planter felt despised, an object of ridicule. Owning even a slowfooted saddle horse made the common planter more of a man in his own eyes as well as in those of his neighbors; he was reluctant to venture forth on foot for fear of making an adverse impression. As the Rev. Hugh Jones explained in 1724, "almost every ordinary Person keeps a Horse; and I have known some spend the Morning in ranging several Miles in the Woods to find and catch their Horses only to ride two or three Miles to Church, to the Courthouse, or to a Horse-Race, where they generally appoint to meet upon Business."[35] Such behavior seems a waste of time and energy only to one who does not comprehend the symbolic importance which the Virginians attached to their horses. A horse was an extension of its owner; indeed, a man was only as good as his horse. Because of the horse's cultural significance, the gentry attempted to set its horsemanship apart from that of the common planters. Gentlemen took better care of their animals, and, according to John Clayton, who visited Viriginia in 1688, they developed a distinctive riding style. "They ride pretty sharply," Clayton reported; "a Planter's Pace is a Proverb, which is a good sharp hand-Gallop."[36] A fast-rising cloud of dust far down a Virginia road probably alerted the common planter that he was about to encounter a social superior.

The contest that generated the greatest interest among the gentry was the quarter-horse race, an all-out sprint by two horses over a quarter-mile dirt track.[37] The great planters dominated these events. In the records of the county courts—our most important source of information about specific races—we find the names of some of the colony's most prominent planter families—Randolph, Eppes, Jefferson, Swan, Kenner, Hardiman, Parker, Cocke, Batte, Harwick (Hardidge), Youle (Yowell), and Washington. Members of the House of Burgesses, including its powerful speaker, William Randolph, were frequently mentioned in the contests that come before the courts.[38] On at least one occasion the Rev. James Blair, Virginia's most eminent clergyman and a founder of the College of William and Mary, gave testimony in a suit arising from a race run between Capt. William Soane and Robert Napier.[39] The tenacity with which the gentry pursued these cases, almost continuations of the race itself, suggests the victory was no less sweet when it was gained in court.

Many elements contributed to the exclusion of lower social groups from these contests. Because of the sheer size of wagers, poor freemen and common planters could not have participated regulary. Certainly, the members of the Accomack County Court were embarrassed to discover that one Thomas Davis, "a very poore Man," had lost 500 pounds of tobacco or a cow and calf in a horse race with an adolescent named Mr. John Andrews. Recognizing that Davis bore "a great charge of wife and Children," the justices withheld final judgment until the governor had an opportunity to rule on the legality of the wager. The Accomack court noted somewhat gratuitously that if the governor declared the action unlawful, it would fine Davis five days' work on a public bridge.[40] In such cases country justice ordinarily made no comment upon a plaintiff's or defendant's financial condition, assuming, no doubt, that most people involved in racing were capable of meeting their gaming obligations.

The gentry actively enforced its exclusive control over quarter-horse racing.When James Bullocke,a York County tailor,challenged Mr. Mathew Slader to a race in 1674, the county court informed Bullocke that it was "contrary to Law for a Labourer to make a race being a Sport for Gentlemen" and fined the presumptuous tailor two hundred pounds of tobacco and cask.[41] Additional evidence of exclusiveness is found in early eighteenth-century Hanover County. In one of earliest issues of the colony's first newspaper, the *Virginia Gazette,* an advertisement appeared announcing that "some merry-dispos'd gentlemen" in Hanover planned to celebrate St. Andrew's Day with a race for quarter-milers. The Hanover gentlemen explained in a later, fuller description that "all Persons resorting there are desir'd to behave themselves with Decency and Sobriety, the Subscribers being resolv'd to discountenance all Immorality with the utmost

Rigour." The purpose of these contests was to furnish the county's "considerable Number of Gentlemen, Merchants, and credible Planters" an opportunity for "cultivating Friendship."[42] Less affluent persons apparently were welcome to watch the proceedings provided they acted like gentlemen.

In most match races the planter rode his own horse, and the exclusiveness of these were two ways to set up a challenge. The first was a regularly scheduled affair usually held on Saturday afternoon. By 1700 there were at least a dozen tracks, important enough to be known by name, scattered through the counties of the Northern Neck and the James River valley. The records are filled with references to contests held at such places as Smith's Field, Coan Race Course, Devil's Field, Yeocomico, and Varina.[43] No doubt, many races also occurred on nameless country roads or convenient pastures. On the appointed day the planter simply appeared at the race track and waited for a likely challenge. We know from a dispute heard before the Westmoreland County Court in 1693 that John Gardner boldly "Challeng'd all the horses then upon the ground to run with any of them for a thousand pounds of Tobo and twenty shillings in money."[44] A second type of contest was a more spontaneous challenge. When gentlemen congregated over a jug of hard cider or peach brandy, the talk frequently turned to horses. The owners presumably bragged about the superior speed of their animals, and if one planter called another's bluff, the men cried out "done, and done," marched to the nearest field, and there discovered whose horse was in fact the swifter.[45]

Regardless of the outcome, quarter-horse races in Virginia were exciting spectacles. The crowds of onlookers seem often to have been fairly large, as common planters, even servants, flocked to the tracks to watch the gentry challenge one another for what must have seemed immense amounts of money and tobacco. One witness before a Westmoreland County Court reported in 1674 that Mr. Stone and Mr. Youle had run a challenge for £10 sterling "in sight of many people."[46] Attendance at race days was sizable enough to support a brisk trade in cider and brandy. In 1714 the Richmond County Court fined several men for peddling liquors "by Retaile in the Race Ground."[47] Judging from the popularity of horses throughout planter society, it seems probable that the people who attended these events dreamed of one day riding a local champion such as Prince or Smoaker.

The magnitude of gentry betting indicates that racing must have deeply involved the planter's self-esteem. Wagering took place on two levels. The contestants themselves made a wager on the outcome, a main bet usually described in a written statement. In addition, side wagers were sometimes negotiated between spectators or between a contestant and spectator.[48] Of the two, the main bet was far the more significant. From accounts of disputed races reaching the county courts we know that gentlemen frequently risked very large sums. The most extravagant contest of the period was a race run between John Baker and John Haynie in Northumberland County in 1693, in which the two men wagered 4000 pounds of tobacco and 40 shillings sterling on the speed of their sprinters, Prince and Smoaker.[49] Some races involved only twenty or thirty shillings, but a substantial number were run for several pounds sterling and hundreds of pounds of tobacco. While few, if any, of the seventeenth-century gentlemen were what we would call gambling addicts, their betting habits seem irrational even by the more prudential standards of their own day: in conducting normal business transactions, for example, they would never have placed so much money in such jeopardy.

To appreciate the large size of these bets we must interpret them within the context of Virginia's economy. Between 1660 and 1720 a planter could anticipate receiving about ten shillings per hundredweight of tobacco. Since the average grower seldom harvested more than 1500 pounds of tobacco a year per man, he probably never enjoyed an annual income from tobacco in excess of eight pounds sterling.[50] For most Virginians the conversion of tobacco into sterling occurred only in the neat columns of account books. They themselves seldom had coins in their pockets. Specie was extremely scarce, and planters ordinarily paid their taxes and conducted business transactions with tobacco notes—written promises to deliver to the bearer a designated amount of tobacco.[51] The great preponderance of seventeenth-century planters were quite poor, and even the great planters estimated their income in hundreds, not thousands, of pounds sterling.[52] Fitzhugh, one of the wealthier men of his generation, described his financial situation in detail. "Thus I have given you some particulars," he wrote in 1686, "which I thus deduce, the yearly Crops of corn and Tobo. together with the surplusage of meat more than will serve the family's use, will amount annually to 60000lb. Tobo wch. at 10 shillings per Ct. is 300£ annum."[53] These facts reveal that the Baker-Haynie bet—to take a notable example—amounted to approximately £22 sterling, more than 7 percent of Fitzhugh's annual cash return. It is therefore not surprising that the common planters seldom took part in quarter-horse racing: this wager alone amounted to approximately three times the income they could expect to receive in a good year. Even a modest wager of a pound or two sterling represented a substantial risk.

Gentlemen sealed these gaming relationships with a formal agreement, either a written statement laying out the terms of the contest or a declaration before a disinterested third party of the nature of the wager. In either case the participants carefully stipulated what rules would be in effect. Sometimes the written agreements were quite elaborate. In 1698, for an example, Richard Ward and John Steward, Jr., "Covenanted and agreed" to race at a quarter-mile track in Henrico County known as Ware. Ward's mount was to enjoy a ten-yard handicap, and if it crossed the finish line within five lengths of Steward's horse, Ward would win five pounds sterling; if Steward's obviously superior animal won by a greater distance, Ward promised to pay six pounds sterling.[54] In another contest William Eppes and Stephen Cocke asked William Randolph to witness an agreement for a ten-shilling race: "each horse was to keep his path, they not being to crosse unlesse Stephen Cocke could gett the other Riders Path at the start at two or three Jumps."[55]

Virginia's county courts treated race covenants as binding legal contracts.[56] If a gentleman failed to fulfill the agreement, the other party had legitimate grounds to sue; and the county justices' first consideration during a trial was whether the planters had properly recorded their agreement.[57] The Henrico court summarily dismissed one gambling suit because "noe Money was stacked down nor Contract in writing made[,] one of wch in such cases is by the law required."[58] Because any race might generate legal proceedings, it was necessary to have a number of people present at the track not only to assist in the running of the contest but also to act as witnesses if anything went wrong. The two riders normally appointed an official starter, several judges, and someone to hold the stakes.

Almost all of the agreements included a promise to ride a fair race. Thus two men in 1698 insisted upon "fair Rideing"; another pair pledged "they would run fair horseman's play."[59] By such agreements the planters waived their customary right to jostle, whip, or knee an opponent, or to attempt to unseat him.[60] During the last decades of the seventeenth century the gentry apparently attempted to substitute riding skill and strategy for physical violence. The demand for "fair Rideing" also suggests that the earliest races in Virginia were wild, no-holds-barred affairs that afforded contestants ample opportunity to vent their aggressions.

The intense desire to win sometimes undermined a gentleman's written promise to run a fair race. When the stakes were large, emotions ran high. One man complained in a York County court that an opponent had interfered with his horse in the middle of the race, "by meanes whereof the s[ai]d Plaintiff lost the said Race."[61] Joseph Humphrey told a Northumberland County court that he would surely have come in first in a challenge for 1500 pounds of tobacco had not Capt. Rodham Kenner (a future member of the House of Burgesses) "held the defendt horses bridle in running his race."[62] Other riders testified that they had been "Josselled" while the race was in progress. An unusual case of interference grew out of a 1694 race which Rodham Kenner rode against John Hartly for one pound sterling and 575 pounds of tobacco. In a Westmoreland County court Hartly explained that after a fair start and without using "whipp or Spurr" he found himself "a great distance" in front of Kenner. But as Hartly neared the finish line, Kenner's brother, Richard, suddenly jumped onto the track and "did hollow and shout and wave his hat over his head in the plts [plaintiff's] horse's face." The animal panicked, ran outside the posts marking the finish line, and lost the race. After a lengthly trial a Westmoreland jury decided that Richard Kenner "did no foule play in his hollowing and waveing his hatt."[63] What exactly occurred during this race remains a mystery, but since no one denied that Richard acted very strangely, it seems likely that the Kenner brothers were persuasive as well as powerful.

Planters who lost large wagers because an opponent jostled or "hollowed" them off the track were understandably angry. Yet instead of challenging the other party to a duel or allowing gaming relationships to degenerate into blood feuds, the disappointed horsemen invariably took their complaints to the courts.[64] Such behavior indicates not only that the gentlemen trusted the colony's formal legal system—after all, members of their group controlled it—but also that they were willing to place institutional limitations on their own competitiveness. Gentlemen who felt they had been cheated or abused at the track immediately collected witnesses and brought suit before the nearest county court. The legal machinery available to the aggrieved gambler was complex; and no matter how unhappy he may have been with the final verdict, he could rarely claim that the system had denied due process.

The plaintiff brought charges before a group of justices of the peace sitting as a county court; if these men found sufficient grounds for a suit, the parties—in the language of seventeenth-century Virginia—could "put themselves upon the country."[65] In other words, they could ask that a jury of twelve substantial freeholders hear the evidence and decide whether the race had in fact been fairly run. If the sums involved were high enough, either party could appeal a local decision to the colony's general court, a body consisting of the governor and his council. Several men who hotly insisted that they had been wronged followed this path.For example,Joseph Humphrey, loser in a race for 1500 pounds of tobacco, stamped out of a Northumberland County court, demanding a stop to "farther proceedings in the Common Law till a hearing in Chancery."[66] Since most of the General Court records for the seventeenth century were destroyed during the Civil War, it is impossible to follow these cases beyond the county level. It is apparent from the existing documents, however, that all the men involved in these race controversies took their responsibilities seriously, and there is no indication that the gentry regarded the resolution of a gambling dispute as less important than proving a will or punishing a criminal.[67] It seems unlikely that the colony's courts would have adopted such an indulgent attitude towards racing had these contests not in some way served a significant social function for the gentry.

Competitive activities such as quarter-horse racing served social as well as symbolic functions. As we have seen, gambling reflected core elements of the culture of late seventeenth-century Virginia. Indeed, if it had not done so, horse racing would not have become so popular among the colony's gentlemen. These contests also helped the gentry to maintain group cohesion during a period of rapid social change. After 1680 the great planters do not appear to have become significantly less competitive, less individualistic, or less materialistic than their predecessors had been.[68] But while the values persisted, the forms in which they were expressed changed. During the last decades of the century unprecedented external pressures, both political and economic, coupled with a major shift in the composition of the colony's labor force, caused the Virginia gentry to communicate these values in ways that would not lead to deadly physical violence or spark an eruption of blood feuding. The members of the native-born elite, anxious to preserve their autonomy over local affairs, sought to avoid the kinds of divisions within their ranks that had contributed to the outbreak of Bacon's Rebellion. They found it increasingly necessary to cooperate against meddling royal governors. Moreover, such earlier unrest among the colony's plantation workers as Bacon's Rebellion and the plant-cutting riots had impressed upon the great planters the need to present a common face to their dependent laborers, especially to the growing number of black slaves who seemed more and more menacing as the years passed.

Gaming relationships were one of several ways by which the planters, no doubt unconsciously, preserved class cohesion.[69] By wagering on cards and horses they openly expressed their extreme competitiveness, winning temporary emblematic victories over their rivals without thereby threatening the social tranquility of Viriginia. These non-lethal competitive devices, similar in form to what social anthropologists have termed "joking relationships," were a kind of functional alliance developed by the participants themselves to reduce dangerous, but often inevitable, social tensions.[70]

Without rigid social stratification racing would have lost much of its significance for the gentry. Participation in these contests publicly identified a person as a member of an elite group. Great planters raced against their social peers. They certainly had no interest in competing with social inferiors, for in this kind of relationship victory carried no positive meaning: the winner gained neither honor nor respect. By the same token, defeat by someone like James Bullocke, the tailor from York, was painful, and to avoid such incidents gentlemen rarely allowed poorer whites to enter their gaming relationships—particularly the heavy betting on quarter horses. The common planters certainly gambled among themselves. Even the slaves may have laid wagers. But when the gentry competed for high stakes, they kept their inferiors at a distance, as spectators but never players.

The exclusiveness of horse racing strengthened the gentry's cultural dominance. By promoting these public displays the great planters legitimized the cultural values which racing symbolized—materialism, individualism, and competitiveness. These colorful, exclusive contests helped persuade subordinate white groups that gentry culture was desirable, something worth emulating; and it is not surprising that people who conceded the superiority of this culture readily accepted the gentry's right to rule. The wild sprint down a dirt track served the interests of Virginia's gentlemen better than they imagined.

Footnotes

[1][Durand of Dauphiné], *A Huguenot Exile in Virginia: or Voyages of a Frenchman Exiled for his Religion with a Description of Virginia and Maryland*, ed. Gilbert Chinard (New York, 1934 [orig. publ. The Hague, 1687]), 148.

[2]Rev. James Fontaine, *Memoirs of a Huguenot Family . . .* , ed. Ann Maury (Baltimore, 1967 [orig. publ. 1853]), 265-266; John Mercer, cited in Jane Carson, *Colonial Virginians at Play* (Williamsburg, 1965), 49, n.l; H.R. McIlwaine, ed., *Minutes of the Council and General Court of Colonial Virginia, 1622-1632, 1670-1676 . . .* (Richmond, 1924), 252, 281, 285.

[3]Throughout this essay I use the terms gentry, gentlemen, and great planters as synonyms. In each Virginia county a few gentry families dominated civil, ecclesiastical, and military affairs. While the members of these families were substantially wealthier than the great majority of white planters, they were not a class in a narrow economic sense. Their cultural style as well as their financial position set them apart. The great planters and their families probably accounted for less than 2% of the colony's white population, Louis B. Wright, *The First Gentlemen of Virginia: Intellectual Qualities of the Early Colonial Ruling class* (San Marino, Calif., 1940), 57, estimates their number at "fewer than a hundred families." While entrance into the gentry was not closed to newcomers, upward mobility into that group became increasingly difficult after the 1690s. See Philip A. Bruce, *Social Life of Virginia in the Seventeenth Century* (New York, 1907), 39-100; Aubrey C. Land, "Economic Base and Social Structure: The Northern Chesapeake in the Eighteenth Century," *Journal of Economic History,* XXV (1965), 639-654; Bernard Bailyn, "Politics and Social Structure in Virginia," in James Morton Smith, ed., *Seventeenth-Century America: Essays in Colonial History* (Chapel Hill, N.C., 1959), 90-115; and Jack P. Greene, "Foundations of Political Power in the Virginia House of Burgesses, 1720-1776," *William and Mary Quarterly,* 3d Ser., XVI (1959), 485-506.

[4]These disturbances are described in T.H. Breen, "A Changing Labor Force and

Race Relations in Virginia 1660-1710," *Journal of Social History,* VII (1973), 3-25. The fullest account of Bacon's Rebellion remains Wilcomb E. Washburn, *The Governor and the Rebel: A History of Bacon's Rebellion in Virginia* (Chapel Hill, N.C., 1957).

[5]Several historians have remarked on the unusual political stability of 18th-century Virginia. See, for example, Jack P. Greene, "Changing Interpretations of Early American Politics," in Ray Allen Billington, ed., *The Reinterpretation of Early American History: Essays in Honor of John Edwin Pomfret* (San Marino, Calif., 1966), 167-168, and Gordon S. Wood, "Rhetoric and Reality in the American Revolution," *WMQ,* 3d Ser., XXIII (1966), 27-30.

[6]The phrase "Creole elite" comes from Carole Shammas, "English-Born and Creole Elites in Turn-of-the-Century Virginia," in Thad W. Tate and David L. Ammerman, eds., *Essays on the Seventeenth-Century Chesapeake* (Chapel Hill, N.C., forthcoming). See also David W. Jordan, "Political Stability and the Emergence of a Native Elite in Maryland, 1660-1715," *ibid.* The process of forming a native-born elite is also discussed in Bailyn, "Politics and Social Structure," in Smith, ed., *Seventeenth-Century America,* 90-115; John C. Rainbolt, "The Alteration in the Relationship between Leadership and Constituents in Virginia, 1660 to 1720," *WMQ,* 3rd Ser., XXVII (1970), 411-434; and Martin H. Quitt, "Virginia House of Burgesses 1660-1706: The Social, Educational, and Economic Bases of Political Power" (Ph.D. diss.,Washington University, 1970).

[7]Breen, "Changing Labor Force," *Jour. Soc. Hist.,* VII (1973), 2-25; Edmund S. Morgan, *American Slavery — American Freedom: The Ordeal of Colonial Virginia* (New York, 1975), 295-362; Rainbolt, "Leadership and Constituents," *WMQ,* 3rd Ser., XXVII (1970), 428-429. On the social attitudes of the small planters see David Alan Williams, "Political Alignments in Colonial Virginia, 1698-1750" (Ph.D. diss., Northwestern University, 1959), chap. I.

[8]A sudden growth of gambling for high stakes in pre-Civil War England is discussed in Lawence Stone, *The Crisis of the Aristocracy, 1558-1641* (Oxford, 1965). For the later period see Robert W. Malcolmson, *Popular Recreations in English Society, 1700-1850* (Cambridge, 1973); G.E. Mingay, *English Landed Society in the Eighteenth Century* (London, 1963), 151-153, 249-250; and E.D. Cuming, "Sports and Games," in A.S. Turberville, ed., *Johnson's England: An Account of the Life and Manners of his Age,* I (London, 1933), 362-383.

[9]It is important to stress here that the Virginia gentry did not simply copy English customs. As I argue in this essay, a specific, patterned form of behavior, such as gambling, does not become popular in a society or among the members of a subgroup of that society unless the activity reflects or expresses values indigenous to that culture. In 17th-century Massachusetts Bay, for example, heavy betting did not develop. A small amount of gambling seems to have occurred among the poor, especially among servants, but I can find no incidence of gambling among the colony's social, political, or religious leaders. See Nathaniel B. Shurtleff, ed., *Records of the Governor and Company of the Massachusetts Bay . . .* (Boston, 1853-1854), II, 180, III, 201, IV, pt. I, 366; *Records of the Suffolk County Court, 1671-1680* (Colonial Society of Massachusetts, *Publications* [Boston, 1933]), XXIX, 131-259, 263, XXX, 1162; and Joseph H. Smith, ed., *Colonial Justice in Western Massachusetts, 1639-1702: The Pynchon Court Record* (Cambridge, Mass., 1961), 109.

[10]Two of Clifford Geertz's essays here helped shape my ideas about Virginia society: "Thick Description: Toward an Interpretive Theory of Culture" and "Deep Play: Notes on the Balinese Cockfight" in Geertz, *The Interpretation of Cultures* (New York, 1973), 3-30, 412-453. Also see Erving Goffman's "Fun in Games" in Goffman, *Encounters: Two Studies in the Sociology of Interaction* (Indianapolis, 1961), 17-81;

Raymond Firth, "A Dart Match in Tikopia: A Study in the Sociology of Primitive Sport," *Oceania,* I (1930), 64-96; and H.A. Powell, "Cricket in Kiriwina," *Listener,* XLVIII (1952), 384-385.

[11]Philip A. Bruce, *Economic History of Virginia in the Seventeenth Century* . . . , II (New York, 1935 [orig. publ. 1895]), 151.

[12]"A Letter from Mr. John Clayton Rector of Crofton at Wakefield in Yorkshire, to the Royal Society, May 12, 1688," in Peter Force, ed., *Tracts and Other Papers Relating Principally to the Origin, Settlement, and Progress of the Colonies in North America* . . . , III (Washington, D.C., 1844), no. 12, 21.

[13]Richard Beale Davis, ed., *William Fitzhugh and His Chesapeake World, 1676-1701: The Fitzhugh Letters and Other Documents* (Chapel Fill, N.C., 1963), 15.

[14]On the independence of the Virginia gentry see Gerald W. Mullin, *Flight and Rebellion: Slave Resistance in Eighteenth-Century Virginia* (New York, 1972), chap. I.

[15]William Byrd II to Charles, earl of Orrery, July 5, 1726, in "Virginia Council Journals, 1726-1753," *Virginia Magazine of History and Biography,* XXXII (1924), 27.

[16][Durand], *A Huguenot Exile,* ed. Chinard, 110.

[17]I discuss this theme in greater detail in a paper entitled "Looking Out For Number One: Cultural Values and Social Behavior in Early Seventeenth-Century Virginia" (paper delivered at the Thirty-Second Conference in Early American History, Nov. 1974).

[18]Rev. Andrew Burnaby, *Travels through The Middle Settlements In North America, In the Years 1759 and 1760; With Observations Upon the State of the Colonies,* in John Pinkerton, ed., *A General Collection of the Best and Most Interesting Voyages and Travels in All Ports of the World* . . . , XIII (London, 1812), 715.

[19]According to John Rainbolt, the gentry's "Striving for land, wealth, and position was intense and, at times, ruthless" ("Leadership and Constituents," *WMQ,* 3d Ser., XXVII [1970], 414). See Carole Shammas, "English-Born and Creole Elites," in Tate and Ammerman, eds., *Seventeenth-Century Chesapeake;* Morgan, *American Slavery — American Freedom,* 288-289; and Rhys Isaac, "Evangelical Revolt: The Nature of the Baptists' Challenge to the Traditional Order in Virginia, 1765 to 1775," *WMQ,* 3d Ser., XXXI (1974),345-353.

[20]Louis B. Wright, ed., *Letters of Robert Carter, 1720-1727: The Commercial Interests of a Virginia Gentleman* (San Marino, Calif., 1940), 93-94.

[21]Hugh Jones, *The Present State of Virginia Giving a Particular and short Account of the Indian, English, and Negroe Inhabitants of that Colony* . . . (New York, 1865 [orig. publ. 1724]), 48.

[22]Quoted in Thomas Jefferson Wertenbaker, *The Old South: The Founding of American Civilization* (New York, 1942), 19.

[23]Peter Collinson to John Bartram, Feb. 17, 1737, *WMQ,* 2d Ser., VI (1926), 304.

[24]Davis, ed., *Fitzhugh Letters,* 229, 241-242, 244, 246, 249-250, 257-259. For another example of the concern about outward appearances see the will of Robert Cole (1674), in *WMQ,* 3d Ser., XXXI (1974), 139.

[25]Robert Beverley, *The History and Present State of Virginia,* ed., Louis B. Wright (Chapel Hill, N.C., 1947), 226.

[26]William Fitzhugh to Oliver Luke, Aug. 15, 1690, in Davis, ed., *Fitzhugh Letters,* 280.

[27]William Byrd I to Perry and Lane, July 8, 1686, in "Letters of William Byrd I," *VMHB,* XXV (1917), 132.

[28]Louis B. Wright and Marion Tinling, eds., *The Secret Diary of William Byrd of Westover, 1709-1712* (Richmond, Va., 1941), 223-224.

[29]Gaming was so popular among the gentry, so much an expression of their culture, that it became a common metaphor in their discussion of colonial politics. For example, an unsigned essay entitled "The History of Bacon's and Ingram's Rebellion, 1676" described the relationship between Nathaniel Bacon and Gov. William Berkeley as a card game. Charles M. Andrews, ed., *Narratives of the Insurrections, 1675-1690* (New York, 1915), 57. In another account of Bacon's Rebellion, written in 1705, Thomas Mathew noted that several members of the House of Burgesses were "not docill enough to Gallop the future Races, that Court seem'd dispos'd to Lead 'em." *Ibid.*, 32. In May 1697 William Fitzhugh explained to Capt. Roger Jones: "your self will see what a hard Game we have to play the contrary party that is our Opposers, having the best Cards and the trumps to boot especially the Honor. Yet would my Lord Fairfax there [in England], take his turn in Shuffling and Dealing the Cards and his Lordship with the rest see that we were not cheated in our game, I question not but we should gain the Sett, tho' the game is so far plaid" (Davis, ed., *Fitzhugh Letters*, 352).

[30]Rhys Isaac provides a provocative analysis of the relationship between games and gentry culture on the eve of the Revolution in "Evangelical Revolt," *WMQ*, 3d Ser., XXXI (1974), 348-353. See also Mark Anthony de Wolfe Howe, ed., "Journal of Josiah Quincy, Junior, 1773," Massachusetts Historical Society, *Proceedings,* XLIX (1915-1916), 467, and William Stith, *The Sinfulness and Pernicious Nature of Gaming. A Sermon Preached before the General Assembly of Virginia: At Williamsburg, March 1st 1752* (Williamsburg, 1752), 5-26.

[31]The best discussion of these household games is Carson, *Virginians at Play*, 49-89. See also Charles Cotton, *The Compleat Gamester or Instructions How to Play at Billiards, Trucks, Bowls, and Chess . . .* (1674), in Cyril H. Hartmann, ed., *Games and Gamesters of the Restoration: The Compleat Gamester by Charles Cotton, 1674, and Lives of the Gamesters, by Theophilus Lucas, 1714* (London, 1930).

[32]After 1750, however, the gentry's attitude toward household or tavern games seems to have changed. The betting became so heavy that several eminent planters lost fortunes at the gaming tables. A visitor at Williamsburg in 1765 wrote of these men that "they are all professed gamesters, Especially Colonel Burd [William Byrd III], who is never happy but when he has the box and Dices in hand. [T]his Gentleman from a man of the greatest property of any in america has reduced himself to that Degree by gameing, that few or nobody will Credit him for Ever so small a sum of money. [H]e was obliged to sel 400 fine Negroes a few Days before my arival." "Journal of a French Traveller in the Colonies, 1765, I," *American Historical Review,* XXVI (1920-1921), 742. Byrd was not alone. Robert Wormeley Carter and Robert Burwell were excessive gamblers, and as the aging Landon Carter (Robert "King" Carter's son) observed the wagering of the gentry on the eve of the Revolution, he sadly mused, "they play away and play it all away." Jack P. Greene, ed., *The Diary of Colonel Landon Carter of Sabine Hall, 1752-1778,* II (Charlottesvile, Va., 1965), 830. On this generation's addiction to gambling see Emory G. Evans, "The Rise and Decline of the Virginia Aristocracy in the Eighteenth Century: The Nelsons," in Darrett B. Rutman, ed., *The Old Dominion: Essays for Thomas Perkins Abernethy* (Charlottesville, Va., 1964), 68-70.

[33]Wright and Tinling, eds., *Secret Diary,* 75, 442, 449.

[34]Only one mention of cockfighting before 1730 has come to my attention, and that one refers to contests among the "common planters." Jones, *Present State of Virginia,* 48. See Carson, *Virginians at Play,* 151-152.

[35]Jones, *Present State of Virginia,* 48. This observation was repeated in other accounts of Virginia society throughout the 18th century. William Byrd II wrote "my

Dear Countrymen have so great a Passion for riding, that they will often walk two miles to catch a Horse, in Order to ride One." William K. Boyd, ed., *William Byrd's Histories of the Dividing Line Betwixt Virginia and North Carolina* (Raleigh,N.C., 1929), 258. See also Carson, *Virginians at Play.* 102-105.

[36]"A Letter From Clayton," in Force, ed., *Tracts and Other Papers,* no. 12, 35.

[37]On the development of racing in Virginia, especially the transition from the quarter-mile straight track to the oval course, see W.G. Stanard, "Racing in Colonial Virginia," *VMHB,* II (1894-1895), 293-305, and Fairfax Harrison, "The Equine F.F.V.'s: A Study of the Evidence for the English Horses Imported into Virginia before the Revolution," *ibid.,* XXXV (1927), 329-370. I suspect that quarter-horse racing was a sport indigenous to Virginia.

[38]Besides Randolph, there were John Stone, William Hardidge, Thomas Yowell, John Hardiman, Daniel Sullivant, Thomas Chamberlain, Rodham Kenner, Richard Kenner, William Soane, and Alexander Swan.

[39]Aug. 1690, Henrico County, Order Book, 1678-1693, 340. All references to manuscript county records are to the photostat copies at the Virginia State Library, Richmond.

[40]Jan. 16, 1666, Accomack Co., Orders, 1666-1670, 9.

[41]Sept. 10, 1674, York Co., Deeds, Orders, Wills, 1672-1694, 85.

[42]*Virginia Gazette,* Nov. 19-26, 1736, Sept. 30-Oct. 7, 1737.

[43]Bruce, *Social Life,* 195-209; Carson, *Virginians at Play,* 108-110.

[44]Apr. 7, 1693, Westmoreland Co., Order Book, 1690-1698, 92; "Racing in Virginia in 1700-05," *VMHB,* X (1902-1903), 320.

[45]Aug. 1683, Henrico Co. Records [Deeds and Wills], 1677-1692, 254.

[46]Oct. 16, 1674, Westmoreland Co., Deeds, Patents, Etc., 1665-1677, 211; Bruce, *Social Life,* 197-198; Carson, *Virginians at Play,* 109.

[47]Beverley Fleet, ed., *Richmond County Records, 1704-1724,* Virginia Colonial Abstracts, XVII (Richmond, Va., 1943), 95-96.

[48]Carson, *Virginians at Play,* 105. See Aug. 29, 1694, Westmoreland Co., Order Book, 1690-1698, 146.

[49]Aug. 22, 1695, Northumberland Co., Order Book, 1678-1698, Pt. 2, 707-708.

[50]Morgan, *American Slavery — American Freedom,* 142, 108, 204.

[51]Bruce, *Economic History,* II, 495-512.

[52]Aubrey Land's analysis of the probate records in a tobacco-producing area in nearby Maryland between 1690 and 1699 reveals that 74.6% of the estates there were worth less than 100 sterling. According to Land, the differences between the social structures of Maryland and Virginia at this time were not "very great." Land, "Economic Base and Social Structure," *Jour. Econ. Hist.,* XXV (1965), 641-644.

[53]William Fitzhugh to Dr. Ralph Smith, Apr. 22, 1686, in Davis, ed., *Fitzhugh Letters,* 176.

[54]The full covenant is reproduced in Stanard, "Racing in Colonial Virginia," *VMHB,* II (1894-1895), 296-298.

[55]*Ibid.,* 296.

[56]Virginia law prohibited fraudulent gaming, certain kinds of side bets, and gambling by persons who had "no visible estate, profession, or calling, to maintain

themselves." William Waller Hening, ed., *The Statutes at Large; Being a Collection of all the Laws of Virginia* . . . , IV (Richmond, 1820), 214-218; George Webb, *Office and Authority of A Justice of Peace* . . . (Williamsburg, Va., 1736), 165-167. Wagers made between two gainfully employed colonists were legal agreements and enforceable as contracts. The courts of Virginia, both common law and chancery, apparently followed what they believed to be standard English legal procedure. Whether they were correct is difficult to ascertain. Sir William Holdsworth explains that acts passed by Parliament during the reigns of Charles II and Anne allowed individuals to sue for gaming debts, but he provides no evidence that English courts regularly settled disputed contests such as horse races. Holdsworth, *A History of English Law* (London, 1966), VI, 404, XI, 539-542.

[57]Not until the 1750s did Virginians begin to discuss gambling as a social vice. See Stith, *The Sinfulness* . . . *of Gaming;* R.A. Brock, ed., *The Official Records of Robert Dinwiddie,* I (Richmond, Va., 1883), 30-31; Samuel Davies, *Virginia's Danger and Remedy. Two Discourses Occasioned by The Severe Drought* . . . (Williamsburg, 1756).

[58]Oct. 1690, Henrico Co., Order Book, 1678-1693, 351. See also Aug. 28, 1674, Northampton Co., Order Book No. 9, 1664-1674, 269, and Nov. 4, 1674, *ibid.,* No. 10, 1674-1679.

[59]Stanard, "Racing in Colonial Virginia," *VMHB,* II (1894-1895), 267; Henrico Co. Records [Deeds and Wills], 1677-1692, 466.

[60]Carson, *Virginians at Play,* 109-110.

[61]"Some Extracts from the Records of York Co., Virginia," *WMQ, 1st Ser., IX (1900-1901),* 178-179.

[62]*Jan. 1694, Northumberland Co., Order Book, 1678-1698, Pt.2, 643.*

[63]*Aug. 29 1694, Westmoreland Co., Order Book, 1690-1698, 146-146a. Also see Oct. 1689, Henrico Co., Order Book, 1678-1693, 313, and Stanard, "Racing in Virginia," VMHB,* II (1894-1895), 296.

[64]A gentleman could have challenged an opponent to a duel. Seventeenth- and early 18th-century Virginians recognized a code of honor of which dueling was a part, but they did everything possible to avoid such potentially lethal combats. I have found only four cases before 1730 in which dueling was even discussed. County courts fined two of the challengers before they could do any harm. ("A Virginian Challenge in the Seventeenth Century," *VMHB,* II [1894-1895], 96-97; *Lower Norfolk County Antiquarian,* IV, [1904], 106.) And two comic-opera challenges that only generated blustery rhetoric are described in William Stevens Perry, ed., *Historical Collections Relating to the American Colonial Church,* I (Hartford, Conn., 1870), 25-28, and Bond, ed., *Byrd's Histories of the Dividing Line,* 173-175. On the court system see Philip A. Bruce, *Institutional History of Virginia in the Seventeenth Century* . . . , I (Gloucester, 1910), 484-632, 647-689.

[65]Aug. 29, 1694, Westmoreland Co., Order Book, 1690-1698, 146a.

[66]Jan. 1694, Northumberland Co., Order Book, 1678-1698, Pt. 2, 643.

[67]Sometimes the courts had an extremely difficult time deciding exactly what had occurred at a race. A man testified in 1675 that he had served as the official judge for a contest, and that while he knew which horse had finished first, he was "not able to say much less to Sweare that the Horse did Carry his Rider upon his back over the path." Sept. 16, 1675, Surry County, Deeds, Wills and Orders, 1671-1684, 133. For another complex case see Mar. 5, 1685, Rappahannock Co. Orders [no. 1], 1683-1686, 103, 120, 153.

[68]For evidence of the persistence of these values among the gentry in the Revolutionary period see Isaac, "Evangelical Revolt," *WMQ,* 3d Ser., XXXI (1974), 348-353.

[69]The planters' aggressive hospitality may have served a similar function. Hospitality in Virginia should be analyzed to discover its relationship to gentry culture. Robert Beverley makes some suggestive comments about this custom in his *History and Present State of Virginia,* 312-313. An interesting comparison to the Virginia practice is provided in Michael W. Young, *Fighting with Food: Leadership, Values and Social Control in a Massim Society* (Cambridge, 1971).

[70]A.R. Radcliffe-Brown, *Structure and Function in Primitive Society: Essays and Addresses* (New York, 1964), chaps. 4, 5.

Suggestions For Further Reading.

Brailsford, Dennis. *Sport and Society: Elizabeth to Anne* (London: Routledge & Kegan Paul, 1969).

Carson, Jane. *Colonial Virginians at Play* (Charlottesville, Va.: University of Virginia Press, 1965).

Dulles, Foster Rhea. *A History of Recreation: America Learns to Play* (N.Y.: Appleton-Century-Crofts, 1965).

Ewing, William C. *The Sports of Colonial Williamsburg* (Richmond: Diety Press, 1937).

Guttmann, Allen, *From Ritual to Record, The Nature of Modern Sports* (N.Y.: Columbia University Press, 1978).

Hervey, John. *Racing in America, 1665-1865,* Vol. I (N.Y.: Jockey Club, 1944).

Hill, Phyllis J. "A Cultural History of Frontier Sport in Illinois, 1673-1820." (Ph. D. dissertation, University of Illinois, 1967).

Hole, Christina, *English Sports and Pastimes* (N.Y.: Batsford, 1949).

Kennard, June, "Maryland Colonials at Play: Their Sports and Games." *Research Quarterly* 41 (October 1970): 389-95.

Krout, John A. *Annals of American Sport* (New Haven: Yale University Press, 1929).

Ledbetter, Bonnie S. "Sports and Games of the American Revolution." *Journal of Sport History* 6 (Winter 1979): 29-40.

Malcolmson, Robert W. *Popular Recreations in English Society, 1700-1850* (Cambridge: Cambridge University Press, 1973).

Mook, H. Telfer. "Training Day in New England." *New England Quarterly* 2 (December 1938): 675-697.

Standard, William C. "Racing in Colonial Virginia." *Virginia Magazine of History and Biography* 2 (1894-1895): 293-305.

Stone, Lilly C. *English Sports and Recreations* (Washington, D.C.: Folger, 1960).

Struna, Nancy. "The Cultural Significance of Sport in the Colonial Chesapeake and Massachusetts." (Ph.D. dissertation, University of Maryland, 1979).

Strutt, Joseph. *Sports and Pastimes of the People of England* (London: T. Bensely, Bolt Court for J. White at Horace's Head, 1801).

Tait, James. "The Declaration of Sports for Lancashire (1617)." *English Historical Review* 32 (October 1917): 561-68.

Thompson, E.P. "Time, Work-Discipline, and Capitalism." *Past and Present* 38 (December 1967): 56-97.

Wagner, Peter. "Literary Evidence of Sport in Colonial New England: The American Puritan Jeremiad." *Station* 2 (1976): 233-49.

Wagner, Peter. "Puritan Attitudes Toward Physical Recreation in Seventeenth Century New England." *Journal of Sport History* 3 (Summer 1975): 139-51.

Sport In Antebellum America

Introduction

Until his death in 1971, John R. Betts of Boston College was the most distinguished scholar of American sport history. He published many valuable monographs which derived from the research for his extensive doctoral dissertation, "Organized Sport in Industrial America," completed at Columbia University in 1951. Much of his work was later summarized in his text *America's Sporting Heritage, 1850-1950* published posthumously in 1974. Betts was mainly concerned with explaining the reasons for the rise of American organized sport in the second half of the nineteenth century (see Section III). In addition, Betts sought to establish the background for the rise of sport. In "Mind and Body in Early American Thought," Betts argued that even though there was not much sporting activity during the antebellum era, there were important changes occurring in the way American thinkers and reformers were viewing physical fitness, health, and sport. He asserted that these changing perspectives, along with the influence of German gymnastics, had a significant impact on the subsequent growth of sports. Educators, physicians, health faddists, and social reformers of the 1830s and 1840s supported sport as a positive good which enhanced health, morality, the mind, and the spirit. This fulfilled the traditional American criterion of utilitarianism for its leisure pursuits. Consequently, sports became increasingly acceptable to middle-class Americans and helped pave the way for the explosive growth of organized sports after the Civil War.

Thomas Wentworth Higginson was one of the essayists whom Betts believed contributed greatly to the reevaluation of American attitudes to sport and physical fitness. Higginson was an elite Bostonian, a graduate of Harvard College, and a Unitarian minister. Like many members of his social class, Higginson was actively involved in a wide variety of social reform movements, including abolitionism, temperence, women's suffrage, and health. His attitude on physical culture is presented in his famous essay "Saints and Their Bodies," which appeared in 1858 in the first volume of the *Atlantic Monthly,* a periodical that would be widely read by opinion makers in the future. Higginson argued that physical vitality was a positive good, and recommended vigorous exercise for all Americans regardless of age or sex. Higginson especially focused on the idea of muscular Christianity, a philosophy that was gaining popularity in Great Britain. Muscular Christianity emphasized the union of physical activity and spiritual sanctity. It asserted that there was a positive relationship between sound health and sound morals.

The most popular spectator sport in the antebellum period until about 1845 was undoubtedly horse racing. The highlight of the racing calendar between 1820 and 1850 were the fifty-odd intersectional races which attracted huge crowds coming to wager on their favorite steed and to marvel at the endurance and speed of American-bred horses. The most important contests were the so-called "Great Races" which were match races between carefully screened representative horses from the North and South. The first Great Race occurred in 1823 at New York's Union Course when Eclipse, representing the North, took the best of the South's Sir Henry. The next two races were taken by southern mounts, which reflected the decline in northern racing. The North regained its self-esteem in the 1842 match race between the southern champion, Boston, and the North's favorite, Fashion. The race generated enormous public attention and it was reported in the press that approximately 70,000 spectators were on hand, including congressmen and other dignitaries. The final Great Race occurred in 1845 when Fashion, aged eight, was challenged by the six-year-old Peytona, who raced to victory in straight heats. An extract from the extensive front page report of the race by correspondents for the *New York Herald* is included below.

The *Herald* was one of the first penny papers and covered subjects of popular interest like sports in order to get the largest possible readership. The article on the Fashion-Peytona race captured the ambiance of that exciting event and foreshadowed the development of sporting journalism. It described in rich detail various aspects of the grand spectacle, including crowd behavior, the rituals engaged in by the spectators, and, of course, the race itself.

By the mid-nineteenth century, harness racing had become the leading American spectator sport. Unlike horse racing, which had agrarian roots, harness racing developed in an urban setting, particularly in New York, which was the breeding and training center. The development of harness racing in New York is deftly examined by Melvin L. Adelman in his essay, "The First Modern Sport in America: Harness Racing in New York City, 1825-1870." Adelman asserts that harness racing in the 1820s was a premodern sport characterized by informal or no organization, simple unwritten rules based on local custom, local competition, limited role differentiation between participants and spectators, little publicity, and no records or statistics. These were the characteristics of sport in traditional societies, which are stable, localistic, ascriptively organized, and lack role differentiation. Adelman traces the processes by which harness racing would become highly modernized. By 1870 the sport was very organized, with formal and uniform rules and national competition. Roles had become highly specialized with the rise of professionalism, there was substantial coverage of contests by the press, and statistics and records were carefully maintained and publicized. This occurred in a society which was itself undergoing modernization and urbanization, which contributed to the development of harness racing.

It should be pointed out that not all sports became modernized or even began modernizing at the same time and speed. By 1870, when harness racing had become modernized, other sports, like baseball, were only beginning to become modernized and certain pre-modern games, like the popular Scottish game of hurling the caber, were still played in their historic form in traditional settings.

4

Mind And Body In Early American Thought

by John R. Betts

American interest in physical fitness was largely the culmination of the educational movement and the urban-industrial development of the latter half of the nineteenth century. But the origins of American thought about the relationship of mind and body can be traced to the Enlightenment of the eighteenth century, the romantic spirit of the early republic, and the recurring appeals of educators, physicians, health advocates, journalists, and sports enthusiasts of the Middle Period. The wisdom of ancient as well as modern philosophers who saw the fulfillment of man only in the unity of body, mind, and spirit was long confined to an intellectual elite and only began to win a wider audience in an era of democratic upsurge and mounting concern over health in an urbanizing society.

Ministers, doctors, and planters in colonial times had access to Greek and Roman classics, the works of some medieval scholars, and the literature of the Renaissance, Reformation, Elizabethan age, and Enlightenment. Among modern writers who had published scattered fragments and discourses on physical training were Martin Luther, Girolamo Mercuriale, John Comenius, Richard Mulcaster, Michel de Montaigne, John Milton, John Locke, Francis Fuller, and Jean Jacques Rousseau.[1] Before the end of the colonial era the Encyclopedists were investigating man's knowledge of hygiene and exercise, and Scottish physicians were publishing works on physic and health.[2]

New England Calvinists, however, remained cool toward all the appetites of the flesh, except for an occasional Harvard student who went skating, hunting, or fishing. The gospel of work was rooted in the Protestant ethic; it was believed that innocent play was too easily

John R. Betts was with the Department of History, Boston College. He authored America's Sporting Heritage, 1850-1950 *(Reading, Mass.: 1974).*

From John R. Betts, "Mind and Body in Early American Thought," Journal of American History, LIV (March 1968), pp. 787-805. Copyright © 1968 by the Organization of American Historians. Reprinted by permission.

turned to frivolous amusement, and rural sports and youthful games were discarded in manhood according to the Biblical injunction. Dutch Calvinists in New Netherland were somewhat different; they smoked their pipes, played at bowls, and skated on the wintry ice. Southern gentlemen mastered the arts of horsemanship and fencing or collected books on hunting and fishing in good Cavalier tradition. When Sir Francis Nicholson, governor of Virginia in 1691, proclaimed an annual field day for contests of strength and skill among "the better sort of Virginians only, who are bachelors," he established a precedent for similar festivals in the region. Physical training was a necessary attribute of the gentleman,[3] and planters who engaged in fox hunting and the wild sports of the woods set an example later imitated in the middle colonies.

By the middle decades of the eighteenth century, signs of interest in sport and exercise were the cricket matches in Georgia, Maryland, and New York and Benjamin Franklin's references to running, leaping, wrestling, and swimming for boys in his *Proposals Relating to the Education of Youth in Pennsylvania* (1749).[4] Among the anglers following in the footsteps of Isaak Walton were the Philadelphia sportsmen who formed the Schuylkill Fishing Company in 1732. Samuel Moody of the Dummer School at Byfield, Massachusetts, championed swimming as a release from the rigors of the classroom, while Bostonian readers of the *Chronicle* were alerted to the values of exercise expounded in Dr. George MacKenzie's *Art of Preserving Health.* At least a decade before the American Revolution James Rivington of New York advertised the "best racquets for tennis and fives" — indicative of the increasing popularity of ball games. Even during the winter of Valley Forge, Revolutionary troops drilled and exercised or played the ball game called "base."[5] After the war Americans returned to their normal pursuits and recreations, among which were horse racing, target shooting, and quoits.

There was a continuing flow of writings on recreation. Thomas Jefferson in 1785 recommended two hours of daily exercise, including gunning, walking, and horseback riding. The *Virginia Almanack* of 1787 favored outdoor exercise in the months of November and December. In an address to the young men of Hartford in 1790 on the virtues of athletics, Noah Webster claimed "a fencing skool is, perhaps, as necessary an institution in a college as a professorship of mathematics." Dr. Benjamin Rush approved all exercises "calculated to import health, strength and elegance to the human body" in his proposals for a federal university. The prize-winning essay of the American Philosophical Society in 1797 was written by Samuel Harrison Smith, Jeffersonian editor of the *National Intelligencer,* who believed military drills and exercises would cultivate a "national spirit." At the end of the century, Samuel Knox of the Frederick Academy in Maryland encouraged dancing, fencing, and spontaneous activity: "Exercise and temperance are necessary both for the vigor of body and mind . . . ."[6]

After 1800 the tempo of publication on educational theory, health, and physical training quickened. Dr. Shadrach Ricketson cited various "authorities" on exercise in his *Means of Preserving Health and Preventing Diseases* (1806). Philadelphia printers published English children's manuals. From Edinburgh came *The Code of Health and Longevity* (1807), in which Sir John Sinclair cited ancient critics of athletics like Euripides and Galen as well as such expositors as Herodicus and Hippocrates. Sinclair referred to Locke, Rousseau, Fuller, and Strett (author of *The Sports and Pastimes of the People of England,* 1808); he recorded an interview with the celebrated pugilist James Jackson; and he sanctioned French, English, and Scottish games and sports, such as fives, tennis, cricket, shinty, golf, rowing, angling, and hunting. Games were espoused as remedies for defects in respiration, digestion, posture, and complexion. All the mental faculties were brightened and preserved: "The mind also becomes more courageous . . . ." Every sport seemed to win approval — sailing, riding, bowling, dumbbells, and billiards.[7] In the second decade of the century, less literature on the subject appeared. Exceptions were the reprinting of Franklin's thoughts on swimming, John Frost's *Art of Swimming* (1818), and Emma Willard's comments on dancing in her proposals for a female seminary. And after the War of 1812 farmers raced their trotters, pedestrians appeared at race courses, and the prize fighter made his bow before a disapproving public.

Politics in the 1820s mirrored the energy, turbulence, and aspiration of a generation conditioned by Jeffersonian ideals and the westward movement. Education became the watchword of National Republicans and Jacksonian Democrats, and concern for the interdependence of mind and body grew out of the fusing of ideas from several intellectual sources. Rousseau's *Emile* and Pestalozzi's pedagogical insights played a vital role in forming American romantic ideals for the education that would liberate and elevate the masses. Perfectible man, free of original sin, was almost divine — his impulses and desires were true to Nature. Self-improvement and self-fulfillment were imperatives popularized by educators influenced by European ideas on child training and by reformers on the lyceum platform, or by philanthropists helping to establish libraries for school children and apprentices. An intellectual prejudice against the exaltation of muscle prevailed among most academicians, and fashion dictated that the lady of breeding be sleek and delicate; but national pride was wounded when foreign critics referred to the undeveloped physiques, wan complexions, and premature aging of Americans. Classicists and romanticists alike were inspired by the Greek Revolution; and ancient history was featured in the curriculum, which reminded the young of the gymnasiums of Athens and the vigor of Sparta.

The Enlightenment only gradually broke through the confines of an intellectual aristocracy, but the rationalist emphasis on sensory experience tied the brain even more firmly to bodily functions. Environmentalism and materialism, with a strong Christian bent, crept into American thought through Deism, the American Philosophical Society, and the writings of Joseph Priestley and Thomas Cooper. A scientific approach to hygiene appeared in the medical works of Benjamin Rush and others, following the lead of Edinburgh. The Enlightenment had accented the power of knowledge but had also assumed man's essential goodness and potential improvement. Man, if not the center of the cosmos, was ascending and gaining mastery over Nature. The secularization of society encouraged the state to move into the area of popular education. While orthodox and evangelical Christianity thrived in an era of democratic aspirations, the old Calvinist assumption of man's sinful nature was eroded with the diffusion of knowledge, a spreading individualistic philosophy, and a utilitarian acceptance of society's responsibility for controlling disease and disseminating education according to the Benthamite dictum of the greatest good for the greatest number. By the 1820s the European educational developments of the late-eighteenth and early nineteenth centuries were becoming known to a core of American scholars and pedagogues.[8]

One innovation of the late-eighteenth century ws the development of gymnastic systems by J.K.F. Guts Muths, Christian Salzmann, Franz Nachtegall, and Henrik Ling.[9] Salzmann's work, in particular, had been printed in this country; but it would be the authoritative name of Pestalozzi that would persuade American educational reformers of the goodness of childish instincts and of the need to allow the child a freedom of action and expression heretofore impossible in schools dedicated to memory work and discipline by the rod. A disciple of Rousseau, Pestalozzi went beyond the master. As early as 1804 he opened a gymnasium in his school at Statz, Switzerland. Like a number of his contemporaries, he emphasized the natural development of the child but also included the improvement of society as an educational objective. During the German nationalistic reaction to Napoleonic conquest, patriotic feeling in the era of Fichte and Stein spilled over into educational theory. Pestalozzi wrote a tract on physical education in 1807, and Fichte encouraged him to reorganize Berlin's schools toward German regeneration. John Griscom's *A Year in Europe* (1819) noted the Pestalozzian influence and was considered an educational classic by Jefferson. Educators traveling abroad visited Pestalozzi's Yverdun and Emmanuel Fellenberg's Hofwyl, where gymnastics and outdoor exercise were featured. The gymnastic movement gradually penetrated American school circles in the twenties as knowledge of Prussian educational reforms spread.

The single most influential figure in the German revival was Friedrich Jahn, who had organized Turnplatz schools, fought in the War of Liberation, and emerged the "father" of the Turner movement. Throughout western Europe experiments with gymnastics continued. Ling reformed Swedish national education with a system of free movements; Francisco Amoros and Charles Junod in Paris, Captain P.H. Clias in Berne and London, Carl Voelker in London, and J.A. Beajeu in Dublin became active proponents.[10] Captain Alden Partridge of West Point was introducing exercises as part of American military training. Thus in many countries Jahn became the symbol of physical training as an instrument in national educational reform.

Medical and educational leaders were alerted. In 1826-1827 William Russell's *American Journal of Education* discussed the work of Salzmann, Jahn, Clias, Voelker, and their American adherents. The *Journal* pointed out the need for city playgrounds and gymnasiums, as well as the benefits of hunting, cricket, handball, and golf. Boston's *North American Review* cited James G. Carter's *Essays upon Popular Education,* while the Boston *Medical Intelligencer* described the decline of gymnastics during the Middle Ages and its revival by Guts Muths, Jahn, and company. Robert Dale Owen had been a student at Fellenberg's Hofwyl, where he joined in the public games, annual walking tours, and daily gymnasium exercises, which he considered so conducive to vigor, health, good temper, morality, and intellectual vitality. Francis Neefe, the Pestalozzian, was attracted to New Harmony, Indiana, whose *Gazette* discussed the values of gymnastics. For those enslaved by the dictates of fashion, the *Ladies Magazine* prophesied: "Strengthen their physical powers, and you may then give energy to their intellects, brilliant links of beauty to their persons, animation to their spirits, and grace to their manners."[11]

Gymnastics were introduced in Massachusetts, New York, and Virginia almost simultaneously. Jefferson and the organizing trustees provided for gymnastic exercises at the University of Virginia in 1824; William Bentley Fowle of the Boston Monitorial School declared, "I hope the day is not far distant when gymnasiums for women will be as common as churches in Boston"; John Griscom, who had visited the schools of Pestalozzi and Fellenberg, introduced gymnastics into his New York high school; and George Bancroft, acquainted with the influence of Pestalozzi and Fichte in Berlin's schools, joined with Joseph Cogswell in organizing the Round Hill School in Northampton, Massachusetts. Round Hill played an historic role. Though they would provide a liberal education, Cogswell and Bancroft announced, "We would also encourage activity of body, as the means of promoting firmness of constitution and vigor of mind, and shall appropriate a regular portion of each day to healthy sports and gymnastic exercises. In the *Prospectus* of 1823, they said they were "deeply impressed with the necessity of uniting physical with moral education" and claimed they were "the first in the new continent to connect gymnastics with a purely literary establishment." Calisthenics, the mile run on the school's own track, archery, tumbling, games, and long walking trips were part of the daily schedule.[12] To Round Hill came a disciple of Jahn, Charles Beck, who constructed a gymnasium and translated his master's *Treatise on Gymnasticks,* saying that play and enthusiasm could counteract pecuniary ambitions absorbed early in life.

Emigré scholars followed Beck in extending the movement. Charles Follen, newly appointed at Harvard, opened a school gymnasium and then founded the Boston (Tremont) Gymnasium in 1826.[13] When he resigned his position, he expressed the hope that the gymnasium would "spread over all this free and happy land." In his *Lectures on Moral Philosophy,* the young German scholar claimed that "this methodical exercise of every part of the human frame, is the only way to make the body a sure and well-trained servant of the mind, always ready to obey its master's call." German idealism had influenced a number of intellectuals, including Ralph Waldo Emerson, Theodore Parker, and Margaret Fuller; and Follen was one of the links to idealist literature.[14]

Francis Lieber, who was familiar with the idea of the gymnasium and the Turner movement, accepted an invitation extended by a group in Boston to come to that American city from London in 1827. The German scholar wrote, "Believe me, Sir, I only want benevolent and sincere intention from those citizens, who declared to patronize the Gymnastics, this important branch of education." In a visit with Lieber at Boston, the sixty-one-year-old President John Quincy Adams plunged into Lieber's swimming pool from a six-foot springboard. Adams remarked that he hoped there would be many similar establishments to improve public health. The President thought that swimming was superior to gymnastic exercise, after hard intellectual exertion.[15]

New Englanders were adopting gymnastics. Henry and Sereno Dwight opened a New Haven gymnasium. Apparatus was secured by the Mount Pleasant Classical Institute in Amherst, the Berkshire Gymnasium at Pittsfield, and the Woodbridge School at South Hadley. Amherst, Brown, Williams, Bowdoin, and Andover Seminary students participated in the sport. School journals deplored the endless hours of rigid posture in tiny, overheated classrooms. Philip Lindsley from Princeton, the new president of the University of Nashville, advised: "Attach to each school house a lot of ten acres of land, for the purpose of healthful exercise, gardening, farming, and the mechanical arts." The true university would teach a broad spectrum of literary and scientific subjects and would include fencing, riding, swimming, and gymnastics.[16] Frontiersmen had their rail splitting, ploughing, turkey shoots, and brawls on county-court day; but physical education was moving into the West and South on the coattail of the educator.

College enthusiasm waned as manual-labor experiments were introduced, and apparatus on some school and academy greens rusted with age. Even so, Richard Henry Dana found Harvard students exercising at cricket, football, boxing, fencing, and swimming. Academies, well-established by 1820, entered their golden age in the next two decades, years marked by a rising middle class as well as more education-oriented rural communities. Typical of the most progressive academies, in terms of physical education, were the Dummer School, Phillips Andover, Exeter, Chauncy Hall, and Salem Latin in New England; in New Jersey there was the Lawrenceville School; and more than two thousand academies, many military in nature, appeared in the South. Football (soccer style) was popular at Exeter by 1800, and after-school games proved a diversion to boarding students everywhere. Both Emma Willard at Middlebury, Vermont, and Zilphah Grant at Derry, New Hampshire, sprained ligaments during calisthenics.[17]

Educators and physicians were increasingly cognizant of the dependence of mental health upon physical well-being. Even the decline in the mortality rate was ascribed, in part, to physical education. Dr. William P. Dewees of the University of Pennsylvania Medical School urged imitating European educators in promoting exercise: "The play of a child is a sort of intellectual occupation. The mind at this age prompts to perpetual exercise and noisy motion." Gymnastic exercise, he concluded, gives "tone and vigour to all parts of the body," and improve morality as well.[18] Though public concern for health had been limited in the past,[19] reformers were now aroused by George Combe's *Constitution of Man* (1828) and by Dr. Andrew Combe's *Principles of Physiology* (1834). The latter recalled Sinclair's *Code of Health* and declared that social play and sports were more meaningful than aimless walking. One scholar has observed, "American health reformers cited the Combes [book] as theologians cited the Bible."[20]

The *Journal of Health,* published by an association of Philadelphia physicians, proposed following the example of Sheffield, England, and providing public gymnasiums and baths open to the laboring classes at a minimal fee. An advocate of *mens sana in corpore sano,* the *Journal* printed articles on calisthenics, riding, and sports, paid court to the goddess of health, cited Strutt's *The Sports and Pastimes of the People of England,* and apparently approved John Frost's lecture to Middlebury students on the benefits of sparring. Mind and body were indissolubly linked in human development. The young woman was urged to dance in moderation and to ride horseback without corset and buckles (which prevented "the free expansion of her chest") as a cure for nervousness, tremors, palpitation, paleness, headache, indigestion, and poor appetite. Such riding often did "more good than all the art medicinal." The *Journal* saw a variety of benefits of exercise: gymnastics were an antidote for hypochondria, and golfers in Scotland had frequently lived an extra decade. It also ranked the lack of exercise with such "poisons of modern invention" as rum, tobacco, and tea as a cause of the physical decline of modern man.[21]

Physical strength of Americans in an urban society was inferior to that of their ancestors of the colonial era and to that of frontiersmen, according to many reformers. The New York *Mirror* became concerned over health and physical degeneration, claimed a "healthy man in New York would be a curiosity," regretted the early fading of women's beauty, deplored the routine of schools, colleges, and seminaries, noted the total neglect of exercise in all social classes, and appealed for more writing on the subject of health. Businessmen foolishly excused their inactivity as the result of lacking time, and thousands were going to unnecessarily early graves.[22]

Health faddists were on the march. Sylvester Graham, a temperance lecturer, concerned himself with vegetarianism, overindulgence, adequate sunlight, bathing, dress reform, sex hygiene, and exercise. The *Graham Journal of Health and Longevity* appeared in 1837 and related physical fitness to great achievement. Plato, Aristotle, Cicero, and Caesar had appreciated the dependence of a sound mind on a healthy body, it was argued, and so had Shakespeare, Gibbon, Byron, Scott, and Davy. *The Boston Health Journal and Advocate of Physiological Reform* carried Graham's appeal. He found exercise a tonic, thought horseback riding a preventive of pulmonary consumption, and warned, "Aged people, after they have retired from the active employments of life, must keep up their regular exercise, or they will soon become feeble and infirm."[23]

Medical men rivaled health cultists in discussing physical fitness. Dr. William A. Alcott edited the *Moral Reformer* and *Teacher on the Human Constitution.* His *Library of Health* encouraged swimming and gymnastics and praised exercise as a means of avoiding consumption.[24] The profession was especially concerned with the war on cholera, yellow fever, influenza, and other epidemics, but the well-being of individuals was thought to hinge in good part on exercise. Dr. John Collins Warren spoke to the American Institute of Instruction on the importance of physical education and lectured annually thereafter on the value of exercise in the development of the organic structure of the body. A study of muscular action was presented in *Human Physiology* by Dr. Robley Dunglison of the University of Virginia, while Dr. John Jeffries discussed "Physical Culture The Result of Moral Obligations" in the *American Quarterly Observer.*

The plight of the American woman's physical development and health was emphasized in the medical and physiological writings of such physicians as William Alcott, E.W. Duffin, J.M. Keagy, Charles Caldwell, John Bell, Caleb Ticknor, and Abel L. Peirson. Alcott cited the English girl's vigor in his *Young Woman's Guide to Excellence* as a curative for deformity of the spine and noted Pestalozzi's influence. Caldwell, a student of Benjamin Rush, had toured Europe and held the chair of medical and clinical practice at Transylvania University when he published *Lectures on Physical Education* in 1834 and *Thoughts on Physical Education* in 1836. The doctor noted the increase of insanity and dyspepsia, which he blamed on political and religious agitation and the pursuit of wealth. Observing Dr. William Beaumont's discovery of the role of gastric juices in digestion, Caldwell recommended abandonment of excessive mental exertion, regulation of passion, and the practice of muscular exercise. Physical education, he contended, was vital to the destiny of the republic: "Its aim should be loftier and more in accordance with the destiny and character of its subject — to raise man to the summit of his nature. And such will be its scope in future and more enlightened ages."[25] John Bell related exercise to femininity and grace in *Health and Beauty: An Explanation of the Laws of Growth and Exercise.* Caleb Ticknor discussed walking and riding in his *Philosophy of Life.*

Abel Peirson, who had studied in Paris, edited the *Medical Magazine.* The prejudice against girls exercising in the open air, he declared, was aggravated by the passing of the spinning wheel with its muscular demands and by the imposition of a social code which permitted only sledding and battledore as feminine sport. Poor girls! "There is no amusement which could be contrived, better suited to improve the shape of females, by calling into action all the muscles of the back, than the game of billiards. But this game has unfortunately come into bad repute, from being the game resorted to by profligate men of pleasure, to destroy each other's health and pick each other's pockets." According to the learned doctor, French women surpassed the Europeans in lightness of step, symmetry of form, and retention of agility and vivacity into old age. From duchess and leader of *ton* to chambermaid and peasant girl, this vitality was due to the French love of dancing.[26] Feminist leaders also championed physical education for women. Catherine Beecher pioneered with *Suggestions Respecting Improvements in Education* (1829) and *Course of Calisthenics for Young Ladies* (1831); Mary Lyon at Mount Holyoke inaugurated a calisthenic quadrille; and Margaret Coxe featured exercise in her *Young Lady's Companion* as an antidote to the ravages inflicted by a half century of increasing luxury.

The wakening spirit caught hold of the educational movement. Professor Edward Hitchcock of Amherst cited the case of President Timothy Dwight of Yale as an example of the restorative powers of walking. He claimed that three or four hours daily were not too much to devote to moderate outdoor activity. Statistically, he found that 186 great men of ancient, medieval, and modern times had lived to the average age of seventy-eight, possibly due to physical culture as well as constitutional endowments. Andover seminarians heard Dr. Edward Reynolds of Boston deplore "the measured ministerial walk." "Look at Germany," he advised, and imitate the ancients: "The same necessity which sent Plato and Aristotle to the gymnasium after severe mental labor, still exists with the hard students of our day." Princeton's *Biblical Repertory* lauded the intellectual benefits of rational gymnastics:

They not only minister present health, but look forward prospectively to firmness of constitution in subsequent life.

Most of the Gymnastic games, also, are of a social kind, and awaken an intense interest in the competitors; absorbing the attention, sharpening the perception, and communicating alertnesss to the motions of the mind as well as the body. Thus they become invaluable auxiliaries to the more direct methods of promoting intellectual culture.[27]

Theodore Weld's Society for Promoting Manual Labor in Literary Institutions encouraged active sports: "Their effects upon the economy are universal — are felt everywhere. A glow of pleasure, as indescribable as it is exquisite, diffuses itself over all the organs . . . . The vigor of the intellect is revived, and study once more becomes easy and successful." Publisher Mathew Carey acknowledged the importance of Weld's work.

Other testimonials to exercise were given by numerous professors, ministers, and leading citizens. Thomas Grimké of Charleston declared the habit of exercise "creates a greater capacity for mental labor, a more enduring energy, a loftier enthusiasm, a more perfect harmony in the whole system of intellectual powers." Francis Wayland, president of Brown University, recommended three hours of exercise per day: "No man can have either high intellectual action, or definite control over his mental faculties, *without regular physical exercise*. The want of it produces also a feebleness of will, which is as fatal to moral attainment as it is to intellectual progress." In his inaugural address, Mark Hopkins of Williams claimed many students spent too much time in drinking, smoking, and eating rather than in exercises such as sawing wood, walking, or gardening. "It is now agreed," he observed, "that the health of the body is to be one great object of attention, not only for it own sake, but from its connection with a sound state and vigorous action of the mind."[28] The editor of the *American Annals of Education and Instruction,* William Channing Woodbridge, duly recorded the views of the *Boston Medical and Surgical Journal* and discussed the sports of children. Samuel R. Hall recognized play as the only source of pleasure for some school children, because "brilliancy and force of thought are the natural fruits of activity." And Orestes Brownson commented on the "Necessity and Means of Physical Education" at the American Institute of Instruction.[29]

Thought on exercise in the age of Jackson focused upon the common schools. The *New York Mirror* in 1833 warned:

> The seeds of many diseases, which sweep hundreds and thousands of our most estimable men into premature graves, are planted at school by the injudicious ambition of teachers, who entirely overlook the body in their efforts to overcultivate the mind. Parents forget, in their zeal to clothe the brows of their children with the early laurel for the triumphs of learning that learning itself is valueless without health . . . .

Pedagogues became aware of the refreshment of the mind provided by exercise. Victor Cousin's widely discussed *Report on the State of Public Instruction in Prussia* revealed that all Prussian primary schools supported gymnastic exercises, for graceful carriage strengthened "the good qualities of the soul." Jacob Abbott's *The Teacher* recommended battledore and softball at recess. The Essex County Teachers' Association in Massachusetts called for a quarter-acre for play and exercise at each schoolhouse. Alexander Dallas Bache asserted, "A system of education, to be complete, must combine moral, intellectual, and physical education." Commissioned by Nicholas Biddle and the trustees of Girard College to study European schools, Bache noted the presence of commons or playground for every school on the Rugby model. Central High School in Philadelphia and Houston Public School in New York featured the playground.[30] Entering upon his historic superintendency of Massachusetts schools and aware of the new conditions of urban life, Horace Mann read the *Constitution of Man* in 1837. Thus he commenced a long friendship and correspondence with George Combe, whom he considered the greatest living man. The first issue of Mann's *Common School Journal* appeared in 1838, asserting the involvement of mind and body and expressing dismay over the deterioration of the health of people:

> Mental power is so dependent for its manifestations on physical power, that we deem it not extravagent to say, that if, amongst those who lead sedentary lives, physical power could be doubled, their mental powers would be doubled also. The health and constitutional vigor of a people is a blessing not to be lost—certainly not to be regained—in a day . . . . Gradually and imperceptibly a race may physically deteriorate, until their bodies shall degenerate into places, which without being wholly untenantable, are still wholly unfit to keep a soul in.[31]

During the 1830s sports gained a foothold in the press because of the rising interest in horse racing, prize fights, and walking matches. Popular publications were the *American Turf Register,* the *Spirit of the Times,* Horatio Smith's *Festivals, Games and Amusements,* Robin Carver's *Book of Sports,* and a few manuals on archery and games, treasured by lucky youngsters.

The rise of sports coincided with the social changes of the times — for example with the growth of an affluent middle class in the North and a leisured aristocracy in the South. It coincided with the emergence of a spirit of reform: interest in Utopian experiments, women's rights, penal legislation, capital punishment, a peace crusade, care of the insane, temperance, public education, and the abolition of slavery. Greater attention to outdoor recreation may also have been related to unemployment and the depression of the late thirties and early forties. At any rate, labor editors concerned themselves with health and with the shorter work day. Men puzzled over the flaws in an urbanizing society. Albert Brisbane, a popularizer of Fourierism, charged American schools with hostility to both Nature and health; corporal dexterity and health, he thought, "were sources of Internal riches."[32] Only a few reformers, however, seriously advocated increased attention to public health and better conditions for the working classes and the poor. Such was recommended by William Ellery Channing in 1840, by Dr. Lemuel Shattuck in his study of the overcrowding and the tenement life of Boston, and by the first report of the New York Association for the Improvement of the Condition of the Poor (1845).

Sporting and athletic interest increased in the early forties as reports of English activities became more common.[33] Pierce Egan's *Book of Sports* and Donald Walker's *British Manly Exercises* capitalized on the acquaintance of many with *Bell's Life in London,* the *Sporting Magazine,* and James Gordon Bennett's *Herald,* which pioneered in sports news. The transcendentalist *Dial* even published Henry David Thoreau's translation of Pindar's *Olympic Odes.* Walt Whitman used the columns of the Brooklyn *Daily Eagle* in the mid-forties as a forum for discussing school playgrounds. In a pre-Freudian speculation on a young boy's drive for power, Emerson observed: "In playing with bat-balls, perhaps he is charmed with some recognition of the movement of the heavenly bodies, and a game of base or cricket is a course of experimental astronomy, and my young master tingles with a faint sense of being a tyrannical Jupiter driving spheres madly from their orbit."[34] In the early forties, too, Caldwell's *Thoughts on Physical Education* (1836) and Dr. J. Lee Comstock's *Outlines of Physiology* (1837) were reissued and remained popular. Shortly before his historic surgical experiment with Dr. William Morton's ether at Massachusetts General Hospital,

Dr. Warren published his lecture in expanded book form and urged open-air exercise for factory workers.

Though specialization had begun to crowd discussion of personal hygiene and exercise out of professional medical journals, popular interest seemed to persist and grow.[35] The water-cure system of Vincent Priessnitz of Silesia, who came to the United States in 1831, stressed walking, skipping, jumping, and running, "but what lady dare do these things in these days of refinement?" The perils of urban comfort brought a revival of the gymnasium. Sheridan's gymnasium in New York catered to clergymen, lawyers, physicians, merchants, artists, artisans, and schoolboys. Harvard scholars in 1842 worked out under T. Belcher Kay, instructor in "the art of self-defense" to Francis Parkman, who prided himself on "a rapid development of frame and sinews."[36] In New Haven, however, activity lagged badly. A student commented on the contrast with Cambridge in England:

There is one great point in which the English have the advantage over us: they understand how to take care of their health . . . every Cantab takes his two hours' exercise *per diem,* by walking, riding, rowing, fencing, gymnastics, &c. How many Yalensians take *one* hour's regular exercise? . . . The gymnasium has vanished, wicket has been voted ungenteel, scarce even a *freshman* dares put on a pair of skates, and there have never been rideable horses in New Haven within the memory of "the oldest inhabitant."[37]

Taking note, men of Yale and Harvard formed sculling crews in 1843 and 1844.

Despite obstacles and even some religious objections, progress in physical culture continued. Playgrounds were adopted in Cincinnati and received the support of Henry Barnard. New York state schools recognized the need of muscular exercise, and teachers "in almost every school district" were said to have access to Andrew Combe's *Principles of Physiology.* Illustrative of professional activity were the work of the American Physiological Society by 1837 and the publication of *Human Physiology for the use of Elementary Schools* by Dr. Charles A. Lee. Charles Dickens, though noting the American deficiency in exercise and being shocked by the emaciated prisoners of New York's Tombs, visited the Perkins Institute in Boston and found blind boys engaged in active sports, games and gymnastics.[38] George B. Emerson lent the prestige of his name to the encouragement of walking, riding, gardening, sleighing, and general exercise in the open air and sunlight.[39] In the *Sixth Annual Report of the Board of Education* Mann expounded on the oxygenizing of the blood through "the athletic exertions of manual labor or of gymnastic sports," far superior to passive activities like sailing. Lack of space in cities led to physical degeneration, Mann thought, but he was pleased with recreational improvements in the schools during the decade up to 1845.

Dr. David Thayer's gymnasium, he observed, was a boon to Boston clerks, students, lawyers, and clergymen; and he similarly praised Mrs. Hawley's gymnastic school for young misses.[40] The Michigan superintendent of education, O.C. Comstock, declared exercise was "essential to physical health, mental vigor and delightful study."[41].

Urban people, grappling with the need for schools and sound pedagogy, also faced mounting sanitation, housing, and health problems in a society marked by its high mortality rate. The labor of immigrant workers on canals and railroads and in factories and the vigorous life of farmers and frontiersmen more than met their requirements of physical activity. But there were impediments for others, such as old myths about night air and fashionable prejudices against athletic women. Early Victorian society in England, having reached a more advanced stage of industrialism, might hunt the fox, attend Ascot, encourage schoolboy games, introduce athletics and rifle shooting into the army and the military academies, and become disciples of Isaak Walton; but their contemporaries in America required an extra generation or two before the leisure provided by a maturing industrial system would become general enough to extend the health and sporting interests of the privileged classes to the populace at large. Religous hostility to amusement and recreation proved to be a continuing deterrent, and social acceptance of the machine raised doubts about the value of bodily strength and muscle. Still, the development of a nationwide system of education, the encouragement of child-centered educational programs, the immigrant's fondness for his active games, and the fear of physical degeneration made a breakthrough in attitudes toward recreation and sport by the late thirties and early forties. Rowing clubs in Boston, New York, Philadelphia, Savannah, and Detroit; throngs attending thoroughbred racing and trotting; matches between runners, pedestrians, and prize fighters; formation of numerous hunting and fishing clubs; sailing and yachting clubs in Atlantic coastal communities and on the Great Lakes; adoption of mass football, gymnastics, cricket, or crew at eastern colleges — all bore witness to the sporting fever.[42]

Mind and body were more intimately related to one another by the development of a native literature of pedagogues and physicians, by an awareness of English concern for exercise and German educational reforms, and by a mounting public recognition that the Puritan gospel of work lost some of its validity in a highly commercial, urban environment. Outdoor life took on greater appeal in the romantic call back to the solitude or to the primitive challenge of Nature; the woodland haunts of "Frank Forester" (Henry William Herbert) lured the angler and the hunter. Emulation of the frontiersman's vigor contributed to the mounting concern over the debility of college students, the fair sex, office workers, and children in the crowded tenement.

Soon the voices of Edward Everett, Thoreau, Oliver Wendell Holmes, and others would aid the cause.

Events of the mid-forties were prophetic of things to come. As the nation looked to the threat of war with Mexico, the New York Yacht Club organized, and the Knickerbocker Club established the rules of baseball. In the near future German forty-eighters would establish Turner societies, Scottish Caledonians would introduce their native games, the Irish crewmen would race in city regattas. Only in the generation after the Civil War would expectations be realized; but in the quarter century between 1820 and 1845 educators, physicians, and reformers had begun to develop a philosophical rationale concerning the relationship of physical to mental and spiritual benefits derived from exercise, games, and sports. From the diffusion of ideas developed by the medical profession under the influence of the Enlightenment and by educators and reformers affected by the romantic spirit, Americans were alerted to the threat against their physical and mental powers that came with the confinement of the home and school and the more sedentary habits of the city.

Footnotes

[1]The Renaissance broadened the concept of education, and scholars like Sir Thomas Elyot and Roger Asham endorsed gymnastics, sports, and games as antidotes to mental weariness. Pope Pius II recommended games of ball and skill; Luther, the vigorous life and wrestling. Mercuriale wrote the *Celebrated Gymnastic Art of the Ancients* (1569). In *Of Education* John Milton declared that young men must be ". . . practised in all the locks and grips of wrestling, wherein Englishmen were wont to excel, as need may often be in fight to tug, or grapple, and to close." As sensory experience was more widely acknowledged as the basis for education, John Locke opened *Some Thoughts Concerning Education* with the assertion, "A sound mind is a sound body, is a short but full description of a happy state in this world." In 1704 Francis Fuller published *Medicina Gymnastica;* and other eighteenth-century writers on physical education included Friedrich Hoffmann, Johann Peter Frank, Gerhard Vieth, Simon Tissot, C.J. Tissot *(Gymnastique Medicale,* 1781), and Pierre Cabanis. From Vesalius and Harvey onward, physiological writing spread the new knowledge of the skeleton and the muscular system; and in eighteenth-century Virginia, Kenneth McKenzie, Alexander Reade, John Sutherland, and William Fleming owned extensive medical libraries.

[2]In 1751 Jean D'Alembert declared that hygiene dealt with the health, beauty, or strength of the body and that *"athletics* will produce *gymnastics,* or the art of *exercising* . . . ." Richard N. Schwab and Walter E. Rex, eds., *Preliminary Discourse to the Encyclopedia of Diderot and Jean D'Alembert (1751)* (Indianapolis, 1963), 155-62. As the Encyclopedists' model, Francis Bacon had visualized the science of the human body as constituting medicine, cosmetics, athletics, and the pleasures of the senses. Hallé discussed Greek gymnastics from Homer and the early Greeks to Herodicus and his pupil Hippocrates. He also noted the contemporary French *collège* enthusiasm for handball, football, and tennis, while French physicians were acquainted with the exercising interests of Sydenham,

Baglivi, Stahl, and Boerhaave, N.F.J. Eloy, ed., *Dictionnaire Historique de la Médecine Ancienne et Moderne* (3 vols., Paris, 1778), II, 420-22. Jean J. Rousseau contended, "Nature wills that they should be children before they are men." Cliff climbing, swimming, and carefree sports and games helped develop the child: "A debilitated body enfeebles the soul . . . . If you would cultivate the intelligence of your pupil, cultivate the power which it is to govern." *Émile, ou Traité de l'Éducation (1762).*

³*Louis B. Wright, The First Gentlemen of Virginia: Intellectual Qualities of the Early Colonial Ruling Class* (San Marino, 1940), 87, 153.

⁴Examples of children's manuals published in the colonies were Edward Blackwell, *A Compleat System on Fencing* (Williamsburg, 1734) and Hugh Gaine, *A Little Pretty Book* (Philadelphia 1762). Benjamin Rush in his "Sermon on Exercise" encourged mountain climbing, swimming, skating, bowling, quoits, jumping, and such games as golf and tennis. Dagobert D. Runes, ed., *The Selected Writings of Benjamin Rush* (New York, 1947), 360-63.

⁵*The Military Journal of George Ewing: 1754-1824* (Yonkers, 1938), 31; Robert W. Henderson, *Ball, Bat and Bishop: The Origin of Ball Games* (New York, 1947), 102.

⁶Edward M. Hartwell, *On Physical Training* (Washington, 1904), 746; Runes, *Selected Writings of Benjamin Rush,* 101-05. See also Mathew Carey's *American Museum: or Repository of Ancient and Modern Fugitive Pieces etc. Prose and Poetical,* IV (Dec. 1788), VI (July 1789), XI (April 1792); Frederick Rudolph, ed., *Essays on Education in the Early Republic* (Cambridge, 1965), 222; Samuel Knox, *An Essay on the Best System of Liberal Education, Adapted to the Genius of the Government of the United States* (Baltimore, 1799), 134; Allen Oscar Hansen, *Liberalism and American Education in the Eighteenth Century* (New York, 1965), 110, 125.

⁷Robert W. Henderson, comp., *Early American Sport: A Chronological Check-List of Books Published Prior to 1860, Based on an Exhibition Held at the Grolier Club* (New York, 1937); Shadrach Ricketson, *Means of Preserving Health and Preventing Diseases* (New York, 1806), 152-71; John Sinclair, *The Code of Health and Longevity* (4 vols., Edinburgh, 1807), I, 575-611, 707-10, II, 83-93.

⁸The romantic spirit in American culture and education has been treated by many writers, including Ellwood P. Cubberley, *Public Education in the United States, A Study and Interpretation of American Educational History* (Boston, 1934), 344-66, and Stuart G. Noble, *A History of American Education* (New York, 1938), 197-211.

⁹Johann Basedow had opened his "Philanthropium" at Dessau in 1776, the first modern educational institution to give prominence to physical education. Christian Salzmann established his institute at Schnepfenthal in Saxony in 1786, where Johann K.F. Guts Muths pioneered in the pedagogy of gymnastics and wrote *Gymnastik für die Jugend* (1793) as well as *Spiel zur Uebung und Erholung des Korpers und Giestes für die Jugend* (1796). A Philadelphia imprint of *Gymnastics for Youth* (1802-1803) was attributed to Salzmann. In 1803 Immanuel Kant published his *Pedagogy,* in which he claimed, "Playing ball is one of the best sports for children, since it involves running, which is very healthful." Edward Franklin Buchner, trans. and ed., *The Educational Theory of Immanuel Kant* (Philadelphia, 1904), 160. After the War of Liberation, Friedrich Jahn wrote *Die Deutche Turnkunst,* the guide of the Turner movement.

¹⁰Francisco Amoros, *Gymnase Normal, Militaire et Civil* (Paris, 1821); Charles Junod, *Considérations sur la Gymnastique* (Paris, 1825); P.H. Clias, *An Elementary Course of Gymnastic Exercises, or Calisthenics* (Dublin, 1828). Johann Heinrich Pestalozzi

had published a tract on physical education in 1807 and had set off a Swiss movement about 1815 at the Academy of Berne. A French journal referred to the decline of gymnastics in past ages with the spiritual emphasis of early Christianity and with the expulsion of the Moors, who had brought exercises to Spain, France, and Italy. *Journal de Médecine, Chirurgie, Pharmacie, &c.,* LXXXVI (Jan. 1791), 457. Later popularizers included Adolph Spiess and Ernst Eiselen. Sandhurst introduced athletic games in 1812, and the Grenelle gymnasium opened in Paris in 1818.

[11]Richard G. Boone, *A History of Education in Indiana* (New York, 1892), 80-81; *Ladies Magazine,* I (Jan. 1828), 26. Boston *Medical Intelligencer,* IV (Oct. 24, 1826), 195-99, (Dec. 12, 1826), 314-15, (Feb. 13, 1827), 459-61. *North American Review,* XXIV (Jan. 1827), 159-63; *American Journal of Education,* I (Jan. 1826), 19-23, (July 1826), 430-32, (Nov. 1826), 698-701, II (May 1827),I 289-92, (Aug. 1827), 466-67.

[12]Thomas Woody, *A History of Woman's Education in the United States* (2 vols., New York, 1929), II, 111; *American Journal of Education,* X (June 1861), 608, XV (June 1865), 232; George Bancroft to Caleb Cushing, June 5, 1823, Cushing Family Papers #1 (Massachusetts Historical Society); Joseph G. Cogswell and George Bancroft, *Prospectus of a School to be Established at Round Hill, Northampton, Massachusetts* (Cambridge, 1823), 17; M.A. DeWolfe Howe, *The Life and Letters of George Bancroft* (2 vols., New York, 1908), I, 167-73; Russel B. Nye, *George Bancroft, Brahmin Rebel* (New York, 1944), 67-70.

When Thomas Jefferson wrote George Ticknor for a set of Harvard's rules of government, the Boston scholar sent the Round Hill School *Prospectus* as a preferable model for the University of Virginia. Henry A. Pochmann, *German Culture in America, Philosophical and Literary Influences 1600-1900* (Madison, 1957), 67.

[13]Daniel Webster expressed his approval: "I am highly pleased with the idea of a Gymnasium. It is a subject which has occupied my thoughts . . . . Those who have charge of education seem sometimes to forget that the body is part of the man. The number of young men who leave our colleges, emulous indeed, and learned, but with pale faces and narrow chests, is truly alarming. The common rustic amusements hung about our literary institutions for a long time, but they at length seem to have been entirely abandoned, and nothing, at least nothing useful, has succeeded them. If it be desirable that there should be cultivated intellect, it is equally so, as far as this world is concerned, that there should be a sound body to hold it in." See Paton Stewart, Jr., *Warren's Recommendation of Gymnastics* (Boston, 1856), 4.

[14]*The Works of Charles Follen* (5 vols., Boston, 1841), III, 243; E.L. Follen, *The Life of Charles Follen* (Boston, 1844), 107-19.

[15]Francis Lieber to Dr. John C. Warren, April 3, 1827, John C. Warren Paper (Massachusetts Historical Society); Boston *Medical Intelligencer,* V (July 10, 1827), 134; Thomas Sergeant Perry, ed., *The Life and Letters of Francis Lieber* (Boston, 1882), 78.

[16]Philip Lindsley, *The Cause of Education in Tennessee* (Nashville, 1833), 12; *North American Review,* XXIV (Jan. 1827), 219-24; George P. Schmidt, "Intellectual Crosscurrents in American Colleges, 1825-1855," *American Historical Review,* XLII (Oct. 1936), 58-59.

[17]Emmet A. Rice, *Physical Education* (New York, 1939), 152; Russel Blaine Nye, *The Cultural Life of the New Nation, 1776-1830* (New York, 1960), 187; Harriett Webster Marr, *The Old New England Academies Founded Before 1826* (New York, 1959), 155-63. Manual-labor programs, usually stressing Fellenberg's ideas on industrial education rather than his concern for exercise, are described in Charles Alpheus Bennett, *History of Manual and Industrial Education Up to 1870* (Peoria, 1926), 128-209.

[18]Review of William P. Dewees, *A Treatise on the Physical and Medical Treatment of Children,* in the New England Journal of Medicine and Surgery, XV (April 1826), 173-79.

[19]On early public health measures in Boston, Philadelphia, and Baltimore, see Ralph Chester Williams, *The United States Public Health Service 1798-1950* (Washington, 1951), 162-64.

[20]Robert Samuel Fletcher, *A History of Oberlin College From Its Foundation Through the Civil War* (2 vols., Oberlin, 1943), I, 317.

[21]*Journal of Health,* I (Sept. 9, 1829), 4, 14-15, (Oct. 7, 1829), 58, (Nov. 11, 1829), 78, 92-93, (Dec. 23, 1829), 118-21, (Jan. 13, 1830), 132-34, (May 12, 1830), 262-67, (Aug. 24, 1830), 372-74, II (Jan. 11, 1832), 145-46.

[22]*New York Mirror,* X (April 6, 1833), 317-18, 343, 375, 392.

[23]Richard H. Shryock, "Sylvester Graham and the Popular Health Movement, 1830-1870," *Mississippi Valley Historical Review,* XVIII (Sept. 1931), 172-83; *Graham Journal of Health and Longevity,* 1 (June 20, 1837) 92-93, III (July 20, 1839), 298-99; Sylvester Graham, *Lectures on the Science of Human Life* (2 vols., Boston, 1839), II, 658-59. Temperence advocates stressed the drinking of water, abstinence from or moderate use of liquor, wine, and tobacco, and the moral obligations of the pledge as keys to good health. Only a few linked exercise to temperance, although anatomy professor Reuben Mussey of Dartmouth listed exercise as a substitute for "ardent spirits" in the cure of dyspepsia. Mussey noted J.B. Buckingham's story of Himalayan "athletae" in Calcutta who far surpassed British grenadiers and sailors in wrestling, boxing, and lifting of weights. Reuben J. Mussey, *Prize Essay on Ardent Spirits* (Washington, 1837), 44; G.J. Grosvenor, *An Address on the Importance of Female Influence to the Temperance Reformation* (Geneva, N.Y., 1842), 20.

[24]William A. Alcott, *The Library of Health* (5 vols., Boston, 1837-1841), I, 250-53, II, 346; see also *Health Tract No. 2* (n.p., n.d.), 19 (American Antiquarian Society, Worcester).

[25]Charles Caldwell, *Thoughts on Physical Education and the True Mode of Improving the Condition of Man* (Edinburgh, 1836), 77-91.

[26]Abel L. Peirson, *On Physical Education* (Boston, 1840), 18-23.

[27]Edward Hitchcock, *Dyspepsy Forestalled and Resisted* (Amherst, 1831), 203; *American Annals of Education,* II (Sept. 1832), 449-59.

[28]*Promotion of Health in Literary Institutions* (New Haven, 1833), 20-21; Mathew Carey, *Societies for Promoting Manual Labor in Literary Institutions* (Philadelphia, 1834); Mark Hopkins, *An Inaugural Discourse* (Troy, 1836), 13-19.

[29]*American Annals of Education and Instruction,* III (Jan. 1833), 32-36, VI (Feb. 1836), 84-86, (Nov. 1836). 496; S.R. Hall, *Lectures to Female Teachers on School-Keeping* (Boston, 1832), 110.

[30]*New York Mirror,* X (May 25, 1833), 375; M. Victor Cousin, *Report on the State of Public Instruction in Prussia* (New York, 1835), 194-98; Jacob Abbott, *The Teacher* (Boston, 1833), 205-06; supplement to the *Report of the Board of Education on the Subject of School Houses* (Boston, 1838), 35; J. Orville Taylor, *The District School* (New York, 1834), 213, 230; *Common School Journal,* I (June 1836), 45, II (Feb. 1837), 16; Franklin Spencer Edmonds, *History of the Central High School of Philadelphia,* (1902), 248; Alexander Dallas Bache, *Report on Education in Europe* (Philadelphia, 1839), 402; review of and extracts from George Combe, *Notes on the United States of North America, during a Phrenological Tour in 1838-39-40* (2 vols., Philadelphia, 1841)in *Connecticut Common School Journal,* III (June 1, 1841), 173.

[31]Mary Peabody Mann, *Life of Horace Mann* (Boston, 1865), 59; *Common School Journal for the Year 1839,* I (Nov. 1838), 11.

[32]Albert Brisbane, *Social Destiny of Man, or, Association and Reorganization of Industry* (Philadelphia, 1840), 427-29.

[33]The writings on sport for this period are extensive. Among the best general, yet critical, treatments are John Allen Krout, *Annals of American Sport* (New Haven, 1929); Jennie Holliman, *American Sports 1785-1835* (Durham, N.C., 1931); and Foster Rhea Dulles, *America Learns to Play, A History of Popular Recreation, 1607-1940* (New York, 1940). See also John R. Betts, "Organized Sport in Industrial America" (doctoral dissertation, Columbia University, 1951).

[34]Herman Melville, *White-Jacket: The World in a Man-of-War* (New York, 1860), 322-25; *Dial,* IV (Jan. 1844), 379-82; Edward Waldo Emerson and Waldo Emerson Forbes, eds., *Journals of Ralph Waldo Emerson with Annotations* (10 vols., Boston, 1909-1914), V, 410.

[35]Among these were *Guardian of Health; Health, a Home Magazine* devoted to *Physical Culture; Boston Health Journal and Advocate of Physiological Reform; Monthly Miscellany and Journal of Health; Water-Cure Journal;* and *Journal of Health and Practical Educator.*

[36]Mason Wade, *Francis Parkman, Heroic Historian* (New York, 1942), 20.

[37]*Yale Literary Magazine,* VII (Nov. 1841), 36-37.

[38]*Common School Journal of the State of Pennsylvania,* I (Nov. 15, 1844), 340; *Eleventh Annual Report of the Condition of the Common Schools, to the City Council fo Cincinnati* (Cincinnati, 1840), 6; Henry Barnard, *School-Houses* (Providence, 1844), 31, 45; *District School Journal,* II (Sept. 1, 1841), 21-22; Charles Dickens, *American Notes for General Circulation* (London, 1842), 15, 33-34.

[39]George B. Emerson, *The Schoolmaster* (New York, 1842), 290.

[40]*Common School Journal,* V (Nov. 1, 1843), 323, VII (June 16, 1845), 177-80. Mann was said to appreciate "the great value of institutions for developing the muscular system in cities." *Boston Medical and Surgical Journal,* XXXII (June 25, 1845), 844.

[41]Comstock's 1845 report is quoted in Francis W. Shearman, ed., *System of Public Instruction and Primary School Law of Michigan* (Lansing, 1852), 457.

[42]The athletic movement was still in a formative stage. College men, in general, were not yet persuaded of the necessity of exercises and games; and many were guilty of "intense physical indolence." Francis Wayland, *Thoughts on the Present Collegiate System in the United States* (Boston, 1842), 118.

5

Saints And Their Bodies

by Thomas Wentworth Higginson

Ever since the time of that dyspeptic heathen, Plotinus, the saints have been "ashamed of their bodies." What is worse, they have usually had reason for the shame. Of the four famous Latin fathers, Jerome describes his own limbs as misshapen, his skin as squalid, his bones as scarcely holding together; while Gregory the Great speaks in his Epistles of his own large size, as contrasted with his weakness and infirmities. Three of the four Greek fathers—Chrysostom, Basil, and Gregory of Nazianzen—ruined their health early, and were wretched invalids for the remainder of their days. Three only of the whole eight were able-bodied men,—Ambrose, Augustine, and Athanasius; and the permanent influence of these three has been far greater, for good or for evil, than that of all the others put together.

Robust military saints there have doubtless been, in the Roman Catholic Church; George, Michael, Sebastian, Eustace, Martin, and Christopher the Christian Hercules. But these have always held a very secondary place in canonization. . . . The mediaeval type of sanctity was a strong soul in a weak body; and it could be intensified by strengthening the one or by further debilitating the other. The glory lay in contrast, not in combination . . . . It was reserved for the modern Pre-Raphaelites to attempt the combination of a maximum of saintliness with a minimum of pulmonary and digestive capacity.

It is to be reluctantly recorded, in fact, that the Protestant saints have not ordinarly had much to boast of, in physical stamina, as compared with the Roman Catholic. They have not got far beyond Plotinus. We do not think it worth while to quote Calvin on this point, for he, as everybody knows, was an invalid for his whole lifetime. But we do take it hard, that the jovial Luther, in the midst of his ale and skittles, should have deliberately censured Juvenal's *mens sana in corpore sano,* as a' pagan maxim!

If Saint Luther fails us, where are the advocates of the body to

From Thomas Wentworth Higginson, "Saints and Their Bodies," Atlantic Monthly, 1 (March 1858): 82-95.

look for comfort? Nothing this side of ancient Greece, we fear, will afford adequate examples of the union of saintly souls and strong bodies . . . .

It would be tedious to analyze the causes of this modern deterioration of the saints. The fact is clear. There is in the community an impression that physical vigor and spiritual sanctity are incompatible. We knew a young Orthodox divine who lost his parish by swimming the Merrimac River, and another who was compelled to ask a dismissal in consequence of vanquishing his most influential parishioner in a game of ten-pins; it seemed to the beaten party very unclerical. We further remember a match, in a certain sea-side bowling-alley, in which two brothers, young divines, took part. The sides being made up, with the exception of these two players, it was necessary to find places for them also. The head of one side accordingly picked his man, on the presumption (as he afterwards confessed) that the best preacher would naturally be the worst bowler. The athletic capacity, he thought, would be in inverse ratio to the sanctity. We are happy to add, that in this case his hopes were signally disappointed. But it shows in which way the popular impression lies.

The poets have probably assisted in maintaining the delusion. How many cases of consumption Wordsworth must have accelerated by his assertion, that "the good die first!" Happily, he lived to disprove his own maxim. We, too, repudiate it utterly. Professor Pierce has proved by statistics that the best scholars in our colleges survive the rest; and we hold that virtue, like intellect, tends to longevity. The experience of the literary class shows that all excess is destructive, and that we need the harmonious action of all the faculties . . . . No doubt, many of the noble and the pure were dying prematurely at the same time; but it proceeded from the same essential cause: physical laws disobeyed and bodies exhausted. The evil is, that what in the debauchee is condemned as suicide, is lauded in the devotee, as saintship. The *delirium tremens* of the drunkard conveys scarcely a sterner moral lesson than the second childishness of the pure and abstemious Southey.

But, happily, times change, and saints with them. Our moral conceptions are expanding to take in that "athletic virtue" of the Greeks, which Dr. Arnold, by precept and practice, defended. The modern English "Broad Church" aims at breadth of shoulders, as well as of doctrines. Kingsley paints his stalwart Philammons and Amyas Leighs, and his critics charge him with laying down a new definition of the saint, as a man who fears God and can walk a thousand miles in a thousand hours. Our American saintship, also is beginning to have a body to it, a "Body of Divinity," indeed. Look at our three great popular preachers. The vigor of the paternal blacksmith still swings the sinewy arm of Beecher; — Parker performed the labors, mental and physical, of four able-bodied men, until even his great strength temporarily yielded;—and if ever dyspepsia attacks the burly frame of Chapin, we fancy that dyspepsia will get the worst of it.

This is as it should be. One of the most potent causes of the ill-concealed alienation between the clergy and the people, in our community, is the supposed deficiency, on the part of the former, of a vigorous, manly life. It must be confessed that our saints suffer greatly from this moral and physical *anhoemia,* this bloodlessness, which separates them, more effectually than a cloister, from the strong life of the age. What satirists upon religion are those parents who say of their pallid, puny, sedentary, lifeless, joyless little offspring, "He is born for a minister," while the ruddy, the brave, and the strong are as promptly assigned to a secular career! . . . . We distrust the achievements of every saint without a body; and really have hopes of the Cambridge Divinity School, since hearing that it has organized a boat-club.

We speak especially of men, but the same principles apply to women. The triumphs of Rosa Bouheur and Harriet Hosmer grew out of a free and vigorous training, and they learned to delineate muscle by using it.

Everybody admires the physical training of military and naval schools. But these same persons never seem to imagine that the body is worth cultivating for any purpose, except to annihilate the bodies of others. Yet it needs more training to preserve life than to destroy it . . . . Do not waste your gymnastics on the West Point or Annapolis student, whose whole life will be one active exercise, but bring them into the professional schools and the counting-rooms. Whatever may be the exceptional cases, the stern truth remains, that the great deeds of the world can be more easily done by illiterate men than by sickly ones. Wisely said Horace Mann, "All through the life of a pure-minded but feeble-bodied man, his path is lined with memory's gravestones, which mark the spots where noble enterprises perished, for lack of physical vigor to embody them in deeds.

Physical health is a necessary condition of all permanent success. To the American people it has a stupendous importance, because it is the attribute of power in which they are losing ground. Guaranty us against physical degeneracy, and we can risk all other perils,— financial crisis, Slavery, Romanism, Mormonism, Border Ruffians, and New York assassins; "domestic malice, foreign levy, nothing" can daunt us. Guaranty us health, and Mrs. Stowe cannot frighten us with all the prophecies of Dred; but when her sister Catherine informs us that in all the vast female acquaintance of the Beecher family there are not a dozen healthy women, we confess ouselves a little tempted to despair of the republic.

The one drawback to satisfaction in our Public-School System is the physical weakness which it reveals and helps to perpetuate. One seldom notices a ruddy face in the school-room, without tracing it back to a Transatlantic origin. The teacher of a large school in Canada went so far as to declare to us, that she could recognize the children born this side the line by their invariable appearance of ill-health joined with the intellectual precocity, — stamina wanting, and the place supplied by equations. Look at a class of boys or girls in our Grammar Schools; a glance along the line of their backs affords a study of geometrical curves. You almost long to reverse the position of their heads, as Dante has those of the false prophets, and thus improve their figures; the rounded shoulders affording a vigorous chest, and the hollow chest an excellent back.

There are statistics to show that the average length of human life is increasing; but it is probable that this results from the diminution of epidemic diseases, rather than from any general improvement in *physique*. There are facts also to indicate an increase of size and strength with advancing civilization . . . . It is also known that the strongest American Indians cannot equal the average strength of wrist of Europeans, or rival them in ordinary athletic feats. Indeed, it is generally supposed that any physical deterioration is local, being peculiar to the United States . . . .

No one can visit Canada without being struck with the spectacle of a more athletic race of people than our own. On every side one sees rosy female faces and noble manly figures. In the shop-windows, in winter weather, hang snow-shoes, "gentlemen's and ladies' sizes." The street-corners inform you that the members of the "Curling Club" are supposed to meet to-day at "Dolly's" and the "Montreal Fox-hounds" at St. Lawrence Hall to-morrow. And next day comes off the annual steeple-chase, at the "Mile-End Course," ridden by gentlemen of the city with their own horses; a scene, by the way, whose exciting interest can scarcely be conceived by those accustomed only to "trials of speed" at agricultural exhibitions. Everything indicates out-door habits and athletic constitutions.

We shall assume, as admitted, therefore, the deficiency of physical health in America, and the need of a great amendment. But into the general question of cause and cure we do not propose to enter . . . .

Who, in this community, really takes exercise? Even the mechanic commonly confines himself to one set of muscles; the blacksmith acquires strength in his right arm, and the dancing-master in his left leg. But the professional or business man, what muscles has he at all? The tradition, that Phidippides ran from Athens to Sparta, one hundred and twenty miles, in two days, seems to us Americans as mythical as the Golden Fleece. Even to ride sixty miles in a day, to walk thirty, to run five, or to swim one, would cost most men among us a fit of illness, and many their lives. Let any man test his physical condition, we will not say by sawing his own cord of wood, but by an hour in the gymnasium or at cricket, and his enfeebled muscular apparatus will groan with rheumatism for a week. Or let him test the strength of his arms and chest by raising and lowering himself a few times upon a horizontal bar, or hanging by the arms to a rope, and he will probably agree with Galen in pronouncing it *robustum validumque laborem.* Yet so manifestly are these things within the reach of common constitutions, that a few weeks or months of judicious practice will renovate his whole system, and the most vigorous exercise will refresh him like a cold bath.

To a well-regulated frame, mere physical exertion . . . . is a great enjoyment, which is, of course, enhanced by the excitement of games and sports. To almost every man there is joy in the memory of these things; they are the happiest associations of his boyhood. It does not occur to him, that he also might be as happy as a boy, if he lived more like one. What do most men know of the "wild joys of living," the daily zest and luxury of out-door existence, in which every healthy boy beside them revels? — skating, while the orange sky of sunset dies away over the delicate tracery of gray branches, and the throbbing feet pause in their tingling motion, and the frosty air is filled with the shrill sound of distant steel, the resounding of the ice, and the echoes up the hillside? — sailing, beating up against a stiff breeze, with the waves thumping under the bow, as if a dozen sea-gods had laid their heads together to resist it? — climbing tall trees, where the higher foliage, closing around, cures the dizziness which began below, and one feels as if he had left a coward beneath and found a hero above? — the joyous hour of crowded life in football or cricket? — the gallant glories of riding and the jubilee of swimming?

The charm which all have found in Tom Brown's "School Days at Rugby" lies simply in this healthy boy's-life which it exhibits, and in the recognition of physical culture, which is so novel to Americans. At present, boys are annually sent across the Atlantic simply for bodily training. But efforts after the same thing begin to creep in among ourselves. A few Normal Schools have gymnasiums (rather neglected, however); the "Mystic Hall Female Seminary" advertises riding-horses; and we believe the new "Concord School" recognizes boating as an incidental;—but these are all exceptional cases, and far between . . . . Tradition spoke of Dr. Follen and German gymnastics; but the beneficent exotic was transplanted prematurely, and died. The only direct encouragement of athletic exercises which stands out in our memory of academic life was a certain inestimable shed on the "College Wharf," which was for a brief season the paradise of swimmers, and which, after having been deliberately arranged for their accomodation, was suddenly removed, the next season, to make room for coal-bins. Manly sports were not positively discouraged in our day,—but that was all.

We cling still to the belief, that the Persian curriculum of studies—to ride, to shoot, and to speak the truth—is the better part of a boy's education. As the urchin is undoubtedly physically safer for having learned to turn a somerset and fire a gun, perilous though these feats appear to mothers,—so his soul is made healthier, larger, freer, stronger, by hours and days of manly exercise and copious draughts of open air, at whatever risk of idle habits and bad companions. Even if the balance is sometimes lost, and play prevails, what matter? . . . .

The hours the idle schoolboy squandered
The man would die ere he'd forget.
Only keep in a boy a pure and generous heart, and, whether he work or play, his time can scarcely be wasted.

Should it prove, however, that the cultivation of active exercises diminishes the proportion of time given by children to study, we can only view it as an added advantage. Every year confirms us in the conviction, that our schools, public and private, systematically over-task the brains of the rising generation. We all complain that Young America grows to mental maturity too soon, and yet we all contribute our share to continue the evil. It is but a few weeks since we saw the warmest praises, in the New York newspapers, of a girl's school, in that city, where the appointed hours of study amounted to nine and a quarter daily, and the hours of exercise to a bare unit. Almost all the Students' Manuals assume that American students need stimulus instead of restraint, and urge them to multiply the hours of study and diminish those of out-door amusements and of sleep, as if the great danger did not lie that way already. When will parents and teachers learn to regard mental precocity as a disaster to be shunned, instead of a glory to be coveted? We could count up a dozen of young men who have graduated at Harvard College, during the last twenty years, with high honors, before the age of eighteen; and we suppose that nearly every one of them has lived to regret it . . . .

One invaluable merit of out-door sports is to be found in this, that they afford the best cement for childish friendship. Their associations outlive all others. There is many a man, now perchance hard and worldly, whom we love to pass in the street simply because in meeting him we meet spring flowers and autumn chestnuts, skates and cricket-balls, cherry-birds and pickerel. There is an indescribable fascination in the gradual transference of these childish companionships into maturer relations. We love to encounter in the contests of manhood those whom we first met at football, and to follow the profound thoughts of those who always dived deeper, even in the river, than our efforts could attain . . . .

Luckily, boy-nature is too strong for theory. And we admit, for the sake of truth, that physical education is not so entirely neglected among us as the absence of popular games would indicate. We suppose, that, if the truth were told, this last fact proceeds partly from the greater freedom of field-sports in this country. There are few New England boys who do not become familiar with the rod or gun in childhood . . . .

Again, the practice of match-playing is opposed to our habits, both as a consumer of time and as partaking too much of gambling. Still, it is done in the case of "firemen's musters," which are, we believe, a wholly indigenous institution. We have known a very few cases where the young men of neighboring country parishes have challenged each other to games of base-ball, as is common in England; and there was, if we mistake not, a recent match at football between the boys of the Fall River and the New Bedford High Schools. And within a few years regattas and cricket-matches have become common events. Still, these public exhibitions are far from being a full exponent of the athletic habits of our people; and there is really more going on among us than this meagre "pentathlon" exhibits.

Again, a foreigner is apt to infer, from the more desultory and unsystematized character of our out-door amusements, that we are less addicted to them than we really are. But this belongs to the habit of our nation, impatient, to a fault, of precedents and conventionalisms. The English-born Frank Forrester complains of the total indifference of our sportsmen to correct phraseology . . . . And yet, careless of these proprieties, Young America goes "gunning" to good purpose. So with all games. A college football-player reads with astonishment Tom Brown's description of the very complicated performance which passes under that name at Rugby. So cricket is simplified; it is hard to organize an American club into the conventional distribution of point and cover-point, long slip and short slip, but the players persist in winning the game by the most heterodox grouping. This consititutional independence has its good and evil results, in sports as elsewhere. It is this which has created the American breed of trotting horses, and which won the Cowes regatta by a mainsail as flat as a board.

But, so far as there is a deficiency in these respects among us, this generation must not shrink from the responsibility. It is unfair to charge it on the Puritans. They are not even answerable for Massachusetts; for there is no doubt that athletic exercises, of some sort, were far more generally practised in this community before the Revolution than at present. A state of almost constant Indian warfare then created an obvious demand for muscle and agility. At present there is no such immediate neccessity. And it has been supposed that a race of shopkeepers, brokers, and lawyers could live without bodies. Now that the terrible records of dyspepsia and paralysis are disproving this, we may hope for a reaction in favor of bodily exercises. And when we once begin the competition, there seems no reason why any other nation should surpass us. The wide area of our country, and its variety of surface and shore, offer a corresponding range of physical training . . . .

We have shown, that, in one way or another, American schoolboys obtain active exercise. The same is true, in a very limited degree, even of girls. They are occasionally, in our larger cities, sent to gymnasiums, — the more the better. Dancing-schools are better than nothing, though all the attendant circumstances are usually unfavorable. A fashionable young lady is estimated to traverse her three hundred miles a season on foot; and this needs training. But out-door exercise for girls is terribly restricted, first by their costume, and secondly by the remarks of Mrs. Grundy. All young female animals unquestionably require as much motion as their brothers, and naturally make as much noise, but what mother would not be shocked, in the case of her girl of twelve, by one-tenth the activity and uproar which are recognized as being the breath of life to her twin brother? Still, there is a change going on, which is tantamount to an admission that there is an evil to be remedied. Twenty years ago, if we mistake not, it was by no means considered "proper" for little girls to play with their hoops and balls on Boston Common; and swimming and skating have hardly been recognized as "lady-like" for half that period of time.

. . . American men, how few carry athletic habits into manhood! The great hindrance, no doubt, is absorption in business; and we observe that this winter's hard times and consequent leisure have given a great stimulus to outdoor sports. But in most places there is the further obstacle, that a certain stigma of boyishness goes with them. So early does this begin, that we remember, in our teens, to have been slightly reproached with juvenility, because, though a Senior Sophister, we still clung to football. Juvenility! We only wish we had the opportunity now. Full-grown men are, of course, intended to take not only as much, but far more active exercise than boys. Some physiologists go so far as to demand six hours of out-door life daily, and it is absurd in us to complain that we have not the healthy animal happiness of children, while we forswear their simple sources of pleasure.

Most of the exercise habitually taken by men of sedentary pursuits is in the form of walking. We believe its merits to be greatly overrated. Walking is to real exercise what vegetable food is to animal; it satisfies the appetite, but the nourishment is not sufficiently concentrated to be invigorating. It takes a man out-doors, and it uses his muscles, and therefore of course it is good; but it is not the best kind of good. Walking, for walking's sake, becomes tedious. We must not ignore the *play-impulse* in human nature, which, according to Schiller, is the foundation of all Art. In female boarding-schools, teachers uniformly testify to the aversion of pupils to the prescribed walk. Give them a sled, or a pair of skates, or a row-boat, or put them on horseback, and they will protract the period of exercise till the teacher in turn grumbles. Put them into a gymnasium, with an efficient teacher, and they will soon require restraint, instead of urging.

Gymnastic exercises have two disadvantages: one, in being commonly performed under cover; . . . another, in requiring apparatus, and at first a teacher. These apart, perhaps no other form of exercise is so universally invigorating. A teacher is required, less for the sake of stimulus than of precaution. The tendency is almost always to dare too much; and there is also need of a daily moderation in commencing exercises; for the wise pupil will always prefer to supple his muscles by mild exercises and calisthenics, before proceeding to harsher performances on the bars and ladders . . . . The feats once learned, a private gymnasium can easily be constructed, of the simplest apparatus, and so daily used; though nothing can wholly supply the stimulus afforded by a class in a public institution, with a competent teacher. In summer, the whole thing can partially be dispensed with; but we are really unable to imagine how any person gets through the winter happily without a gymnasium.

For the favorite in-door exercise of dumb-bells we have little to say; they are not an enlivening performance, nor do they task a variety of muscles,—while they are apt to strain and fatigue them, if used with energy. Far better, for a solitary exercise, is the Indian club, a lineal descendant of that antique one in whose handle rare medicaments were fabled to be concealed. The modern one is simply a rounded club, weighing from four pounds upwards, according to the strength of the pupil; grasping a pair of these by the handles, he learns a variety of exercises, having always before him the fears of the marvellous Mr. Harrison, whose praise is in the "Spirit of the Times," and whose portrait adorns the back of Dr. Trall's Gymnastics. By the latest bulletins, that gentleman measured forty-two and a half inches round the chest, and employed clubs weighing no less than forty-seven pounds.

It may seem to our non-resistant friends to be going rather far, if we should indulge our saints in taking boxing lessons; yet it is not long since a New York clergyman saved his life in Broadway by the judicious administration of a "cross-counter" or a "flying crook," and we have not heard of his ex-communication from the Church of the Militant. No doubt, a laudable aversion prevails, in this country, to the English practices of pugilism; yet it must be remembered that sparring is, by its very name, a "science of self-defence"; and if a gentleman wishes to know how to hold a rude antagonist at bay, in any emergency, and keep out of an undignified scuffle, the means are most easily afforded him by the art which Pygmalion founded. Apart from this, boxing exercises every muscle in the body, and gives a wonderful quickness to eye and hand. These same remarks apply, though in a minor degree, to fencing also.

Billiards is a graceful game, and affords, in some respects, admirable training, but is hardly classed among athletic exercises. Tenpins afford, perhaps, the most popular form of exercise among us, and have become almost a national game, and a good one, too, so far as it goes. The English game of bowls is less entertaining, and is, indeed, rather a sluggish sport, though it has the merit of being played in the open air. The severer British sports, as tennis and rackets, are scarcely more than names, to us Americans.

Passing now to out-door exercises (and no one should confine himself to in-door ones,) we hold with Thalesian school, and rank water first . . . . A square mile even of pond water is worth a year's schooling to any intelligent boy. A boat is a kingdom. We personally own one,—a mere flat-bottomed "float," with a centre-board. It has seen service, — it is eight years old, — has spent two winters under the ice, and been fished in by boys every day for as many summers. It grew at last so hopelessly leaky, that even the boys disdained it. It cost seven dollars originally, and we would not sell it to-day for seventeen. To own the poorest boat is better than hiring the best. It is a link to Nature; without a boat, one is so much less a man.

Sailing is of course delicious; it is as good as flying to steer any-thing with wings of canvas, whether one stand by the wheeel of a clip-pership, or by the clumsy stern-oar of a "gundalow." But rowing has also its charms; and the Indian noiselessness of the paddle, beneath the fringing branches of the Assabeth or Artichoke, puts one into Fai-ryland at once, and Hiawatha's *cheemaun* becomes a possible pos-session. Rowing is peculiarly graceful and appropriate as a feminine exercise, and any able-bodied girl can learn to handle one light oar at the first lesson, and two at the second; this, at least, we demand of our own pupils.

Swimming has also a birdlike charm of motion. The novel ele-ment, the free action, the abated draper, give a sense of personal contact with Nature which nothing else so fully bestows. No later tri-umph of existence is so fascinating, perhaps, as that in which the boy first wins his panting way across the deep gulf that severs one green bank from another, (ten yards, perhaps,) and feels himself thence-forward lord of the watery world. The Athenian phrase for a man who knew nothing was, that he could "neither read nor swim." Yet there is a vast amount of this ignorance; the majority of sailors, it is said, can-not swim a stroke, and in a late lake disaster, many able-bodied men perished by drowning, in calm water, only half a mile from shore. At our watering-places it is rare to see a swimmer venture out more than a rod or two, though this proceeds partly from the fear of sharks, — as if sharks of the dangerous order were not more afraid of the rocks than the swimmers of being eaten. But the fact of the timidity is unquestionable; and we were told by a certain clerical frequenter of a watering-place, himself a robust swimmer, that he had never met but two companions who would venture boldly out with him, both being ministers, and one a distinguished Ex-President of Brown University. We place this fact to the credit of the bodies of our saints.

But space forbids us thus to descant on the details of all active exercises. Riding may be left to the eulogies of Mr. N.P. Willis, and cricket to Mr. Lillywhite's "Guide." We will only say, in passing, that it is pleasant to see the rapid spread of clubs for the latter game, which a few years since was practised only by a few transplanted English-men and Scotchmen; and it pleasant also to observe the twin growth of our indigenous American game of base-ball, whose briskness and unceasing activity are perhaps more congenial, after all, to our national character, than the comparative deliberation of cricket. Football, bating its roughness, is the most glorious of all games to those whose animal life is sufficiently vigorous to enjoy it. Skating is just at present the fashion for ladies as well as gentlemen, and needs no apostle; the open weather of the current winter has been unusu-ally favorable for its practice, and it is destined to become a perma-nent institution.

For, after all, the secret charm of all these sports and studies is simply this, — that they bring us into more familiar intercourse with Nature. They give us that *vitam sub divo* in which the Roman exulted, — those out-door days, which, say the Arabs, are not to be reckoned in the length of life.

We know persons who, after years of abstinence from athletic sports or the pursuits of the naturalist or artist, have resumed them, simply in order to restore to the woods and the sunsets the zest of the old fascination. Go out under pretence of shooting on the marshes or botanizing in the forests; study entomology, that most fascinating, most neglected of all the branches of natural history; go to paint a red maple-leaf in autumn, or watch a pickerel-line in winter; meet Nature on the cricket ground or at the regatta; swim with her, ride with her, run with her, and she gladly takes you back once more within the horizon of her magic, and your heart of manhood is born again into more than the fresh happiness of the boy.

6

The Great Contest: Fashion v. Peytona (1845)

THE GREAT CONTEST.
Between the North and the South.

PEYTONA, THE SOUTHERN MARE.
VICTORIOUS.

Tremendous Excitement on the Race Course.
Immense Concourse of People.

The Morning.

At a very early hour yesterday morning, New York showed by evident and significant signs, that it was no common day. It is well known that her industrious citizens are no long sleepers when business calls to resume the daily task. But say what we will, there is a difference between work and play, toil and enjoyment, care and sport. Yesterday was a day dedicated to the latter, and we again repeat that the thousands and tens of thousands who turned out for the Long Island races, showed clearly the meaning of the phrase, "life let us cherish."

It was an exciting, but very beautiful morning; exciting because the contest between the North and the South for the dominion of the turf was to be settled, before the shades of evening closed on the well-trodden race ground. It is well understood that the ambiguity of the relative pretensions of the two great sections of the country to this honor, is the natural result of former well balanced successes. The North beat the South twice, and twice the South returned the compliment; their yearnings then for victory were as keen as Damascus sword blades. In addition to the sectional feeling and the strong rivalry of sportsmen, and in one sense partizans—the vast sums of money pending on the race, attached a degree of absorbing interest to the result, quite proportionate to the great demonstration that took place.

From New York Herald, 5 May 1845

Scene at the Ferries—Going to the Races.

More than three thousand persons crossed the South Ferry yesterday morning before 8 o'clock, for the races. As the morning progressed, the crowd increased rapidly, and a scene of tumult, disorder, and confusion ensued. Apple women's stands were overturned, an omnibus upset, fighting, swearing, pushing, screaming and shouting in abundance.—All seemed eager to reach the ground. Long trains of carriages, filled with all sorts of people, reaching to Broadway, lined Whitehall Street. Here was the magnificent barouche of the millionaire, full of gay, laughing, dark-eyed *demoiselles,* jammed in between a Bowery stage and a Broadway hack—here were loafers and dandies, on horseback and on foot—sporting gentlemen in green coats and metal buttons—Southerners from Louisiana, Mississippi and Alabama, with anxious faces, but hearts full of hope, "a pocket full of rocks," and a calm determination to await the result. The whole Union had in fact sent delegates to represent it in the grand contest which this day ushered in—all business seemed laid aside—one spirit animated the vast multitude. Omnibusses of all dimensions, cabriolets, chariots, drays, wagons, and every description of vehicle were put in requisition.

"Bill," said a singular specimen of humanity, whose slouch cap, plaistered soap-locks, and "forty inch" trowsers, denoted him as belonging to that class of our citizens commonly styled the "Boys"—"Bill, I tell yer *Petuny's* the crack hoss o' the track—she's bound to beat, she is, and if you want to bet, I'll go ye anything from an oyster stew to a new top piece at Tice's, or a hot supper at Sweeny's.

"By the blood and bones of old Gineral Putnam vat rid down the stone steps of the Old Bowery (said Bill) if I hadn't no more patriotism than you've got I'd never call myself von of the Boys again. Talk about *Petuny.* I tell ye Fashion's a York hoss, and a Southern hoss cant begin to touch her, no how. Go way from me, I vont talk to a boy that vants to bet agin his own country; go vay vid you." Here a great rush. took place towards the gate, in which several persons were more or less injured, draymen cursing, cabmen roaring—"I say, Jack, tell that ere gentleman with the telegraphic nose to leave my way, or if he doesn't, I'm blowed if I don't drive through both him and the gate, without giving him the trouble of opening it."

Another scene took place at the Railroad Ticket window. A gentleman while purchasing a ticket had his pocket picked by one of the light-fingered tribe, who was pursued through the battery into Castle garden, and after giving chase for some time, was finally captured and delivered of a cotton pocket handkerchief, an empty purse and a small piece of pigtail. "Thimble-rig" and "trick o' the loop," seemed in great demand, and in some cases, early as the sport began, a sure game was made.

In short, the whole scene was of a very exciting and disorderly character. At the Fulton ferry somewhat similar occurrences took place, though no blame is to be attached to the proprietors of the ferries, or the gate-keepers. By 12 'clock about 30,000 persons had passed over the South and 20,000 over Fulton ferries.

We saw many distinguished sporting characters, politicians, editors, reporters, managers, actors, printers' devils, &c., among the group. Tryon, of the New Bowery Theatre came down in a splendid vehicle—and "Mi Boy and the Brigadier" followed on the look out for news.

The first train started from the terminus of the railway, Brooklyn, at 7 o'clock, followed by others at 8, 9, 9 1/4, 9 3/4, and 10 1/2 o'clock. With each of these trains one of our corps started, to not only note whatever might occur, but to afford the voyageurs the benefit of their presence, and also because it is fitting that the *Herald* should be represented, if not identified with all marvellous progressive movements of our race. A terrific rush from the ferry boats to the cars was the work of a moment, and another sufficed to pile them in, and about the cars, in all sorts of postures and attitudes. A large number of cars had been fitted up with temporary seats made of deal scantlings; some were placed transversely, others parallel with the length; whatever were their directions, however, happy was the wight, who got a seat, here or there, for forty minutes or so, for the lawful consideration of twenty-five cents. Our reporters on comparing notes found that there was no casualty of sufficient importance to publish to the world, and they were immensely gratified to learn that the vast migration of citizens took place under their judicious supervision, without any accident or misfortune to damp the ardor of the day's sport. It was observed that the moment the trains halted, the passengers bolted as though they were in danger of being blown up by retaining their seats one second after the wheels of the cars had ceased to revolve. It was moreover ascertained from accurate observations, that for the most part each passenger the instant his feet touched the ground, turned round and gave a parting glance of rather a contemptuous cast at the vehicles, and without an exception, save one each and every individual who had passed the time going out in smoking, threw away the stumps of their cigars; but he who persisted in tugging away at his, had his whiskers much singed by reason of the united heat of the weather, at the Course, and the blaze of the cigar. Having nothing to add further to this section of our narrative, we will proceed to describe . . .

The Course.

On the arrival of the two earlier trains, there was not a very remarkable degree of bustle. The passengers were set down immediately beside the course, to which admittance was procured through narrow entrances, about three or four hundred yards from the railway, on the edge of which are half a dozen of dwelling houses. These were all converted into dram shops and places of refreshment, and if they did not do more than their share of the business, they had the honor of an early call from a large portion of the race-going blades, who, after their dusty and perilous journey, per railway, were ready for a grateful draught of something or other to wash down the dust. From this point to the entrance of the course, and, as far beyond it, equal, perhaps to a fifth of the circumference of the course, was a continuous line of tents on one side of the thoroughfare—the other being bounded by the fence of the Course. This passage was about twenty yards wide, so that, there being a good deal of room to spare, it was occupied by all sorts of irregular forces, and indescribable camp followers, sutlers, loungers, rowdies, gamblers, and twenty other species of the genus loose fish. Here you saw a bucket of water, with two or three little negro boys for an escort; there baskets of oranges as thick as yellow gowans; piles of oysters reared their rough exteriors in huge profusion, and the confectionery peered up in tempting masses, albeit in rather a melting mood on account of the sun's vertical rays, which spared nothing, sweet or sour, that memorable day. Business in the tents—the wigwams—the culinary camps and conventicles commenced at an early hour, and was carried on with a briskness that betimes looked like voracity, and fears were occasionally excited that the impetuosity of the hungry crowd might find a melancholy end in the prodigious tubs of lemonade and brandy punch that lay in elegant negligence around the tables, whose extended surfaces supported masses of ham, sandwiches, lobsters, loaves, decanters, glasses, and all the paraphernalia of drinking that could be condensed into the space. The rap of the hammer in erecting these tents mingled incessantly with the popping of corks, for a couple of hours, when the music of mastication reigned triumphant. During all this time, from the very beginning of the arrivals, gamblers of all descriptions swarmed about in every direction. In the space of a hundred yards we counted no less than seventeen ill-looking wretches, using their utmost cunning to cajole the natives with three cups and one ball. Various unfavorable characteristics made them conspicuous; but what was particularly striking, hardly one of these thimble-riggers had a table or stand, but as a substitute carried on their operations on their knees, which were raised to a horizontal direction and supported them on the curved heads of their walking-sticks; the look of these worthies in this attitude was quite in keeping with their appearance, character and habits—all of which are as graceless—to use the word in any sense—as can possibly be imagined. Each of them had his jackall or attendant to raise his game, with whom a continual rhapsody of slang sentences was kept up, something like this:—"I'll bet ten or twenty dollars which ball the pea's under." "I'll bet you I do—it's under that middle one." "What will ye bet." "I'll lay you $50 you don't tell me which it's under." "I'll not bet this time." "Let me try." "I'll bet you or any body can't tell which cup has the pea under; here's fifty dollars in gold, who'll take me up." "I'll bet you five it's under that one." "I'll not bet five, I'll stake fifty no one tells where the pea is; its neither there, nor there, but its here, gentlemen, &c." In every part of the space outside the wall, this jargon kept grating on the ear. Of sweat tables, too, there were no scarcity, presided over by gentlemen of all hues of color, whose invitation to passers by to "come and win and lose a dollar," were part of the floating harmony.

The enclosed area, whose circumference of a mile formed the Course, was the resort of the carriages and horsemen; and those pedestrians who declined to pay for a place on the stand, or who were able to screw up their self denial to leave the enticing precincts of the booths and tents we have spoken of to witness the potent contest between the horses. On first casting the eye over this field, its outlines and occupants were quite indistinctly seen, as enormous clouds of dust floated over it like the smoke of artillery over a bombarded city. In attempting to wend your way to it countless obstacles impeded your steps. The crowd moving in counter currents, the carriages hastening to take up a favorable position, and the oppressive masses of pulverized clay that bounded in mid air, all contributed to make the progress to the Course slow indeed. Immediately on the right of the Judge's stand, and opposite to the great stand for spectators, on the other side of the course, a dense mass of vehicles of all descriptions congregated. Among these, the most striking were a number of the city omnibusses, which had been engaged for the day by a full complement of passengers, who, from the roofs of them were enabled to have a capital view of the race. As may be expected, the occupants of them were of a more mixed class than those who lolled in private carriages, or those engaged *special* for the occasion; accordingly, our friends of the omnibuses managed to while away time in a right free and easy manner. Here and there out of the windows might be seen protruding a rubicund visage, smiling complacently down on a jar of Old Jamaica, whose contents were being dispensed to a knot of thirsty looking souls beneath the shadow of the high carriage; in another quarter, the bowl of a huge Dutch pipe kept steaming away with less noise but more uniformity than the chimney of the locomotives on the road contiguous; whilst now and again a willing hand was stretched out to lay hold on that sparkling glass of grog, that the boun-tiful dispenser of the beverage below had raised to his friend inside. All over the face of the field the crowd was continually in motion; hundreds seated themselves on the grass, but by far the larger number went roaming up and down, seeking rest but finding none, until finding spirits more wicked than themselves, they entered into the swept and garnished groggery, and "verily, the last state of these men was worse than the first." Around the whole field dense masses of human beings were observed in different postures. On the slate roof of the houses already mentioned, situated at the entrance to the Course from the railroad, there could not be fewer than three or four hundred perched for four consecutive hours in the sultry sun; two or three trees also of a considerable size, which grew on the margin of the field now referred to, afforded an observatory to several scores, many of whom ascended to the very summit, and the extremities of the branches fit to bear them. In all this enterprise in search of accommodation, it is pleasing that no accident occurred, for, consid-ering the vast mass of human beings, and their varied methods of dis-posing of themselves, nothing was more apparently probable than hurt to life and limb. The nearest approach to it before the race was from a horse that broke away with a light wagon or gig; he started from near the centre of the course, headed at a hard pace towards the main approach from the Brooklyn high road, turned to the right at an increased speed, making every thing fly before him. At last two or three resolute individuals expertly seized the lines, and brought him to a dead halt, without hurt or molestation to any one. A most fortunate and strange thing considering the number of persons that were exposed to injury from such a cause. As the hours flew past, the crowd increased with amazing rapidity. Every train brought its full quota, and the roads leading to the course were every one of them covered with a continuous torrent of men, horses, wagons, omnib-uses and carriages, up to two o'clock. About this hour the multitude had got to its maximum strength, and if would seem an exaggeration, but it is a fact, that the cessation of arrivals was followed by a sensible amelioration in the state of the atmosphere; for the direction of the wind being parallel with that of the approach to the Course from New York, the air was thoroughly impregnated with the dust set in motion on the trodden and thronged roads, and as soon as they disem-bogued their myriads, the southerly breeze came pure and balmy and refreshing. It would be out of the bounds of possibility, to convey a graphic sketch of the scene on this field, where we have been wand-ering in fancy for the last few minutes, but where, yesterday forenoon, we were in the body, and witnesses of as large an accumulation of the realities of life, as could be seen by human eye in one day.

On the stand there could not be fewer than thirty thousand persons; every train added countless hosts, for the first race of everybody who obtained admission, was to the grand stand, and the solicitude to secure places increased in the direct ratio of the difficulty of finding them, so that the onset of the last was impetuous in the extreme. A harder day's labor no men performed that day, than those who had charge of the stairs. We saw several altercations with fellows who attempted to get on the stand without tickets, but they were invariably foiled. More fortunate by far, however, was the onset made on its left extremity, at about one o'clock. At that hour it became desirable to remove some of the boards of the back wall to give free admission to the air to those below; the rowdies no sooner got a foothold, than they attacked and carried the outer wall, thirty feet high, by escalade. By a species of affinity their chums above collected in sufficient force to co-operate in the movement, and in about two minutes our reporter counted fifty who either rolled over, or were hoisted by the coat collar and inexpressibles, to a place among the 30,000. At last the trick was detected and stopped, but not before a strong posse of boys had profitted by the example set them; and for the ensuing half hour, hordes of irregular troops kept prowling about the wall, like a tribe of Bedouins around a doomed caravan. It was understood that the horses were to start at one o'clock, and from this hour the excitement on the stand became intense, and until two, each individual kept his position, or looked for one that was better; with eye constantly bent to the Judge's stand. We saw several persons from Canada among the crowd, and we understand that every section of the Union was largely represented. The lower portion of the stand was occupied by refreshment tables on one side and farb and roulette, and all sorts of gaming tables on the other. Betting and gambling and guzzling went on at a rapid rate, and the work of Satan here progressed with a celerity and promptitude that must have been greatly pleasing to his infernal highness.

At about 2 o'clock the excitement which had been gathering like a thunder cloud all day, was tremendous. In the vicinity of the judges' stand, and the enclosed space before the grand stand, the multitude heaved and fell like the billows of the ocean in a mighty storm; and from amidst this excited throng, looking up at the stands, the immense sea of faces, and the hoarse murmur of expectation that spread through the thronged buildings, was one of the most extraordinary scenes that can well be imagined. Here might be seen representatives from all parts of the Union, and the countenances of all betokened that their whole spirit was awakened, and their entire attention, for the time, given to the anxiously expected scene that was about to be enacted. In one corner might be heard the Bowery boy arranging his final bet of a five on Fashion, and in another the Southerner concluding his bet with a Northern blood, for some cool hundreds on Peytona. In the general eagerness to obtain a favorable position to view the coming race, many, at the peril of life and limb, were climbing on the different parts of the buildings, and the efforts of those who, though "not shaped for sportive tricks," still persisted in climbing to the roof and eaves, afforded much amusement to the expectant multitude. Two tall trees that stand toward the head of the course, were filled with those who, probably not relishing the idea of paying for grand stand or jockey club tickets, selected this commanding situation, and patiently waited in their perches for hours previous to the race. One of them, we observed, caused considerable annoyance to his fellows, by swinging about with the activity of a cat. The track all round was lined inside by vehicles of every description and shape, from the rickety oyster cart, with its skeleton of a horse, to the aristocratic turn-out of the "upper ten thousand." Omnibusses, farm-wagons, carryalls—in fact every kind, and on the top of them were perched the gazing many.

In the club stand there was about this time, all the symptoms of an incipient disturbance. The crowd, perceiving that the entrance of a female, in charge of a gentleman, was disputed by the officers, with the inherent gallantry that is so characteristic of this nation, an immediate excitement was created in her favor, and an angry rush took place, for the purpose of insisting on her admissal; but on finding that the cause of the difficulty was a person of questionable character, the feeling was changed, and she retired to a carriage within the area.

On the Course itself there was the utmost difficulty in preserving the track clear from intruders, and to the efficiency of a few may be ascribed the comparative order which was at length established. A young gentleman, mounted on a black horse, was quite conspicuous in the part he took, riding up and down, and most fearlessly charging the intruding multitude with his whip. The indomitable Captain Isaiah Rynders, mounted on his famous white charger, rendered most valuable services, and never have we seen such perfect self-possession and invincible good humor as was displayed on this occasion by the leader of the Empires. He was loudly cheered by the members of the Jockey Club, and by his address to the crowd, appealing to their feelings of pride as northerners, to show the southerners assembled that fair play could be given to their horse, succeeded in obtaining a clear course. Country McClusky also appeared on horseback, and used his hands, feet and legs, most liberally. Yankee Sullivan, and others, including Bill Harrington, who, with the rest, preserved their temper and feelings most admirably midst the hundred provocations so plentifully given them, most ably seconded the efforts of the rest. Justice Matsell, by his appearance, was of most essential service, and, where-ever a notorious character, or suspicious-looking individual, fell under the influence of his eye, their stay was short. The worthy Recorder, by his influence and presence, was most efficient in two or three emergencies.

We observed Mr. Prescott Hall in the Judge's stand exerting his lungs to the utmost to preserve the necessary order, but beyond that we did not see any particular action on his part. There was also the tall form of another gentleman who is quite prominent in sporting affairs, looming up in the same place, but the exertions requisite appeared to have been left entirely to the twenty or thirty constables who were expected to control the hundred thousand people on the Course. The indefatigable Mr. Toler, the Treasurer of the Club, appeared to take the whole of its work on his shoulders, and he was so occupied with discharging his multifarious duties, that our reporter was unable to obtain from him even the names of the Stewards of the day and the Judges of the occasion.

The booths and temporary stands with refreshments that were erected outside were crowded during the whole day, and we should judge that, be the result of the race what it may to northern men in general, the proprietors of these establishments at least, returned to town to the tune of "money in both pockets." The gambling fraternity were by no means inactive on the occasion, and the extraordinary force of example that always tempts people to gamble at a race course was fully followed here. Roulette, sweat-cloth, thimble-rig and all the usual games were in full operation during the whole day, and many a one felt the full truth, of the old adage touching a fool and his money being soon parted. There was one feature we noticed with pleasure, which was the almost universal absence of all the gross scenes of intemperance that used formerly to disgrace our race-courses, and despite all the attractions of the various drinkables in the different booths, the crowd generally seemed to partake more of the eatables and the different temperance beverages of soda water, lemonade and the like.

In the meantime all eyes were turned towards the judges' stand, where it was expected the horses would be led out previous to being saddled, and when we mention this stand, we should say that we were surprised to see it occupied by some sixteen or seventeen individuals, amongst whom was one of very questionable character, shouting and cheering, cap in hand. Last year our reporter was refused the accommodation of this stand for the public interest, whilst on this occasion some dozen strangers had free admission, and the reporters had to get their information and obtain a sight as best they could.

The Race.

About half past two o'clock, the bugle sounded to bring forth the horses. They shortly after showed themselves, and each were received with shouts that might have almost been heard from one end of the isle to the other. We have so often described them that it is almost needless to repeat it; suffice it to say that both looked as fine as silk, in first rate condition. Mr. J. Laird topped the pit-skin across Fashion, dressed in a purple jacket and red and gold cap. The "indomitable Barney" mounted Peytona. Two finer animals and abler jockies it is supposed there is not in the States. Having gone to the scales Laird made up his weight to 125 lbs.; and Barney his to 118. Many thought that Fashion had "a leetle" too much upon her, but she appeared the same as ever.

After some endeavors on the part of those in authority, the track was well cleared as could be expected under the circumstances, thanks to the indefatigable Capt. Rynders, Bill Harrington, Country McClusky, Yankee Sullivan, Don Casseau, or some such name, on his blind black mare. At 33 minutes past two o'clock the horses were saddled and mounted, and at the first tap they went forth in gallant style, Peytona having the poll, but a most beautiful start—nose and nose. They kept thus together round the bottom, Peytona gently falling off, but yet keeping her nose close to the tail of her rival, evidently waiting attendance. They kept thus to the first quarter, the same to the half. At the third quarter they were close together, Peytona making up, evidently waiting attendance; at the drawgate she came in front, and led to the judges stand a length and a half in front. For the second mile they appeared to keep in this position round the bottom, but owing to the clouds of dust prevailing just then, only an occasional glimpse could be caught of them; but they seemed to maintain a similar position round the top to the drawgate, where Fashion appeared to come in front, but on reaching the judge's chair, Fashion's nose was close up with that of Peytona, on the inside. For the third mile they kept well thus together round, to the nearing of the half mile post, where the heavy patch before alluded to occurs, Fashion appeared to gain somewhat, but shortly after Peytona reached her flank, nipping her hard, but Fashion appeared immediately afterwards to make the gap wider. At the drawgate, Fashion appeared two lengths in front, but on nearing the judge's stand, Peytona had her nose close on the flank of her opponent. It was now pretty evident that Barney had it all his own way, and could do just as he pleased with the affair, and faces became elongated, while others could scarce keep their feet . . . . Round the bottom they kept well together, but owing to dust, &c, there was no seeing further, until they reached the drawgate towards home, where Fashion appeared to have the lead, but it was immediately taken from her, and Peytona came home two lengths in front, making the first heat in 7 m. 39 s., amid the most unbounded cheers.

The betting now took a very different turn—50 to 30 was offered on Peytona, but there was great shyness; 50 to 25 was taken to some extent. The course was kept in the best order possible, previous to the second heat, under all the circumstances.—This was owing to the indefatigable exertions of Bill Harrington and others. A few light skirmishes took place previous to the commencement of the next heat, but after a sufficient dose of punishment having been administered, pro, and con, matters were adjusted, and every preparation was made for the succeeding heat.

The Second Heat.—

At the first attempt they did not go forth, and were pulled short up, owing to what appeared a rather premature tap. They returned and commenced again, *de novo.* At the second attempt they went forth Peytona leading a neck, Laird well up round the bottom to the quarter; on approaching the half Fashion went in front, and led to the three-quarter. Here the crowd broke in at the lower drawgate, which caused some confusion for a few moments, but owing to the vigilance of those now engaged, was soon got under. Fashion led to the draw-gate, where they came together to the Judge's chair, head and head, no telling who had the lead. For the second mile Fashion appeared to have the lead to the quarter, the other well up; they kept so up the back stretch; at the three-quarter it was just so. Fashion still kept the lead, closely waited upon by Peytona; it was thus round the top, but at the drawgate they were again well together, Fashion having the track, but at the end of the second mile, notwithstanding Fashion's advantage Peytona led to the Judge's stand a head in front. For the third mile they kept so so to the quarter; a table cloth might have covered the pair to the half-mile post. They kept just so to the three-quarters; at the drawgate Fashion led on the inside, but Peytona had got her and led her home a length in advance. "Now comes the tug of war." Peytona maintained her position, both well together; she gained a little on her round the bottom, but apparently with little effect; at the half they were well together, which was maintained to the three-quarters, but here the mob closed in so as to obscure sight from the club stand.— Fashion appeared to have the lead, but on approaching the draw-gate, notwithstanding the mob closing on the track, Peytona led the way a clear length in advance in 7:45¼. We have only time to say that it was quite a waiting race; "Barney" knew what he had to do, and did it nobly, and doubtless more he would have done if it had been required.

The following is the summary of the whole affair:

Miles	First Heat	Second Heat
First	1:54	1:58
Second	1:53	1:54
Third	1:57	1:55¼
Fourth	1:55¾	1:58
Total	7:39¾	7:45¼

SPEED OF PEYTONA, THE WINNER OF THE GREAT RACE:

Distance, miles	Distance, feet	Time, seconds	Distance pr sec'd	Strides pr sec'd
First Heat 4	21,120	459¼	46	2
Second Heat .. 4	21,120	465¼	45 2/5	2

Remarks —

The horses at length appeared, and after the close of the first heat (an account of which we have given), when the word passed round that Peytona, the southern favorite, was the conqueror, a most exciting scene was presented on the ground. The southern gentry having their most anxious expectations thus so nearly consummated, were loud in their rejoicing and hearty congratulations and warm hand shakings were seen on all sides among them, whilst the more cool and deliberate Northerners remained perfectly cool and easy, though certainly their spirits were not quite so buoyant as before this damper to their sanguine expectation however, the general excitement of the crowd on the Course was by no means allayed; in fact, if possible, it was more intense than ever, and the various groups walking up and down might be heard discussing with the greatest earnestness the chances and probabilities for and against their respective favorites, and in some instances waxing so high in dispute as to cause apprehensions of a breach of the peace—but a few instances of fighting however came under our immediate notice, and as far as we could ascertain, but very few took place altogether. In the interim between the heats, quite an alarm was created in the gambling establishments underneath the stand by an ominous crack of the rafters overhead, and a most terrific rush from the tables took place, money and game being alike forgotten in the horror of being crushed by the superincumbent mass of people on the stand. Luckily the alarm was a false one, and except the descent of a couple of sightseers from the stand above to the room below and the astonishment of a roulette table keeper at their landing on the top of his apparatus and disturbing his game, no damage was done. In the early part of the day, one of the stair cases leading to the stand broke down, but also in this instance the damage was slight, as all we could gather was the loss one unfortunate gentleman sustained in his wig, which, considering the warmth of the day, must have been no slight loss to the owner.

After the interval of twenty minutes the horses were again ready, and the crowd resumed their positions round the course; this time wound up to the pitch of frenzy, and, on the announcement of Peytona being again the conqueror, we can compare the universal cheer that broke forth to nothing that we have ever heard. The southerners appeared perfectly beside themselves with joy, and afforded quite a striking contrast to the northerners, whose lengthened faces were indicative of the shortening their purses and fame had undergone within the last few minutes. The result was soon announced from the judge's stand, and the time of the different heats marked in front of that building, and thus the south was declared the victor of the turf.

The Return.

Both heats having been won by Peytona, and the necessity of a third heat being precluded, every one was busily engaging in making preparations for their return to town, and it was marvellous to see the astonishing celerity with which the ground was cleared of its thousands and thousands of spectators. One after another the various vehicles disappeared, and in a quarter of an hour the ground was almost deserted; though the booths and gambling establishments outside still had a number of customers, who remained till the train started for Brooklyn, at six o'clock, and though we thought the crowded state of the cars in the morning could not be exceeded, yet they were far more crammed, and it not only required much agility to obtain a seat, but a good share of strength to keep it. However good, bad and indifferent, we all rolled off together, and a more dust-begrimed, dirty looking set of passengers we doubt have ever travelled on one train before. In consequence of the length of the train, it was seven o'clock before it arrived at the tunnel at Brooklyn, and the horrid screeches, yells and noises which they kept up during their passage through it, were well calculated to give an idea of Pandemonium. As might be supposed, the boats were crowded down with vehicles and passengers of every kind, and the day must have proved very profitable to the railroads and ferry boats on the route. Not the least gratifying fact is, the absence of any material accident among such an immense concourse of people.

The Evening in the City.

The general excitement that prevailed during the day was continued throughout the evening, and our city presented a scene of general vivacity, similar to that seen on public anniversaries, which was kept up until a late hour. The various places of public amusement were crammed to excess, and the different hotels were filled to overflowing. Much diplomacy must have been exercised by the landlords in disposing of their guests, and though it has been said that "poverty makes strange bed-fellows," last night it could not have been charged to that score, for among the Southern strangers, at least the *embarras du richesse,* must have been more in vogue than the former, yet from the different accounts we have heard, of the crowded state of the houses, many strangers must have been bed-fellows.

7

The First Modern Sport in America: Harness Racing in New York City, 1825-1870

by Melvin L. Adelman

Historians have assigned the rise of sport in America to the last three decades of the nineteenth century. Although they found antecedants to this development in the antebellum period, especially during the 1850s, they presented the era as one of limited sporting activity.[1] This perspective of the pre-Civil War years is unfortunately based on only a handful of studies and most of these examine the changing atti-tudes towards athletics.[2] The sporting patterns in New York City between 1820 and 1870 revealed, however, a much more active sporting life than heretofore thought to have existed at that time. Far from mere prefigurings, the framework of modern sport was estab-lished during this half century.[3]

The modernization of harness racing between 1825 and 1870 exemplifies the growth and transformation of sport during this period. An examination of the modernization of trotting[4] can proceed by employing two ideal sporting types: one premodern and the other modern.[5] These ideal sporting types need not be perfect representa-tions of actual historical stages, but they may be distinguished by six polar characteristics (see Table 1). The modernization of sport entails the movement of the activity in the direction of the modern ideal type This movement is generally, although not always, accompanied by a shift in the playing arena from an open to a close one, the increasing presence of spectators and the commercialization of the sport.

Prior to 1825, harness racing was a premodern sport. Trotting consisted primarily of informal road contests which took place mainly in the northeastern section of the country. The sport was unorgan-ized, lacked standardized rules, attracted limited public attention and

Melvin Adelman is Assistant Professor, Department of Physical Education, Ohio State University.

From Melvin L. Adelman, "The First Modern Sport in America: Harness Racing in New York City, 1825-1870," Journal of Sport History 8 (Spring 1981): 5-32. Copyright © 1981 by the North American Society for Sport History. Reprinted with permission.

possessed no permanent records. By 1870, harness racing had become a modern sport. The creation of the National Trotting Association in that year indicates the development of harness racing into a highly organized sport, with fairly uniform rules and with contests taking place throughout the country. The modernization of trotting is further illustrated by the coverage harness racing received in the daily and sporting press, the emergence of statistics and records and the appearance in 1871 of the first stud book devoted exclusively to trotting. Finally, harness racing emerged as the first sport to be successfully commercialized. By the mid-nineteenth century, trotting replaced thoroughbred racing as this country's number one spectator sport. Not until after the Civil War did baseball challenge the supreme position of trotting; but by 1870, if not for awhile longer, harness racing remained the nation's leading spectator sport.

The contention that harness racing was the first modern sport in American does not mean that it was the initial sport to assume modern characteristics. Thoroughbred racing began to modernize during the eighteenth century when permanent jockey clubs were established. The modernization of this sport reached its pre-Civil War peak during the 1830s when the sport enjoyed a period of unprecedented growth and prosperity. By the mid-1840s, however, the process grounded to a halt when the sport collapsed throughout the North. With horse racing confined mainly to the South during the subsequent two decades, the modernization of the sport remained dormant until the revival of thoroughbred racing in the North in the years immediately following the Civil War. By 1870, nevertheless, the gestalt of horse racing was not as yet modern despite the significant steps in this direction during the antebellum period.[6]

Conversely, the claims that harness racing had become a modern sport by 1870 does not mean to suggest that the modernization of trotting was complete by this date. Rather a key point of this article is that a certain stage is reached as a sport moves along the continuum from the premodern to the modern ideal form in which modern characteristics are sufficiently present to shape the structure and direction of the sport. At this juncture, the sport presents a modern configuration, one which shares more in common with its future than its premodern past. It is in this sense that harness racing had become America's first modern sport by 1870.

Harness racing conjures up a rural image, the sport of the county fair. Trotting was, however, an urban product. The sport first emerged on urban roads and developed its most salient modern characteristics in the city. New York played a more critical role in the development of harness racing than any other city. As early as 1832, the *Spirit of the Times* recognized that New York was the premier city in the breeding and training of trotting horses. Nearly a quarter of a century later, one frequent correspondent to this sporting journal maintained that trotting was indigenous to the Empire City and that there were "more fine horses here than can be found any where else in the world."[7] The importance of New York to the growth of the sport did not derive solely from the concentration of the best stock in the metropolitan region. New York was the hub of harness racing throughout the period 1825 to 1870. In the nation's most populated city, there were more trotting tracks, more races, including a disproportionate number of the leading contests, and more prize money offered than in any other place in the country. Equally significant, the characteristics of modern harness racing initially appeared in New York. Here the sport was first organized and commercialized. As a result, New York set the pattern that was to be followed on a national scale.[8]

Table 1.
The Characteristics of Premodern and Modern Ideal Sporting Types

PREMODERN SPORT	MODERN SPORT
1. ORGANIZATION—is either non-existent or at best informal and sporadic. Contests are arranged by individuals directly or indirectly (e.g., tavern-owners, bettors) involved.	1. ORGANIZATION—formal organizations, institutionally differentiated at the local, regional and national level.
2. RULES—are simple, unwritten and based upon local customs and traditions. Variations exist from locale to locale.	2. RULES—are formal, standardized and written. Rules are rationally and pragmatically worked out and legitimized by organizational means.
3. COMPETITION—locally meaningful contests only; no chance for national reputation.	3. COMPETITION—national and international superimposed on local contests; chance to establish national and international reputation.
4. ROLE DIFFERENTIATION—low role differentiation among participants and loose distinction between playing and spectating roles.	4. ROLE DIFFERENTIATION—high role differentiation; emergence of specialists (professionals) and strict distinctions between playing and spectating roles.
5. PUBLIC INFORMATION—is limited, local and oral.	5. PUBLIC INFORMATION—is reported on a regular basis in local newspapers, as well as national sporting journals. The appearance of specialized magazines, guidebooks, etc.
6. STATISTICS AND RECORDS—non-existent.	6. STATISTICS AND RECORDS—are kept, published on a regular basis and are considered important measure of achievement. Records are sanctioned by national associations.

I

Harness racing emerged as a popular pastime in New York and in other parts of the northeast in the first quarter of the nineteenth century.[9] Sport historians have maintained that the growth of trotting was directly related to the anti-racing legislation passed by several northern states, including New York State, during this era. Denied the race course, lovers of fast horses took to the "natural track"—the highway. While the road was ill suited for the feet of the running horse, it was the natural home of the trotter. "It is no accident," a leading historian of the sport contended. "that the racing of trotters began in regions where horses could be 'raced' only in defiance of law."[10]

New York State's anti-racing law, passed in 1802, neither directly nor indirectly influenced the growth of trotting in the Empire City. As enforcement had been lax, horsemen did not have to take to the road as a substitute for the prohibited race course.[11] Rather, trotting emerged at this time because improvements in the roads now made the sport possible. One historian noted that "it was only natural that the speed of the harness horse found its first testing ground upon the smooth hard roads whose networks radiated from the northeastern cities . . . especially those of the Boston-New York-Philadelphia regions."[12]

Sportsmen began racing their "roadsters" (as street trotters came to be called) because it provided them with an amusement which was convenient, participatory and relatively inexpensive. Third Avenue quickly emerged as New York's major trotting area. Beginning outside the residential portion of the city at that time, the approximately five mile road was perfectly suited for these informal trials of speed. In close proximity to the homes of the horsemen, it was a convenient location for these contests which started upon the completion of the day's work and which usually lasted until dark. Moreover, numerous taverns dotted the highway where reinsmen could stop, arrange contests and discuss the latest sporting developments.[13]

These impromptu contests appealed to the city's horsemen because they allowed personal participation. Unlike thoroughbred racing, where the owner and the rider of the horse had long been separated, trotting permitted the sportsman to demonstrate the prowess of his horse, as well as his own skill as a reinsman. Finally, the pastime did not require the capital outlay of thoroughbred racing. The trotter was not a "pure breed," but rather a horse drawn from the common stock that had the ability to trot. The plebian horses that engaged in these road races, moreover, were almost always used by their owners in their day-to-day activities.[14]

Although early nineteenth century trotting consisted almost exclusively of these impromptu contests, permanent structures began to emerge. The first trotting tracks in the New York metropolitan region were mere extensions of the courses used for thoroughbred racing. The most significant of these tracks was located in Harlem and the first recorded performance by an American trotter took place there in 1806. Several years later, the first track constructed exclusively for trotting was built in Harlem next to the Red House Tavern. The course was the major resort for the Third Avenue road racing crowd and the track was probably constructed for their benefit. While racing took place on both courses, these tracks remained essentially training grounds for the city's roadsters.[15]

More formalized matches, either on the city's roads or tracks, were a natural outgrowth of the impromptu races, or "brushes" as they were called, which took place on Gotham's streets. Since the press paid scant attention to these matches information exists on only a few of them. Probably the most important took place in 1818 when William Jones of Long Island, a prominent horseman, wagered Colonel Bond of Maryland a thousand dollars that he could produce a horse that would trot a mile in less than three minutes. The race caused great excitement among the city's sporting crowd. With odds against success, a horse named *Boston Pony* accomplished the feat in just less than the required time.[16]

The formation of the New York Trotting Club (NYTC) in the Winter of 1824-1825 marks the first critical step in the modernization of harness racing.[17] The first organized trotting club in America, there is no information on its members, although most were probably drawn from the men who raced their roadsters on Third Avenue and other roads in the New York metropolitan region. The creation of the NYTC was inspired by the success thoroughbred racing had enjoyed in New York after the State revoked its anti-racing legislation in 1821. The NYTC drew its objectives and methods heavily from the experience of horse racing. Similar to the racing organization of its sister sport, the NYTC justified its association on utilitarian grounds (the sport's contribution to the improvement of the breed); instituted regular meetings twice yearly; and, constructed a race course (in Centerville, Long Island) to facilitate the growth of the sport.[18]

Trotting in New York made significant advances as both a participatory and spectator sport in the two decades following the formation of the NYTC. In 1835, the *Spirit* noted that the "number of fast horses for which our city is so celebrated is steadily accumulating." With some exaggeration, one contemporary observer claimed that "there was scarcely a gentleman in New York who did not own one or two fast (trotting) horses."[19] The rising cost of good roadsters further indicated the increasingly appeal of the sport. During the 1830s, the price of the best trotting horses doubled.[20] In addition, trotting races on the city's tracks, especially the major ones, generated considerable excitement among New York's sporting crowd. In 1838, the *New York Herald* reported that the contest between *Dutchman* and *Ratner* created "as much interest in our city and neighborhood" as the intersectional horse race between *John Bascombe* and *Post Boy* held in New York two years earlier.[21]

The emerging commercialization of trotting most accurately dramatizes the growth of the sport. By the mid-1830s, entrepreneurs began to tap the public interest in harness races that took place on New York's streets and tracks. The experience of the Beacon Course in nearby Hoboken, New Jersey, illustrates the early introduction of the profit motive into trotting. This course was constructed in 1837 for thoroughbred racing. When the sport proved unprofitable the following year, the proprietors of the track started to promote harness racing for the sole purpose of reaping the financial rewards from the gate receipts. By the early 1840s, businessmen had replaced the original sponsors of trotting—the road runners and their associations—as the major promoters of the sport.[22]

Although organized trotting made important progress in its first twenty years, it continued to take a back seat to horse racing. The coverage harness racing received in the press defined the secondary status of this turf sport. While trotting won the polite endorsement of New York newspapers, reports of races, even important ones, remained limited. Similarly, harness racing won the approval of sports editors John Stuart Skinner and Cadwallader Colden, but their monthly journals were devoted almost exclusively to thoroughbred racing and provided only the barest summaries and details of the developments on the trotting track. Only William T. Porter's *Spirit* paid any significant attention to trotting and even there the extent of the coverage did not correspond to the growth of the sport.

II

As thoroughbred racing collapsed throughout the North in the decade following the Depression of 1837, the sporting press took increasing note of the activities of the trotting horse. By the early 1840s, they suggested that the "ugly duckling" had become the legitimate rival of her more respected sister. In 1847, the *Herald* pointed out that "for several years past, trotting has been gradually taking the precedence of running in this part of the country; while one specie of amusement has been going into decay, the other has risen to heights never before attained.[23]

Contemporaries claimed that the corresponding fates of the two turf sports were closely linked to the characteristics associated with the two different horses. In contrast to the aristocratic and foreign thoroughbred, the trotter was perceived as the democratic, utilitarian, and, by logical extension, the American horse. Implicit was the belief that harness racing surpassed horse racing as the leading turf sport because it more accurately captured the spirit of the American experience.

Henry W. Herbert (better known as Frank Forester) recognized the close connection between the nature of the horses and the popularity of the respective sports. Since cost restricted the ownership of thoroughbreds to wealthy men, horse racing could never be a popular sport. By contrast, the trotter was common to all and the "most truly characteristic and national type of horse" in America. In this country, the transplanted Englishman concluded, trotting "is the people's sport, the people's pastime, and consequently, is, and will be, supported by the people."[24]

This perspective provides a good starting point in understanding the maturation of trotting if such terms as democratic, utilitarian and even American are broadly conceived. While contemporaries grossly exaggerated the extent to which the masses owned trotters, ownership of thes plebian and relatively inexpensive horses was far more widespread than thoroughbreds.[25] Precise data on the owners of trotting horses in New York is non-existent, but available information does permit a profile to be logically deduced. The evidence indicates that only a small number of trotting men came from the "upper crust."[26] Conversely, the cost and upkeep of trotting horses were still sufficiently high to generally exclude individuals who fell below the middle class. While broad parameters still exist, it appears that trotting owners came from the more prosperous segments of the middle class—men who lived a comfortable, but hardly opulent, lifestyle. Nevertheless, individuals of more moderate means could still own a roadster as a result of the limited price of the horse and their usage in daily activities. This was particularly the case for men working in New York's various food markets. Their involvement in harness racing gave credence to the common adage that "a butcher rides a trotter" often used to illustrate the democratic nature of the horse."[27]

The fortunes of the two turf sports, the *Herald* repeatedly insisted, were connected to their utilitarian functions. The decline of horse racing stemmed from the fact that the thoroughbred had little practical benefit. The newspaper conceded that trotting "may not be attended with all the high zest and excitement" of running races, but it is "a more useful sport, as the qualities in the horse which it is calculated to develop are more intimately connected with the daily business of life.[28] The growth of harness racing did reflect shifting patterns of travel. With the improvement of roads and wagons, the driving horse increasingly replaced the saddle horse as the basic means of convoy in the northeastern and Middle Atlantic states. As one scholar pointed out, there was "a direct correlation between the improved modes of transportation and their popular manifestations seen on the trotting track."[29]

Since Americans believed that the true nature of the trotter—democratic and utilitarian—could only be developed in this country, they perceived the trotter as a native product although they were familiar with English antecedents. In 1853, the *Herald* wrote, "We are the first who have attached particular importance to the breeding of trotting horses, and in this respect . . . have shown the practical nature of our character."[30] The assumptions may be passed off as American chauvinism, but the contention that both the horse and the sport were indigenous product does contain merit. Harness racing had been a popular pastime in England, but its emergence as a sport first occurred in the United States.[31] Similarly, the establishment of a distinct breed of trotting race horse was an American creation, although this process was not completed until the late nineteenth century. More significantly, it was the perception of the trotter as the American horse, more than the reality, which was of critical importance to the growth of the sport. While harness racing never wrapped itself in the flag to the extent that baseball did, nationalistic overtones gave trotting a sanction absent in horse racing.[32] Oliver Wendell Holmes, Sr., captured these sentiments. He noted that the running horse was a gambling toy, but the trotting horse was a useful animal. Furthermore, "horse racing is not a republican institution; horse-trotting is."[33]

While the contemporary explanation provides a starting point, other critical factors must also be examined if a comprehensive analysis of the maturation of trotting is to be constructed. Trotting's supreme position in the turf world can be more productively analyzed in terms of three interacting forces: the increasing potential for commercialized amusements made possible by urban and economic expansion; the greater susceptibility of trotting to commercialization than any of its sporting counterparts; and, the more innovative nature of trotting.

The absence of surplus wealth and concentrated populations traditionally restricted the development of commercialized amusements. During the antebellum period, these two major barriers began to dissolve under the impact of urban and economic growth. The expanding economy throughout these years not only produced a significant rise in wealth, but, more importantly, broadened the availability of discretionary income among a wider segment of the population. The concentration of large numbers of people in one area facilitated the creation of a greater number of permanent institutions devoted to commercialized amusements.[34] These newer forms of popular entertainment shared three essential properties: they were cheaper, depended on volume, and appealed to a wider segment of the populace. While commercialized amusements increased throughout the first four decades of the nineteenth century, their numbers multiplied rapidly in the two decades preceding the Civil War. As one scholar pointed out, commercialized amusements underwent "an expansion of new proportions" during the lengthy era of general prosperity between 1843 and 1860[35]

The plebian character of the trotter and its relatively inexpensive price made the sport more susceptible to commericalization. Since the trotter cost less than the thoroughbred, the prize money offered by track proprietors did not have to be as great for the owners of the trotters to cover their cost and make a profit. As late as 1860, purses in New York rarely exceeded $250 and contests could be run for as low as $10. The stakes were naturally higher in match or privately arranged races. By the 1850s, a few contests went for as much as five thousand dollars per side. In general, however, the amounts fell below that which existed for similar kinds of thoroughbred races. Clearly one does not find anything comparable to the stakes placed on the major intersectional thoroughbred contest, such as between *Eclipse* and *Henry* or *Boston* and *Fashion,* or for that matter the money that could be won in horse racing's larger sweepstake races.

The nature of the trotter facilitated the commercialization of the sport by making more races possible. Whereas a good thoroughbred might race six or seven times a year, the more durable trotter started at least twice as many races annually. Furthermore, a trotter's career lasted long, many racing into their teens. More importantly, the trotter came from the common horse stock. Consequently, there were simply more of them to race. The impact of the greater numbers can be seen in terms of the respective racing sessions in New York. There were at most three weeks of thoroughbred racing in the city annually; but hardly a week would pass, except in the Winter months, without a trotting match taking place somewhere in the New York metropolitan region.

Finally, harness racing was not bogged down in the "aristocratic" trappings which characterized horse racing. In 1843, the *Spirit* recognized that trotting men were more innovative and aggressive than their horse racing counterparts. As a result of their greater "enterprise, industry and go *aheadiveness*," the sporting journal predicted, harness racing "will soon be a formidable rival to thoroughbred racing in the North." Nearly a quarter of a century later, *Turf, Field and Farm,* essentially a thoroughbred journal, gave the same basic reasons and used exactly the same words in explaining the greater popularity of harness racing.[36]

Trotting was more innovative than horse racing in two critical ways. The first was a product of the different social backgrounds of those involved in the respective sports. Engaged in thoroughbred racing were wealthy men and/or people from established families. Most of the owners of trotting horses and the proprietors of trotting tracks, however, appear to have been middle class in origin. The different social origins affected the entire tone of the two turf sports. While thoroughbred racing was run for and by the upper class, harness racing enticed a broader segment of the populace. The commercially minded proprietors of trotting tracks catered more readily to all ticket holders than those involved in their sister sport. One does not find connected with trotting complaints of exclusiveness, aristocracy and snobbishness levelled by the press against the leaders of thoroughbred racing. As a leading sporting journal noted, "Racing will never succeed in New York until it and its attended arrangements are put on a more democratic basis—something approaching the order of the first class trotting races. Then, like the trots, it will get the support of the people."[37]

In addition, trotting was more innovative because the comparatively new sport was not inhibited by tradition. By the 1840s, horse racing in America had a long heritage on how a thoroughbred race should be conducted. The absence of institutional confinements made it easier for trotting to adjust to commercialization. Similar to their horse racing counterparts, trotting men initially valued a horse which combined speed and endurance. Early trotting contests were raced in heats from one to five miles. By the early 1840s, trotting men broke with this pattern. Most major contests were now one mile heats with the winner required to win three heats. Since the new system placed less strain on the trotter, the horse could race more frequently and thereby more races were possible. Furthermore, harness racing contests took place in a wider variety of styles, giving the sport greater diversity and interest.

Harness racing surged to the forefront of not only the turf world, but modern sport in general, because more than any other sport of the day it captured the flow of the American experience. In common with other forms of popular entertainment, the emergence of trotting as a spectator sport was a product of the two dynamic forces—urbanization and economic expansion—transforming and modernizing American life. The impact of these agents of change would have been far less had not trotting possessed properties which predisposed it towards commercialization. Here the nature of the horse played a critical role. Of equal significance was the fact that those who governed trotting, at least from the standpoint of sport, internalized the values of modern society. As such, they put a greater premium on innovation rather than tradition, and cash rather than class.

III

Harness racing progressed rapidly as a popular spectator sport both in New York and throughout the country in the two decades preceding the Civil War. While the change in the social and economic conditions, discussed in the previous section, created the setting for the growth of the sport, performers attracted the crowds. During the early years of organized trotting, numerous horses left their mark on the history of the sport, but it was *Lady Suffolk* who set the standard of excellence and was the sport's first hero.[38] The fifteen year career of *Lady Suffolk* (1838-1853), moreover, illustrates the condition and development of trotting during this period.

Foaled in 1833, *Lady Suffolk* was bred by Leonard Lawrence of Suffolk Country, Long Island, from whence she drew her name. The *Lady* was a descendant of imported *Messenger*, the founding father of the American trotter, but no preparation was made for the trotting career.[39] As a weanling she was sold for $60, then resold as a two year old for $90. At age four she was pulling a butcher or oyster cart when David Bryan purchased her for $112.50 for use in his livery stable. The prowess of the horse went undiscovered until none other than William T. Porter by chance rented her for a tour of the Long Island tracks. The editor of the *Spirit* was impressed with the *Lady*'s speed and good gait. He told Bryan that she had too much potential as a racer to be wasted in his stable. In the Spring of 1838, Bryan entered the *Lady* in her first race. The "Old Grey Mare," as she was later affectionately called, completed the mile contest in three minutes flat, winning the fabulous sum of eleven dollars.

Bryan owned *Lady Suffolk* until his death in 1851. Of Irish or Celtic origin, little is known of his background, save for his previous occupation. It is clear, however, that Bryan was the embodiment of the professional ethic which came to dominate the sport. As one historian wrote, "For Bryan, his *Lady Suffolk*, the most loved as well as the most admired horse of her time, was not, first and foremost, a sporting animal—she was a mint of money, a nugget of rich metal to be melted by him in the heat of competition and struck off into dollars."[40] Bryan raced his grey mare mainly in the New York metropolitan area because this is where he lived and, even more importantly, because the city's courses provided the best financial opportunities. Similar to other professional trotting men of his day, however, Bryan campaigned with *Lady Suffolk* on the growing number of tracks throughout the country, going as far west as St. Louis and as far south as New Orleans.

Bryan had the reputation of being a poor reinsman and he placed excessive demands on *Lady Suffolk*. Nevertheless, he was an unqualified success by the new professional standards. He entered the *Lady* in 162 races, and won between $35,000 and $60,000.[41] The ability of *Lady Suffolk* to achieve victory, despite the clumsy and inept driving of her owner, derived from her saintly patience, an unbreakable spirit and a remarkable endurance. At age nineteen, her last full year on the turf, the Old Grey Mare demonstrated her tremendous stamina by coming to the start twelve times.

Harness racing had emerged as the nation's leading spectator sport by the time *Lady Suffolk* was retired in the early 1850s. During this decade, the sport emerged as an integral part of the county fair and the public's desire to see harness races resulted in the creation of an ever increasing number of trotting tracks throughout the country. By 1858, one sporting journal estimated that over seventy trotting courses existed in America.[42]

Expanding coverage of harness racing corresponded with its growth. In New York, the daily newspapers naturally focused on contests within the metropolitan region, but the city-based sporting journals reported on races throughout the country. While trotting men had always been preoccupied with "time" as a measure of their horses' abilities and performances, statistics and records took on new importance when horsemen began touring the increasing number of tracks in search of fame and fortune. That these measurements served the interest of track promoters and fans of the sport was to a large extent responsible for their expanding value. Since a trotter might visit a city only once a year, proprietors of the courses could use the statistical reputation of a horse to encourage people to come to see the race even though they may have never seen him perform. Similarly, statistics nourished fan interest by providing them with a method of evaluating a horse in the absence of personal observation or witnessing the horse race on only a handful of occasions.

Trotting men were not only familiar with unsurpassed performances, but were already cognizant of the concept of the record. In 1860, for example, *Flora Temple,* who succeeded *Lady Suffolk* as the "princess of the turf," sought to break *Dutchman*'s record (7:32.5) for three miles. Since the "watch never breaks and never tires," Wilkes' *Spirit of the Times* reported, the effort of *Flora Temple* (eventually unsuccessful) to surpass the time of the then dead horse evoked considerable speculation and discussion.[43]

New York continued to dominate the development of harness racing even though the sport expanded nationally. At least seven trotting tracks existed in the metropolitan region, with three—Union, Fashion and Centerville Courses—hosting first class contests. More significantly, with the ever increasing importance of gate receipts, trotting in the Empire City drew the largest number of spectators. Between six and eight thousand spectators were usually present at each of the four to six leading matches held annually. However, when *Flora Temple* raced, attendance could jump into double figures. Within a period of seventeen days in 1859, her contests with *Ethan Allen* and then *Princess* drew crowds of 12,000 and 20,000, respectively.

The growth of harness racing as a sports spectacle did not occur without problems. As the commercial and professional ethic came to dominate the sport, suspicions of irregularities on the trotting track markedly increased. The question of the integrity of harness racing produced the first extensive discussion and concern about the honesty of professional-commercial sport. Cries of foul play on New York tracks were already heard as early as the 1830s. The *Spirit* claimed that the public are beginning to express concern about the improprieties on the trotting track and insisted that men of character must immediately rule off the track those who disgrace the sport or else the "trotting course and everything pertaining them must 'go to pot.'"[44]

While complaints of irregularities persisted, the city's sporting press began to repeat these charges vociferously only in the 1850s. Fundamentally these statements did not vary from the theme, solution and dire predictions offered by the Spirit over a decade earlier. In 1857, the *New York Times* asserted that many owners of fast trotters would not allow their horses to compete in races since the courses had "fallen under the control of men who made use of them to subserve their own private interest."[45]

During the next two decades, the New York press emphatically argued that the fixing of races was a common practice.[46] So often were the charges made that by their sheer numbers this argument becomes a compelling one. Yet was it accurate? It would be naive to assume that no races were rigged, but the claims of widespread manipulation of contests seems grossly exaggerated. Evidence of these "clandestine arrangements" are significantly lacking. It is not surprising, therefore, that the arguments develop a predictable rhythm and break down into vague generalities. In contrast to the contention of rampant wrongdoings, I was impressed at the number of times the favorite, and especially the outstanding horses, won.[47] Clearly, many of the assertions, which at times border on the incredulous, can be cast aside as sensationalist journalism.[48] From time to time, moreover, statements in the press not only challenged the prevailing view, but often contradicted previous beliefs.[49]

The rise of the "manipulation theory" derived from three interrelated factors: the non-existence of investigative commissions; the nature of professional sport and the attitude towards professional athletes; and the primitive concept of "upset." In absence of effective investigating commissions as we know them today, charges of irregularities were rarely examined. The lack of this critical institutional structure for the governance of sport facilitated the growth or rumor and innuendo and made personal judgment the sole criteria in deciding the honesty of a race. The case brought against James Eoff illustrates the obvious drawbacks of such a method in determining the integrity of a contest. In 1859, *Princess,* a California mare, was the first horse to make the trip from the West Coast to New York. With little time to recoup from the long journey, she was matched against *Flora*

Temple. Hiram Woodruff, the leading antebellum reinsman and a spectator at the contest, wrote that ninety-five percent of the huge crowd felt that *Princess* lost because Eoff, her jockey, pulled the mare. So vociferous was the cry of "fix" at the Union Jockey Club, a thoroughbred organization which owned the course where the race took place, held a rare investigation. There Eoff claimed that the California mare tired because she had not recovered from her trip and could not be pushed any harder. Woodruff felt the explanation was a plausible and truthful one. He further pointed out that not one of the many people who felt the race had been thrown came forward to substantiate their charge.[50]

The nature of professional athletics made creditable the assertion that races were fixed. Since the major purpose of the contest for the professional athlete is to make money, what guarantees exist that he would not manipulate the event to maximize his profit? A certain class bias against the professional athlete accentuated the suspicions inherent within the professional system. While no monolithic view of either the professional athlete or professional athletics existed, the prevailing attitude was that the public was assured honest contests only when the "better class governed the sport.[51]

The strong temptations confronting the professional athlete went far in explaining why the press so vehemently opposed what was known as "hippodroming" — the making of contests for the sole purpose of splitting the gate receipts (in contrast to racing for stakes and purses). With no money depending on the outcome, and therefore with no incentive to win, these "concocted affairs" were perfect races to rig. As the *New York Clipper* pointed out. "Many matches advertised for heavy stakes are merely for 'gate money' and so arranged that the winners are known to the 'initiated' before the event ever took place."[52]

The suspicions of wrongdoing were justifiably heightened by the less than candid policy of track promoters in billing what was essentially an "exhibition" as a match race for large stakes. This less than honest practice does not prove, however, that the contests were fixed. In 1860, the *Spirit* conceded that hippodroming had become a method of scheduling races, but it doubted "if there is one-tenth part of the rascality on a trotting track that many people suppose."[53]

The development of hippodroming was a legitimate response to the financial considerations of both the owners of the horses and the proprietors of the courses rather than being the product of evil intent. Woodruff claimed that *Flora Temple* caused the new system. In a class by herself, the mare "could not get a match on even terms, and was excluded from all purses."[54] It is unlikely that *Flora Temple* or any other horse initiated hippodroming. Instead it emerged from the inadequacy of the prevalent winner-take-all system.[55] The new arrangements made it possible for a horse to be defeated and the owner still be able to cover part of his cost and possibly emerge with a profit. Consequently, it gradually facilitated an expansion in both the number of trotters and races. Equally important for the proprietors, it guaranteed the presence of the super horses that drew the huge crowds. "No matter how these 'little arrangements' are concocted," the *Clipper* was forced to conclude, "it is but fair to say that they generally made interesting races, and in that way the spectators are pleased."[56]

The most striking fact about the literature of the day was the primitive understanding of the concept of "upset." Nineteenth century writers were conscious that luck played a factor in the outcome of athletic contests and that the more talented performer did not always win. On most occasions when the favorite lost, however, the press and the public offered some excuse for his defeat. As I perceive it, the concept of upset does not automatically entail that luck played a part in the underdog winning, although it may and often does. Rather it is premised on the realization that on certain occasions a competitor can achieve a level of performance which is not his usual standard and quite possible may never be reached again.

Today it is axiomatic that on any given day any professional athlete or team could defeat any other professional athlete or team. Over the years, the vicissitudes of sport have sufficiently demonstrated the validity of this idea. The legitimacy of even the most unbelievable developments go unquestioned. Jargon ridden as this perspective has become in our mass communication sporting world, the internalization of this view by the fan and the press alike is mandatory if the integrity of professional sport is to be accepted. Precisely because such an attitude was absent in the early days of professional sport any unexpected occurrence fequently became translated into "fix."[57]

Serious doubts must be raised of the prevalent view that widespread manipulation of races followed on the heels of the growth of professional-commercial harness racing. While dishonest contests occurred in New York, they were the exception rather than the rule. Nevertheless, professionalization did significantly alter the character of these contests. The emphasis of amateur turfmen on style and sportsmanship yielded to the sole objective of success as jockies adopted tricks and tactics which if not outright violations of the rules permitted the drivers to get all he could within them. Such practices were often chastised and contributed to the belief that there was a lack of propriety on the trotting track; but they foreshadowed the pattern which emerged in all professional sports. As one historian pointed out, these techniques were consistent with the dominant American values "in that it was results that counted, not how hard you tried or how sportingly you behaved."[58]

IV

While commercialization became harness racing's leading characteristic by the 1850s, informal trials of speed persisted on New York's streets. With the growth of the city, however, severe restrictions began to be placed on the roadster. By the early 1860s, New York's road runners had moved from Third Avenue to Harlem Lane in the upper part of Manhattan. This location shortly began to succumb to the forces of progress. Dismayed by the prospect of the loss of New York's last good driving area, the editor of *Wilkes' Spirit* believed that it "was incumbent upon the city's authorities to supply the vacancy created by the occupation of Harlem Lane." As the headquarters of the fast trotter, anything less, he suggested, "would be a national loss, as well as a municipal sham and disgrace."[59]

The call for government intervention might be considered a "far sighted" approach, but trotting men took steps more typical of the period. They established private organizations which bought or rented their own tracks. Unlike earlier trotting or jockey clubs, these organizations did not sponsor public or private races, although club members could and probably did arrange contests amongst themselves and their guests. Rather, they were formed to perpetuate an informal pastime no longer possible in the more formalized urban setting.[60] The first of these clubs was the Elm Park Pleasure Grounds Association established in the late 1850s. The majority of the 400 members were prosperous businessmen, although there were a handful of men of considerable wealth, most notably Cornelius Vanderbilt and Robert Bonner.[61]

Of New York's road drivers, none had a more dramatic impact on the development of harness racing than Robert Bonner. Born in Londonderry, Ireland, in 1824, Bonner amassed his fortune by the time he was thirty as the owner of the *New York Ledger,* a weekly family journal.[62] In 1856, his physician advised him to find an outdoor recreation for health reasons. Bonner then bought a horse and began driving it on New York's speedways. There he had a few brushes with Vanderbilt. What emerged was a friendly rivalry between these two for the ownership of the best trotters. The Bonner-Vanderbilt duel, a leading turf historian insisted, "marked the beginning of a change that provided the sport not only with strong financial backing but an efficient leadership."[63] While the confrontation between the steamship and newspaper magnates did not initiate a new era, it symbolized and gave impetus to an already existing process.

In the battle between the two giants, Bonner emerged as the king of the road. He spent lavishly in purchasing some of the best trotters of his era. Between 1859 and 1870, Bonner bought thirteen horses at a total cost of $162,000. His prize purchase was *Dexter*, clearly the number one trotter of his day. By the time he retired in 1890, the newspaper magnate had spent nearly half a million dollars for his horses, including $40,000 each for his stars *Maud S. and Pocahontas.*[64]

Bonner's reputation as a horseman did not derive solely from his ownership of possibly the largest and best stable. A more significant reason, as the *New York Tribune* pointed out, was that he "did more to lift the trotting horse from disrepute to respectability than any other man."[65] According to the universally accepted perspective, prior to Bonner's involvement, acceptable society viewed the owners of trotting horses as fast men "who spent their afternoons trotting from tavern to tavern. . .(and) had too much money in their pockets."[66] Bonner was the critical figure in altering this negative impression. A man of unimpeachable character, the strict Scotch-Presbyterian did not smoke, drink or swear. Moreover, he so violently opposed gambling that he refused to enter his horses in public places. Consequently, Bonner could bring a dignity to the sport that other wealthy *nouveaux,* such as the salty Vanderbilt, never could. Through Bonner's influence, the ownership of trotting horses won an acceptable position in society, with the result that "Men of affairs, men of money, men of social position began to buy trotters, drive them on the road and even enter them for races on the public tracks."[67]

That the possession of trotting horses gradually achieved greater respectability in New York society when men of wealth became involved in the sport is undeniable as it was almost inevitable. This development did not emerge from a shift in the attitude of the city's "upper crust," but rather from a shift in its composition. As older elites gave way to the onslaught of new wealth, they lost their position as the arbiters of culture. The ascending group, from whom trotting men were overwhelmingly drawn, dictated from its new position the acceptability of its own activity.[68] The increasing involvement of New York's affluent in trotting, therefore, can be understood against the background of what a leading scholar of New York elites described as the plutocratic nature of the city's high society. Since New York society was easily accessible to the newly risen who were uncertain of the traditions and prerogatives of their new class and status, it produced an elite structure which encouraged the pursuit of publicity and created a fashionable style of conspicuous luxury. Although these traits did not emerge as the dominant characteristics of New York society until the 1870s, they were strongly present among the city's elite even prior to the Civil War.[69]

Nouveaux riche New Yorkers became involved in trotting, as they would in other sports, as a means of status confirmation. Interesting differences existed, however, between trotting and other sporting activities. In the prevailing pattern, new wealth asserted its position by patronizing those sports which had an upper class heritage and/or could be afforded only by men of wealth. In the early years of trotting, the sport shared none of these characteristics. To function as other upper class sports, therefore, exclusiveness had to be created. Two interrelated processes accomplished this transformation: the purchasing of the best trotters at lavish prices and the rationalization of the breeding industry.

The willingness of wealthy men to pay premium prices resulted in their monopoly of the best trotters by the 1870s.[70] The soaring cost of trotters was in part a product of the growth of the sport and the increasing number of bidders for what is a relatively fixed market; there can be only a few champions per period. However, the law of supply and demand, important though it may be, does not explain the surge in prices. For example, Bonner bought *Dexter* in 1867 for the increditable sum of $33,000 even though his seller, George Trussle of Chicago, had paid only $14,000 for the horse two years earlier. Another subtle but significant reason therefore existed for the rising cost. The fabulous sums trotting horses attracted was a critical part of the status game. To have obtained the best horses at anything less than these fantastic sums would have not satisfied the needs of these *parvenus* to demonstrate their wealth and status.

The rationalizations of the breeding industry further encouraged the concentration of good trotting horses in the hands of the wealthy. In the mid-nineteenth century, this business required little capital, organization or promotion. Some attention was paid to pedigree; however, lineage was usually guesswork, if not outright falsification. The small scale on which the business was run was not conducive to finely selective breeding, but its random nature had the valuable result of diffusing the blood of the best stock widely throughout the country. This haphazard method, one historian noted, "contributed to the sport a delightful element of uncertainty, dicovery and surprise, the satisfaction of making something out of nothing." This business enabled David Bryan and William M. Rysdyk, a former farmhand, to make their fame and fortune from their horses *Lady Suffolk* and *Hambletonian,* respectively, at a cost of less than $250 for the two horses.[71]

Within two or three decades, small breeders yielded to the larger stables owned by wealthy men for pleasure, profit or both. These well capitalized stock farms gathered the best trotters. Similar to other American industries in the latter part of the nineteenth century, the concentration of talent and wealth permitted the breeding of trotting horses to become a more rationalized process. For the small breeder, the swift trotter was essentially a sideline, although an important one, to the general stud services his horses provided. Above all, the major objective was the procreation of the race and the overall improvement of the breed. In the large stables, speed was the sole objective. Using innovative techniques, the big farms "became laboratories of speed." As one turf historian concluded, "A system of breeding that had diffused the qualities of the best sires so widely through the common horse stock was replaced by a system more narrowly concentrated but for that reason more likely to produce exceptional results."[72]

During the 1870s, four more critical steps were taken to rationalize the breeding industry: (1) the creation of the first turf register devoted exclusively to the trotting horse (1871); (2) the appearance of the first sporting journal, *Wallace's Monthly Magazine,* concerned primarily with trotting affairs (1875); (3) the formation of the National Association of Trotting Horse Breeders (1876); and, (4) the establishment of a standard breed of trotting horse (1879).[73] By the end of this decade, the rationalization of the breeding industry solidified the ownership of the leading trotters in the hands of wealthy men. Unable to compete with the big farms, the horses of the smaller breeders found themselves confined to tracks at county fairs. The day that a horse could be removed from a butcher's cart and became a world's champion was relegated to dime novels and serials in popular magazines.

Neither the shift in the social composition of the owners of trotting horses nor changes in the breeding industry undermined the popularity of harness racing. Since the initial growth of the sport was strongly linked to the inexpensive cost of the trotter and its broadly based ownership, why did trotting continue to enjoy widespread popular appeal in the aftermath of these profound alterations? The persistent perception of the trotter as the democratic and utilitarian horse, despite the changes, played a contributory role. As late as 1884, one newspaper insisted that the "millionaire horsemen with their mammoth establishments and invested thousands, represent but a small fraction of the money employed in this special industry."[74] While the contention that the average farmer was the backbone of the sport was inaccurate, the tremendous growth of harness racing at the county fair, with its rural connotations, did give the sport a democratic aura.[75]

The symbiotic relationship which already developed between the growth of harness racing, the changes in the breeding industry and the commercialization of the sport was an even more important factor. This linkage made it virtually impossible for the wealthy owners of trotters to create a sport run solely for their own class. While considerations of status contributed to elite involvement in this sport, financial concerns, for the overwhelming majority of these turfmen, were always present.[76] To offset the surging cost of trotting horses required a corresponding expansion of the economic side of the sport. Consequently, trotting men continued to welcome the public and their money from gate receipts and gambling as a means of defraying their expenses and making a profit.[77] The ongoing willingness of harness racing to cater to a broad segment of the population resulted in the perpetuation of trotting as the "people's pastime."

V

Harness racing underwent tremendous growth as a commercial-spectator sport in New York in the 1860s. The outbreak of the Civil War brought a brief pause to the general prosperity of the sport, but things were back into full swing by the Fall of 1862. During the following years, trotting in New York appeared to be one continuous stream of match races. Symbolized by a series of six races, each for $5,000, between *General Butler* and *George Patchen,* these match races attracted large audiences to the various courses. By 1864, the *Clipper* noted that the previous season was "Successful beyond precedent, alike in the quantity and quality of the sport which it produced."[78]

More significant for the overall development of trotting than these glamorous races was the increasing size of the purses given by the proprietors and clubs of the various tracks. The prize money tendered at the Fashion Course, for example, more than tripled, increasing from $3,750 to $11,500, in the years between 1862 and 1870. By the start of the 1870s, the aggregate sum of the purses offered by New York's three leading tracks during their weekly sessions exceeded $25,000. In addition, the proprietors scheduled other purse contests from time to time.[79] Races which went for not more than $250 during the 1850s, and were run for about $1,000 by the early 1860s, could go for as much as $5,000 by the end of the decade.

An increase in the number of horses coming to the start corresponded with the rise in prize money. Whereas four horses rarely entered a race in the 1850s, this had become the norm by the early 1860s and it was not uncommon to find as many as seven horses in a contest. When there were 78 entries for the ten races held at the Fashion Course in 1864, one sporting journal called it by far the greatest number ever known for a regular meeting.[80] To facilitate the growing number of horses, the proprietors of the courses adopted the policy of sweepstake racing, long used in horse racing, with nominations to these contests sometimes coming as much as a year in advance.

The rapid expansion of harness racing not only in New York but throughout the nation during this decade, and especially after the Civil War, gave rise to several problems. According to the press, the most serious one remained the specter of the "fix." Calling upon the proprietors of the courses to cleanse and reform trotting of its evil element, they continued to prognosticate dire consequences if their advice went unheeded.[81] Nevertheless, no significant action was taken until the Naragansett (RI) Trotting Association called a convention of track operators in late 1869. Meeting in New York the following February, delegates from forty-six tracks in fifteen states established the National Trotting Association for the Promotion of the

Interest of the Trotting Turf, later simplified to the National Trotting Association (NTA).

The dual objectives of the NTA were the creation of uniform government and the prevention and punishment of fraud. To facilitate the former goal, the NTA adopted rules which would be used at all tracks in the association. To expedite the later aim, the NTA attempted to buttress the power of local authorities by creating a board of appeals which would rule on all kinds of infractions. To give muscle to this court, it made the suspension on one track applicable to all courses within the federation.[82]

Turf historians have accepted the desire to reform the evils of the turf as the major factor behind the creation of the NTA. Although they recognized the need for changes in the institutional structure of harness racing, they perceived this development as a means to the larger end.[83] Since the contemporary press and these historians grossly exaggerated the degree to which races were fixed, the lofty ideals assigned by these writers must be questioned. At the time of the creation of the NTA, in fact, several individuals asked how the proprietors of the courses, who had at least tacitly accepted the fraudulent behavior even though they may not have been responsible for it, were going to lead a reform movement. Interestingly, the right of track operators to represent the "trotting fraternity" at this convention was based on their vested economic interest in the sport."[84]

The formation of the NTA can be more appropriately examined as a response to what were the major problems of the turf: the inefficiency of uncoordinated local organizations and local rules to meet the needs of the proprietors of the courses and the owners of the horses. As early as 1858, *Porter's Spirit of the Times,* noting the growth of the sport, called for the creation of a national organization to govern harness racing.[85] Only with the tremendous expansion of trotting in the years following the Civil War, however, did the extant institutional structures of harness racing become incapable of meeting the requirements of the sport. Far from being a means to an end, the new institutions were ends in themselves. The creation of the NTA, to borrow a popular historical phrase, was part of harness racing's "search for order."

Trotting had long been governed solely by local rules. This system did not prove excessively unwieldly when harness racing depended mainly on match races or consisted of contests with small fields comprised largely of neighborhood horses. With the growth of the sport, the older rules became inoperative. In 1862, the Fashion Course rewrote their rules to adjust to the more numerous starters. Such a simple matter as the positioning of the horses on the track prior to each heat, heretofore left to the individual driver, now had to be codified. Moreover, races began to be handicapped to maintain competitive balance between the increasing number of trotters present on the course. In the early 1860s, New York tracks began handicapping by weight, but not until the next decade was the more efficient system of time-classification introduced. The increase in the number of tracks throughout the country was far more significant in producing homogeneity in the rules. To facilitate the easy movement of horses from course to course, standardization of the rules and regulations became necessary.[86]

The NTA drew heavily on the experience of the New York tracks. Since the leading sporting journals were located in Manhattan, New York's rules were the ones published and therefore practiced on a goodly number of courses throughout the country even prior to the convention.[87] Moreover, Isaiah Rynders, the only New Yorker on the nine man committee designated to draft the NTA's regulations, was the chairman of this group. John L. Cassady, a delegate at the convention and a leading commentator on the trotting scene, maintained that Rynders was the busiest and most influential member at the convention.[88]

Rynders' presence and influence in the creation of the NTA raises further questions of those who viewed this association as a reform movement led by men in "white hats." A former Mississippi river boat gambler, the founder of the notorious Empire Club, a major New York gang, an active and influential member of Tammany Hall and a leading "shoulder hitter," he was the man, the *Times* claimed, who was most responsible for the "organized system of terrorism and ruffianism in city politics." Clearly, Rynders was the prototype (gambler, ruffian) of the individual who the press frequently complained wielded undo and negative influence on the sport.[89] If this was the man who was leading the reform, it may be asked from whom were they reforming the turf?

Besides the necessity of uniform rules, the expansion of harness racing made it imperative that the various tracks be coordinated. For New York's major courses it was not so much a question of the need to synchronize their respective schedules as it was the growing competition from the increasing number of tracks emerging outside of Manhattan. With these courses offering good prize money to attract top notch horses to their meetings, even New York lacked the financial resources to meet the combined competition of these tracks. While New York remained the sport's capital, the virtual monopoly it had of the best horses in former days was undermined. In the years immediately following the Civil War, the proprietors of the turf in Gotham were forced to abandon their policy of arranging purses races through the year and adapted a more compact racing season.[90] To guarantee the presence of the best talent, the enlarged market necessitated the creation of some form of systematic scheduling to avoid conflicting engagements.[91]

The subsequent development of the NTA goes beyond the scope of this article. Clearly greater research into this organization, as with all phases of harness racing, is necessary. Nevertheless, the perspective drawn from the experience of New York raises questions concerning the traditional view of the formation of this federation. While New York track operators paid lip service to the need to reform the turf, the desire for order, and thereby profit, motivated them to join the national association. Through collective action they could coordinate the activities of the expanding sport, as well as buttress local authority. While the institutional reform checked some of the persistent problems confronting the turf, they were a product of pragmatic, rather than moral, objectives.[92]

The formation of the NTA symbolized the transformation of harness racing from a premodern to a modern sport. In contrast to the informal road contests which took place in the northeastern section of the country a half century earlier, harness racing evolved into a highly organized sport, with relatively uniform rules and with contests taking place in all sections of the nation. The emergence of a trotting literature (stud books and *Wallace's Monthly Magazine*) and developments in the breeding industry (the formation of the National Association of Trotting Horse Breeders and the creation of a standard breed) in the 1870s further demonstrated the centralizing and modernizing forces at work in the sport. By this decade, one social historian noted, harness racing "had grown to such mammoth proportions and won a greater share of the public attention than any other public pastime which contributed to the enjoyment of the people."[93]

Footnotes

[1]For the general view of the sporting patterns of nineteenth century America, see John R. Betts, *America's Sporting Heritage, 1850-1950* (Reading, Mass.: Addison-Wesley, 1974), pp. 10-246; John A. Krout. *Annals of American Sport* (New Haven: Yale University Press, 1929); Foster R. Dulles, *A History of Recreation: America Learns To Play.* 2nd Ed. (New York: Appleton-Century-Crofts, 1965), pp. 84-99, 136-47, 182-99, 223-29; John A. Lucas and Ronald A. Smith, *Saga of American Sport* (Philadelphia: Lea and Febiger, 1978), pp. 55-302; Dale A. Somers, *The Rise of Sport In New Orleans* (Baton Rouge: Louisiana State University Press, 1972); Frederic L. Paxson, "The Rise of Sport," *Mississippi Valley Historical Review,* 4 (Sept., 1917), 143-68.

[2]For studies dealing with the changing attitudes towards athletics during the antebellum period, see John R. Betts, "Mind and Body in Early American Thought," *Journal of American History,* 54 (Mar., 1968), 797-805; Guy M. Lewis, "The Muscular Christianity Movement," *Journal of Health, Physical Education and Recreation,* 37 (May, 1966), 27-28,42; John A. Lucas, "A Prelude To The Rise of Sport: Antebellum America, 1850-1860," *Quest,* 11 (Dec., 1968), 50-57; Roberta J. Park, "'Embodied Selves': The Rise and Development of Concern For Physical Education, Active Games and Recreation Among American Women, 1776-1865," *Journal of Sport*

History, 5 (Summer, 1978), 5-41; Arthur C. Cole, "Our Sporting Grandfathers: The Cult of Athletics At Its Source," *Atlantic Monthly,* 110 (July, 1932), 88-96. For other works touching on this period, see Jennie Holliman, *American Sport, 1785-1835* (Durham, N.C.: Seeman Press, 1931); Sorern S. Brynn, "Some Sports In Pittsburgh During The National Period," *Western Pennsylvania Historical Magazine,* Part I, 51 (Oct. 1968), 345-68, Part II (Jan. 1969), 57-79.

[3]Melvin L. Adelman, "The Development of Modern Athletics: Sport In New York City, 1820-1870," (Unpublished Ph.D. dissertation: University of Illinois, 1980).

[4]For the purpose of simplicity and convenience the terms "trotting" and "harness racing" will be used interchangably, although technically there are differences between the two. Trotting is a style of racing and may occur "in saddle" (the dominant form until the 1840s) or in harness. Harness racing is a method of racing and consists of trotting and pacing gaits.

[5]My thoughts on the characteristics of premodern and modern ideal sporting types were influenced by Eric Dunning, "The Structural-Functional Properties of Folk Games and Modern Sport," *Sportwissenschaft.* 3 (Jahrgang, 1978), 215-38; Allen Guttmann, *From Ritual to Record: The Nature of Modern Sports* (New York: Columbia University Press, 1978), pp. 15-55. For a discussion of the usage of ideal sporting types, see Alan G. Ingham, "Methodology in the Sociology of Sport: From Symptoms of Malaise to Weber for a Cure," *Quest,* 31 (1979), 198-211. Also of value was Richard D. Brown, *Modernization: The Transformation of American Life, 1600-1865* (New York: Hill and Wang, 1976), pp. 3-22.

[6]For the limited commercialization and modernization of horse racing prior to 1870, see Adelman, "Modern Athletics," pp. 74-77, 162-65.

[7]*Spirit of the Times* 1 (May 12, 1832): 26 (Mar. I, 1856): 38.

[8]I recognize that an essential characteristic of modern sport is its national dimension. Nevertheless, the evolution of sport from pre-modern to modern can be revealed at a local level. While this paper focuses mainly on the changing pattern of harness racing in New York, I have united, when necessary, my discussion of trotting there with similar developments taking place nationally.

[9]For the development of harness racing during the first quarter of the nineteenth century, see Dwight Akers, *Drivers Up: The Story of American Harness Racing* (New York: G.P. Putnam's Sons, 1938), pp. 27-36.

[10]Ibid., p. 29 (27-30); Holliman, *American Sport,* p. 121; John Hervey, *The American Trotter* (New York: Coward McCann, 1947), p. 27.

[11]For the continuation of horse racing in New York, see John Hervey, *Racing in America, 1665-1865.* 2 vols. (New York: The Jockey Club, 1944), 1: 136-40, 253-60; Adelman, "Modern Athletics," P. 33. The anti-racing legislation also prohibited trotting and pacing. See *Laws of New York, 25th Session* (Albany, 1802). pp. 69-70. That the bill prohibited these sports illustrates that New Yorkers were familiar with them even prior to the nineteenth century. Nevertheless, there is no evidence that the sport enjoyed any degree of popularity prior to 1800.

[12]Hervey, *American Trotter,* p. 19.

[13]For a discussion of racing and taverns on Third Avenue, see Akers, *Drivers Up,* pp. 30-31; Abram C. Dayton, *Last Days of Knickerbocker Life in New York* (New York: G.P. Putnam's Sons, 1897), pp. 237-58; Charles Astor Bristed, *The Upper Ten Thousands: Sketches of American Society* (New York: Stringer and Townsend, 1852), pp. 23-24; *American Turf Register and Sporting Magazine* 8 (Sept., 1836): 41.

[14]Until the creation of the Standard-bred light harness horse in 1879, the trotter was a "mongrel horse" although certain well recognized families, such as the Morgans,

Bellfounders and Messangers, emerged in the second quarter of the nineteenth century. Consequently, the trotting horse during this period was at best "a group of horse families that had a common characteristic, their ability to trot." [Akers, *Drivers Up*, pp. 106-9; Hervey, *American Trotter*, p. 12].

[15]Frank A. Wrench, *Harness Horse Racing In The United States and Canada* (New York: D. Van Nostrand, 1948), p. 21; Hervey, *American Trotter*, pp. 21-2; Akers, *Drivers Up*, p. 28; Dayton, *Last Days*, pp. 245-60. As late as 1847, the Harlem Course was still viewed as the beginner's school for the city's roadsters. See *New York Herald* 28 Apr. 1847.

[16]Thomas Floyd-Jones, *Backward Glances: Reminiscence of An Old New Yorker* (Somerville, N.J.: Unionist Gazette Association, 1941), p. 71; Akers, *Drivers Up*, p.13; Hervey, *American Trotter*, pp. 22-23.

[17]For the formation of the NYTC, see Akers, *Drivers Up*, pp. 37-38; Krout, *Annals*, p. 48; Holliman, *American Sport*, p. 122. Johan Huizinga saw the creation of permanent organizations as the starting point of modern sport. See his *Homo Ludens: A Study of the Play Element In Culture* (Boston: Beacon Press, 1955), p.196.

[18] For the relationship between the formation of the NYTC and the reemergence of horse racing in New York after 1821, see the speech of the president of the NYTC, *New York Evening Post* 20 May 1825. For the parallel developments in horse racing in New York, see Adelman, "Modern Athletics," pp. 38-39.

[19]*Spirit* 5 (Dec. 12, 1835); Henry W. Herbert, *Frank Forester's Horse and Horsemanship Of The United States and the British Providence of North America*. 2 vols. (New York: Stringer and Townsend, 1857), 2:158. Also see *Turf Register* (Sept., 1836): 41; Dayton, *Last Days*, pp. 245-47; Akers, *Drivers Up*, pp. 59-60.

[20]Peter C. Welsh, *Track and Road: The American Trotting Horse. A Visual Record 1820 to 1900 From The Harry T. Peters "America On Stone" Lithography Collection* (Washington, D.C.: Smithsonian Institute Press, 1967), p. 18.

[21]*Herald* 11 Oct. 1838. For popularity of trotting as a spectator sport, also see *Post* 19 Sept. 1832; *Spirit* 1 (Sept. 15, 1832), 11 (July 32, 1841): 258; *New York Spectator* 9 Oct. 1829; *New York American* 2 Oct. 1832. For discussion of the race between *Post Boy* and *John Bascombe*, see Hervey, *Racing in America*, 2:117-19.

[22]For the experience of the Beacon Course, see Adelman. "Modern Athletics," pp. 56-57; Hervey, *Racing in America*, 2:99-100, 103; Harry B. Weiss and Grace M. Weiss, *Early Sports and Pastimes In New Jersey* (Trenton: The Pass Time Press, 1960), p. 124. Also see Akers, *Drivers Up*, p. 152.

[23]*Herald* 28 Apr. 1847. Also see *Turf Register* 14 (Apr. 1843): 227; *Spirit* 13 (Mar. 18, 1843): 25. For the decline of thoroughbred racing in New York and throughout the North following the Depression of 1837, see Adelman, "Modern Athletics," pp. 57-64; Hervey, *Racing in America*, 2:153-54.

[24]Herbert, *Frank Forester's*, 2:123, 126-27. Also see, *Turf Register* 14 (Apr., 1843): 216-217; *Turf, Field and Farm* 4 (June 12, 1867):387.

[25]In contrast to the view that the trotter was the horse of the masses, only one New Yorker in thirty in 1826 even owned a horse and by 1853 this ratio increased to only one in twenty-three. for figures, See *Herald* 25 Apr. 1853.

[26]Frank Forester maintained that prior to 1840 (or before commercialization), trotting was "as completely in the hands of gentlemen sportsmen, as the turf proper." [Herbert, *Frank Forester's*, 2:158]. The evidence does not confirm this thesis. While the owners of thoroughbreds in the New York metropolitan region were from wealthy and/or eminent families, only three New Yorkers actively involved in trotting came from the city's upper crust. To make this assessment the names of individuals

involved in trotting were extracted from the newspapers and then checked against Edward Pessen's list of the wealthiest New Yorkers in 1828 and 1845. For this list, see his article "The Wealthiest New Yorkers of the Jacksonian Era: A New List," *New York Historical Society Quarterly,* 53 (April, 1970), 155-72. for the social composition of thoroughbred men in New York between 1821 and 1845, see Adelman, "Modern Athletics," pp. 66-67.

[27]For the involvement of men in New York's various food markets with trotting, see Floyd-Jones, *Backward Glances,* p. 9.

[28]*Herald* 25 Apr.,16 May.1849, 30 May 1848, 21 June 1853, 4, 10 June 1859, 15 Mar. 1869.

[29]Welsh, *Track and Road,* p. 75.

[30]*Herald* 25 Apr. 1853.

[31]For the differences in the development of harness racing in the United States and England, see Hervey, *American Trotter,* p. 19.

[32]For the view of the trotter as an American development, see Robert Bonner, "Papers," Box 12, 19 Feb. 1895, New York Public Library: Hervey, *American Trotter,* p. 20; Akers. *Drivers Up,* p. 29. Harness racing also suffered from the religious opposition which checked the growth of horse racing in various regions of the country. See ibid., p. 29; Peter C. Welsh, "The American Trotter," *American Heritage,* 23 Dec., 1966), 31.

[33]For Holmes' statement, see Lucas and Smith, *Saga,* p. 93.

[34]For the urbanization of America during the antebellum period, see Charles N. Glaab and A. Theodore Brown, *A History of Urban America* (New York: Macmillan, 1967), p. 26; Blake McKelvey, *American Urbanization: A Comparative Perspective* (Glenview, Ill.: Scott, Foreman and Co., 1973), p. 14. for changing economic develoments during this period, see George R. Taylor, *The Transportation Revolution, 1815-1860* (New York: Harper and Row, 1968); Douglass C. North, *Growth and Welfare In The American Past: A New Economic History* (Englewood Cliffs, N.J.: Prentice-Hall, 1966), pp. 75-89; Stuart Bruchey, *The Roots of American Economic Growth, 1607-1861* (New York: Harper and Row, 1965), pp. 141-207.

[35]Arthur H. Cole, "Perspectives on Leisure-Time Business," *Explorations in Entrepreneurial History,* 2nd series, 1 (Summer, 1964), 23, 27-8. It would be erroneous to perceive these commercialized "popular" amusements as being "mass" institutions. Rarely were they patronized by large number of men from the working class. Their suport was overwhelmingly drawn from the middle class.

[36]*Spirit* 13 (Mar. 18,1843):25; *Turf, Field and Farm* 4 (June 22, 1867): 387.

[37]*Porter's Spirit of the Times* 1 (Oct. 25, 1856): 132.

[38]For the career of *Lady Suffolk,* see John Hervey, *The Old Grey Mare of Long Island* (New York: Derrydale Press, 1936); Hiram Woodruff, *The Trotting Horse of America: How To Train and Drive Him. With Reminiscences of The Trotting Turf.* Edit. by Charles J. Foster, 19th Ed. (Philadelphia: Porter and Coates, 1874), pp.211-47; Akers, *Drivers Up,* pp. 49-56.

[39]For the impact of *Messenger* on American trotting, see Hervey, *American Trotter,* pp. 28-43; Akers, *Drivers Up,* p. 26.

[40]Akers, *Drivers Up,* p. 49. Bryan's continual ownership of *Lady Suffolk* was a rarity. During this period, most trotters, including some of the best horses, passed through several owners during their careers.

[41]For Bryan's reputation as a reinsman and his demands on *Lady Suffolk,* see Akers, *Drivers Up,* p. 50. By comparing the earnings, number of races and miles raced of

Lady Suffolk and the three competitors in the intersectional horse races of the 1840s—Fashion, Boston and Peytonia—the differences between trotting and thoroughbred racing can be illustrated. In a nine year career, Fashion won $41,500, by winning 32 out of 36 races. In eight years, Boston was triumphant in 40 of his 45 contests winning $51,700. Peytonia won $62,400, although no figures were available for the length of her career or the number of her victories. Furthermore, Fashion raced no more than 260 miles and Boston no more than 324 miles during their careers. (Both probably raced much less). By contrast, Lady Suffolk ran at least 500 miles and quite possibly as much as 800 miles. The figures on thoroughbreds were drawn from Hervey, Racing In America, 2: 175-76, 217-19, 299.

[42]Porter's Spirit 3 (Jan. 23, 1858): 329. For the emergence of harness racing at the county fair, see Betts, Sporting Heritage, pp. 34-36; Akers, Drivers Up, pp. 105-8; Welsh, "The Trotter," p. 31.

[43]Wilkes' Spirit of the Times 3 (Sept. 22, 1860): 54, (Oct. 6, 1860):76. For the career of Flora Temple, see Woodruff, Trotting Horse, pp. 247-335; Akers, Drivers Up, 78-89.

[44]Spirit 7 (Oct. 21, 1837): 284

[45]New York Times 16 Apr. 1857.

[46]For the complaints of irregularities on the trotting track between 1850 and 1870, see New York Clipper 1 (June 25, 1853), (Mar. 25, 1854), 5 (Sept. 26, 1857): 117, 7 (June 25, 1859): 74, 6 (Apr. 9, 1859): 402, 9 (Aug. 10, 1861): 130, (Aug. 31, 1861): 154, 17 (Nov. 20, 1869): 258; Herald 17 Sept. 1853, 4 June 1859, 3 Aug. 1860, 25 Sept., 3 Oct., 11 Nov. 1869; Times 5 June 1863; Wilkes' Spirit 2 (Aug. 13, 1860): 360, 4 (Aug. 10, 1861): 36, 5 (Nov. 23, 1861): 184, (Dec. 7, 1861): 213, 6 (June 21, 1862): 249, (Aug. 2, 1862): 344, 7 (Nov. 8, 1862): 153, 14 (July 7, 1866): 297.

[47]Restrictions of time did not permit me to investigate the accuracy of this impression, but the performance of four leading trotters—Lady Suffolk, Flora Temple, Dexter and Goldsmith Maid—during this period provides some insights. Of these trotters, Dexter won 92 percent of his races, Flora Temple 84.82 percent and Goldsmith Main 79.8 percent. These outstanding records minimize the number of opportunities that they could have thrown a race and gives credence to the belief that their defeats were the product of other factors. On the other hand, Lady Suffolk won 54.9 percent of her races. Her record could be blamed on Bryan's mismanagement of the horse, but no one questioned his integrity. "Money grubber though he was," Akers noted, Bryan "was too jealous of his grey mare's reputation ever to throw a race." [Drivers Up, p. 154]. In contrast to the above horse, George Wilkes, a trotter of outstanding potential and in turn an immensely successful progenitor, won 39.15 percent of his races. Such a poor performance record could give credence to Hervey's contention that he "was manipulated in the most discreditable way was an open secret." Nevertheless, the same historian brought compelling evidence that his poor record could be explained as a product of other factors. He noted that George Wilkes' owners made great demands on the horse and that the horse regularly performed stud service in conjunction with his trotting campaigns. Furthermore, many of his defeats came at the expense of the leading trotters of his day. Finally, George Wilkes had a notorious reputation as a quitter and sulker, a point which this scholar readily accepts as valid. [American Trotter, pp. 106-8]. The winning percentages were drawn from the records in ibid., pp. 453-61.

[48]In his work on harness racing, Akers devoted an entire chapter, entitled "Sharps and Flats," to the crisis the fixing of races created for the sport. Nevertheless, he conceded that "Not all races, probably not most of them, were dishonestly driven . . . Much of the ugly gossip could be set down as the malicious imagination of fanatics who looked upon racing and betting as vices." Despite the presence of this brief statement, Akers left the impression, through the choice of his chapter title and the

disproportionate amount of space devoted to the fixing of races, that he believed that the manipulation of contests was a widespread practice on trotting tracks. [*Drivers Up,* ch. 11]. Harold Seymour is also guilty of the same type of analysis in his treatment of corruption in baseball. See his *Baseball, The Early Years* (New York: Oxford University Press, 1960), pp. 52-54. For a different view of duplicity on the diamond, see Adelman, "Modern Athletics," pp. 412-420.

[49]*Spirit* 30 (July 28, 1860): 298; *Turf, Field and Farm* 5 (Nov. 30, 1867): 338; *Herald* 6 Apr. 1860.

[50]Woodruff, *Trotting Horse,* pp. 296-98. for somewhat similar incident, see ibid., 262-63.

[51]In contrast to trotting, there were almost no charges of fixing of contests in thoroughbred racing in New York between 1820 and 1870 even though jockies were professional athletes and large amounts of money depended on the outcome. Upper class control of the sport was largely responsible for the different attitudes.

[52]*Clipper* 6 (Apr. 9, 1859): 402, 1 (Mar. 25, 1854), 7 (June 25, 1859): 74; *Wilkes' Spirit* 2 (Aug. 11, 1860): 356; *Herald* 4 June 1859, 6 Apr., 3 Aug. 1860.

[53]*Spirit* 30 (July 28, 1860): 298. While the *Spirit* did not believe that races were fixed, it nevertheless opposed races for gate money.

[54]Woodruff, *Trotting Horse,* p. 288.

[55]Unlike today, where the purses are divided, albeit unequally, among a certain number of horses, the winners, in the overwhelming number of races, were rewarded the entire purse in the antebellum period. Both thoroughbreds and trotting men recognized the economic problems created by this system as early as the 1830s; however, this method of reward continued to prevail in both turf sports until after the Civil War.

[56]*Clipper* 7 (July 16, 1859): 103.

[57]Nothing more coherently indicates that nineteenth century writers did not understand the concept of "upset" than the absence in their works of any term which resembles in any way the meaning the term has today.

[58]Seymour, *Baseball,* p. 60. For the changing style of professional drivers, see Akers, *Drivers Up,* p. 152.

[59]*Wilkes' Spirit* 12 (Mar. 25, 1865): 57, (Mar. 18, 1865): 41, (Mar. 11, 1865): 24. For road racing in New York between 1850 and 1870, see Akers, *Drivers Up,* pp. 90-92; Krout, *Annals,* p. 55: Wheaton J. Lane, *Commodore Vanderbilt, An Epic of the Steam Age* (New York: Alfred A. Knopf, 1942), pp. 162-63; *Clipper* 18 (Apr. 16, 1870): 13.

[60]For discussion of this theme, see Adelman, "Modern Athletics," pp. 639-640, 709-710.

[61]While there is no comprehensive list of EPPGA members, there was a register book for the year 1859-1860. It is perfectly clear that not all the signees of this book were members of the club; one being Senator Stephen Douglas of Illinois. Nevertheless, the repetition of names does indicate that the majority were. The occupation of these members were then examined in the New York City directories. Data could be found on 53 members. Of this group, 25 (47.1%) were either merchants or brokers. Twenty-three (43.3%) other members engaged in service occupations with the majority of this group (12) associated with the food and drink industry. Of the remaining five, three were lawyers and two were clerks. Biographical data on these turfmen was unfortunately limited, but what evidence does exist indicates that they originated mainly from the middle class. In only one case was a member the son of an upper-middle class New Yorker and it is perfectly evident that none of the EPPGA members came from the city's upper class. While more data is still necessary, the evidence

tends to support the earlier contention that New York's road runner came mainly from the prosperous segments of the middle class. For the register book, see Elm Park Pleasure Garden Association, "Visitors Book," New York Historical Society.

[62]For background material on Bonner, see his own "Scrapbook of Newspaper Clippings, 1850-1899," 2 vols. New York Public Library; Stanwood Cobb. *The Magnificent Partnership* (New York: Vintage Press, 1945); Charles Morris (ed.), *Makers of New York* (Philadelphia: L.R. Hamersly, 1895), p. 236. Notices of Bonner's death (July 6, 1899) can probably be found in every major American newspaper.

[63]Akers, *Drivers Up,* p. 95. For the Bonner-Vanderbilt battle, see ibid., pp. 90-104; Lane, *Commodore Vanderbilt,* p. 163; Adelman. "Modern Athletics," 112-13.

[64]Bonner, "Papers," v.1,p.66; Hervey, *American Trotter,* p. 77; Akers, *Drivers Up,* p. 95.

[65]*New York Tribune* 7 July 1899.

[66]Akers, *Drivers Up,* p. 93; Lane. *Commodore Vanderbilt,* p. 164. While New York's upper crust were never supporters of trotting, it is doubtful that its opposition to either the sport or trotting men was as monolithic as these writers suggested. See Dayton, *Last Days,* pp. 237-58; Bristed, *Upper Ten Thousands,* pp. 23-24.

[67]Akers, *Drivers Up,* p. 95

[68]I found only one individual involved in trotting prior to 1870 (excluding the three noted in the 1830s, see fn. 26) who was a descendant of the city's antebellum elite. The lone case, George B. Alley, moreover, was not a product of the new respectability of trotting horses won. Involved with trotting prior to Bonner, Alley was "one of the most prominent patrons of the trotter in the Metropolis, if not the foremost among them all" between 1850 and 1870. [Hervey, American Trotter, p. 131]. For biographical material on Alley, see *Times* 17 Oct. 1883.

[69]For a discussion of New York elites, see Frederic C. Jaher, "Style and Status: High Society in Late Nineteenth-Century New York," in *The Rich, the Well Born, and the Powerful: Elites and Upper Classes in History* (Urbana, Ill.: University of Illinois Press, 1973), pp. 258-84; idem., "Nineteenth-Century Elites In Boston and New York," *Journal of Social History,* 6 (Fall, 1972), 32-77. For the view that New York's upper class during the antebellum period was a stable group, see Edward Pessen, *Riches, Class and Power Before The Civil War* (Lexington, Mass.: D. C. Heath, 1973), pp. 84-85, 146. For criticism of this view, see Whitman Ridgway, "Measuring Wealth and Power in Antebellum America: A Review Essay," Historical Methods Newsletter 8 (Mar., 1975),Frederic C. Jaher,"Elites and Equality In Antebellum America,"*Reviews In American History,* 2 (Mar., 1974), 86-87.

[70]John Elderken, "Turf and Trotting Horse of America," in *Every Horse Owners' Cyclopedia,* edit. by Robert McClure (Philadelphia, 1872), p. 553, quoted in Welsh, *Track and Road,* p. 18: Akers, *Drivers Up.* pp. 168-69.

[71]Akers, *Drivers Up,* p. 105. For the story of William M. Rysdyk and *Hambletonian,* see ibid., 115-19; Hervey, *American Trotter,* pp. 44-48.

[72]Akers, *Drivers Up,* pp. 168-69.

[73]For a very good discussion of these developments, see Hervey, *American Trotter,* pp. 277-92.

[74]The quote can be found in Betts, *Sporting Heritage,* p. 145. For the persistance of the utilitarian argument, see Adelman, "Modern Athletics," pp. 118-120.

[75]For the tremendous popularity of harness racing at county fairs in the immediate post-Civil War years, see Betts, *Sporting Heritage,* p. 144.

[76]Until recently historians have designated wealthy participants in athletics as "sportsmen." The inference they expected to be drawn from this term was that these rich men eschewed financial considerations and were involved in sport solely for its own sake. The evidence on New York turfmen, both thoroughbred and trotting, between 1820 and 1870 testifies to the inaccuracy of this impression. While many of these turfmen did not feel compelled to profit from their involvement, they were not out to lose money either. When they could no longer cover their costs, as had been the case with the owners of the thoroughbreds in New York in the 1840s, their involvement in the sport ceased. For further discussion of this theme, see Adelman, "Modern Athletics," pp. 65-68. For other recent challenges to the traditional view, see Steven A. Riess, "The Baseball Magnate and Urban Politics in the Progressive Era, 1895-1920," *Journal of Sport History*, 1 (Spring, 1974), 41-62; Jonathan Brower, "Professional Sports Team Ownership: Fun, Profit and Ideology of the Power Elite," *Journal of Sport and Social Issues*, (1976), 16-51.

[77]As early as 1862, the proprietor of the Fashion Course sold to a gambling "auctioneer" the right to handle all the betting on the track. For this privilege, the "pool-seller," as these gamblers were called, paid the proprietor a flat fee. See *Times* 24 July 1862. For a discussion of the "pool system" of wagering, see William H. P. Robertson, *A History of Thoroughbred Racing in America* (Englewood Cliffs, N.J.; Prentice Hall, 1964). pp. 93-94.

[78]*Clipper* 12 (Dec. 17, 1864): 282, 11 (June 6, 1863): 63; *Herald* 11 Sept. 1862; *Times* 11 Sept. 1862, 16 Oct. 1864, 8 Sept. 1865; *Wilkes' Spirit* 8 (May 1863): 140, 10 (July 16, 1864): 313. 11 (Oct. 8, 1864): 78-79, 12 (Apr.29, 1865): 132-33.

[79]For the figures, see *Times* 18 Mar 1862; *Wilkes' Spirit* 22 (Apr. 16, 1870).

[80]*Wilkes' Spirit* 10 (Mar. 26, 1864); 56.

[81]*Clipper* 17 (Nov. 20, 1869): 258, 9 (Aug. 10, 1861): 130 (Aug. 31, 1861): 154: *Herald* 6 Apr. 1860, 25 Sept., 9.; 17 Nov. 1869; *Times* 5 June 1863; *Wilkes' Spirit* 2 (Aug. 11, 1860): 360, 4 (Aug. 10, 1861): 36, 7 (Nov. 8, 1862): 153, 14 (July 7, 1866): 297.

[82]National Association for the Promotion of the Interest of The Trotting Turf, *Rules and Regulations. Adopted February 4, 1870* (Providence: Providence Press. 1870), p. 19; John Hervey, "American Harness Horse and Horsemen," in *American Harness Racing* (New York; Ralph F. Hartstein, 1948), p. 32.

[83]Hervey, "American Harness Horse," p. 32; Wrench, *Harness Horse Racing*, pp. 16-18; Akers, *Drivers Up*, pp. 161-66

[84]*Wilkes' Spirit* 21 (Jan 29, 1870): 370-71.

[85]*Porter's Spirit* 3 (Jan 23, 1858): 370.

[86]*Wilkes' Spirit* 21 (Jan. 29, 1870): 370; *Times* 12 June 1862. For a discussion of the emergence of the time classification system, see Akers, *Drivers Up,* pp. 138-39.

[87]For the publication of the New York rules, see *Spirit* 8 (Apr. 21, 1838): 80, 11 (Jan 29, 1842): 569, 13 (June 3, 1843): 156, 18 (May 6, 1848): 128, Dale Somers informs us that the New Orleans Trotting and Pacing Club adopted the rules used at the Beacon Course. See his *Rise of Sport,* p. 35.

[88]*Wilkes' Spirit* 22 (Feb. 26, 1870): 20-21, John L. Cassady wrote under the name of "Larkin."

[89]*Times* 14 Jan. 1885. For additional information on Rynders and his political involvement, see Alexander B. Callow, Jr. *The Tweed Ring* (New York: Oxford University Press, 1966), p. 58; Herbert Asbury, *The Gangs of New York: An Informal History Of The Underworld* (New York: Capricorn Books, 1970), pp. 43-44. Rynders was not the only man of this "ilk" to have sporting associations with the "better class." John Morrissey—the one time heavyweight champion, casino operator and

member of the notorious Tweed Ring—and the creme de la creme of New York society were co-partners in establishing racing in Saratoga, New York in 1863. For this connection, see Hugh Bradley, *Such Was Saratoga* (New York: Doubleday, Doran and Co. 1950), pp. 142-45; Bernard Livingston, *Their Turf: America's Horsey Set And Its Princely Dynasties* (New York: Arbor House, 1973), pp. 229-30.

[90]*Wilkes' Spirit* 19 (Jan 30, 1869): 337; *Times* 31 Jan. 1870. The newer racing schedule affected only purse races. Match races, sweepstakes and some specially arranged contests continued to be held throughout the year.

[91]I have found no evidence that the NTA in 1870 or afterwards emerged with a *formal* racing calendar. Nevertheless, the creation of systematic schedules, through the federation of local trotting clubs began in the 1870s. The first and by far the most important of these associations was the Grand Circuit established in 1873. The success of this organization "led local associations elsewhere to form similar combinations." In time, an organizational pattern emerged that remains in existence today. "In a truer sense than before, harness racing became a 'national sport.'" [Akers, *Drivers Up*, p. 141]

[92]It is significant to note that Akers conceded that the NTA did not immediately succeed in reforming the trotting turf even though he judged the organization's effort to cleanse the sport of its abuses an overall success. [*Drivers Up.*. pp. 164-65].

[93]Marshal B. Davidson, *Life In America*, 2 vols. (Boston: Houghton Mifflin, 1951), 2:35.

Suggestions For Further Reading.

Adelman, Melvin L. "The Development of Modern Athletics: Sport in New York City, 1820-1870." (Ph.D. dissertation, University of Illinois, 1980).

Akers, Dwight. *Drivers Up: The Story of American Harness Racing* (N.Y.: G.P. Putman and Sons, 1938).

Bennett, Bruce. "The Making of Round Hill School." *Quest 4* (April 1965): 53-64.

Betts, John R. "Agricultural Fairs and the Rise of Harness Racing." *Agricultural History* 27 (April 1953): 71-75.

Betts, John R. "American Medical Thought on Exercise as the Road to Health, 1820-1860." *Bulletin of the History of Medicine* 45 (March-April 1971): 238-52.

Cole, Arthur C. "Our Sporting Grandfathers—The Cult of Athletics at its Source." *Atlantic Monthly* CL (July 1932): 88-96.

Dulles, Foster Rhea. *A History of Recreation: America Learns to Play* (N.Y. Appleton-Century-Crofts, 1965).

Farrand, Max. "The Great Race—Eclipse Against the World!" *Scribner's Magazine* LXX (October 1921): 547-64.

Geldbach, Erich. "The Beginnings of German Gymnastics in America." *Journal of Sport History* 3 (Winter 1976): 236-72.

Green, Margaret D., "The Growth of Physical Education for Women in the United States in the Early Nineteenth Century (Ed. D dissertation, UCLA, 1950).

Henderson, Robert W. *Ball, Bat and Bishop: The Origin of Ball Games* (N.Y.: Rockport Press, 1947).

Hervey, John. *American Trotter* (N.Y. Coward-McCann, 1947).

Hervey, John. *Racing in America, 1665-1865,* Vol. II (N.Y.: Jockey Club, 1944).

Higginson, Thomas Wentworth. "Gymnastics." *Atlantic Monthly* VII (March 1861): 283-302.

Holliman, Jennie. *American Sport, 1785-1835* (Durham, N.C.: Seeman Press, 1931).

Holmes, Oliver W. *The Autocrat of the Breakfast Table* (1815, reprinted, N.Y.: Heritage Press, 1955).

Krout, John A. *Annals of American Sport* (New Haven: Yale Univesity Press, 1929).

Levine, Peter. "The Promise of Sport in Antebellum America." *Journal of American Culture* 2 (Winter 1980): 623-34.

Lewis, Guy M. "The Beginning of Organized Collegiate Sport." *American Quarterly* 22 (Summer 1970): 222-29.

Lucas, John A. "A Prelude to the Rise of Sport: Ante-bellum America, 1850-1860." *Quest* 11 (December 1968): 50-57.

Mathews, Joseph J. "First Harvard-Oxford Boat Race." *New England Quarterly* 33 (March 1960): 74-82.

Nugent, William H. "Sports Section." *American Mercury* XVI (March 1929): 329-38.

Park, Roberta J. "The Attitude of Leading New England Transcendentalists Toward Healthful Exercise, Active Recreation and Proper Care of the Body: 1830-1860." *Journal of Sport History* 4 (Spring 1977): 34-50.

Park, Roberta J. "Embodied Selves:" The Rise and Development of Concern for Physical Education, Active Games and Recreation for American Women, 1776-1865." *Journal of Sport History* 5 (Summer 1978): 5-41.

Swanson, Richard A. "The Acceptance and Influence of Play in American Protestantism." *Quest II* (December 1968): 58-70.

Vertinsky, Pastricia. "Sexual Equality and the Legacy of Catherine Beecher." *Journal of Sport History* 6 (Spring 1979). 39-49.

Wiggins, David K. "The Play of Slave Children in the Plantation Communities of the Old South, 1820-1860." *Journal of Sport History* 7 (Summer 1980): 21-39.

Wiggins, David K. "Sport and Popular Pastimes: Shadow of the Slavequarter." *Canadian Journal of the History of Sport and Physical Education (May 1980): 61-88.*

Wittke, Carl F. *"The Turners."* In Carl F. Wittke, *Refugees of Revolution* (Philadelphia: University of Pennsylvania Press, 1952), 147-60.

The Rise of American Sport: 1870-1900

Introduction

The fundamental question of American sport historiography is: Why did organized sports develop and start to boom in the late nineteenth century? The first historian who sought to answer this basic issue was Frederick L. Paxson. Paxson's essay, "The Rise of Sport," written in 1917, was the first article on sport history published in the major professional journal of American history, the *Mississippi Valley Historical Review* (now the *Journal of American History*). Paxson was a noted historian at the University of Wisconsin who was a follower of the school of history developed by Frederick J. Turner. Turner was renowned for his frontier thesis, a theory which argued that the character of the American nation had been developed on the moving frontier. Paxson did not think it was a coincidence that the period when American sport developed, the late nineteenth century, was also the era when the American frontier had disappeared. He argued that since the cities had lost their principal safety-valve, an open frontier for their overcrowded inhabitants, they needed a new safety-valve to maintain social order. Paxson asserted that sports had developed in the late nineteenth century as a means of managing urban tensions and maintaining order in the densely populated cities. This theory was for many years the standard interpretation for the rise of American sport.

The second article published in the *MVHR* on sport history did not appear until 1953. It was John R. Betts' seminal essay "The Technological Revolution and the Rise of Sport, 1850-1900." Until recently, sport history was not regarded as a subject meriting serious scholarship, and for many years Betts was virtually the only historian studying the American sporting experience. He saw the sporting movement of the late nineteenth century as an antidote for the confinements of city life, but did not go as far as Paxson's unicausal interpretation for the rise of sport. Betts did not assert that urbanization and industrialization by themselves simply caused the rise of sport, but he did vigorously demonstrate how essential they were as factors in that development. Urbanization provided large aggregates of potential customers for commercialized sports. Technology supplied many new inventions and improvements in sporting equipment, electric lighting for indoor arenas, improved forms of communication for reporting results, and revolutionized transportation, enabling competitors to travel around the country and fans to travel within the city to the local ballparks, race tracks, or other sports facilities.

The sporting world in late nineteenth century America was dominated by participatory sports rather than spectatorial sports, but opportunities to play were restricted to white-collar workers or skilled craftsmen. Such factors as discretionary time, income, and the availability of facilities curtailed participation. This era was dominated by the amateur sportsmen who played for healthful or recreational purposes, unlike the low status professional who played for financial rewards. Winning and the striving for excellence was very important to these athletes because competition was a cornerstone of American sport and American social life in the post-Darwinian era. However, nearly as important was the way one played, because athletes were expected to comport themselves as gentlemen. The qualities of a gentleman sportsman are described in the selection taken from *Walter Camp's Book of College Sports,* published in 1893. Walter Camp was not only one of the leading spokesmen for amateur sport, but he himself was a major figure in the history of college football. He was the coach of the powerful Yale football teams which dominated the gridiron in the late nineteenth century, and was instrumental in amending the rules of the sport to make it more popular for the spectators. Camp regarded sportsmanship as an essential ingredient of sport. Gentlemen athletes were amateurs who sought only glory and self-satisfaction from competitive sport. They were expected to be courteous and never mock or belittle their opposition. Gentlemen played fairly and if they lost, accepted defeat with dignity.

Football at this time was predominantly a sport played by well-to-do young men from elite eastern colleges. The game was characterized by brutal mass team play in which the ball was seldom advanced more than a few yards a try. The sport was so violent that more athletes died from playing football than by boxing. Historian John H. Moore has called the period from 1893 to 1913 "Football's Ugly Decades." In his article, Moore points out that besides the problems of violence and boring play (which hurt its box office appeal), football was also being harmed by its over-commercialization and underemphasis on academics. The crisis in the sport was so great that essential reforms had to be introduced in 1906 and 1910 to save the game from self-destruction. One of the most important changes instituted was the legalization of the forward pass. The potential value of this offensive weapon was first demonstrated in 1913 when an obscure Notre Dame team defeated a powerful Army eleven 35-13 by using the forward pass. By this time, football was no longer the exclusive preserve of the elite eastern institutions who found theirpreeminence challenged by public and private midwestern institutions.

One of the most popular participatory sports of the late nineteenth century was bicycle riding. Its widespread success depended on a new technological innovation called the safety bicycle. This vehicle had equal sized wheels, was lightweight, easy to ride, comfortable, and equipped with good brakes. Previous bicycles like the boneshaker and the ordinary (an odd looking vehicle with a small front wheel and a larger rear wheel) had been difficult to ride, cumbersome, and dangerous. Historian Richard Harmond examines the impact of the safety bicyle in his influential essay "Progress and Flight." Harmond argues that a veritable bicycle craze began in the early 1890s once a safe, comfortable, and relatively easy to ride vehicle was introduced which was not too expensive. The bicycle became a great fad between 1893 and 1896. Millions were manufactured and sold in America by innovative and imaginative entrepreneurs. Its popularity resulted in the development of an entire subculture of cycling fanatics as middle class urbanites used the bicycle to escape their daily routine and the problems of a crowded city. This innovation was particularly liberating for middle class women whose prior sporting experiences had been strictly limited. Cycling provided an opportunity for women to participate in physical exertion and encouraged dress reforms, like loosening corsets and wearing sporty clothing like bloomers.

8

The Technological Revolution And The Rise Of Sport, 1850-1900

by John Rickards Betts

The roots of our sporting heritage lie in the horse racing and fox hunting of the colonial era, but the main features of modern sport appeared only in the middle years of the nineteenth century.[1] Organization, journalistic exploitation, commercialization, intercommunity competition, and sundry other developments increased rapidly after 1850 as the agrarian nature of sport gave way gradually to the influences of urbanization and industrialization. Just as the Industrial Revolution was to alter the interests, habits, and pursuits of all classes of society, it was to leave a distinct impress on the development of sport.

Many other factors were responsible for the directions taken by sport in the half century from 1850 to 1900. Continuing rural influences, the decline of Puritan orthodoxy, the English athletic movement, the immigrant, frontier traditions of manliness and strength, and the contributions of energetic sportsmen were to have a significant effect on the sporting scene. Industrialization and urbanization, however, were more fundamentally responsible for the changes and developments in sport during the next generation than any other cause. Manufacturers, seeking cheap labor, encouraged immigration; factories were most efficiently run in larger towns and cities; urban masses, missing the rustic pleasures of hunting and fishing, were won to the support of commercialized entertainment and spectator sports; the emergence of a commercial aristocracy and a laboring class resulted in distinctions every bit as strong in sport as in other social matters; and the urgency of physical exercise as life became more sedentary was readily recognized.

The revolution in manufacturing methods, which had such profound social consequences for the American way of life, derived from a powerful inventive spirit which flourished throughout the nineteenth

From John Rickards Betts, "The Technological Revolution and the Rise of Sport, 1850-1900," Mississippi Valley Historical Review *XL (September, 1953): 231-56. Copyright © by the Organization of American Historians. Reprinted by permission.*

century. From England and western Europe we borrowed many mechanical innovations and most of our scientific theory, but Americans demonstrated a native ability soon recognized everywhere as "Yankee ingenuity." These inventions were to revolutionize transportation, communication, manufacturing, finance, and all the many facets of economic life. Although the tendency in narrating the history of sport has been to emphasize the role of individuals, the changing social scene was of equal importance in directing sport into the channels it eventually took in modern society. The impact of invention had a decisive influence on the rise of sport in the latter half of the century. By 1900 sport had attained an unprecedented prominence in the daily lives of millions of Americans, and this remarkable development had been achieved in great part through the steamboat, the railroad, the telegraph, the penny press, the electric light, the streetcar, the camera, the bicycle, the automobile, and the mass production of sporting goods.

The transformation of the United States from a rural-agrarian to an urban-industrial society, of course, affected the development of sport in other ways. Urbanization brought forth the need for commercialized spectator sports, while industrialization gradually provided the standard of living and leisure time so vital to the support of all forms of recreation. But it is the relationship of invention to sport, and that alone, which constitutes the theme of this study.

Early American interest in outdoor exercise was largely confined to hunting, fishing, horse racing, field sports, and the informal games of the local schoolyard. As the nation became more commercially minded in the decades after the War of 1812, many of those who lived in rapidly growing cities became concerned over the sedentary habits of clerks, office workers, and businessmen. In the years before 1850 there emerged a limited interest in rowing, running, prize fighting, cricket, fencing, and similar activities, but the only organized sport which excited the minds of most Americans was the turf. A more general interest in horse racing appeared in the 1820s and 1830s, and many jockey clubs held meetings attended by throngs of spectators in their carriages and barouches.[2]

From the early years of the century steamboat captains engaged in racing on the Hudson, Ohio, Mississippi, and other rivers, and the steamboat served as a common carrier of sports crowds. By the 1850s it became an indispensable means of transport to the races along the eastern seaboard and in the Mississippi Valley. As one of the first products of the age of steam it played a significant role in the rise of the turf and outdoor games.[3]

In the years preceding the Civil War the turf was also encouraged by the development of a railroad network. As early as 1838 Wade Hampton was transporting race horses to Charleston by rail;[4] in 1839 the Nashville Railroad was carrying New Orleans crowds to the

Metairie Course;[5] in 1842 the Long Island Railroad was already suffering the abuse of irate passenges swarming to the races; and three years later it carried some 30,000 passengers to the Fashion-Peytona race at more than fifty cents each.[6] Kentucky became the leading breeding center for thoroughbreds and Louisville could announce in 1851: "Lexington, Georgetown, Frankfort, Paris and other towns in this State, are now but a short ride from our city by railroad conveyance. Horses can come from Lexington here in five hours."[7] The famous trotter Flora Temple began barnstorming tours; racing and trotting benefited from the cooperation of railroad lines; and "speed trials" at agricultural fairs during the 1850s were attended by excursionists.[8] Other outdoor sports also profited from the interest shown by certain lines. When excitement over rowing began to catch on in the late 1830s the first boat shipped west of the Appalachians went by way of the Erie Canal.[9] It was a railroad, however, which encouraged the holding of the first intercollegiate rowing race between Harvard and Yale in 1852.[10] Baseball clubs were organized throughout the East and Midwest during the decade and ·the National Association of Base Ball Players was formed in 1857, soon after both sections had been connected by rail. Chicago had its first baseball team in 1856, two years after it was linked by rail to Baltimore, Maryland, and Portland, Maine. In 1860 the Excelsior Club of Brooklyn made a tour of upper New York state. Most of the early prize fights were held along the rivers served by steamboats; the Harlem Railroad carried fight crowds in the early 1850s to the Awful Gardiner-William Hastings (*alias* Dublin Tricks) match sixty miles north of New York City and to a highly publicized championship fight at Boston Four Corners, New York,[11] and the John Morrissey-John Heanan match on the Canadian shore near Niagara Falls in 1858 was advertised by the Erie Railroad.[12]

The Civil War failed to halt turf meetings and outdoor recreation in the North. It was, however, only with the return of peace that the nation felt a new sporting impulse and began to give enthusiastic support to the turf, the diamond, the ring, and other outdoor activities. The game of baseball, spreading from cities to towns and villages, became a national fad, and matches were scheduled with distant communities. A tournament at Rockford, Illinois, in 1866 was attended by teams from Detroit, Milwaukee, Dubuque, and Chicago.[13] In 1869 Harry Wright's Cincinnati Red Stockings were able to make a memorable transcontinental tour from Maine to California; a New Orleans club visited Memphis, St. Louis, and Cincinnati; and eastern teams condescended to travel as far west as the Queen City. The Erie line offered to convey a New Orleans club, then visiting Cincinnati, to New York and return at half-fare rates. When the Cincinnati Red Stockings made their tour by boat, local lines, and the Union

Pacific in 1869 it was reported: "The boys have received every attention from the officers of the different roads . . . At all the stations groups stare us almost out of countenance, having heard of the successful exploits of the Club through telegrams of the Western Associated Press."[14]

Baseball clubs made use of the rapidly expanding networks of the 1870s, and the organization of the National League in 1876 was only possible with the continued development of connecting lines. In the 1886 edition of *Spalding's Official Base Ball Guide* the Michigan Central advertised: "The cities that have representative clubs contesting for the championship pennant this year are—Chicago, Boston, New York, Washington, Kansas City, Detroit, St. Louis and Philadelphia. All of these cities are joined together by the Michigan Central Railroad. This road has enjoyed almost a monopoly of Base Ball travel in former years." Throughout the 1870s and 1880s the expanding railroad network played an indispensable role in the popularization of the "national game."[15]

A widespread interest in thoroughbred and trotting races also was in great part sustained by railroad expansion. In 1866 the Harlem, Rensselaer and Saratoga Railroad Company, realizing the advantage of encouraging the racing public, arranged to convey race horses at cost by express train from New York to Saratoga. *Turf, Field and Farm* pointed to the need for better transportation arrangements and predicted, "The completion of the Pacific Railroad will not be without effect upon the blood stock interests of the great West."[16] Jerome Park, Long Branch, and Gravesend catered to New York crowds, Baltimore attracted huge throngs of sportsmen, and in California racing was encouraged by the building of lines into the interior of the state. In the 1870s western turfmen began sending their horses by rail to eastern tracks, the Grand Circuit linked Hartford, Springfield, Poughkeepsie, and Utica with Rochester, Buffalo, and Cleveland, and racing associations formed in virtually every section. When Mollie McCarthy and Ten Broeck raced at Louisville in 1877, "Masses of strangers arrived by train, extra trains and steamboats." People from "all over the land" attended the Kentucky Derby in 1885, the City Council declared a holiday, and sixteen carloads of horses were sent from Nashville to Louisville.[17] Agricultural fairs, with the cooperation of numerous companies, drew thousands to their fairground tracks, and the railroads encouraged intersectional meetings by introducing special horse cars in the middle eighties.[18]

In the decades after the Civil War an apologetic but curious public acquired a "deplorable" interest in prize fighting, and railroad officials were not slow to capitalize on the crowd appeal of pugilism despite its illegality. When Mike McCoole met Aaron Jones in 1867 at Busenbark Station, Ohio, "Tickets were openly sold for excursion trains to the bout" and sporting men from the East were in attendance, while another McCoole fight in 1869 encouraged the lines to run specials from Cincinnati and other nearby cities.[19] After 1881 John L. Sullivan, the notorious "Boston Strong Boy," went on grand tours of the athletic clubs, opera houses, and theaters of the country, his fights in the New Orleans area with Paddy Ryan, Jake Kilrain, James J. Corbett luring fans who jammed the passenger coaches. When the Great John L. met Kilrain near Richburg, Mississippi, in 1889, the Northeastern Railroad carried a tumultuous crowd from New Orleans to the site, even though Governor Robert Lowry of Mississippi issued a proclamation against the affair and called out armed guards to prevent any invasion of the state. After the brawl the Governor requested the attorney general "to begin proceedings to forfeit the charter of the Northeastern railroad."[20] Railroad companies expressed only a minor concern for such sporadic events, it is true, but the prize ring was greatly aided by their cooperation.[21]

Poor connections, uncomfortable cars, and the absence of lines in rural sections remained a problem for some years.[22] Many of the difficulties and inconveniences of travel remained throughout these expansive years of railroading, but all sports were encouraged by the improved transportation of the post-bellum era. Immediately after the war a New York crew visited Pittsburgh to participate in a regatta held on the Monongahela River.[23] The first intercollegiate football game between Rutgers and Princeton was attended by a group of students riding the train pulled by "the jerky little engine that steamed out of Princeton on the memorable morning of November 6, 1869.[24] Intercollegiate athletics depended on railroad service for carrying teams and supporters to football, baseball, and rowing, as well as track and field contests.

Harvard's crack baseball team made the first grand tour in 1870, "the most brilliant in the history of college baseball," according to Henry Chadwick almost two decades later. Playing both amateur and professional clubs, Harvard won a majority of the games played in New Haven, Troy, Utica, Syracuse, Oswego (Canada), Buffalo, Cleveland, Cincinnati, Louisville, Chicago, Milwaukee, Indianapolis, Washington, Baltimore, Philadelphia, New York, and Brooklyn.[25] Amateur and professional cycling races were held throughout the country,[26] while rod and gun enthusiasts relied on branch lines into rural preserves.[27] By the closing years of the century virtually every realm of sport had shared in the powerful impact of the railroad on American life.

Almost contemporaneous with the development of a continental railroad system came the diffusion of telegraph lines throughout the nation. From its invention in 1844 the electric telegraph rapidly assumed a significant role in the dissemination of news.[28] When the

Magnetic Telegraph Company's line reached New York, James Gordon Bennett's *Herald* and Horace Greeley's *Tribune* installed apparatus in 1846. Direct contact was made between the East and New Orleans two years later, largely to meet the urgent demand for quicker news from the Mexican War front. By 1861 San Francisco was connected by wire with the Atlantic coast, and throughout the war years use of the telegraph was extended in military operations.

During the pioneer years telegraphic messages were both costly and brief, and sports events were reported on a limited scale. One of the first reports by wire was that of the Tom Hyer-Yankee Sullivan brawl at Rock Point, Maryland, in 1849. A New York dispatch read, "We hope never to have to record a similar case of brutality in this country," and even Greeley, an inveterate foe of the prize ring, permitted the printing of dispatches of this brutal encounter. Interest was not confined to Baltimore, Philadelphia, and New York, for some newspapers in the West noticed it. In the next decade several fights were widely reported by telegraph. When Morrissey and Heanan fought for the American championship in Canada in 1858, anxious crowds waited at Western Union offices for the news; when Heanan met Tom Sayers in England two years later the news was spread by wire after it was brought to America by the *Vanderbilt*.[29] Horse racing and yachting news was less novel and less sensational, but Lady Suffolk's appearance on the course at the Rochester, New York, fair in 1851, the victory of Commodore John Cox Stevens' yacht *America* at Cowes in the same year, and the exciting trotting races of the decade were given extensive wire coverage.[30] When Lexington met Lecomte at New Orleans in 1855, however, there seems to have been little reporting of the race in the North. Newspapers of that section were primarily concerned in that year with the trouble in Kansas, the rise of the Republican party, the heat of the abolitionist crusade, and the public furor over the murder of pugilist William Poole.

The expansion of sporting news in ensuing years was directly related to the more general usage of telegraphy, which made possible instantaneous reporting of ball games, horse races, prize fights, yachting regattas, and other events. Box scores, betting odds, and all kinds of messages were relayed from one city to another, and by 1870 daily reports were published in many metropolitan papers. In that year the steamboat race of the *Natchez and the Robert E. Lee* was reported throughout the country in one of the most extensive telegraphic accounts of any nonpolitical event prior to that time.[31] Not only did the newspapers make a practice of publishing daily messages from all corners of the sporting world, but crowds formed around Western Union offices during any important contest.[32] When the Associated Press sent its representatives in 1889 to the Sullivan-Kilrain fight in New Orleans, reporters appeared from "every prominent journal in the Union," and Western Union was said to have employed 50 operators to handle 208,000 words of specials following the fight. Poolrooms and saloons were often equipped with receiving sets to keep customers and bettors posted on baseball scores and track results, while newspapers set up bulletin boards for the crowds to linger around.[33] And the business transactions of sporting clubs and associations were often carried on by wire.

Sport had emerged into such a popular topic of conversation that newspapers rapidly expanded their coverage in the 1880s and 1890s, relying in great part on messages sent over the lines from distant points. Among the leaders in this field during these formative years of "yellow journalism" were such New York papers as Bennett's *Herald,* Charles Dana's *Sun,* and Joseph Pulitzer's *World.* The sports page was not solely the result of improvements in telegraphy, however, for popular interest had encouraged the employment of specialists who were extremely quick, as were the publishers, to capitalize on the news value of sporting events. Chicago produced the pioneers in baseball writing in such masters of breezy slang and grotesque humor as Leonard Washburne, Charles Seymour, and Finley Peter Dunne. Cincinnati newspapers, staffed by experts like Harry Weldon, O.P. Caylor, and Byron (Ban) Johnson, were among the most authoritative journals in the diamond world. In 1895, when William Randolph Hearst invaded the New York field and bought the *Journal,* he immediately brought in western writers and, within a few years, developed the first sports section.[34] The telegraph retained its functional importance in recording daily box scores and racing statistics, but it was not longer the one indispensable factor it had been in earlier decades.

The Atlantic cable, successfully laid in 1866 by Cyrus Field, had overcome the mid-century handicap of reporting two- or three-week-old English sporting news. At the end of that year James Gordon Bennett, Jr., with the aid of the Associated Press, featured cable dispatches of the great ocean race. When the Harvard crew rowed against Oxford in a highly publicized race in 1869, "the result was flashed through the Atlantic cable as to reach New York about a quarter past one, while the news reached the Pacific Coast about nine o'clock, enabling many of the San Franciscans to discuss the subject at their breakfast-tables, and swallow the defeat with their coffee!"[35] The combination of cable and telegraph aroused a deeper interest in international sport. Nor must we ignore that forerunner of the modern radio, the wireless which was demonstrated publicly in America for the first time in the yacht races of 1899. From Samuel F.B. Morse to Guglielmo Marconi the revolution in communication had encouraged the rise of sport.

Public interest in sport was also aroused by the enlarged format and greater circulation achieved by numerous inventions which revolutionized the printing process. By 1830 the Napier double-cylinder press was imported from England and developed by R. Hoe and Company, printing those cheap and sensational papers which were the first to feature horse races, prize fights, and foot races—the New York Sun, the New York Transcript, and the Philadelphia Public Ledger.[36] James Gordon Bennett, Sr., recognized the value of catering to the whims of the masses and occasionally featured turf reporting in the Herald of the 1840s.[37] In 1846 the Hoe type-revolving cylinder press was introduced by the Public Ledger, enabling newspaper publishers, after improvements were made in the machine, to print 20,000 sheets an hour.[38] Other inventions facilitated the mass publication of the daily paper, making possible the sensationalized editions of Bennett, Pulitzer, and Hearst.[39] With the arrival of the new journalism of the 1880s, sporting news rapidly became a featured part of the metropolitan press.[40]

Publishers also aided in the popularization of outdoor sport throughout this whole era. From the 1830s onward sporting books appeared, the most famous of prewar authors being Henry William Herbert, whose illustrious psuedonym was Frank Forester. After the Civil War cheap methods of publication gave a great stimulus to the dime novel and the athletic almanac. While the vast majority of the thrillers and shockers concerned the Wild West or city crime, athletic stories and manuals were put out by Beadle & Adams, the leading publisher of the paper-backed dime novel.[41] After the establishment of A.G. Spalding & Brothers the Spalding Guide developed into the leading authority on rules of play, and all sorts of handbooks were included in the Spalding Library of Athletic Sports. The New York Clipper began publishing a theatrical and sporting Clipper Almanac in the 1870s, and newspapers like the New York World, the New York Tribune, the Chicago Daily News, the Washington Post, and the Brooklyn Daily Eagle issued almanacs listing athletic and racing records and sporting news. Richard Kyle Fox of the National Police Gazette published Fox's Athletic Library and sporting annuals. By the end of the century book publication had grown to astronomic proportions when compared to the Civil War era, and the Outing Publishing Company issued more than a hundred titles on angling, canoeing, yachting, mountain climbing, hunting, shooting, trapping, camping, cycling, and athletics.

A few dime novels had taken up the athletic theme in the 1870s, but more mature stories like Mark Sibley Severance's Hammersmith: His Harvard Days (1878), Noah Brooks's Our Baseball Club (1884), and, of course, Thomas Hughes's English classics, Tom Brown at Rugby and Tom Brown at Oxford, were responsible for the rising desire for sports fiction. By the 1890s a demand for boys' athletic stories was met in the voluminous outpouring of the heroic sporting achievements of Gilbert Patten's "Frank Merriwell." [42] Along with the newspaper and the sporting journal the field of publishing, with its improved techniques and expanded output, did much to attract attention to athletics at the turn of the century.

Much of the angling and hunting equipment and horseman's supplies came from England in the colonial era, but in the years before and after the American Revolution several dealers in sporting wares appeared in Philadelphia, New York, and Boston. From the early years of the nineteenth century merchants and gunsmiths in Kentucky supplied the settlers west of the Appalachian range.[43] Field sports were still enjoyed mainly by schoolboys and sportsmen with their simple rods in the 1840s and 1850s, but from the 1830s onward fishing and hunting purely for recreation developed into a sporting fad, the end of which is not in sight. Charles Hallock, noted sportsman, conservationist, and journalist of the post-Civil War era recalled how the rural folk of Hampshire County, Massachusetts, responded to a visiting sportsman of the 1840s who brought with him a set of highly finished rods, reels, and fly-fishing equipment.

Ah! those were the halcyon days. No railroads disturbed the quiet seclusion of that mountain nook...Twice a week an old-fashioned coach dragged heavily up the hill into the hamlet and halted in front of the house which was at once post-office, tavern, and miscellaneous store . . . One day it brought a passenger . . . He carried a leather hand-bag and a handful of rods in a case. The village *quidnuncs* said he was a surveyor. He allowed he was from Troy and had "come to go a-fishing." From that stranger I took my first lesson in fly-fishing.[44]

By the 1850s the manufacture of cricket bats and stumps, billiard tables, archery equipment, guns, fishing tackle, and other sporting accessories was carried on by a host of individual craftsmen and by such concerns as J.W. Brunswick & Brothers of Cincinnati, Bassler of Boston, Conroy's of New York, and John Krider's "Sportsmen's Depot" in Philadelphia.

Mass-production methods of manufacture were still in their infancy in post-Civil War decades, but the factory system became ever more deeply entrenched. While the sporting goods business never attained any great economic importance in the nineteenth century,[45] much of the popularity for athletic games and outdoor recreation was due to standardized manufacturing of baseball equipment, bicycles, billiard tables, sporting rifles, fishing rods, and various other items.[46] Although most American youths played with restitched balls and minimum of paraphernalia, college athletes, cycling enthusiasts, and professional ballplayers popularized the products of George B. Ellard of Cincinnati, Peck & Snyder of New York, and other concerns.[47]

By the end of the century A.G. Spalding & Brothers was the nationally recognized leader in this field. As a renowned pitcher for the Boston and Chicago clubs and then as the promoter of the latter, Albert Spalding had turned to the merchandising of athletic goods in 1876.[48] One of the most avid sponsors of the national game, he branched out into varied sports in the 1880s, and acquired a virtual monopoly over athletic goods by absorbing A.J. Reach Company in 1885, Wright & Ditson in 1892, as well as Peck & Snyder and other firms. By 1887 the Spalding "Official League" baseball had been adopted by, the National League, the Western League, the New England League, the International League, and various college conferences, and balls were offered to the public ranging in price from 5 cents to $1.50. To gain an even greater ascendancy over his rivals A.G. Spalding published a wide range of guides in *Spalding's Library of Athletics Sports,* in which his wares were not only advertised but those of rivals were derided as inferior.

The sewing machine was one of many inventions which made possible the more uniform equipment of the last decades of the century when local leagues and national associations took shape throughout the United States. Canoeing and camping were other diversions which gave rise to the manufacture of sporting goods on an ever larger scale. In the latter years of the century the mail-order house and the department store began to feature sporting goods. Macy's of New York began with ice skates, velocipedes, bathing suits, and beach equipment in 1872, although all sporting goods were sold by the toy department. By 1902, with the addition of numerous other items, a separate department was established. Sears, Roebuck and Company, meanwhile, devoted more than eighty pages of its 1895 catalog to weapons and fishing equipment, and within a decade not only hunting and fishing equipment but also bicycles, boxing gloves, baseball paraphernalia, and sleds were featured.[49]

When Thomas A. Edison developed the incandescent bulb in 1879 he inaugurated a new era in the social life of our cities. Although the first dynamo was built within two years, gas lighting did not give way immediately, and the crowds which jammed the old Madison Square Garden in New York in 1883 to see John L. Sullivan fight Herbert Slade still had to cope not only with the smoke-filled air but also with the blue gas fumes. The Garden had already installed some electric lights, however. At a six-day professional walking match in 1882 the cloud of tobacco smoke was so thick that "even the electric lights" had "a hard struggle to assert their superior brilliancy" over the gas jets. Even "the noisy yell of programme, candy, fruit and peanut venders who filled the air with the vilest discord" failed to discourage the crowd, according to a philosophically minded reporter who wondered what Herbert Spencer would think of "the peculiar phase of idiocy in the American character" which drew thousands of men and women to midnight pedestrian contests.[50]

Within a few years electric lighting and more comfortable accommodations helped lure players and spectators alike to Y.M.C.A.'s athletic clubs, regimental armories, school and college gymnasiums, as well as sports arenas. In 1885, at the third annual Horse Show in Madison Square Garden, handsomely dressed sportswomen reveled in the arena, "guady with festoons of racing flags and brilliant streamers, lighted at night by hundreds of electric lights," while visitors to the brilliantly lighted New York Athletic Club agreed that "fine surroundings will not do an athlete any harm."[51] The indoor prize fight, walking contest, wrestling match, and horse show were a far cry from the crude atmosphere of early indoor sport. In 1890 carnivals were held at the Massachusetts Mechanics' Association by the Boston Athletic Association and at the new Madison Square Garden in New York by the Staten Island Athletic Club; the horse show attracted fashionable New Yorkers to the Garden; and indoor baseball, already popular in Chicago, was taken up in New York's regimental armories.[52] A decade of electrification, paralleling improvements in transportation and communications, had elevated and purified the atmosphere of sport. The saloon brawls of pugilists in the 1850s and 1860s were gradually abandoned for the organized matches of the 1880s and 1890s. At the time of the Sullivan-Corbett fight in the New Orleans Olympic Club in 1892, an observer wrote in the Chicago *Daily Tribune,* September 8, 1892: "Now men travel to great boxing contests in vestibule limited trains; they sleep at the best hotels . . . and when the time for the contest arrives they find themselves in a grand, brilliantly lighted arena."

Basketball and volleyball, originating in the Y.M.C.A. in 1892 and 1895, were both developed to meet the need for indoor sport on winter evenings. The rapid construction of college gymnasiums and the building of more luxurious clubhouses after the middle eighties stemmed in great part from the superior appointments and more brilliant lighting available for athletic games, and much of the urban appeal of indoor sport was directly attributable to the revolution which electric lighting made in the night life of the metropolis.

Electrification, which transformed everything from home gadgets and domestic lighting to power machinery and launches, exerted an influence on the course of sport through the development of rapid transit systems in cities from coast to coast. Horse-drawn cars had carried the burden of traffic since the 1850s, but the electric streetcar assumed an entirely new role in opening up surburban areas and the countryside to the pent-up city populace. Soon after the Richmond, Virginia, experiment of 1888, the streetcar began to acquaint large numbers of city dwellers with the race track and the ball diamond.[53] Experimental lines had been laid even earlier in the decade, and Chicago crowds going to the races at Washington Park in 1887 were jammed on "the grip," one reporter noting the "perpetual stream of track slang," the prodding and pushing, and the annoying delay when it was announced that "the cable has busted."[54] Trolley parks, many of which included baseball diamonds, were promoted by the transit companies; ball teams were encouraged by these same concerns through gifts of land or grand-stands; and the crowds flocked to week-end games on the cars.[55] At the turn of the century the popular interest in athletic games in thousands of towns and cities was stimulated to a high degree by the extension of rapid transit systems, a development which may possibly have been as significant in the growth of local sport as the automobile was to be in the development of intercommunity rivalries.

Numerous inventions and improvements applied to sport were of varying importance: the stop watch, the percussion cap, the streamlined sulky, barbed wire, the safety cycle, ball bearings, and artificial ice for skating rinks, among others. Improved implements often popularized and revolutionized the style of a sport, as in the invention of the sliding seat of the rowing shell, the introduction of the rubber-wound gutta-percha ball which necessitated the lengthening of golf courses, and the universal acceptance of the catcher's mask.

Vulcanization of rubber by Charles Goodyear in the 1830s led to the development of elastic and resilient rubber balls in the following decade, and eventually influenced the development of golf and tennis balls as well as other sporting apparel and equipment. The pneumatic tire, developed by Dr. John Boyd Dunlop of Belfast, Ireland, in 1888, revolutionized cycling and harness racing in the next decade. Equipped with pneumatic tires, the sulky abandoned its old highwheeler style, and the trotter and pacer found it made for smoother movement on the track. Sulky drivers reduced the mile record of 2:08¾ by Maud S. with an old highwheeler to 1:58½ by Lou Dillon in 1903 with a "bicycle sulky." According to W.H. Gocher, a racing authority, the innovation of pneumatic tires and the streamlining of the sulky cut five to seven seconds from former records, which was "more than the breeding had done in a dozen years."[56] The pneumatic tire, introduced by racing cyclists and sulky drivers, went on to play a much more vital role in the rise of the automobile industry and the spectacular appeal of auto racing.

The camera also came to the aid of sport in the decades following the Civil War. Professional photography had developed rapidly in the middle period of the century, but nature lovers became devotees of the camera only when its bulkiness and weight were eliminated in the closing years of the century. Development of the Eastman Kodak after 1888 found a mass market as thousands of Americans put it to personal commercial use. Pictorial and sporting magazines which had been printing woodcuts since the prewar era began to introduce many pictures taken from photographs, and in the late 1880s and early 1890s actual photographic prints of athletes and outdoor sportsmen came into common usage. *Harper's Weekly, Leslie's Illustrated Weekly, Illustrated American,* and the *National Police Gazette* featured photography, and by the end of the century the vast majority of their pictures were camera studies.[57] Newspapers recognized the circulation value of half-tone prints, but because of paper and technical problems they were used sparsely until the New York *Times* published an illustrated Sunday supplement in 1896, soon to be imitated by the New York *Tribune* and the Chicago *Tribune.* The year 1897 saw the half-tone illustration become a regular feature of metropolitan newspapers, rapidly eliminating the age-old reliance on woodcuts. At the turn of the century sport was available in visual form to millions who heretofore had little knowledge of athletics and outdoor games.[58]

It was in 1872 that Eadweard Muybridge made the first successful attempt "to secure an illusion of motion by photography." With the help of Leland Stanford, already a noted turfman, he set out to prove whether "a trotting horse at one point in its gait left the ground entirely."[59] By establishing a battery of cameras the movements of the horse were successively photographed, and Muybridge later turned his technique to "the gallop of dogs, the flight of birds, and the performances of athletes." In his monumental study entitled *Animal Locomotion* (1887) he included thousands of pictures of horses, athletes, and other living subjects, deomonstrating "the work and play of men, women, and children of all ages; how pitchers throw the baseball, how batters hit it, and how athletes move their bodies in record-breaking contests."[60] Muybridge is considered only one among a number of the pioneers of the motion picture, but his pictures had presented possibly the best illusion of motion prior to the development of flexible celluloid film. A host of experimentors gradually evolved principles and techniques in the late 1880s which gave birth to the true motion picture. Woodville Latham and his two sons made a four-minute film of the prize fight between Young Griffo and Battling Barnett in 1895, showing it on a large screen for an audience, an event which has been called "the first flickering, commercial motion picture."[61] When Bob Fitzsimmons won the heavyweight championship from James J. Corbett at Carson City, Nevada, in 1897, the fight was photographed for public distribution. With the increasing popularity in succeeding years of the newsreel, the short subject, and an occasional feature film, the motion picture came to rival the photograph in spreading the gospel of sport.[62]

When sport began to mature into a business of some importance and thousands of organizations throughout the country joined leagues, associations, racing circuits, and national administrative bodies, it became necessary to utilize on large scale the telephone, the typewriter, and all the other instruments so vital to the commercial world. Even the phonograph, at first considered a business device but soon devoted to popular music, came to have an indirect influence, recording for public entertainment such songs as "Daisy Bell," "Casey at the Bat," "Slide, Kelly, Slide" and, early in the present century, the theme song of the national pastime, "Take Me Out to the Ball Game." All of these instruments created a great revolution in communication, and they contributed significantly to the expansion of sport on a national scale.

The bicycle, still an important means of transport in Europe but something of a casualty of the machine age in the United States, also had an important role. After its demonstration at the Philadelphia Centennial, an interest was ignited which grew rapidly in the 1880s and flamed into an obsession in the 1890s.[63] Clubs, cycling associations, and racing meets were sponsored everywhere in these years, and the League of American Wheelmen served as a spearhead for many of the reforms in fashions, good roads, and outdoor exercise. Albert H. Pope was merely the foremost among many manufacturers of the "velocipede" which became so popular among women's clubs, temperance groups, professional men, and, at the turn of the century, in the business world and among the trades. Contemporary observers speculated on the social benefits to be derived from the cycle, especially in enticing women to the pleasures of outdoor exercise. Bicycling was discussed by ministers and physicians, it was considered as a weapon in future wars, police squads in some cities were mounted on wheels, mail carriers utilized it, and many thought it would revolutionize society.[64]

As a branch of American industry the bicycle was reputed to have developed into a $100,000,000 business in the 1890s. Mass-production techniques were introduced, Iver Johnson's Arms and Cycle Works advertising "Every part interchangeable and exact." The Indiana Bicycle Company, home of the Waverley cycle, maintained a huge factory in Indianapolis and claimed to be the most perfect and complete plant in the world: "We employ the highest mechanical skill and the best labor-saving machinery that ample capital can provide. Our methods of construction are along the latest and most approved lines of mechanical work."[65]

Much of the publicity given to competing manufacturers centered around the mechanical improvements and the speed records of their products. Between 1878 and 1896 the mile record was lowered from 3:57 to 1:55-1/5. While recognizing the effect of better riding styles, methodical training, improved tracks, and the part of pacemaking, one critic contended, "The prime factor . . . is the improvement in the vehicle itself. The racing machine of 1878 was a heavy, crude, cumbersome affair, while the modern bicycle, less than one-sixth its weight, equipped with scientifically calculated gearing, pneumatic tires, and friction annihilators, represents much of the difference."[66] Roger Burlingame has pointed out the impact of the bicycle on the health, recreation, business, and the social life of the American people, and on the manufacture of the cycle he claimed that "it introduced certain technical principles which were carried on into the motor car, notably ball bearings, hub-breaking and the tangential spoke."[67] Little did cycling enthusiasts realize that in these same years a much more revolutionary vehicle, destined to transform our way of life, was about to make its dramatic appearance on the national scene.

One of the last inventions which the nineteenth century brought forth for the conquest of time and distance was the automobile. During the 1890s the Haynes, Duryea, Ford, Stanley Steamer, Packard, and Locomobile came out in quick succession, and the Pierce Arrow, Cadillac, and Buick were to follow in the next several years.[68] Manufacturers of bicycles had already turned to the construction of the motor car in a number of instances. As early as 1895 Herman H. Kohlsaat, publisher of the Chicago *Times-Herald,* sponsored the first automobile race on American soil. One of the features of this contest, run through a snowstorm and won by Charles Duryea, was the enhanced reputation achieved for the gasoline motor, which had not yet been recognized as the proper source of motor power. A number of European races inspired American drivers to take to the racecourse, and the experimental value of endurance or speed contests was immediately recognized by pioneer manufacturers. Nor were they slow to see the publicity value of races featured by the newspapers.[69]

Henry Ford "was bewitched by Duryea's feat," and he "devoured reports on the subject which appeared in the newspapers and magazines of the day." When other leading carbuilders sought financial backing for their racers, Ford determined to win supremacy on the track. After defeating Alexander Winton in a race at Detroit in 1902, "Ford's prowess as a 'speed demon' began to appear in the columns of the widely circulated trade journal *Horseless Age.*"[70] In later years he was to contend, "I never thought anything of racing, but the public refused to consider the automobile in any light other than as a fast toy. Therefore later we had to race. The industry was held back by this initial racing slant, for the attention of the makers was diverted to making fast rather than good cars." The victory over Winton was his first race, "and it brought advertising of the only kind that people cared to read." Bowing to public opinion, he was determined "to make an automobile that would be known wherever speed was known," and he set to work installing four cylinders in his famous "999." Developing 80 horse power, this machine was so frightening, even to its builders, that the fearless Barney Oldfield was hired for the race. Oldfield had only a tiller with which to drive, since there were no steering wheels, but this professional cyclist who had never driven a car established a new record and helped put Ford back on his feet. The financial support of Alex Y. Malcomson, an admirer of "999," gave him a new start: "A week after the race I formed the Ford Motor Company."[71]

The next few years witnessed the establishment of Automobile Club of America races, sport clubs in the American Automobile Association, the Vanderbilt Cup, and the Glidden Tour. Reporting on the third annual Glidden Tour in 1906, *Scientific American* defended American cars, heretofore considered inferior to European models: "Above all else, the tour had demonstrated that American machines will stand fast driving on rough forest roads without serious damage to the cars or their mechanism. Engine and gear troubles have practically disappeared, and the only things that are to be feared are the breakage of springs and axles and the giving out of tires. Numerous shock-absorbers were tried out and found wanting in this test; and were it not for the pneumatic tires, which have been greatly improved during the past two years, such a tour would be impossible of accomplishment."[72]

The Newport social season featured racing, Daytona Beach soon became a center for speed trials, and tracks were built in various parts of the nation, the first of which may have been at Narragansett Park in 1896.[73] Not until the years just prior to World War I did auto racing attain a truly national popularity with the establishment of the Indianapolis Speedway, but the emphasis on speed and endurance in these early years spurred manufacturers to build ever faster models and advertisers to feature the record performances of each car. Henry Ford had long since lost interest, while the Buick racing team was discontinued in 1915. by then mass production had turned the emphasis toward design, comfort, and economy. Racing was not abandoned and manufacturers still featured endurance tests in later years, but the heated rivalry between pioneer builders had become a thing of the past.[74]

Technological developments in the latter half of the nineteenth century transformed the social habits of the Western World, and sport was but one of many institutions which felt their full impact. Fashions, food, journalism, home appliances, commercialized entertainment, architecture, and city planning were only a few of the facets of life which underwent rapid change as transportation and communication were revolutionized and as new materials were made available. There are those who stress the thesis that sport is a direct reaction against the mechanization, the division of labor, and the standardization of life in a machine civilization,[75] and this may in part be true, but sport in nineteenth-century America was as much a product of industrialization as it was an antidote to it. While athletics and outdoor recreation were sought as a release from the confinements of city life, inustrialization and the urban movement were the basic causes for the rise of organized sport. And the urban movement was of course, greatly enhanced by the revolutionary transformation in communication, transportation, agriculture, and industrialization.[76]

The first symptoms of the impact of invention on nineteenth-century sports are to be found in the steamboat of the ante-bellum era. An intensification of interest in horse racing during the 1820s and 1830s was only a prelude to the sporting excitement over yachting, prize fighting, rowing, running, cricket, and baseball of the 1840s and 1850s. By this time the railroad was opening up new opportunities for hunters, anglers, and athletic teams, and it was the railroad, of all the inventions of the century, which gave the greatest impetus to the intercommunity rivalries in sport. The telegraph and the penny press opened the gates to a rising tide of sporting journalism; the sewing machine and the factory system revolutionized the manufacturing of sporting goods; the electric light and rapid transit further demonstrated the impact of electrification; inventions like the Kodak camera, the motion picture, and the pneumatic tire stimulated various fields of sport; and the bicycle and automobile gave additional evidence to the effect of the transportation revolution on the sporting impulse of the latter half of the century. Toward the end of the century the rapidity with which one invention followed another demonstrated the increasingly close relationship of technology and social change. No one can deny the significance of sportsmen, athletes, journalists, and pioneers in many organizations, and no one can disregard the multiple forces transforming the social scene. The technological revolution is not the sole determining factor in the rise of sport, but to ignore its influence would result only in a more or less superficial understanding of the history of one of the prominent social institutions of modern America.

Footnotes

[1]Among the most useful works to be consulted on early American sport are John A. Krout, *Annals of American Sport* (New Haven, 1929); Jennie Holliman, *American Sports, 1785-1835* (Durham, 1931); Foster R. Dulles, *America Learns To Play: A History of Popular Recreation, 1607-1940* (New York, 1940); Robert B. Weaver, *Amusements and Sports in American Life* (Chicago, 1939); and Herbert Manchester, *Four Centuries of Sport in America, 1490-1890* (New York, 1931). For certain aspects of ante-bellum sport, see Arthur M. Schlesinger and Dixon R. Fox (eds.), *A History of American Life,* 13 vols. (New York, 1927-1948).

[2]See the New York *American,* May 27, 1823; New Orleans *Daily Picayune,* March 27, 1839; New York *Weekly Herald,* May 17, 1845, July 11, 1849; and accounts of many races in the *Spirit of the Times* (New York) for prewar years. In an era when bridges were more the exception than the rule the ferry was an indispensable means of transportation. See, for example, Kenneth Roberts and Anna M. Roberts (eds.),

Moreau de St. Méry's American Journey, 1793-1798 (Garden City, 1947), 173; New York *American,* May 27, 1823.

[3]For examples of the steamboat in early sport, see the New York *Herald,* June 17, 1849; *Wilkes' Spirit of the Times* (New York), XII (August 5, 1865), 380; New Orleans *Daily Picayune,* December 1, 1855, December 10, 1859; *Spirit of the Times,* XX (June 19, 1869), 276; New York *World,* June 19, 1869. When the passenger lines began converting to steam in the Civil War era, the development of international sport was facilitated to a considerable degree. In the latter decades of the century the steam yacht became the vogue among American millionaires.

[4]John Hervey, *Racing in America, 1665-1865,* 2 vols. (New York, 1944), II, 101.

[5]New Orleans *Daily Picayune,* March 27, 1839.

[6]*American Turf Register and Sporting Magazine* (Baltimore), XIII (July, 1843), 367; New York *Daily Tribune,* May 14, 1845.

[7]*Spirit of the Times,* XXI (July 12, 1851), 246.

[8]Albert L. Demaree, *The American Agricultural Press, 1819-1860* (New York, 1941), 203-204. Specific instances of such aid can be found in the *Cultivator* (Albany), IX (March, 1842), 50; *American Agriculturist* (New York), II (October 16, 1843), 258; New York *Daily Tribune,* September 18, 1851; *Transactions of the Illinois State Agricultural Society* (Springfield), I, 1853-54 (1855, 6; II, 1856-57 (1857), 24-32; *Report and Proceedings of the Iowa State Agricultural Society . . . October, 1855* (Fairfield, 1856), 24; *Fifth Report of the Indiana State Board of Agriculture. . . For the Year 1856* (Indianapolis, 1858), 34, 482-83; *Kentucky Farmer* (Frankfort), I, (July, 1858), 12: *Wisconsin Farmer and North-Western Cultivator* (Madison), IX (October, 1857), 873; XI (October, 1859), 386-87; Springfield *Weekly Illinois State Journal,* September 5, 19, 1860. The "ploughing matches" of the ante-bellum era attracted large crowds seeking both entertainemnt and the latest improvements in agricultural implements.

[9]Samuel Crowther and Arthur Ruhl, *Rowing and Track Athletics* (New York, 1905), 11.

[10]James N. Elkins, superintendent of the Boston, Concord and Montreal Railroad, agreed to pay all transportation costs for the crews and their equipment to the New Hampshire lake where the race was to be held. Robert F. Kelley, *American Rowing: Its Background and Traditions* (New York, 1932), 100-101.

[11]New York *Daily Times,* October 13, 1853; Boston *Advertiser,* October 14, 1853.

[12]New York *Herald,* October 23, 1858.

[13]Wilkes' *Spirit of the Times,* XIV (July 7, 1866), 294. More rural areas felt the impact somewhat later, Warrenton, Mississippi, holding a tourney in 1885 to which special trains were sent. New Orleans *Daily Picayune,* July 19, 1885.

[14]New York *World,* August 21, 1869; Cincinnati *Commercial,* September 22, 1869, San Francisco *Evening Bulletin.* October 5, 1869. Their use of Pullman cars set a precedent in sports circles. Advertising by local lines for an approaching game appeared in the Cincinnati *Commercial,* August 24, 1869.

[15]See *Spalding's Official Base Ball Guide* (New York, 1886), appendix. The Memphis Reds Base Ball Association sent a printed circular to Harry Wright of the Boston team in 1877 in which it stressed the reduced rates to any club visiting St. Louis or Louisville. Harry Wright Correspondence, 7 vols., I (1865-1877), 40, Spalding Baseball Collection (New York Public Library). In the 1880s enthusiastic crowds turned out to the railroad station to welcome home the victorious nines. *Frank Leslie's Boys' and Girls' Weekly* (New York), XXXV (October 6, 1883), 174; New York *Sun,* September 7, 1886.

[16]*Turf, Field and Farm* (New York), I (September 2, 1865), 69; VIII (May 28, 1869), 344.

[17]*Wilkes' Spirit of the Times,* XIV (May 19, 1866), 185; San Francisco *Evening Bulletin,* October 15, 1869; Baltimore *American and Commercial Advertiser,* October 25, 1877; New Orleans *Daily Picayune,* April 20, 1884, May 9, 15, 1885; Charles E. Travathan, *The American Thoroughbred* (New York, 1905), 371.

[18]New York *World,* April 29, 1884.

[19]Alexander Johnston, *Ten—And Out! The Complete Story of the Prize Ring in America* (New York, 1947), 42-43.

[20]Dunbar Rowland (ed.), *Encyclopedia of Mississippi History,* 2 vols. (Madison, 1907), II, 142; St. Paul and Minneapolis *Pioneer Press,* February 8, 1882; New Orleans *Daily Picayune,* August 6, 1885; New York *Sun,* May 12, 1886.

[21]Railroad interest in sport was illustrated by the *New York Railroad Gazette:* "Horse-racing tracks of the violest [sic] character are encouraged (indirectly, it may be) in more than one case by railroads normally law-abiding. Sunday excursions patronized chiefly by roughs who conduct baseball games of a character condemned by all decent people are morally the same as prize fights in kind though not in degree." Quoted in the New Orleans *Daily Picayune,* August 6, 1885.

[22]For illustrations of the difficulties of railroad travel, see the Walter Camp Correspondence, Box 64 (Yale University Library, New Haven).

[23]*Wilkes' Spirit of the Times,* XIII (October 14, 1865), 102.

[24]Parke H. Davis, *Football, The American Intercollegiate Game* (New York, 1911), 45.

[25]*Outing* (New York), XII (August, 1888), 407-408.

[26]By the 1890s many railroads carried bicycles as free freight and professional cyclists could tour their National Circuit in luxury cars. New York *Journal,* September 18, 1897.

[27]Scores of railroads in every section of the country served those seeking to hunt or fish in the rustic countryside. See, particularly, Charles Hallock (ed.), *The Sportsman's Gazetteer and General Guide* (New York, 1877), Pt. II, 1-182. See also the Chicago and Northwestern Railway advertisement in the *Spirit of the Times,* SCII (August 19, 1876), 53.

[28]For the early development of the telegraph, see James D. Reid, *The Telegraph in America and Morse Memorial* (New York, 1887); Waldemar Kaempffert (ed.), *A Popular History of American Invention,* 2 vols. (New York, 1924); and Robert L. Thompson, *Wiring a Continent: The History of the Telegraph Industry in the United States, 1832-1866* (Princeton, 1947).

[29]Boston *Daily Journal,* February 7, 8, 9, 1849; New York *Daily Tribune,* February 8, 9, 1849; Milwaukee *Sentinel and Gazette,* February 10, 1849; Boston *Daily Courier,* October 21, 1858; New York *Times,* October 21, 1858; New Orleans *Daily Picayune,* May 6, 7, June 29, 1860; Nashville *Daily News,* April 29, 1860.

[30]New York *Daily Tribune,* September 19, 1851; Natchez *Courier,* September 19, 1851.

[31]New Orleans *Daily Picayune,* July 6, 1870.

[32]*Ibid.* See also New York *Times,* October 21, 1858; *Harper's Weekly* (New York), XXVII (October 13, 1883), 654.

[33]Oliver Gramling, *AP; The Story of News* (New York, 1940), 232; New Orleans *Daily Picayune,* July 10, 1889. For poolrooms, saloons and bulletin boards, see the New York *Sun,* October 6, 1878; New York *Herald,* February 7, 1882; New Orleans *Daily Picayune,* May 17, 1884, July 6, 1885; New York *World,* September 8 1892. Also see *Harper's Weekly,* XXVII (October 13, 1883), 654; XXXVI (April 2, December 17, 1892),

319, 324, 1210. Henry L. Mencken, in *Happy Days, 1880-1892* (New York, 1940), 225 nostalgically recalled how, since there were few sporting "extras" in Baltimore in the 1880s, "the high-toned saloons of the town catered to the [baseball] fans by putting in telegraph operators who wrote the scores on blackboards."

[34]The New York *Transcript* and the *Sun* sensationalized the news as early as the 1830s and began reporting prize fights. James Gordon Bennett's *Herald* exploited sporting interests in pre-Civil War years and his son continued to do so in the period following the war. Magazines which capitalized on sport included the *American Turf Register and Sporting Magazine*, the *Spirit of the Times*, the *New York Clipper*, and the *National Police Gazette* (New York), as well as a host of fishing and hunting journals. Through the 1880s and 1890s the New York *Sun* and the *World competed for the sporting public, only to be outdone by the Journal* at the end of the century. Among the prominent writers of the era were Henry Chadwick, Timothy Murnane, Harry Weldon, Harry C. Palmer, Al Spink, Sam Crane, Walter Camp, Casper Whitney, and Charles Dryden. See William H. Nugent, "The Sports Section," *American Mercury* (New York), XVI (February, 1929), 329-38; and Hugh Fullerton, "The Fellows Who Made the Game," *Saturday Evening Post* (Philadelphia), CC (April 21, 1928), 18 ff.

[35]New York *Herald*, December 30, 31, 1866; Cincinnati *Commercial*, August 24, 28, 1869; *Frank Leslie's Illustrated Newspaper* (New York), XXIX (September 28, 1869), 2.

[36]The origins of the penny press are ably discussed in Willard G. Bleyer, *Main Currents in the History of American Journalism* (Boston, 1927), 154-84; and in Frank L. Mott, *American Journalism, A History* (New York, 1941), 228-52.

[37]Bleyer, *History of American Journalism*, 197, 209; Alfred M. Lee, *The Daily Newspaper in America* (New York, 1937), 611; New York *Weekly Herald*, May 15, 17, 1845, and *Herald* files for the 1840s.

[38]Bleyer, *History of American Journalism*, 394.

[39]*Ibid.*, 394-98.

[40]Joseph Pulitzer's New York *World* began an intensive exploitation of sport as a front-page attraction almost immediately after its purchase in 1883, and by the following year first-page accounts of pedestrian matches, dog shows, and similar topics became regular features.

[41]Albert Johannsen, *The House of Beadle and Adams and its Dime and Nickel Novel: The Story of a Vanished Literature*, 2 vols. (Norman, 1950), 1, 260, 377-79.

[42]John L. Cutler, *Gilbert Patten and His Frank Merriwell Saga*, University of Main Studies (Orono), Ser. II, No. 31 (1934).

[43]Charles E. Godspeed, *Angling in America: Its Early History and Literature* (Boston, 1939), 285 ff.

[44]Charles Hallock, *The Fishing Tourist: Angler's Guide and Reference Book* (New York, 1873), 18.

[45]In 1900 the value of sporting goods manufactured was only $3,628,496. United States Bureau of the Census, *Statistical Abstract of the United States* (Washington, 1909), 188.

[46]See the *Spirit of the Times*, XX (May 4, 1850), 130; Natchez *Courier*, November 26, 1850; Madison *Daily State Journal*, March 26, 1855; New Orleans *Daily Picayune*, April 4, 1856. As midwestern merchants began to purchase large stocks from the East, John Krider advertised widely. Madison *Daily State Journal*, April 13, 1855. Michael Phelan, who in 1854 developed an indiarubber cushion permitting sharp edges on billiard tables, joined with Hugh W. Collender in forming Phelan and

Collender, the leading billiards manufacturer until the organization of the Brunswick-Balke-Collender Company in 1884. Gymnastic apparatus, created by Dudley A. Sargent and other physical educators, was featured by many dealers, while the readers of *American Angler* (New York), *Forest and Stream* (New York), and other sporting journals were kept informed of the latest models of rifles, shotguns, and fishing reels.

[47]George B. Ellard, who sponsored the Red Stockings, advertised his store as "Base Ball Headquarters" and "Base Ball Depot," with the "Best Stock in the West." Cincinnati *Commercial*, August 24, 1869. Other merchandisers included Horsman's Base Ball and Croquet Emporium in New York and John H. Mann of the same city. Peck & Snyder began dealing in baseball equipment in 1865 and by the 1880s claimed to be the largest seller of sporting goods.

[48]Moses King (ed.), *King's Handbook of the United States* (Buffalo, 1891), 232; Arthur Bartlett, *Baseball and Mr. Spalding; The History and Romance of Baseball* (New York, 1951), *passim; Fortune* (New York), II (August, 1930), 62 ff.; Arthur Bartlett, "They're Just Wild About Sports," *Saturday Evening Post*, CCXXII (December 24, 1949), 31 ff.; *Spalding's Official Base Ball Guide for 1887* (New York and Chicago, 1887), *passim.*

[49]It was on mass manufacture of baseballs and uniforms that Spalding gained such a leading position in the sporting goods field. Since the business was restricted in these early years certain difficulties had to be overcome. To make the most out of manufacturing bats Spalding bought his own lumber mill in Michigan, while Albert Pope received little sympathy from the rolling mills in his first years of manufacturing bicycles. *Wheelman* (Boston), I (October, 1882), 71. For department and mail-order stores, see Ralph M. Hower, *History of Macy's of New York, 1858-1919* (Cambridge, 1946), 103, 162, 234-35, 239; Boris Emmet and John C. Jeuck, *Catalogues and Counters: A History of Sears, Roebuck and Company* (Chicago, 1950), 38; David L. Cohn, *The Good Old Days* (New York, 1940), 443-60.

[50]New York *Herald*, October 23, 1882; New York *Sun*, August 7, 1883. The introduction of electric lighting in theaters was discussed, while the opposition of gas companies was recognized. *Scientific American*, Supplement (New York), XVI (November 10, 1883), 6535-36.

[51]*Harper's Weekly*, XXIX (February 14, November 14, 1885), 109, 743.

[52]See *ibid.*, XXXIV (March 1, 8, 1890), 169, 171, 179. A new Madison Square Garden with the most modern facilities was built in the years 1887-1890; the California Athletic Club in San Francisco featured a "powerful electric arc light" over its ring; and electric lights in the Manhattan Athletic Club's new gymnasium in 1890 "shed a dazzling whiteness." *Ibid.*, XXXIV (April 5, 1890), 263-64; New York *Daily Tribune*, November 2, 30, 1890.

[53]After the completion of the Richmond line rapid transit spread throughout the country. Although in 1890 there were only 144 electric railways in a national total of 789 street lines, by 1899 there were 50,600 electric cars in operation as compared to only 1,500 horse cars. Gilson Willets *et al., Workers of the Nation*, 2 vols. (New York, 1903), I, 498. For the suburban influence, see the *Street Railway Journal* (New York), XVII (November 23, 1901), 760-61.

[54]Chicago *Tribune*, July 5, 1887.

[55]*Street Railway Journal*, XI (April, 1895), 232; XII (May, November, 1896), 317, 319, 708; *Cosmopolitan* (New York), XXXIII (July, 1902), 266; *Collier's (New York), CXXV (May, 1950), 85;* Oscar Handlin. This *Was America* (Cambridge, 1949), 374; New Orleans *Daily Picayune*, February 27, 1899.

[56]W. H. Gocher, *Trotalong* (Hartford, 1928), 190.

[57]Robert Taft, *Photography and the American Scene: A Social History, 1839-1889* (New York, 1910), II, 534-35.

[58]Photography developed throughout the nineteenth century as an adjunct of the science of chemistry. Chemical and mechanical innovations were also responsible for the improvements of prints and all kinds of reproductions. Woodcuts were featured in the press, engravings were sold widely, and lithographs were found in the most rural rural home. Nathaniel Currier (later Currier & Ives) published hunting, fishing, pugilistic, baseball, rowing, yachting, sleighing, skating, trotting, and racing scenes for more than half a century. Cheap prints, calendars, and varied reproductions of sporting scenes did much to popularize the famous turf champions and sports heroes of the era. See Harry T. Peters, *Currier & Ives: Printmakers to the American People* (Garden City, 1942).

[59]Frank L. Dyer and Thomas C. Martin, *Edison: His Life and Inventions*, 2 vols. (New York, 1910), II, 534-35.

[60]Kaempffert, *Popular History of American Inventions*, I, 425.

[61]Lloyd Morris, *Not So Long Ago* (New York, 1949), 24.

[62]The pioneer years of the motion picture industry are described by numerous other works, among them Deems Taylor, *A Pictorial History of the Movies* (New York, 1943), 1-6; Leslie Wood, *The Miracle of the Movies* (London, 1947), 66 ff.; George S. Bryan, *Edison: The Man and His Work* (Garden City, 1926), 184-94; Josef M. Eder, *History of Photography*, trans. by Edward Epstean (New York, 1945), 495 ff.; Taft, *Photography and the American Scene*, 405-12; Morris, *Not So Long Ago*, 1-35.

[63]There was a brief craze in 1869, during which year, according to Albert H. Pope, "More than a thousand inventions were patented for the perfection and improvement of the velocipede." *Wheelman*, I (October, 1882), 70. Interest declined, however, until the Philadelphia celebration of 1876. Although race meetings and cycling clubs were widely reported in the 1880s, there were only 83 repair establishments in 1890 and the value of products of bicycle and tricycle repairs was only about $300,000. By 1900 there were 6,378 repair shops and the value in repairs exceeded $13,000,000. United States Bureau of the Census, *Statistical Abstract of the United States* (Washington, 1904), 516.

[64]For summaries of the impact of the bicycle, see E. Benjamin Andrews, *History of the Last Quarter-Century in the United States, 1870-1895*, 2 vols. (New York, 1896), II, 289-90; Arthur M. Schlesinger, *The Rise of the City* 1878-1898 (New York, 1933), 312-14; Roger Burlingame, *Engines of Democracy: Inventions and Society in Mature America* (New York, 1940), 369-74.

[65]*Harper's Weekly*, XL (April 11, 1896), 365. It is interesting that the "father of scientific management," Frederick W. Taylor, a tennis champion and golf devotee, was said to have learned through sport "the value of the minute analysis of motions, the importance of methodical selection and training, the worth of time study and of standards based on rigorously exact observation." Charles De Freminville, "How Taylor Introduced the Scientific Method Into Management of the Shop," *Critical Essays on Scientific Management*, Taylor Society *Bulletin* (New York), X (February, 1925), Pt. II, Mass-produced techniques, however, were only partially responsible for the outpouring of athletic goods which began to win wider markets at the turn of the century. The manufacture of baseball bats remained a highly specialized trade, while Scotch artisans who came to the United States maintained the personalized nature of their craft as makers of golf clubs. Despite the great improvements in gun manufacture, Elisha J. Lewis asserted in 1871 that there were thousands of miserable guns on the market: "The reason of this is that our mechanics have so many tastes and fancies to please, owing principally to the ignorance of those who order fowling-pieces, that they have adopted no generally-acknowledged standard style to guide them in the

getting up of guns suitable for certain kinds of sport." Elisha J. Lewis, *The American Sportsman* (Philadelphia, 1871), 435. Although numerous industries had taken up the principle of interchangeable parts, mass-production techniques were to come to the fore only with the assembly lines of Henry Ford and the automobile industry in the years before World War I.

[66]*Harper's Weekly*, XL (April 11, 1896), 366.

[67]Burlingame, *Engines of Democracy: Inventions and Society in Mature America*, 3.

[68]Herbert O. Duncan, *World on Wheels*, 2 vols. (Paris, 1927), II, 919 ff.

[69]Lawrence H. Seltzer, *A Financial History of the American Automobile Industry* (Boston, 1928), 91; Pierre Sauvestre, *Histoire de L'Automobile* (Paris, 1907), *passim*; Ralph C. Epstein, *The Automobile Industry, Its Economic and Commercial Development* (Chicago, 1928), 154; Reginald M. Cleveland and S. T. Williamson, *The Road Is Yours* (New York, 1951), 175-76, 194-97.

[70]Keith Sward, *The Legend of Henry Ford* (New York, 1948), 14.

[71]Henry Ford and Samuel Crowther, *My Life and Work* (Garden City, 1927), 36-37, 50-51.

[72]*Scientific American*, XCV (August 11, 1906), 95.

[73]G. F. Baright, "Automobiles and Automobile Races at Newport," *Independent* (New York), LIV (June 5, 1902), 1368.

[74]In these years the motorcycle and the motorboat also created interest, Sir Alfred Harmsworth (later Lord Northcliffe) establishing the Harmsworth Trophy for international competition in 1903. Air races also won widespread publicity in the press from 1910 onward. Glenn H. Curtiss achieved an enviable reputation as an aviator, newspapers sponsored air meets, and considerable attention was given to the "new sport of the air." *Ibid.*, LXIX (November 3, 1910), 999.

[75]Lewis Mumford, *Technics and Civilization* (New York, 1934), 303-305; Arnold J. Toynbee, *A Study of History*, 6 vols. (London, 1934-1939),IV, 242-43.

[76]Technological developments throughout the business world transformed the pattern of city life. The electric elevator and improvements in the manufacture of steel made possible the skyscrapers of Chicago and New York in the late 1880s. Concentration of the business community in the central part of the city was increased also by the telephone switchboard and other instruments of communication. Less and less open land remained for the youth living in the heart of the metropolis, and it was to meet this challenge that the Y.M.C.A., the settlement house, the institutional church, the boys' club, and other agencies expanded their athletic facilities. The playground movement and the public park grew out of the necessity for recreational areas for city dwellers, and public authorities early in the twentieth century began to rope off streets for children at play. The subway, the streetcar, and the automobile made possible the accelerated trend toward suburban development, where the open lot or planned play area offered better opportunities to participate in sport. The more general implications of the impact of the technological revolution on society, already considered by several outstanding scholars, are not discussed here, the principal aim of this study being to describe the interrelationship of sports and invention in the latter half of the nineteenth century. Although the account of the auto slightly transgressed the limits of this study, it was felt necessary to give it an abbreviated treatment. The twentieth century, and the rule of improved sporting equipment, racing and training devices, the radio, television, improved highways, and bus and air transport, would require an equally extensive study.

9

Walter Camp on Sportsmanship

"Be each, pray God, a gentleman!" It is an easy word, and a pleasant one. I don't doubt but that you all pronounce it trippingly enough, and have each one his own high ideal of what a gentleman should be. Do you live up to it? Or are you letting it come down a little here and there; so little, perhaps, that you hardly notice it until you make comparison? A gentleman against a gentleman always plays to win. There is a tacit agreement between them that each shall do his best, and the best man shall win. A gentleman does not make his living, however, from his athletic prowess. He does not earn anything by his victories except glory and satisfaction. Perhaps the first falling off in this respect began when the laurel wreath became a mug. So long as the mug was but the emblem, and valueless otherwise, there was no harm. There is still no harm where the mug or trophy hangs in the room of the winner is indicative of his skill; but if the silver mug becomes a silver dollar, either at the hands of the winner or the donor, let us have the laurel back again.

A gentleman never competes for money, directly or indirectly. Make no mistake about this. No matter how winding the road may be that eventually brings the sovereign into the pocket, it is the price of what should be dearer to you than anything else, — your honor. It is quite the fashion to say "sentimental bosh" to any one who preaches such an old-fashioned thing as honor; but among true gentlemen, my boy, it is just as real an article as ever, and it is one of the few things that never ring false. The man who tells you that insufferable rot about being practical and discarding sentiment, is not the man you would choose as a friend. He wouldn't stand by you in a pinch, and when we come to the reality, it is only the man who believes in such a thing as honor that is worth anything. So stick to it, my boy, and keep it bright. Carry it down into the small affairs of school and college.

From Walter Camp, Walter Camp's Book of College Sports *(New York: Century, 1893), pp. 1-9.*

If you are enough of a man to be a good athlete, and some one asks you to use that athletic ability upon their behalf, don't take money for it, or anything that amounts to pay. If you are on the school team or nine and go into training, don't break faith with your captain, yourself, and your fellows by surreptitious indulgences. This doesn't mean that if you see some other fellow smoke on the sly you are obliged to tell of it, nor does it mean that you must call him to account, unless you are the captain. If his standard is not so high as yours, that is his misfortune. If he asks your opinion, give it to him, if you like, but not in such a way as to leave the impression that you are put out by your own longing for a similar indulgence. If you are the captain and you find a man breaking training in spite of your orders, and you consider it advisable to put him off, don't be afraid to do it. Gentlemen are not cowards, mentally or physically.

If a man comes to you and endeavors to affect your choice of a college by offers of a pecuniary nature, he does not take you for a gentleman or a gentleman's son, you may be sure. Gentlemen neither offer nor take bribes.

Now, my young college friend, it is your turn. Remember it is upon you that the eyes of the preparatory school-boy are fixed, it is toward you that the younger brother looks for example, and whatever you do in your four years' course, you will see magnified by the boys who come after you. Support your class and your college in every way compatible with your position. Gentlemen are not stingy, nor are they selfish. Play it if you can and your class or college needs you. Pay if you can afford it, but do not allow a false pride to lead you into subscriptions beyond your means. Don't be ashamed of enthusiasm. A man without it is a man without a purpose.

I remember a little incident of my own college course. I was a freshman, and knew almost no one in college except a certain junior. I had entered in two events in the fall athletic games, one a quarter mile, the other a hurdle race. I had run the quarter and been beaten, although I finished second. My opponents had all been upper classmen, and I received no little encouragement from their friends. I felt very lonely and disgusted with myself and life in general when I got on the mark for the hurdle. I had but two competitors, and both had been cheered when they came to the scratch. Suddenly as we were getting on our marks I heard a voice half-way down the course call out, "You can do 'em," and I saw my junior friend waving his hat to me. It was not a classical remark, but it made me feel better. I was clumsy in getting off, and when we came to the sixth hurdle was nearly five yards behind the other two, but from that time on I could hear my friend roaring out, "Go in!" "You've got 'em yet!" "Now you're over," as I went up each flight. I *did* finish first, and I had hardly touched the tape before he was patting me on the back. I don't suppose it cost him much to yell for a poor freshman, but I know that I always thought of him as one of the best fellows I ever knew, and in after years I have remembered enough of the feeling that was in my heart toward him, to go out and try to make some others feel that even a freshman has friends.

Apropos of this, a word to non-contestants. In a boat-race or a foot-ball match the chances are that your own men will not hear you cheer, but the men who may try for the team or crew the next season do, and they are encouraged to better efforts by it. Now about the treatment of your rivals. A gentleman is courteous. It is not courtesy upon a ball-field to cheer an error of the opponents. If it is upon your grounds, it is the worst kind of boorishness. Moreover, if there are remarkable plays made by your rivals you yourselves should cheer; conceal any chagrin you may feel at the loss it may be to your side, but be courteous to appreciate and applaud an exceptional play by the opponents.

After winning a race or a match, there is no reason why a good, healthy lot of young men should not do plenty of cheering, but there is every reason why they should not make their enjoyment depend upon insulting those who have lost. You cannot take your hilarity off into a corner and choke it to death, and no one wants you to; but gratuitous jibes and jeers at the crestfallen mark you as a man who does not know how to bear a victory, a man whose pate is addled by the excitement or whose bringing up has been at fault.

Finally, to non-contestants, I want to say a word regarding "celebrating." Primarily, do not, I beg of you, do anything because it looks smart. Enjoy yourselves, but do not try to "show off." Don't be "tough." A little unusual hilarity, a tendency to believe that everything is expressly for the collegian, can be upon these occasions overlooked and forgiven, but be ready to appreciate the point beyond which it is carried too far; be ready to apologize quickly and instantly where offense is taken. Show that behind the jolly fun there is the instinct and cultivation of a gentleman's son, and that the ebullition of enthusiasm, although it may be a bore to those who fail to kindle at it, has nothing of the vicious element, and is thoroughly innocent of intentional offense to any one. If you find you are losing your head, go home; you will not be sorry for it.

Now for the contestants. I wish I could impress indelibly upon your minds the fact that with you rests the most enduring standard for amateur sports. With no disrespect to any class or condition — with the best regard for all strong legislation in outside athletic bodies — I say that the collegian's standard of purity in his sports should be the highest. The very fact of having the leisure to devote four years to a higher education, should be taken to involve the duty of acquiring a keener perception of right and wrong in matters where right and wrong depend upon a delicacy of honor. Gentlemen do not cheat, nor do they deceive themselves as to what cheating is. If you are elected the captain of a nine, team, or crew, read over your rules, and note exactly who are allowed as contestants by those rules, not by the custom of some predecessor, nor by what you think some rival will do, but by the rules themselves. Having done that, never let a thought enter your head of making use of any man not clearly and cleanly eligible. You will save yourself many a future worry if you start fairly by looking into the record of every one of every candidate at the outset. It is your duty to know that every one of your men is straight and square. I know what I am talking about when I say that a college captain can, in ninety-nine cases out of a hundred become possessed of the exact truth regarding any man he thinks of trying. Don't investigate to see how much your opponent could prove, but investigate for your own satisfaction. In legislating, remember that what a gentleman wants is fair play and the best man to win. When it is possible, without losing sight of this, to legislate for improvements in method, so much the better; but primarily make every rule such that the probability of unfinished, drawn, or disputed contests is reduced to a minimum.

What if, at the time, your side may be the weaker? Don't be a coward on that account. Face it like a man, and say with your whole heart that you are on the side of the men who want no chance of retreat or escape, only a fair contest and certain victory or defeat at the end of it. To what do all the technicalities amount when compared with the sincerity of men who come together to effect that result? When the delegates earnestly desire rules that shall ensure such a contest and such an issue, their work is more than half done. Don't take the coward's part and try to legislate means of avoiding the issue.

Perhaps if you, sir, the father of these boys, have had patience to listen thus far to me, you will allow me to put in a word for the love they bear these sports and the pride they take in their school and college. Talk with them about these interests. You will lose no dignity by it, and you will gain a confidence from them worth having. When you see anything in their speech or conduct that betokens a lowering of the high ideal of gentlemanliness, don't hesitate to say so. You don't want your boy "hired" by any one. If he plays, he plays as a gentleman, and not as a professional; he plays for victory, not for money; and whatever bruises he may have in the flesh, his heart is right, and he can look you in the eye as a gentleman should.

Be each, pray God, a gentleman!

10

Football's Ugly Decades, 1893-1913

by John Hammond Moore

The opening years of this century witnessed a crisis in American football — a crisis which almost proved fatal. The sport was savagely attacked by editors, legislators, and educators. Ministers and female orators saw a pigskin mania corrupting American youth and ruining the true goals of academic life. Muckrakers assailed it, yellow journalism had a field day, and the President of the United States even threatened to ban the sport. The outcry subsided only when those within collegiate ranks decided *something* had to be done. In fact utilization of the forward pass by some boys from South Bend did much more for football than the outraged denunciations of college presidents, hack writers, and professional do-gooders.

Battle lines began to form in the 1890s. Edward L. Godkin of the *Nation* saw America caught up in a football frenzy. In his words it was just another "craze" like the Greenbackers, Silverites, and Grangers. Now there was an "athletic craze," and the leading colleges were becoming "huge training grounds for young gladiators, around whom as many spectators roar as roared in the Flavian amphitheatre."[1] Such spectacles not only hurt scholarship, they frightened "plain people" away from college campuses. Ordinary folk feared what went hand-in-hand with such extravaganzas — debt, drink, dice, and debauchery. As the 1893 season came to a gory close, Godkin pointed out that English football players who broke rules of the game were hailed into court, whereas here in America anything was permitted above the belt except slugging. Merely amending rules as some suggested would not do. "So long as a man can be treated as a simple package to be removed by pushing, pulling, rolling, kicking, or 'slugging,' there will always be great danger of his being in some way maimed."[2]

J. Hammond Moore has taught at the University of Mississippi and Georgia State college. He has written two books on southern history.

Walter Camp, Yale's famous athletic director, also deplored the excessive number of accidents. He blamed "overdevelopment of mass plays." Many spectators found the flying wedge especially offensive. It horrified a reporter of the austere *Manchester Guardian.* He said Americans had "spoiled and brutalized" Rugby. "This is not football as we know it in England!"[3] Invented at Harvard in 1892, the flying wedge was soon copied by other colleges. The play was arranged so that nine players withdrew about twenty yards and on a given signal converged at a point directly ahead of the ball carrier. Needless to say their momentum provided unusual interference. John Heisman called the wedge something wonderful to behold and terrible to stop.

Writing in *Harper's Weekly,* Teddy Roosevelt said such brutality must cease. Roosevelt, who was learning about life in Washington as a member of the Civil Service Commission, urged university officials and faculty members — perhaps through cooperative efforts among various colleges — to do away with mass play and blatant professionalism. "It should be distinctly understood among the academies and the colleges that no team will have anything to do with another team upon which professionals are employed."[4]

These comments by Godkin, Camp, and the man who in 1905 would call a White House conference on football highlight the key issues. Godkin, one of the sport's severest critics, condemned football because, in his opinion, it undermined scholarship, scared away potential students, and attracted depraved elements of society. Roosevelt, who represented a middle ground, was disturbed by increasing brutality and obvious professionalism. Not too surprisingly, Walter Camp was the man who would change football least. He was merely concerned lest "overdevelopment" of mass formations might give the game a bad name.

Football had, of course, numerous defenders. Speaking in Boston early in 1894, the Honorable Charles Francis Adams, son of Lincoln's minister to Great Britain, struck a chord which would be echoed many times by those who shared his views. Football built character. Even death on the gridiron was cheap if it educated youth "in those characteristics that have made the Anglo-Saxon race pre-eminent in history."[5] Members of Philadelphia's Art Club heard two college professors debate the question, "Ought football to be encouraged?"[6] Woodrow Wilson of Princeton stressed the moral qualities to be gained on the gridiron. Although all sports developed precision, presence of mind, decision, and endurance, football fostered the additional virtues of cooperation and self-subordination, and should be encouraged so as to insure continued control by colleges themselves. In Wilson's opinion, this was the only way "gentlemen" would be able to keep the sport "manly and clean." (Actually it was difficult for Wilson to be impartial. As a Princeton undergraduate he was secretary of a student board directing football, and during the late 1880's he had coached the Wesleyan [Conn.] eleven. Now, back at Princeton, he was chairman of the faculty committee on outdoor sports.) The future president . . . could not resist ridiculing Harvard's elective system — a plan of academic study subsequently adopted by nearly all colleges and universities. No wonder Harvard lost so many games each fall. The "elective" man lacked self-discipline. Wilson's adversary, Burt Wilder of Cornell, bypassed such matters as electives and control of the game and centered his attack on a simple query which apparently baffled Wilson: If football developed "moral qualities," why were referees necessary?

In February of 1894, the Cambridge representative in the Massachusetts lower house introduced a bill designed to prohibit public football games throughout the Bay State. In March, concerned over mounting injuries, West Point and Annapolis limited football to the grounds of their respective academies. An alarmed Walter Camp took the offensive. He mailed a questionnaire to scores of former grid heroes. How many years did they play? What was the most serious injury received? Was it permanent? Was it received in a game or in practice? Were they properly trained? One can easily predict the results of any such poll.

Nevertheless, under the pressure of these attacks there was some reform. The flying wedge was outlawed, and since critics pointed out that nearly all serious injuries occurred during the waning moments of play, playing time was cut from ninety to seventy minutes, and the game divided into halves. Godkin was still scornful. Colleges promised spectators a more "open" game minus the flying wedge, but "new" football reminded one of Tammany Hall — *"Plus ça change, plus c'est la même chose."*[7] He attacked the Yale-Harvard game of 1894 as the most brutal ever. If not, why were surgeons and litter bearers necessary? Seven of the twenty-two men who began the game were injured; that was thirty-three percent! Much worse than even Union losses at Cold Harbor! He claimed that Yale's captain, a youth named Hinkey, broke the collarbone of a Harvard player by repeatedly jumping upon him as he lay on the ground. Apparently Godkin's charges were all too true. Tempers were so short that this famous series was canceled for three seasons.

The weekend following the Harvard debacle, Walter Camp's eleven were scheduled to meet Princeton in New York City, and many feared another rough and tumble affair. The New York *Times* expressed relief when Manhattan police threatened to lock up any player involved in mayhem, even if he failed to commit a legal offense under the new rules. In view of this development, the *Times* predicted that the game would probably be "so quiet and gentlemanlike that Hinkey, John L. Sullivan, and Jack the Ripper will find it mawkish, and even a well-regulated kinescope would disdain to record it."[8] Twenty thousand rain-drenched fans saw Yale win 24-0, some watching the rather dull contest from the security of horse-drawn coaches. It was a clean, honest game, Hinkey behaved himself, and the police made no arrests.

One spectator at Yale's victory, Reverend John L. Scudder of Jersey City, was thoroughly converted. He saw at Manhattan field a manly contest, not, as he had been told, "twenty-two human battering rams engaged in fiendish combat."[9] Actually, said Congregationalist Scudder, there was much more danger in the stands where one faced the hazards of pneumonia, consumption, and drink. Still shuddering, he asked a question which thousands have repeated every autumn: "Why don't they play the game in better weather?"

There were still those, however, who thought that football should not be played at all, regardless of weather. Early in 1895, Indiana's college presidents prohibited intercollegiate contests, and Harvard's Charles W. Eliot stated in his annual report that, as played, football was "unfit" for college life. If the answer to the current dilemma was more referees, then this was no sport for gentlemen! "A game which needs to be so watched," he concluded, "is not fit for genuine sportsmen."[10] Although Godkin applauded these reports from Indiana and Cambridge, he emphasized that the players themselves were not really responsible for prevailing evils,

> They are swayed by a tyrannical public opinion — partly ignorant and partly barbarous — to the formation of which graduates and undergraduates, fathers, mothers and sisters, leaders of society, and the veriest of gamblers and rowdies all contribute. The state of mind of the spectators at a hard-fought football match at Springfield, New York, or Philadelphia cannot but suggest the query how far these assemblages differ at heart from the throngs which enjoy the prize-fight, cock-fight, or bull-fight, or which in other centuries delighted in the sports of the Roman arena.[11]

In the fall of 1895 the "veriest" gamblers were at it again — on the floor of the New York Stock Exchange itself! On the eve of the Yale-Princeton game odds makers favored Eli, 100-75. Yale won as expected, 20-10, and perhaps inspired a hearty meal or the prospect of one, a *Times* reporter presented readers with a picture which did little to enhance the appeal of football,

> Slap! Two masses of humanity would come together with a sound like the cracking of the bones of a tasty hot bird between the teeth of some hungry giant. Legs and arms and heads and feet would be apparently inextricably intermingled, until it looked as if not even the fondest mother would be able to sort out the right parts of her one and only son. The whistle of the referee would blow

sharply, and the lot of legs and arms and hands and heads would sort themselves out once more, and there would be something like the sixteen or eighteen of the boys that seemed to be human beings once more, with all the members of their bodies intact.

The rest of the men that had been in the collision lay prone on the field and Drs. Josh Hartwell and Boviard would rush on the field, followed by assistants with packages of sticking plaster, buckets of water, and cases of surgical instruments. A big gap in someone's head would be patched together with plaster, another man's leg would be pulled back until it assumed its normal shape, sprained wrists would be bandaged, and wrenched ankles bound up. Then the crowd would yell itself hoarse with the rival cries of the colleges, possibly because no one had been killed outright. Roaring bulls of Bashan never made one-half the noise!

Sharply the whistle of the referee would ring out its orders and then another human cyclone would be set in motion, and possibilities of carnage can be suggested by the merry cries of "Eat 'em up, Princeton!" and "Kill 'em in their tracks, Yale!"[12]

Editorially, however, the *Times* commented that while players must not "maim and slay each other," critics should realize that football was not "checkers or dominoes." Football men should develop skill and dexterity, not sheer brawn. If the game's severest critics had their way, it would deteriorate into little more than "button-button."[13]

The debate raged on during the closing years of the 19th century. In January 1897, New York's august University Club spoke out sharply against metropolitan extravaganzas which encouraged sensationalism in the press and injured the good name, not only of the sport, but of the colleges involved. There were also complicating factors — ticket scalpers, rowdy folk, and unstable bleachers. To save football from unfavorable publicity and unsavory elements, contest should be staged only on college playing fields. Actually, much of the bad publicity resulted from injuries to precollege players. All too frequently it was the light, inexperienced youth, poorly dressed and inadequately coached, who was hurt. Nevertheless, the newspapers, eager for readers, lumped *all* injuries and deaths together. One had to proceed past glaring headlines. "FOOTBALL CLAIMS ANOTHER VICTIM," to discover that the player was a twelve-year-old engaged in a sandlot fracas.

As the 1897 season got underway, fans saw more and more of their heroes decked out in what sports writers called "football armor." The outfit reminded one observer of "a cross between a baseball catcher and a deep sea diver."[14] It included several pounds of horsehair padding, fearsome mask, rubber mouthpiece, heavy canvas blouse, thick-ribbed socks, and sturdy shoes. Despite such precautions, it was another unhappy fall. Referees seemed uncertain as to what constituted slugging, but the president of the University of Chicago made it clear that any player who did so would be dropped from the team *and* from college. The Syracuse-Colgate game ended in a wild exchange of punches. Commenting upon accidents on the gridiron, Cornell's president noted that "a far larger number traveling for pleasure on railways have recently been killed."[15] (editorially the *Nation* questioned President Jacob G. Schurman's logic and expressed the hope that this was not "a fair specimen of the style of reasoning he teaches his students.") Eliot of Harvard retorted that football injuries were *not* accidents! Unlike most sports, the nature of football, the slugging and clashing of players of unequal size and weight made serious injuries inevitable.[16]

Late in October five thousand Atlanta fans watched in silence as Virginia's Cavaliers trounced their Georgia Bulldogs,17-4."Everything went smoothly," wrote one reporter, "and there was a surprising absence of slugging until near the game's end." Then, Richard Von Gammon, a Georgia player, tripped while making a tackle. He suffered a severe concussion and died a few hours later. Although an accident, Gammon's death caused a widespread sensation. The University of Georgia abandoned football and announced plans to convert its playing field into a bicycle track. Atlanta prohibited the sport and the state legislature concurred. Governor William Atkinson vetoed the bill, however, and thanks to some parliamentary maneuvering, his wishes eventually prevailed. (Arkansas and Virginia also considered a ban on football, but neither state took any action.) There are indications that Populist sentiment — hostility toward the "aristocratic" state university — was involved in this fight. Despite a public plea by Gammon's mother deploring any ban on football and Atkinson's words terming the bill "petty, tyrannical, and useless," Georgia's House of Representatives voted 107-45 (with twenty abstentions) to override the veto. The speaker, however, stepped into the breach and ruled that support by two thirds of the total membership of the House was needed to disregard the governor's wishes. In the parliamentary confusion which ensued, the speaker was upheld and the bill killed. A ban on football within Atlanta's city limits was short-lived. Passed shortly after Gammon's death, it was repealed in February 1898.

In an editorial dedicated to young Gammon, the New York *Times* agreed that football could not be made a sedentary sport. "It may properly call for a greater muscular activity than croquet, even. But that mayhem and homicide should become its familiar accompaniements [sic] will not be permitted. That point is not yet reached, but it cannot be denied that the rapid development of modern methods of play tend in that direction."[17] The real evil was money, and academic studies were being neglected as rising gate receipts commercialized a *college* sport. In true Victorian tone the *Times* thundered, "There is something not quite nice in the notion of young gentlemen exhibiting themselves in contests for money."[18]

On November 23, 1897, this same daily carried one of the strangest messages ever to appear in its editorial columns. In one salvo it told how to deal with "Two Curable Evils" — *lynching and football!* The family of anyone lynched should recover damages from the community where the offense occurred, "say not more than 1% of the assessed property, real and personal...." That would halt lynching! If degenerates continued these outrages, local citizens would deal with them rather than continuing to pay damages. As for football, take away gate receipts and the sport would revert to its proper status. After all, "the great public jousts and massacres yield fifteen to twenty thousand dollars each from the sale of seats." These funds were used to train and equip teams. Cut out this revenue and football would become merely a game for relaxation and exercise. It was all so simple: "Make lynching expensive and public football unprofitable."

With the new century debate grew hotter. Despite promises that rule changes would end brutality, the death toll continued to mount. A dozen deaths during the 1902 season precipitated an avalanche of criticism. Play seemed fully as brutal as before. This is how one observer described a memorable moment in the Yale-Harvard game of that year:

I saw a Yale man throttle — literally throttle — Kernan, so that he dropped the ball; the two hands reached up in plain view of every one — and all saw but the umpire — and choked and choked; such a man would cheat at your cardtable, if he thought he could do so without detection. The dirty players in football are the thugs of society, and the disgrace of the university that tolerates their presence on the team.[19]

A substantial number of educators agreed that mass play must cease. As the *Nation* so succinctly put it, "Who will bell the football cat?" Eliot of Harvard, according to that publication, was the logical man for the job. If he demanded reform, other schools would fall into line.[20] The *Nation* also suggested increasing the distance in a series of downs to ten yards instead of five, and limiting the backfield to four men on defense to end short dangerous line plunges and brutal power plays. Meanwhile, the headmasters of some seventy preparatory schools denounced football as "too severe and too dangerous."[21]

Eliot Hubbard of "Message to Garcia" fame saw five men carried from the field during the Purdue-Notre Dame game on Thanksgiving Day, 1902. One, apparently suffering from a concussion, rushed back onto the field, screaming as he ran. Although Hubbard did not know what happened to that unfortunate youth, he assured readers of *Cosmopolitan* that he knew two other boys who were in mental asylums because of gridiron injuries. "The practical world," he wrote, "has no use for football. The game will have to go, and its passing will not be regretted by those who love books and ideas, and prize the mintage of mind which manifests itself in courage, kindness, and a just appreciation for all that is beautiful and true."[22]

In April 1903, a University of Illinois professor published a thorough survey of football.[23] After tabulating returns from some sixty colleges, Edwin Dexter concluded that one college man in ten played football, and larger schools had nearly twice as many men actively participating in the game. One player in thirty-five lost class time because of injuries, but the number of men permanently disabled or killed seemed negligible. (Although this study revealed only three deaths during the previous decade, Dexter questioned the accuracy of these figures.) College authorities favored football 17-1, and small schools were more emphatic in approval or disapproval of the sport. According to Dexter, press accounts of college injuries were "grossly exaggerated." This was not the case, however, with mishaps in high school and athletic club leagues.

Despite attacks, pleas for reform, and surveys, the rules committee of the National Intercollegiate Football Conference did little when it met in 1903. A minor concession permitted a back who received the ball to cross the scrimmage line five yards from where the ball had been centered. Previously he had to relay it to another teammate who could then attempt to gain yardage. The game, divided only into halves, was still seventy minutes long. Players had three downs in which to make five yards. The results were mass formations and continued public dismay.

In the midst of the 1903 campaign, George Merril, president of Colgate University, attacked football for different reasons, expressing concern that "assured completion of the play was not an element of the sport." He was especially critical of the scoring system. (At that time, a touchdown and a field goal each counted five points; a safety two; and point after touchdown, one.) Why begin all over again in the second half? Why not start where the first half ended?[24]

In February 1904, President Eliot told the Harvard faculty that the sport conducted at that school with "the least intelligence and success is football — except from a pecuniary point of view."[25] Deploring the extent to which it interrupted academic work, he insisted something be done. Nevertheless, when the fall season began, a wave of alarming headlines again greeted the American public. A youth in Tarrytown, New York, had an ear "kicked off almost completely" in an athletic club meet.[26] Jere Delaney, Northwestern's trainer, said many players suffered from an affliction similar to "softening of the brain."[27] He blamed the physical and nervous strain of three months training which he thought more dangerous than games themselves. It seemed to promote "daydreaming and childishness." As Harvard ended another disastrous season, the Crimson coach blamed injuries and lack of experience. He admitted that only one man went through the entire season unhurt, and several magazines and newspapers cited his words as tacit admission of gridiron hazards.

On November 24, 1904, the New York *Times* agreed with the new state superintendent of schools, Andrew Draper (former president of the University of Illinois), that large gate receipts and student gambling must cease. Draper had blasted football for fostering "loafing, gambling, and drinking!" He noted that so far in 1904 fourteen players had been killed and 296 injured. "Had such losses been incurred in one battle in the Philippines," he added, "the public would have been much exercised."[28] But faculties across the nation *could not* and *would not* act against football, because they were engaged in a "game" of their own! That "game," said the *Times*, was fierce competition for the students. No college or university dared tamper with football. Big games, winning teams, and enthusiastic alumni were keys to growth. It seemed that reputations as centers of learning were being built on athletic prowess.

Two days later, in an editorial entitled "Facilis Descensus," the *Times* launched a searing indictment of football. Going the way of boxing, the sport had "degenerated into pugilism in the mass" and unfortunately "few of the vices of the prize ring" were lacking. Many players, little more than "temporary professionals," had an unhealthy effect upon youth who worshipped them. Parents who kept their sons off the gridiron must also consider their daughters. Proper young ladies should not witness such "sordid carnage." New rules had done little but make the sport "an immensely dull and stupid performance."

> One's sincere sympathy goes out to the Presidents and professors of our colleges at this ruin of a gallant and health-giving game, which it has been beyond their power to avert. It may be doubted whether reform be possible; the evil will have to cure itself and football disappear for a time. That it can go on in its present state is impossible. The descent to Avernus is too steep and the slope is greased with greed. The sooner the game is discontinued, the better.

In December, fifty-four Harvard alumni petitioned for a paid coach. It would be better to drop the sport entirely than continue losing games. "The object, then, of football," noted the *Nation*, "is merely to beat Yale."[29] Crimson grads had until this time talked much of exercise, wholesome recreation, and moral development, but exercise in defeat apparently did not count. Couldn't a Harvard man demonstrate moral restraint while losing? Would a "paid" coach and a "succession of Harvard victories restore the game to divine favor and invoke upon the players the blessings of Heaven?"

When the Harvard faculty met a few weeks later, Eliot repeated his charges of the previous year. The undergraduate mind was too absorbed with the gridiron. Each fall the University ate, talked, and breathed football. He pleaded for the assistance of the "educated public," but the *Nation* — in contrast to an opinion expressed two years earlier — doubted if even Eliot with all of his prestige could accomplish anything. College presidents, fearing for the prosperity of their institutions, would remain silent. "We have been deluded hitherto by the Roosevelts and other worshippers of brute force into thinking that there is something noble, inspiring, and uplifting in the crashing together of twenty-two men."[30]

One Harvard graduate suggested that a national board be set up to rule on roughness and unfair play. He recommended banning unruly players for the remainder of the game, for a season, or for life. University of Nebraska officials decided no man could play until he had been in college at least one year. He would also have to maintain passing grades, reveal all sources of income, and face suspension if guilty of immorality, breaches of training rules, or improper play. Such measures, cried Ralph Paine, a former war correspondent busily churning out books for boys, were ridiculous! It would be better to simply abolish college sports and forget them entirely.

In June 1905, *McClure's* muckraking staff unleashed a stinging, two-part volley: "The College Athlete."[31] The author, Henry Beach Needham, noted that on February 18, 1898, seven northeastern colleges met to discuss athletic policies. These schools — Brown, Columbia, Cornell, Penn, Harvard, Dartmouth, and Princeton — agreed that no student should be paid for athletic ability. This practice, they affirmed, was "degrading to amateur sport." Yale, conspicuously absent, later signed substantially the same agreement with Harvard. Yet, wrote Needham, in these very schools *commercialism was rampant!* In 1899, Columbia decided to plunge into big-time football. The Lions got themselves a "paid" coach who in turn "hired" players. A scandal resulted when these men beat both Yale and Princeton.

Needham charged that the Ivy League frequently raided prep schools in its search for talent. James J. Hogan, who entered Exeter at 23, was now captain of the Yale eleven, living in great style at New Haven. Among his sources of income were commissions from the American Tobacco Company. Students down at Mory's often referred to "Egyptian Deities" and "Turkish Moguls" as "Hogan's Cigarettes." James J. Conney, an Exeter product now at Princeton, was operating a baseball concession worth thousands of dollars. While these men were smart, top honors went to Andrew Smith, a stellar performer at Penn. On October 4, 1902, Smith played a fine game for Penn State against the Quakers. The following Monday he was practicing with Penn. According to Needham, Penn had also "drafted" players from Middlebury, Colorado College, Lafayette, and Peddie. And in his opinion, Harvard had little reason for its "holier than thou" attitude. That school had threatened to drop Penn from its schedule unless "decisive" victories ceased. Nevertheless, Harvard alumni gave their gridiron heroes substantial aid, and the Crimson baseball nine was studded with semipros. These men, despite specific provisions to the contrary, played in the White Mountains each summer under assumed names. For the service academies, West Point and Annapolis, Needham had special praise. There one found no frills, no special training tables, no trophies. It was simply "sport for sport's sake."

The schools' faculties were to blame for these conditions, said Needham, and he saw little hope of reform being started by the colleges of the northeast. Midwestern schools, however, might show older and more corrupt institutions the way from commercialism and brutality. In addition, he charged that excessive brutality was both calculated and intentional. A Princeton player told him that he and his teammates were trained to eliminate dangerous opponents during the first five minutes of each game.

These articles in *McClure's* and a photograph which caught the eye of the President of the United States led to the climax of over a decade of agitation. On October 7, 1905, Swarthmore and Penn tangled in an extremely rough game. Penn won, 11-4, but only by "eliminating" a huge lineman named Bob Maxwell. When Teddy Roosevelt say a picture of Maxwell's mangled face, he exploded. Rough play must cease, or he would abolish football forever! . . . One cartoonist [conceived] of Roosevelt beginning still another campaign — this one against football brutality. "The man who brought peace to Russia and Japan," said the Richmond (Va.) *Dispatch,* "now seeks to save life and limb of people in the United States."[32] Within a few days athletic advisers and coaches of Harvard, Yale, and Princeton were lunching at the White House. On October 12, Walter Camp and his counterparts issued this statement:

At a meeting with the president of the United States, it was agreed that we consider an honorable obligation exists to carry out in letter and in spirit the rules of the game of foot-ball [sic], relating to roughness, holding, and foul play, and the active coaches of our universities being present with us, pledged themselves to so regard it and to do their utmost to carry out that obligation.[33]

For many Americans these were welcome words. During the 1904 season twenty-one players had been killed and over two hundred injured. Sickened by what he had seen, Dr. F.R. Oastler, surgeon of the Columbia squad for six years, blasted football: "I think it is the most brutal exhibition I have ever seen or heard of to [be] call[ed] a sport. The players go on the field expecting to be hurt, and are glad if they come off with nothing worse than a broken bone."[34] Professor

Shailer Mathews of Chicago's Divinity School denounced football as "a social obsession — a boy-killing, education-prostituting, gladitorial [sic] sport. It teaches virility and courage, but so does war. I do not know what should take its place, but the new game should not require the services of a physician, the maintenance of a hospital, and the celebration of funerals."[35]

Meanwhile, to be sure that football moguls would not forget his warning, Roosevelt continued to prod them. On November 20, Dr. J.W. White, professor of surgery at the University of Pennsylvania, lunched at the White House. As White emerged, he told reporters that Mr. Roosevelt wanted to end brutality, increase the power of officials, and set up a simple eligibility code. The president was still a loyal fan, but it was clear, in his opinion, that "brutality and foul play in football should receive the same summary punishment given to a man who cheats at cards or strikes a foul while boxing."[36]

In the face of these stern words, some institutions abolished football — hinting broadly that its future depended upon what new rules were adopted during the winter months. Meeting in Chicago, the "Big Nine" agreed upon a five game schedule, outlawed training tables, and limited varsity competition to unergraduates who had been in residence for at least six months. Harvard, Yale, and Princeton conceded that freshmen and graduate students should be banned from varsity play. The Midwestern conference also limited admission to fifty cents and stressed faculty control of athletics. Professors, not alumni and undergraduates, must handle finances; coaches should be regularly employed staff members not professionals.

Late in February 1906, the powerful rules committee of the National Inter-collegiate Football Conference held the first of several stormy sessions at New York's Murray Hotel. Walter Camp vehemently opposed demands for a legalized forward pass and a weaker defense. When a second eight-hour session ended in deadlock, Columbia spokesmen said the Lions had played their last game. Despite considerable grumbling by alumni and students, that school did not play football for over a decade, only resuming the game in earnest after World War I.

While football's future was being debated, prominent citizens in and out of collegiate ranks voiced their opinions. Among these individuals were Groton's Endicott Peabody, Brown's William H. Faunce, William Howard Taft, and Charles Evans Hughes. Peabody and Faunce admitted that football was dangerous but after all it was not supposed to be dominoes or authors! Peabody said that prohibiting a sport because some players were dishonest was like dropping political economy from the curriculum because some students cheated in exams in the subject.[37] President Faunce sternly maintained that every college should have at least one "rough game. . . one game in which men come into personal contact with one another." He noted that "the old drinking and carousing . . . , the smashing of window-panes and destruction of property" of previous generations no longer existed on college campuses, and he credited the rise of athletics, especially football.[38]

Addressing Yale alumni in St. Louis, Taft advocated a ten-yard series of downs and advised grid heroes to "play hard, respect your opponents; then win or lose you have done your part to preserve the game which has too much good in it to sacrifice."[39] On the other hand, while speaking to Brown alumni, Hughes attacked the commercial spirit of the game. It fostered the same evils which created bossed and insurance scandals.[40]

The rules committee met on March 4 and, amid charges and countercharges, came to an agreement. One more official was added, making a total of four. (The *Nation* contemptuously remarked that now another "blind umpire" would be on the field.) Playing time was reduced to sixty minutes; hurdling and mass play formations were prohibited, and as Taft and others had suggested, the now familiar ten-yard series of downs was approved, but a team still had only three chances, not four. The forward pass was made legal, but with one great drawback. If incomplete, the team attempting to pass was penalized fifteen yards on the first and second down. On the third down they lost possession, regardless of who recovered the loose ball.

Although few critics were satisfied, during the 1906 season football was very obviously a changed game. On October 20, *Harper's Weekly* expressed relief that the revised sport seemed to be succeeding. Play was more open; there were fewer injuries, and even the *Nation* conceded that there was some improvement. There was, however, room for much, much more. Columbia had lost nothing, the editors caustically observed, by abolishing football.

As the 1907 campaign got underway, Walter Camp, glumly resigned to "new" football, told youthful readers of *St. Nicholas* that colleges had been forced to change football because mass play proved too tiring. Roughness, he admitted, could be concealed in mass formations. Spectators had seen a more attractive game in 1906, and he predicted that the current season would be equally as fine if not better.[41] Camp was not the only person to change his views. Speaking at Harvard University on February 23, 1907, Teddy Roosevelt said.

It is to my mind simple nonsense, a mere confession of weakness, to desire to abolish a game because tendencies show themselves . . . which prove that the game ought to be reformed. Take football, for instance. The preparatory schools are able to keep football clean and to develop the right spirit in the players without the slightest necessity ever arising to so much as consider the question of abolishing it. There is no excuse whatever for colleges failing to show the same capacity, and there is no real need for considering the question of abolition of the game.[42]

Although American football reached its nadir in 1905, true reform came slowly. During the next few years players, coaches, and officials slipped back into old habits. Mass play reappeared; the forward pass was ignored as too difficult or too risky, and black headlines tell of mounting injuries and fatalities. In the fall of 1909, another crisis occurred — one almost as serious as that of 1905. A total of thirty killed (eight of them college men) and 216 injured gave critics plenty of ammunition. Ever alert to such statistics, the *Nation* charged, "Football is not merely a sport, now; it is a contrivance for injuring and maiming."[43] The *Review of Reviews,* while agreeing that football was more combat than sport, attacked parents for remaining silent. Weekend orgies went hand-in-hand with bruising play on the gridiron — any metropolitan policeman could attest to that.

The outcry might have been less potent if it had not been for two very unfortunate deaths. Eugene Byrne, acting captain of the Army team, was fatally injured in the Harvard game on October 31. Play was immediately halted; Byrne buried with military honors, and the Army-Navy game for that year canceled. Two weeks later, a Virginia halfback, Archer Christian, died soon after being hurt in the Georgetown game. Georgetown immediately abandoned football, and a Virginia professor, obviously not familiar with the sport, suggested lacrosse as a less dangerous substitute for football. (During these weeks the District of Columbia banned football and New York City considered similar action.)

Charles Eliot, who had recently stepped down from his post at Harvard, was visiting at the British embassy in Washington when he learned of Christian's death. Ever critical of football, he hurriedly dispatched a note to his friend, Edwin A. Alderman, president of the University of Virginia. He reiterated that football by its very nature meant "deaths, broken bones, sprains, and damaged brains" and concluded with this plea: "May not the calamity of yesterday give you a chance to clarify the public thinking on risks in manly sports."[44]

Eliot was not the only person in Washington who was alarmed. A few blocks from where he was visiting lived a peppery, cantankerous Confederate veteran. Now seventy-six years old, controversial John S. Mosby of Mosby's Raiders issued a call to arms. Virginia was in a sense his alma mater. He had been suspended in 1853 for shooting a fellow student (a fracas which put him in jail for several months). Despite these unpleasant memories, Mosby sent a vigorous letter to University officials. When his words appeared in several newspapers, he felt the wrath of football partisans, and on December 7, 1909, the old warrior informed a member of Virginia's Board of Visitors (Thomas P. Bryan) that the school ought to banish football and all their intercollegiate sports as well!

I do not think football should be tolerated where the youth of the country are supposed to be taught literature, science & humanity. The game seems to overshadow everything else at the University. I believe that cock-fighting is unlawful in Virginia: Why should better care be taken of a game chicken than a school boy? The amusement is a renaissance of the worst days of the Caesars. You say that fox hunting is as dangerous as football but there is no public protest against it. The difference is a Hunt Club is not a public institution supported by the State like the University where the youth are sent to learn not only the Classics and Mathematics, but principles of Ethics. The persons who "ride to the hounds" for amusement are generally men of leisure, not boys. If one occasionally breaks his neck jumping a fence it is the concern of a very few. But what would you think of a University Club with a Professor as master of the Hounds? I think a fox chase every morning around the University would be as dignified and do less harm than the Professors who quit their scholastic duties to see a student killed at a football game. So[,] between football and the hounds I am for the hounds. I do not think any of the schools have been educated up to the point of keeping packs of hounds for their scholars.

If the teams were not school appendages but independent organizations and gave public exhibitions of skill as prize fighters, I would care nothing about them. The more that got killed the better. Football is only a polite term for prize fighting. Old Soldiers avoid useless exposure to danger and preserve themselves for occasions when duty requires it. Courage will keep. They know that "tempted Fate will leave the loftiest Star." People ride automobiles and railroads in spite of the danger for convenience and because the conditions of modern life require it. But unlike football, the danger of this mode of traveling is not the attraction. It has been said that the athletic training that Wellington's soldiers got at the English schools won Waterloo; *per contra*, I say that Jackson's men won their victories without such nursing. "Of two such lessons why forget the nobler and manlier one?"

It is notorious that football teams are largely composed of professional mercenaries who are hired to advertise colleges. Gate money is the valuable consideration. There is no sentiment of Romance for Chivalry about them. The swords of the Old Knights are rust. Ivanhoe broke his lance against the Templar to rescue Rebecca. His reward was the song of the troubadour.[45]

This blast, if flowery and verbose, summarized the public's principal objections to football: too many players were injured or killed, studies were neglected, and professionalism and gate receipts corrupted academic life. Football was once more at the crossroads. Some magazines and newspapers demanded outright abolition. In a vigorous article entitled "The Case Against Football", *Outing* called for more rule changes and suggested that possibly the new Department of Labor and Commerce might say who could play. After all, football wasn't for kids![46] This article cited twenty-five fatalities in the 1909 season, fourteen of them youths about fifteen years of age.

Taking a more direct approach, *Harper's Weekly* asked the presidents of Yale, Harvard, and Princeton if they did not find "football as it is played this year a little rough?" More men had been killed and injured than ever before. They should either ban the game as Columbia had done, or make "Walter Camp and the other rules experts" give some consideration to saving both football and those who play it. "You could do it if you chose. You have the power — the moral power, if no other, and having the moral power, it is for you to consider how far you also have the moral responsibility."[47] Apparently Woodrow Wilson of Princeton and Arthur Hadley of Yale took note of this challenge. Both men considered abolishing football, but A. Lawrence Lowell, Eliot's successor at Harvard, hesitated. Thus no concerted action was possible.

In addition to these familiar cries, football men were alert to new dangers. Rugby was fast gaining favor on the West Coast. Both Stanford and California were fielding teams, and high schools throughout the state were abandoning football in favor of the English sport. Theodore Roosevelt, speaking at Cambridge University in May 1910, took note of this trend and commented upon the need for reform. One of the things he hoped to learn while in England was how to make American football "less homicidal" and more like its parent game. "I would not have football abolished for anything, but I want to have it changed, just because I want to draw the teeth of the men who always clamor for abolition of any manly game. I wish to deprive those whom I put in the mollycoddle class of any argument against good sport."[48]

Columbia's abandonment posed an even more serious threat to the game's promoters. For over two decades colleges had refrained from tampering with football, fearing deemphasis would be reflected in decreased enrollments. But even though Columbia abolished football, the school flourished. In 1903 it had 4,557 students; and in 1909, 6,132. During the same years Harvard's enrollment declined slightly, and Yale, despite success on the gridiron, saw its student body decrease even more sharply. It was obvious that an institutions's success as a center of learning did not depend upon football victories and weekend hoopla.

As football men gathered in New York City early in 1910 to ponder the future of their sport, they were greeted by still more alarming news. Princeton announced that it too was considering Rugby as a substitute for football.[49] Southerners meeting in Atlanta revamped the game completely. They ruled out piling on, approved measures encouraging the forward pass, outlawed swearing on the gridiron, and established an unorthodox scoring system. This Southern scheme, which gained little national support, scrapped field goals and awarded a point for each five-yard advance.

Despite Eliot's personal plea, Edwin Alderman spoke in favor of football at the New York meeting. He demanded drastic rule changes, however. Sixty of the seventy schools represented agreed with the Virginia educator. Revision was imperative! Five schools voted to abandon the game and five others wanted to leave the rules unchanged. Throughout the winter of 1910 the committee argued and haggled. Lengthy sessions in February, March, and April resulted in five specific changes. The flying tackle and pushing or pulling of the ball carrier by his teammates were prohibited. Playing time was divided into four fifteen-minute periods. There must be a seven-man line on offense, and an on-side kick had to travel at least twenty yards. But there was still no decision on the real issue — the forward pass. Many from the northeast were vehemently opposed to it. Robert Kernan, a former all-American at Harvard, contemptuously dubbed it "the diseased vermiform appendix of football, an utterly useless and highly dangerous play!"[50] Walter Camp remained convinced that the pass was much too risky. He stoutly maintained that several seasons of pass play substantiated his views. On the other hand, men from the south and midwest insisted it be made more attractive. This was the *only* way, they said, to achieve open play. (They could have added that with open play and the forward pass they hoped to break the monopoly which the northeast enjoyed.) Eventually their views prevailed, backed of course by public denunciation, the threat of Rugby, and possible abolition of football by stronghold such as Princeton.

On May 13, 1910, the rules committee concluded a heated ten-hour session at New York's Hotel Cumberland. In addition to changes announced earlier, members decided that a ball carrier could cross the line of scrimmage at any point, players caught crawling with a dead ball would be penalized, and the forward pass should continue as a legal play. More important, there was no longer a penalty for an incomplete pass. Play would be resumed at the line of scrimmage. Two years later the length of the playing field was reduced to one hundred yards, four downs replaced three, and the value of a touchdown was increased from five to six points.

It would appear that football had evolved into a game much like the one we know today. Threatened by a hostile press, state legislation, presidential decrees, competition from other sports, and growing independence on the part of college faculties, American football finally put its house in order. As play from 1906 to 1909 clearly demonstrated, however, reform tended to be half-hearted. As soon as reporters got interested in other matters and reformers found other evils to attack, bruising, bone-crushing formations reappeared.

Writing in *Harper's Weekly,* Luther Edwards Price surveyed the 1911 football season and concluded it presented a dismal picture. "Football," he noted, "has become more the art of using up players than using up the ball." It was little more than "a hodgepodge of pugilism, wrestling, and general mauling."[51] Price (Princeton '88) backed up his attack in a rather convincing fashion. During the 1911 season there had been fourteen tie games betweeen major teams. No touchdowns were scored by rushing when Harvard, Yale, Princeton, Dartmouth, Army, and Navy played each other. All tallies had resulted from field goals, fumbles, or intercepted passes. Although Price was critical of bruising play which produced such scores, he was no enemy of football. All he sought was a change in attitude. "We must get rid of the put-him-out-of-business spirit and play the game as fairly and decently as golf or boxing. Then," Price predicted, "will dawn the golden age of the game that makes boys into men eager to undergo hard work, privation, and peril for the sake of a good cause."[52]

A new spirit was infused into football two seasons later, but not in a manner that Price, Walter Camp, or anyone else could have anticipated. Army filled an open date on its 1913 slate with a small Indiana school, and on Friday, October 30, the Irish of Notre Dame arrived at West Point. Both teams were unbeaten. Notre Dame has scored easy wins over Ohio Northern, South Dakota, and Alma. Army had defeated Stevens, Rutgers, Albright, Colgate, and Tufts. The cadets, however, had edged Colgate by only one point, 7-6, and sneaked by Tufts, 2-0. The New York *Times* said that the visitors looked large, but Army wanted a "big score" and would probably get it easily. That Saturday on the Hudson the prayers of those who loved the game of football were finally answered. For, unknown to Army, two Notre Dame players had been practicing all summer in preparation for that afternoon. Let Knute Rockne tell in his own words the electric effect which the first pass had on some 5,000 spectators:

> Finally, Dorais called my number, meaning that he was to throw a long forward pass to me as I ran down the field and out toward the sidelines. I started limping down the field and the Army halfback covering me almost yawned in my face as he was so bored. Suddenly, I put on full speed and left him standing there flat-footed. I raced across the Army goal line as Dorais whipped the ball and the grandstands roared at the completion of a forty-yard pass. Everybody seemed astonished. There had been no hurdling, no tackling, no plunging, no crushing of fibre and sinew. Just a long-distance touchdown plunge by rapid transit.[53]

This is how the game, a stunning 35-13 upset, looked to a reporter:

The Westerners flashed the most sensational football that has been seen in the East this year, baffling the cadets with a style of open play and a perfectly developed forward pass which carried the victors down the field thirty yards at a clip. The Eastern gridiron has not seen such a master of the forward pass as Charley Dorais, the Notre Dame quarterback. A frail youth of 145 pounds, as agile as a cat, and as restless as a jumping jack, Dorais shot forward passes with accuracy into the outstretched arms of his ends, Capt. Rockne and Gushurst, as they stood poised for the ball, often as far as 35 yards away. The yellow leather egg was in the air half of the time with the Notre Dame team spread out in all directions waiting for it.[54]

Needless to say, Army was hopelessly confused. All five Notre Dame touchdowns came on passes. Press reports indicate that the Irish completed thirteen out of seventeen passes for 243 yards. Football men were aghast. Rockne, who said Army was better than the final score indicated, saluted the victory as "the first signal triumph of the new, open game over the old, battering-ram Army play." Still trying to figure out what had happened on the following Monday, a New York *Times* sports writer reflected that "with all its risks and difficulties the forward pass is the best ground-gaining play that can be developed under present gridiron difficulties."

Throughout the remainder of the 1913 season, spectators were treated to more wide-open play. The following weekend Dartmouth used passes to beat Penn, 34-21. The cadets themselves uncorked two passes in a 55-0 rout of Villanova on November 15, and Chicago won the championship of the West by beating Wisconsin, 19-0, again utilizing numerous aerials. The most interesting test of old vs. new football came in the Army-Navy game. During the previous seven years neither team had scored more than six points in a single game. When the teams met in New York City for the first time, some 42,000 spectators, including President Wilson, saw Army triumph, 22-9. Two Army scores came on passes. The cadets had obviously learned a lesson from the Irish.

Years later, as athletic director at the University of Detroit, Charles "Gus" Dorais wrote a small, but important book. *The Forward Pass and Its Defense.* His rules for the pass were simple and terse. Use it as a threat. Pass early in the game to loosen up the opposition's defense. Use the pass when least expected. Although legalized in 1906 and made more attractive in 1910, no one seemed to appreciate the full potential of the pass. True, Yale beat Harvard with a pass in 1906, 6-0, but despite cries for open play, coaches and players clung tenaciously to rough line formations because they knew that — given sufficient weight and size — they could usually batter their opponents into submission. Even after the 1913 season ended there were those who still scoffed. The forward pass was merely a fad. Midwestern schools, in their opinion, put too much faith in the pass play. As for Notre Dame's upset win over Army and the cadets' victory over Navy, those were made possible only by hard line play which wore down the weaker team.

Despite efforts to belittle that stunning 35-13 victory, the Irish must retain the honor of bringing about what so many reformers had long sought. Never again would bruising mass play be quite as attractive to fans, players, and coaches. While it may be too much to claim that the boys from South Bend *saved* football from oblivion it is obvious that they helped to usher in a new era in sports — the age of huge stadiums, Red Grange, and New Year's Day contests. For the true fan, in addition to the Notre Dame team of 1913, there is one other hero. More than any other individual, John Heisman, then coaching at Georgia Tech, led the fight for open play and the forward pass. In 1903 and again in 1904 he wrote to (of all people) Walter Camp, urging that football rules be changed. Receiving no satisfaction, Heisman shifted his appeals to other members of the rules committee.

For those who agree with the denunciations of Eliot and others, this story is a tale of lost opportunities. For two decades (1893-1913) football was in deep trouble. It seems that if such men as Edwin Alderman and Woodrow Wilson *and their faculties* had joined forces with Eliot, the sport might have been eliminated from American academic life. Faced with the realities of their own day, however, many educators chose to compromise their views or even to revel in the new prominence their institutions enjoyed each fall. Emerging from the gray decades of the late 1800s into an era of larger student bodies and increased public interest in higher education, it was easy to conclude that football was somehow responsible, if only partially so. And despite the outraged cries of a few, one could agree with a certain validity (as some still do) that the sport contributed much to college life. Yet if those who temporized, rationalized, or even gloried in the Saturday spectacles had foreseen the "Pandora's Box" which the gridiron held for many of them and their colleges and universities, it seems certain that they would have given President Eliot, Ranger Mosby, and Editor Godkin their unqualified, even enthusiastic support.

Footnotes

[1]"The Athletic Craze," *Nation*, LVII *(December 7, 1893), 422-423.*

[2]*Nation*, LVII (November 30, 1893), 403.

[3]New York *Times* (February 8, 1894).

[4]Theodore Roosevelt, "The Value of Athletic Training," *Harper's Weekly*, XXXVII (December 23, 1893), 1236.

[5]New York *Times* (February 8, 1894).

[6]*Ibid.* (February 18, 1894).

[7]"The New Football," *Nation,* LIX (November 29, 1894), 399-400.

[8]New York *Times* (December 1, 1894).

[9]*Ibid.* (December 3, 1894).

[10]*Nation*, LX (February 7, 1895), 101.

[11]*Ibid.*

[12]New York *Times* (November 24, 1895).

[13]*Ibid.* (November 29, 1895).

[14]Richmond (Va.) *Dispatch* (October 10, 1897).

[15]*Nation*, LXV (November 18, 1897), 387.

[16]*Ibid.* (November 25, 1897), 409.

[17]New York *Times* (November 10, 1897).

[18]*Ibid.*

[19]Caspar Whitney, "The Sports-Man's View Point," *Outing, XLI (January, 1903), 498-510.*

[20]*Nation* LXXVI (January 29, 1903), 83.

[21]*Ibid.* (February 12, 1903), 123.

[22]Elbert Hubbard, "A Gladiatorial Renaissance," *Cosmopolitan,* XXXIV (March, 1903), 597-599.

[23]See Edwin G. Dexter, "Accidents from College Football," *Educational Review,* XXV (April, 1903), 415-420.

[24]George F. Merrill, "Is Football Good Sport," *North American Review,* CLXXVII (November, 1903), 758-765.

[25]New York *Times* (February 2, 1904).

[26]*Ibid.* (November 25, 1904).

[27]*Ibid.* (November 20, 1904).

[28]*Nation* (December 1, 1904).

[29]*Nation* LXXIX (December 29, 1904), 513.

[30]"Football in Its Proper Light," *Nation*, LXXX (February 9, 1905), 108-109.

[31]See Henry Beach Needham, "The College Athlete," *McClure's*, XXV (June, 1905), 115-128; (July, 1905), 260-273.

[32]*Dispatch* (October 10, 1905).

[33]*Ibid.* (October 12, 1905).

[34]"Football Reform by Abolition," *Nation*, LXXXI (November 30, 1905), 437-438.

[35]*Ibid.*

[36]New York *Times* (November 21, 1905).

[37]Endicott Peabody, "After Football—What?, "*Harper's Weekly*, L (January 13, 1906), 56, 64-65.

[38]William H. Faunce, "The Value of College Athletics," *Outlook*, LXXXII (January 27, 1906), 151-152.

[39]New York *Times* (February 25, 1906).

[40]See "Football in Disfavor," *Outlook*, LXXXII (January 27, 1906), 151, for a report of Hughes' speech.

[41]Walter Camp, "Foot-Ball in 1907," *St. Nicholas*, XXXIV (September, 1907), 1012-1013.

[42]*Theodore Roosevelt Cyclopedia*, ed. Albert Bushnell Hart and Herbert Ronald Ferleger (New 41), 182.

[43]"The Football Deaths," *Nation*, LXXXIX (November 4, 1909), 424-425.

[44]Eliot to Alderman (November 14, 1909), Alderman Papers, University of Virginia, Charlottesville, Virginia.

[45]Mosby to Bryan (December 7, 1909), University of Virginia, Charlottesville, Virginia.

[46]"The Case Against Football," *Outing*, LV (January 1910), 514-517.

[47]*Harper's Weekly*, LIII (December 4, 1909), 5.

[48]*Theodore Roosevelt Cyclopedia*, 183.

[49]New York *Times* (January 21, 1910).

[50]Ibid. (March 28, 1910).

[51]Luther Edwards Price, "Spoiling a Great Game," *Harper's Weekly*, LV (December 30, 1911).

[52]*Ibid.*

[53]Knute Rockne, *The Autobiography of Knute Rockne* (Indianapolis, 1931), 89.

[54]New York *Times* (November 2, 1913).

11

Progress And Flight: An Interpretation Of The American Cycle Craze Of The 1890s
by Richard Harmond

The machine cannot be divorced from its larger social pattern; for it is this pattern that gives it meaning and purpose. Every period of civilization carries with it the insignificant refuse of past technologies and the important germs of new ones; but the center of growth lies within its own complex. Lewis Mumford, *Technics and Civilization*, pp. 110-111.

As the nineteenth century neared its close, Americans had good reason to celebrate the technological accomplishments of the past several generations. Conveyor belts and interchangeable parts had sharply altered the system of production; the reaper and other farm machines had expanded enormously the output of food; the steam engine had revolutionized long distance transportation on water and land; and the utilization of electricity was transforming methods of communication, lighting and local travel. For a people who tended to measure progress in quantitative terms, especially by an improvement in physical well-being, an increase in utility, or a growth in power and speed the mechanical advances of the nineteenth century were truly dazzling.[1]

There was another side to the story, though, for the material progress wrought by machines had been costly. Within a brief span, as history measures time, technology had changed the United States from a rustic, primitive land to an industrial giant.[2] That shift, involving as it did great social and economic dislocations required extensive and often wrenching adjustments on the part of the populace. During the 1890s the process of adjustment became particularly painful.

Richard Harmond is Professor of History, St. John's University.

From Richard Harmond, "Progress and Flight: An Interpretation of the American Cycle Craze of the 1890s," Journal of Social History, 5 (Winter 1971): 235-57. Copyright © 1971 by Journal of Social History.Reprinted with permission.

It was no coincidence that the bicycle rose to popularity at this time. Some years before, because it had been difficult and even hazardous to manipulate, Americans had built up a prejudice against the bicycle. But after the appearance of the safety bicycle, their prejudice subsided. Once this was accomplished, Americans discovered the bicycle to be a craft of speed and liberation, as well as an efficient and highly useful device. At the same time, the vehicle enabled them to escape some of the less desirable conditions associated with their technologically oriented society. And it was this paradoxical attraction of the bicycle — as an instance of inventive progress and as a means of flight from the consequences of such progress — which substantially explains the great cycle craze of the years between 1893-96.

I

There is no question about the heightened interest, even the fervor, with which Americans greeted the bicyle in the mid-1890s, though it had not always been a widely popular vehicle. We should not forget that less than a decade earlier, in the era of the ordinary, enthusiasm for the bicycle was distinctly limited. Indeed, in those days the general public entertained serious reservations about the wheel.

The object of these negative sentiments, the ordinary or high wheeler, was the standard bicycle in the years before the rise of the safety. With its tubular steel frame, ball bearings, and hollow or spongy rubber tires, the ordinary of the mid-1880s was a vast technical improvement over the "bone shaker," a vehicle which had exhausted the patience and vigor of riders in the late 1860s.[3] Unfortunately, the high wheeler was hard to master and dangerous to use. The prospective rider usually devoted weeks of effort and endured frequent spills acquiring the knack of mounting the vehicle; and he often spent further months of practice becoming a proficient cyclist.[4]

Nor was this the limit of his trials. Once confident of his ability to remain aloft, the rider ventured out to confront the challenges of the highway (if, that is, his locality permitted him on the highway). Gliding along, perched warily over the large front wheel of his cycle, he had to be prepared for several dangers. Among these might be the frightened reaction to his approach of a bicycle-shy horse, harassment from prankish youngsters or the malicious determination of a teamster to drive him off the road. A more common occurrence was for the cyclist to hear a "yelp" and a "bound" and, turning, see "some large fearless dog" rushing after him. Besides these risks, the rider also continually had to be alert for a jarring encounter with a rock or some other obstruction in the road, which could send him hurtling over the handle bars of his rather unstable vehicle.[5]

All in all, wheeling in the 1880s had its drawbacks. "The greatest wonder to me," one rider aptly recalled, was "that not more cyclers who rode high wheelers were killed." We can readily appreciate why the hazards of riding the ordinary were, according to another contemporary, "commonly imagined to be about the same as those which beset the professional tightrope walker."[6]

Nevertheless, the ordinary had its hardy band of devotees. To those bold and persistent men who were able to manipulate it, the high wheeler was a source of healthy outdoor exercise, pleasure and, if need be, transportation.[7] But the number of such riders, though it grew steadily, was never large and clearly had a limit. Bicycling in the 1880s was an activity restricted to athletically inclined men. Most probably it would have remained so had the ordinary not been supplanted.[8]

Even as those youthful athletes rode about, proud and high on their ordinaries, ingenious men were at work devising a machine for the average person. As early as the 1870s, but more especially in the years 1885-90, the cumulative achievements of a group of largely European inventors resulted in a bicycle that was at once safe to ride and relatively easy to pedal. Its notable features included the tubular construction and ball bearings of the ordinary, along with two equal-sized wheels (thus eliminating headers), chain-gear drive, a diamond-shaped frame and pneumatic tires. This, of course, was the safety bicycle, and it was quickly made available to the American public.[9]

Americans did not, however, become an eager army of buyers. In the first place, early models of the safety were subject to criticisms. The machine was, for instance, quite heavy, some versions weighing seventy pounds or more. The pneumatic tire was also considered overly puncture-prone.[10] Moreover (and the difficulties just mentioned did not help matters here), because of real or vicarious experiences with the old high wheeler, people remained suspicious of any kind of a bicycle.[11] Lastly, at a list price of $125 or more for top grade models, the new vehicle was expensive and seemingly beyond the means of a large part of the public.

All of these problems would have to be resolved before there could be any real boom in bicycling. In one way or another — beginning with the safety's design — the cycle industry did meet them successfully, and, in the process, climbed from obscurity to industrial eminence.[12]

The evolution of the bicycle between 1890 and 1895, though less dramatic than during the previous half decade, was nonetheless impressive. In 1891-1892 an improved pneumatic tire was placed on the market, and well before the end of the latter year it had demonstrated its superiority over the rival cushion tire. The attributes of the new tire were essential to the further development of the safety.

Because it reduced rolling friction, the air-filled tire added to a vehicle's speed; and because it absorbed road shock, the tire not only increased riding comfort, but also enabled manufacturers to cut back on the weight of the bicycle. By 1893 the machine had dropped to thirty-five pounds, and over the course of the next two years it shed another ten to twelve pounds. Moreover, inventors and engineers made other useful changes in the cycle, such as the installation of a more effective coaster brake and the substitution of wooden for metal rims. By the mid-1890s the American bicycle had reached a stage where the *Scientific American* could describe it as "the most beautiful mechanism, and the lightest and easiest running of any wheel manufactured in any country."[13]

The emergence of a safe and, at the same time, light and comfortable machine did much to overcome popular suspicion of the wheel. Equally effective in combating current skepticism was a wide-ranging promotional campaign. The bicycle industry, seeking to infuse wheeling with a sense of excitement and adventure, supported racing tournaments and subsidized top speed riders.[14] Concomitantly, the industry launched an advertising campaign so extensive that, in the opinion of one scholar, it stimulated advertising in other fields. Bicycle interests allocated thousands of dollars annually to instruct the public about the lightness, swiftness, strength and beauty of their product. Some of this sum was spent on catalogues and posters, but most of the money went for advertisements which appeared in trade periodicals (of which at one time there were over eighty), as well as the big daily newspapers and the better magazines. In return, by running editorials and regular columns on the wheel, plus special articles by bicycle enthusiasts and medical men, the press and magazines made cycling an increasingly more discussed and respectable activity.[15]

For anyone convinced by what he read in his favorite daily or magazine, but perhaps slightly hesitant about facing the road alone, companionship was available in a variety of cycling clubs. Riders might sign up with the League of American Wheelmen, a large national organization which, like the American Automobile Association of another era, defended the rights and promoted the broader interests (with special emphasis on better roads) of the riding fraternity. Or, if the League did not seem suitable, a cyclist could enlist in one of the numerous local touring-social clubs that were springing up in cities and towns across the land.[16]

Advertising and clubs by themselves were not enough, however, for there was still the obstacle of price. To overcome this hurdle, the cycle trade presented its clientele with a parcel of options and inducements.

To start with, the customer was not limited to the top grade machines listed at $125 and above. He might also shop around among the medium grades, with prices ranging between $85 and $100; or he might select from among the low grades, marked at about $50. The careful buyer knew, too, that all of these prices were subject to change. He realized, for example, that as a result of overproduction, manufacturers and dealers periodically hawked their wares at sharply reduced prices. And, if he followed trade matters closely, he was aware that, because of the use of mass production techniques in the manufacture of bicycles, the drift of prices was downward.[17]

Again, the patron, if he wished, could make his purchase on the installment plan. He also expected the retailer to give him a liberal trade-in allowance on his old machine. This widely established practice, in turn, laid the basis for a thriving second-hand business, where adequate bicycles were placed within reach even of people earning very modest incomes.[18]

As we can see today, installment buying, trade-ins and the larger engineering and promotional effort of which these were a part, had their intended result. Statistics and some relevant contemporary observations suggest as much. In 1890, at the dawn of the modern bicycle age, there were only about 150,000 riders in the United States. But the new safety began to prove so attractive to segments of the public that in 1891 a columnist for *Sporting Life* felt confident enough to predict that "wheeling is going to be the universal sport." The following year, a writer in the *American Athlete* asserted that bicycling "in the slang vernacular," had " 'caught on,' " and some months later an editorial in the same magazine declared with assurance that the possibilities ahead for cycling were "practically immeasurable judged by the occurrences of the past few years."[19]

Such optimism was well founded. While estimates vary, it seems likely that by 1893 there were close to a million riders in the United States.[20] The old prejudice against the bicycle, as commentators recognized, had finally been overcome.[21] Any lingering doubts on this score were dispelled in the summer of 1894 as society people took to the safety, and cycling became a "marked feature of the Newport season." Moreover, society was joined on wheels by a flock of literary and public figures, including E.L. Godkin, Richard Harding Davis, Owen Wister, Frances Willard, Lillian Russell, Justice Edward D. White of the Supreme Court and Speaker of the House Thomas B. Reed.[22]

And so, with cycling taking on a life and style of its own, the silent steed entered the halcyon years of the mid-1890s. This was a time when it appeared that no one "article of use, pleasure, or sport," in the words of the *American Wheelman,* had ever before retained "such a hold on popular approval, popular taste, or popular fancy as the bicycle." Across the land adults of all ages and both sexes surrendered to the bicycle passion, although it was in the urban-suburban complexes of the northeast and midwest that the largest body of riders was to be found.[23] By 1896, as the cycle craze reached its peak, there were probably four million riders in America. This was a striking figure when compared with the 150,000 or so cyclists of 1890.[24]

In the meantime, the bicycle, once reviled as a dangerous toy, became the subject of songs, poetry, fiction and earnest social commentary. Talk of its being something of a fad was generally dismissed. More commonly, the safety was credited with initiating "a new era in the means of passenger transportation." More than that, it was seen as a "new power" discovered by the human race, and "as a new social force," even a "revolutionary" social force which "could not be abandoned without turning the social progress of the world backward." With characteristic understatement, the *Times* summarized the dominant view by announcing that the wheel had "come to stay," and was to be "one of the powerful elements in shaping social habits."[25]

In the long run, these pronouncements turned out to be somewhat overblown, but at the time they represented the very real popularity and importance which the bicycle had attained in the America of the mid-1890s.

II

Advertising and aggressive merchandising undoubtedly sold a lot of bicycles, but the safety achieved its enormous popularity both for what it proffered and for what it came to represent. On the one hand, the safety promised its riders the pleasures and advantages of speed, good health, greater freedom of movement and utility. On the other hand, it beckoned to them to ride swiftly away from their problems and fears. In short, the bicycle was both a mechanism of progress and a vehicle of flight.

It was not strange that Americans had come to associate speed with the progress of civilization. A mobile, energetic and enterprising people, they knew that swift transportation and communication had been indispensable to the unification and exploitation of their huge and productive land. They had also witnessed the material achievements of such rapidly functioning devices as the sewing machine, typewriter and high-speed press. It may be, too, that, at a different level of consciousness, speed and the closely related desire to save time had become important goals to Americans because, as a people, they were increasingly more concerned with temporal events, rather than those which were to take place in eternity. At any rate, by the 1890s Americans were captivated by the idea of speed, and much of the attraction of the bicycle stemmed from the fact that the vehicle was able to actualize this idea in a highly gratifying fashion.[26]

Riding a bicycle was obviously a pleasurable activity. Since the men and women of the 1890s belonged to the first and *last* generation of adults to learn how to cycle, their initial sense of delight stemmed from encountering a new and exciting kind of motion. One rider vividly related his earliest experience with this new form of motion. He was a trainee at an indoor cycling school in New York; the experience the cyclist describes is after a difficult and frustrating lesson.

Toward the end of my session I discovered that I didn't have to keep a tight rein or to be constantly trying to bend the handlebars, and then, all of a sudden, I was going round and round the place, not pushing pedals, but flying. My world took on a new aspect. I was master, or about to become master of the poetry of motion, of what began to seem there and then the most fascinating and exhilarating method of locomotion that man has ever invented.[27]

As a rider developed more skill and confidence, and as his wheel became "a mechanism of life, the cyclist's other self in steel and rubber," his fascination and exhilaration grew apace. To the joy of motion was now added the delight of a new and "fresh sense of power," which the cyclist received from his relatively effortless passage along the road. Pedaling on, at an "easy and rapid" clip, the rider might be "lifted out" of himself, "up, up from the body that drags." Or, he may have quickened his pace, given himself up to "jolly abandon," and undergone the zestful thrill which inheres in fast and risky flight.[28] In the case of some riders, speed became an irresistible temptation. Contemporaries labelled as "scorchers" those consumed by this passion.

If cycling offered the psychic pleasures of motion and speed, it also conferred other more measurable benefits. One of the most important of these, in the opinion of medical men, was a firm and healthy body.

Doctors and others who studied the subject had grown deeply concerned about the effects which the spreading pattern of sedentary living was having on the population's physical condition. Through most of the nation's history, these authorities asserted, the average American had received all of the exercise he needed in his daily round of chores on the farm or in the shop. "Civilization itself was a gym," as a writer in *Outing* pointed out. But as the nineteenth century progressed, and the wilderness was tamed and cities were established, greater numbers of people began to earn their livelihoods at less physically demanding tasks in factories, offices and stores. Life grew softer in other ways, too. Trolley cars, for example, induced city dwellers to walk less and elevators relieved them of the necessity of climbing stairs. By 1890, according to one alarmed observer, this easier scheme of living had produced a generation of people "prematurely aged," and possessing "easily prostrated physiques."[29]

The medical men of the 1880s and 1890s concluded that exercise was essential to offset the physically debilitating effects of the sedentary life.[30] Hence, they urged Americans to compensate for the missing muscular effort of their forefathers with various forms of artificial activity. And most doctors agreed that among the best of such activities was cycling, for it exercised not only the legs but also the upper parts of the body and, performed regularly and moderately, strengthened the heart and lungs. Moreover, wheeling was fun, exposed the participant to the open air, and engendered "a feeling of brain rest and mental refreshment."[31]

The medical endorsement of cycling played its part in encouraging people to take up the sport. But it is equally apparent that the safety bicycle itself had a very large role in winning converts to what one historian of the Gilded Age calls "the new gospel of physical activity."[32] As a doctor, in a paper read before the New York Academy of Medicine in December, 1894, suggested, the safety was "probably the greatest factor" influencing the extension of the doctrine of physical culture in nineteenth-century America.[33]

This was particularly evident in the case of women. Most medical men contended that physical recreation was every bit as necessary for women as it was for men.[34] Yet an "old and conventional belief," as one lady phrased it, had long limited women's participation in energetic outdoor activities. By the closing decade of the nineteenth century a little progress had been made against this "deep-rooted prejudice." Women, for instance, participated in such sports as archery, tennis, croquet and golf. But these activities had not acquired anything resembling a mass appeal.[35] The generality of women needed an easily learned, enjoyable, outdoor exercise which, at the same time, did not tax their strength nor seriously breach current standards of decorum. Cycling met these conditions. Not surprisingly, then, American women, who had been "starving for sunshine, fresh air" and some sport "to keep their bodies healthy and robust," took eagerly to the wheel. And thus began the widespread participation of women in outdoor athletics.[36]

Not that controversy was absent from the encounter between women and the wheel. The safety was charged with the responsibility of "leading young and innocent girls into ruin and disgrace," and having women assume an "immodest posture." But the strongest objections centered on the bicycle costume which, in the opinion of one typical critic, invited improper remarks from "the depraved and immoral."[37] If some guardians of public virtue cried out in alarm, however, their protests had little effect on the ladies or, for that matter, the general public. Moreover, doctors and leaders of the women's rights movement, enthusiastic cyclists, doffed their confining whalebone corsets, and donned shorter dresses, split skirts and even bloomers. By doing so these riders conquered their inhibitions, improved their health, and enlarged their sense of physical freedom. Without planning it that way, they also advanced the cause of dress reform by making a rational, freer-flowing garb more commonplace.[38]

Many riders, men and women alike, learned that cycling could be much more than a pleasurable and healthy activity. They found that their wheels furnished them with a novel and, in some ways, an unrivaled form of transportation. It was true that cyclists could not surpass the steam railway in speed of locomotion, and they had to make a sustained effort to equal the electric trolley, which averaged about 15 miles per hour. Still, on a smooth, level road they could take sprints of up to 25 miles per hour. Then, too, unlike railroad and trolley passengers, bicycle riders did not have to pay fares or wrestle with jostling crowds; and above all, they were neither bound by time schedules nor confined or fixed routes. They were independent travelers.[39]

Only the horse offered an independence of movement comparable to the bicycle, though on several counts the silent steed was clearly superior to the neighing one. Since a good horse cost about $150 (without a carriage), and another $25 or so each month for upkeep, a safety was far cheaper to own than a horse. Moreover, the practiced cyclist could travel at the same, or even a faster rate of speed, and go much farther than an individual lumbering along in a horse-drawn buggy. And, when the cyclist reached his destination, he did not have to feed, water and bed down his silent steed. He simply picked up his safety and parked it inside the doorway.[40]

Where the roads permitted, cyclists could travel as their mood or mission dictated. Many chose to roam over the world around them. Riders skipped religious services — and thus incurred clerical wrath — to spend their Sundays touring the countryside. People took their vacations on wheels. Some visited neighboring states, and others, more distant parts of their native land. A few even sailed for Europe and, arriving there, set out on their bicycles to explore, in leisurely and independent fashion, the landscape and historic sites of the Old World.[41]

By putting Americans on the move, the bicycle opened up new vistas to its users. This was especially so in the case of young people from culturally limited small towns. One cyclist recalled this of his youth:

On the bicycle you could go where you pleased, fixing your own schedule. It took you to "the city" to attend a theater matinee and be back home in time for the evening meal. Soon after I owned a bicycle I rode with two other boys the sixteen miles from our Ohio town to Dayton and, at a cost of fifty cents for a seat in the peanut gallery, saw Joseph Jefferson in *Rip Van Winkle,* the first good actor any of us had ever seen. That was *living.* Our horizons were broadening.[42]

Others unearthed more practical uses for this new mode of transportation. Thousands of people, some of whom lived in the suburbs, rode back and forth to work each day on their bicycles. Ministers, doctors and salesmen made their calls on wheels. Botanists and geologists found the safety a valuable aid in their field work; while artists, photographers, park commissioners, sanitation foremen, letter carriers, tradesmen and delivery boys, among others, used the vehicle to facilitate their tasks.[43]

With so many pedaling about, New York and other cities established mounted police squads to run down scorchers and bicycling burglars. The men attached to these squads were also adept at capturing runaway horses. Theodore Roosevelt, who was a New York City Police Commissioner in the mid-1890s, observed that the members of that city's bicycle detail

soon grew to show not only extraordinary proficiency on the wheel, but extraordinary daring. They frequently stopped runaways, wheeling alongside of them, and grasping the horses while going at full speed; and, what was even more remarkable, they managed ·not only to overtake but to jump into the vehicle and capture, on two or three different occasions, men who were guilty of reckless driving, and who fought violently in resisting arrest . . . .[44]

As the foregoing discussion indicates, the modern bicycle was a highly versatile device. In an age of utility this alone would have been sufficient to have it counted among the era's distinctive mechanical improvements. But the safety's identification with the forces of progress involved much more than its mere usefulness to the professions, business and government. To contemporaries, it was bettering the people's physical well-being, unifying the nation by breaking down regional and cultural barriers, acting as "the advance agent of personal freedom in locomotion and in costuming" and, most significantly, satisfying the American love of speed. No wonder the wheel was ranked with the great inventions of the age.[45]

To those fascinated by new machines, as most Americans were, the bicycle was even something of a symbol of nineteenth-century technologial advancement. As a cycling book of the time presented the situation, an "individual starting out with a twenty-five pound machine, a light cyclometer, a small bicycle clock, and a compact camera" was indeed a "most wonderful example of the world's progressiveness." In a more philosophical vein, the *Scientific American,* impressed with its speed and power, saw the lithe, two-wheeled machine as "one expression of the great world struggle of mind to overcome the inertia of matter."[46]

Coursing through the cycling literature, however, was another less compelling, but nonetheless insistent theme — escape. The very technological progress which the bicycle typified had brought about a tension-prone, and sometimes strife-torn, industrialized society, and the wheel seemed to assure cyclists an opportunity for forgetfulness and flight.

There were few who protested the opinion of a contemporary that "nervousness" was the characteristic malady of the American nation.[47] It was not considered accidental, either, that this nervousness had appeared after several decades of unprecedented technological changes or that the condition seemed to be such a marked feature of urban life. Economist David A. Wells, for instance, suggested that the replacement of the slow-moving letter by electrical communication had so accelerated the decision-making process of businessmen, that the increased mental and emotional pressure on them had led to an alarming rise in nervous and physical disorders. The *Chicago Tribune,* surveying a broader range of mechanical innovations, remarked that it was the American's "fate to live in an age when railways, telegraphs and fifty other inventions" had added "immeasurably to the wear and tear of the individual and separate units of society." Approaching the matter from a slightly different angle, a Harvard professor explained that his was an age of progress, but that the price had been high. This could be seen, he went on, in the big cities where civilization was most advanced, but where life was most rapid and intense. These urban centers, he believed, were "like so many great furnaces," consuming their inhabitants "in order to keep the machinery of our complex social organism in motion."[48]

There was no dearth of advice for the nerve-wracked Americans of the "great furnaces." Cycling restored one's "confidence and cheerfulness," advised a physician, and caused the future once again to look "bright and full of hope." Or, as the author of *Hygienic Bicycling* informed his readers, on wheels "all morbid thoughts take their flight." Others offered similar counsel.[49] A Boston clergyman, for example, in an address entitled the "Mission of the Bicycle," spoke to his Sunday congregation.

We long to lay aside the dignity of manhood and womanhood, to flee away for a few hours from the serious business of life, but there is no escape.

But suppose you own a wheel. There is your escape. There is your instrument of fun and frolic, and you can take your dignity along. The time for the duties of the day is over. You mount your silent steed, and there is motion and speed and change of scenery; there is forgetfulness, for the time, of cares and duties; you glide along, and lo! you are at the summit of the hill.

You place your feet on the coasters and glide away toward the base, and you are a boy again sliding down hill, only you have no sled to draw up, for you ride both ways. Before you know it laughter comes back. Sunshine fills the soul. The cares of life, and its duties thereafter are cushioned with the pneumatic tires, and the fun of youth becomes projected through our maturer years. Try it, and you will say that the half has never been told.[50]

Devotees of the wheel also reminded overwrought insomniacs that bicycling was a "nerve calming medicine," and a "sweet restorer" and inducer of "nature's sweetest restorer — dreamless sleep." It may even be that for some cyclists, scorching — referred to by a disgusted Englishman as "cyclomania" — was a form of escape.[51]

A physical relief from the tensions of society was one benefit. A number of cyclists, though, looked to Nature for peace of mind. They mounted bicycles, fled the city's " 'maddening crowd,' " and headed for the country. Once there, miles from "so-called civilization," they refreshed themselves with the sights and smells of green fields, brightly colored flowers and stretches of shadowy woods.[52] One poet wrote thusly of the bicycle:

Care-worn city clerks it hurries off to
nature's fairest scenes
Flower-decked meads and, trellised hop-grounds;
babbling brooks and village greens.
Round-backed artisans it bears, too, from
the small and stuffy room,
To the lanes where trailing roses all the
summer air perfumes;
And it makes them grow forgetful of the
stifling, man-made town,
As they climb the breezy roadway o'er
the swelling, God-made down,[53]

In a more prosaic fashion, the Pope Company — the largest of the American bicycle manufacturers — explained the benefits of wheels in one of its cycling catalogues.

The man of sedentary habits throws off the confinements of the office, and seeks relief in an enjoyment of nature. To ride into the country with ever-changing scenery, and to breathe the healthy air is fraught with enjoyment. The nerves are relieved, and sound health and sleep promoted.[54]

Inasmuch as cyclists were able to ride away from their problems and themselves, the wheel acted as an emotional palliative. Though far from a unique occurrence — one thinks, for example, of the motion picture projector — it was no small achievement for a machine to be the means by which people temporarily delivered themselves from the disruptions and stresses of a machine-based society.[55]

Yet some contemporaries seemed more impressed with the bicycle as a possible harmonizer of economic class differences. Perhaps there was something to this. The bicycle craze had hardly begun when, in the spring of 1893, the country was hit by a financial panic which soon deepened into the worst depression in American history. Over the next three years the nation was staggered by labor violence, clashes between troops and workers and a farmers' revolt that culminated in the divisive McKinley-Bryan campaign of 1896. These were bitter years for America, and men talked gloomily about the future of the country.[56] Then the crisis passed. By 1897 the economy had revived, Populism had petered out, and a political peace settled on the land. But during the years 1893-96 — a period which coincided with the cycle craze — there were those who insisted that the bicycle had been a mechanism of stabilization.

The ability to own and drive a carriage was a distinguishing feature of the well-to-do urban resident in late nineteenth-century America — and, as such, beyond the reach of the masses. On the other hand, people in the most moderate circumstances scrimped and saved to buy bicycles.[57] They recognized that they then possessed a means of recreation and transportation which surpassed the horse and trap. And should a rich man purchase a safety, he was no better than anyone else on the road. He had to exert the same physical effort to move his machine and face the same conditions as other riders, and, at a distance or from the rear, his expensive new wheel was indistinguishable from a poor man's second-hand vehicle.

This was why some observers referred to the bicycle as the "great leveler," or as a democratic machine.[58] Here also was one reason why the safety may have served as an agent of social peace in the mid-1890s. Thus, John D. Long, President McKinley's Secretary of the Navy, declared that,

The bicycle is the great safety of modern days. The man who owns a bicycle rides his own steed. He throws his dust in the face of the man in the carriage, so that it is no longer pleasant to ride in a coach and four.[59]

Contemporaries believed, too, that possession of a bicycle gave its owner an opportunity to develop a new and diverting set of interests. A poor man, said Senator George Frisbie Hoar of Massachusetts, used his safety for transportation as well as exercise, and from his machine derived "innocent, healthy and harmless recreation." Moreover, as others suggested, ownership of bicycles admitted rich and poor alike to a new social class — the freemasonry of the wheel. ("There were but two classes of people," explained a contemporary, "those who rode and those who wanted to.") On the road, people from different social strata exchanged friendly greetings, and at rest they might chat about bicycles and related matters.[60]

The safety, according to a columnist of *Bicycling World,* had "made all men brothers." This was claiming too much. But it does seem clear, as a writer in the *Chicago Times Herald* remarked, that the bicycle had cheered "the spirit of man" in a time of economic depression. That we recall the 1890s as gay rather than grim is singular evidence of this observation.[61]

III

The time arrived, however, when adult Americans no longer looked to the safety to cheer their spirits. The cycle craze reached its high point in 1896 when the bicycle industry produced about a million vehicles. The following year manufacturers turned out over a million machines, but twice as many of these vehicles as the year before were shipped for sale abroad. Even better indices of somewhat lessened zeal for the wheel were the reduced coverage given to cycling in the press and magazines, the demise of many of the trade journals (in late 1897, for example, three of the big Chicago bicycle magazines consolidated), and the increasing involvement of prominent bicycle manufacturers in the development of a power-driven horseless carriage.[62]

Between 1898 and 1900, the interest of the American public in the bicycle continued to ebb. The industry manufactured at the rate of a million or more machines annually, but a growing portion of these went into the export trade. By 1901, according to one writer, Americans had even stopped discussing the safety. Three years later the industry's output had fallen to about 225,000 vehicles. The safety remained a factor in adult transportation for a few years more; but the bicycle era had clearly come to an end in the United States.[63] Why was this?

The bicycle won its popularity in part because it had indulged escapist impulses. Its tenure as a vehicle of flight was short-lived, however. To a certain extent this may have been because the feverish class hostility of the mid-1890s subsided with the return of better times and the decline of Populism. Whatever the state of the economy, of course, the stresses and demands of urban-industrial life persisted. But in the Spanish-American War, perhaps those seeking an emotional release from contemporary pressures came upon a more exciting outlet than cycling. As Lewis Mumford argues interestingly in his *Technics And Civilization,* nothing rivals warfare as a release from the tedium and tensions of a mechanistic society.[64]

A weightier consideration was the inability of the bicycle to maintain its place as a progressive machine. For a few years, one cyclist remembered, the safety had fulfilled "the ever-growing desire for greater and greater speed." But by the opening of the new century, people realized that the horseless carriage was superior in this category. Had not a steam-powered vehicle — capable of doing a mile in a minute and four seconds — paced the great Negro cyclist, Major Taylor, when he set the world record for a mile in one minute and nineteen seconds?[65] While it would be some years before the average American could afford an automobile, to a people enamored of speed the bicycle began to seem old-fashioned.

So, though the bicycle had answered the vague longing for a time-saving, distance-conquering, independent mode of transportation, in doing this it had also "whetted" the "public appetite for wheeled contrivances." The bicycle, as inventor Hiram P. Maxim pointed out, created a demand which it could no longer satisfy. "A mechanically propelled vehicle was wanted instead of a foot-propelled one," he wrote, "and we now know that the automobile was the answer."[66]

In this, as in so many other respects, the bicycle had prepared the way for the automobile. The safety, a perceptive contemporary remarked in *Outing,* was "but a single part in a great and widespread movement in transportation which it was in point of time at least, privileged to lead."[67]

The same point could as validly be made about woman's rights and popular recreation, as about transportation. In the long view, the bicycle was only one among many factors promoting the cause of dress reform and female equality. And those who wanted outdoor exercises, or an activity to counter nervous strain, had an increasing variety of sports to choose from in twentieth-century America.[68]

The bicycle had risen from its lowly status as a toy to its lofty station as a mechanical marvel because it had served progressive wants and desires and gratified escapist tendencies. By World War I, no longer able or at least no longer needed to fill these roles, the bicycle returned to its earlier place as an American toy. But it would be a mistake on this account to take lightly the safety's earlier prominence. In the mid-1890s the safety bicycle was an influential force in our national life and, what seems of greater note, a major expression of current beliefs and fears.

Footnotes

[1]Henry Steele Commager, *The American Mind* (New Haven: Yale University Press, 1950), pp. 5-8; Victor C. Ferkiss, *Technological Man: The Myth and the Reality* (New York: George Braziller, 1969), pp. 11, 66. For some contemporary statements, see *Scientific American,* LXXV (July-December, 1896), 50-51, *Century Magazine,* LII (May-October, 1896), 152; David A. Wells, *Recent Economic Changes* (New York and London: D. Appleton and Company, 1889), pp. 67, 370, 366; *North American Review,* CLXI (September, 1895), 299; Edward W. Byrn, *The Progress of Invention* (New York: Russell and Russell, 1900), pp. 4-6; *Munsey's Magazine,* XXIV (October, 1900-March 1901), 36, 40.

[2]Leo Marx, *The Machine in the Garden: Technology and the Pastoral Ideal in America* (New York: Oxford University Press, 1964), p. 343.

[3]C.F. Caunter, *The History and Development of Cycles* (Part I; London: Her Majesty's Stationery Office, 1955), p. 15-17, 20; *Sewanee Review,* V (1897), 50.

[4]Robert P. Scott, *Cycling Art, Energy and Locomotion* (Philadelphia: J.B. Lippincott Company, 1889), p. 118; D.B. Landis, "Evolution of the Bicycle and Its History in Lancaster County," *Historical Papers and Addresses of the Lancaster County Historical Society,* XXXV (1931), 283-84; *Wheel and Cycling Trade Review,* II (August, 1888-February, 1889), 285-433.

[5]Charles E. Pratt, *The American Bicycler: A Manual* (Boston: Houghton, Osgood and Company, 1879), pp. 106, 124, 125; *The Wheel,* May 15, 1885; *Outing,* I (October, 1882-March, 1883),5i; Hannibal Coons, "Bicycles Built For All," *Holiday,* IV (July, 1948), 83; Fred H. Colvin, *60 Years With Men And Machines* (New York and London: McGraw-Hill Book Company, Inc., 1947), p. 87.

[6]*Bicycling World,* XXV (September, 1892-March, 1893), 214; *Century Magazine,* LII (May-October, 1896), 785.

[7]*Outing,* I (October, 1882-March, 1883),204; *Chautauquan,* VIII (October, 1887-July, 1888), 458-59; Colvin, *60 Years With Men And Machines,* pp. 13-14.

[8]Foster Rhea Dulles, *American Learns To Play* (New York and London: D. Appleton-Century Company, 1940), p. 194; *The Living Age,* CCXVII (April-June, 1898), 856; Chauncey M. Depew, ed., *One Hundred Years Of American Commerce* (New York: D.O. Haynes and Company, 1895), p. 551.

[9]Caunter, *History of Cycles,* pp. 33-37; Waldemar Kaempffert, ed., *A Popular History Of American Inventions* 2 vols. (New York and London: Charles Scribner's Sons, 1924), I, 141.

[10]Henry Clyde, *Pleasure-Cycling* (Boston: Little, Brown and Company, 1895), p. 46; *Twelfth Census of the United States,* X (1900), 332.

[11]Cf. *infra.,* note 21.

[12]*Scientific American,* LXXIV (January-June, 1896), 4; LXXVII (July-December, 1897), 292; *Fifty Years of Schwinn-Built Bicycles* (Chicago: Arnold Schwinn and Company, 1945) p. 28. In 1890, the bicycle industry consisted of a few dozen shops and factories, employing 1700 people, and with invested capital of some two million dollars. By 1895 the industry was made up of over 300 shops and factories, employing 25,000 people and an invested capital in excess of twenty million dollars. Between 1890 and 1896 Americans spent over one hundred million dollars for bicycles.

[13]*Twelfth Census,* X, 332-34; *Scientific American,* LXXIV (January-June, 1896), 2.

[14]On the ties between bicycle manufacturers and racing, see the remarks by the President of the League of American Wheelmen in *Wheel and Cycling Trade Review,* XIV (November 2, 1894), 23.

[15]James P. Wood, *The Story of Advertising* (New York: The Ronald Press Company, 1958) pp. 283, 276-78; *Wheel and Cycling Trade Review,* IX (June 10, 1892), 18; *American Wheelman,* VIII (October 29, 1896), 38; XI (February 3, 1897), 14; *American Athlete,* XII (July 21, 1893), 51.

[16]*Outing,* XXX (April-September, 1897), 341-51, 488-94.

[17]*Wheel and Cycling Trade Review,* XI (June 16, 1893), 38; *Bicycling World,* XXXVIII (October-November, 1898), 81; Kaempffert, ed., *Popular History of Inventions,* I, 141; *New York Tribune,* August 8, 1897, p. 6. Thus, in 1895 the top grades were generally reduced to 1200, and two years later the price of these models was cut another $25.

[18]Wood, *Story of Advertising,* p. 282; *Wheel and Cycling Trade Review,* X (February 17, 1893), 44; *Bicycling World,* XXV (September, 1892-March, 1893), 432; XXXI (May-November, 1895), 677; Clyde, *Pleasure Cycling,* p. 45.

[19]*Bicycling World,* XXII (October, 1890-April, 1891), 239; *Sporting Life,* XVI (March 21, 1891), 10; *American Athlete,* IX (June 10, 1892), 489; X (December 9, 1892), 403.

[20]*American Athlete,* XI (March 31, 1893), 285.

[21]*Wheel and Cycling Trade Review,* XI (March 3, 1893), 27; *Bicycling World,* XXVIII (December, 1893-May, 1894), 579; *New York Times,* January 5, 1896, p. 25.

[22]*Scribner's Magazine,* XVII (January-June, 1895), 704-06; "Monthly Record," *Outing,* XXVI (April-September, 1895), 1; *The Critic,* XXIV (New Series: July-December, 1895), 107, 226-28.

[23]*American Wheelman,* VIII (July 2, 1896), 25; Arthur Judson Palmer, *Riding High: The Story of the Bicycle* (New York: E.P. Dutton and Company, 1956), p. 113.

[24]*Bicycling World,* XXXIII (July 10, 1896), 26; *Scientific American,* LXXV (July - December, 1896), 69; *New York Herald,* quoted in *Literary Digest,* XIII (1896). 196.

[25]*The Outlook,* LI (January-June, 1895), 1006; *Bicycling World,* XXXI (May-November, 1895), 137; *The Forum,* XXI (March-August, 1896), 680; *Harper's Weeky,* XL (January-June, 1896), 370; *Century Magazine,* L (May-October, 1895), 374; XLIX (November, 1894-April, 1895) 306; *New York Times,* June 21, 1896, p. 4.

[26]*Cosmopolitan,* XXXIII (May-October, 1902), 136, 131; Roger Burlingame, *Engines of Democracy* (New York and London: Charles Scribner's Sons, 1940), pp. 360, 372.

[27]*Scribner's Monthly,* LXVII (January-June, 1920), 635.

[28]*Outing,* XXIX (October, 1896-March, 1897), 516; Clyde, *Pleasure-Cycling,* p. 28; *Scientific American,* LXXX (January-June, 1899), 292; *American Athlete,* X (October 14, 1892), 278; *Harper's Weekly,* XI (January-June, 1896), 353.

[29]*Atlantic Monthly,* XC (October, 1902), 534; *Outing,* XXXII (April-September, 1898), 383; *North American Review,* CLH (January-June, 1981), 682-83; *Lippincott's Monthly Magazine,* XLV (January-June, 1890), 617.

[30]*Journal of the Franklin Institute, CXXIV (July-December, 1892), 230-35; Hospital,* as quoted in *Scientific American,* IX (January-June, 1889), 185; *Wheel and Cycling Trade Review,* V (February-August, 1890), 34.

[31]*New York Times,* May 21, 1893, p. 12; *Scribner's Magazine,* XVII (January-June, 1895), 708-12; *Scientific American,* LXXII (January-June, 1895), 5.

[32]Arthur M. Schlesinger, Sr., *The Rise of the City, 1878-1898* (New York: The Macmillan Company, 1938), p. 316.

[33]As quoted in Luther H. Porter, *Cycling for Health and Pleasure* (New York: Dodd, Mead and Company, 1895), p. 182. See also, Arthur Train, *Puritan's Progress* (New York: Charles Scribner's Sons, 1931), p. 400.

[34]*Journal of Social Science,* XXII (June, 1887), 46-47; *Literary Digest,* XI (May-October, 1895), 637; XIII (1896), 455-56.

[35]*Outlook,* LII (July-December, 1895), 349; *Nineteenth Century,* XXXIX (April-June, 1896), 797; Schlesinger, *Rise of the City,* p. 318; Train, *Puritan's Progress,* p. 300.

[36]*Bicycling World,* XXXVI (December 17, 1897), 19; Henry Collis Brown, *In The Golden Nineties* (Hastings-On-Hudson: Valentine's Manual, Inc., 1928), pp. 48-49.

[37]*Literary Digest,* XIII (1896), 361; *Bicycling World,* XXXV (July 23, 1897), 5; Dr. C.E. Nash, *Historical and Humorous Sketches of the Donkey, Horse and Bicycle* (Little Rock: Press of Tunnah and Pittard, 1896), p. 200; *New York Times,* May 16, 1899, p. 1.

[38]*New York Tribune,* May 12, 1895, p. 6; *Outlook,* LIII (January-June, 1896) 752; *Century Magazine,* LIV (May-December 1897), 473; *Cosmopolitan,* XIX (May-October, 1895), 394; *Bicycling World,* XXVI (January 14, 1898), 8; Andrew Sinclair, *The Better Half: The Emancipation of the American Woman* (New York: Harper and Row, 1965), p. 107; Dulles, *America Learns to Play,* pp. 266-67.

[39]Hiram Percy Maxim, *Horseless Carriage Days* (New York; Dover Publications, Inc., 1962), pp. 1-2; *Wheel and Cycling Trade Review,* XII (August 3, 1894), 17.

[40]*Bicycling World,* XXX (November, 1894-May, 1895), 957; *Harper's Weekly,* XL (January-June, 1896), 354; Burlingame, *Engines of Democracy,* p. 372.

[41]*The Forum,* XXI (March-August, 1896), 682, *Bicycling World,* XXXIII (May 29, 1896). 11; *The Arena,* VI (1892), 582; *The Living Age,* CCXIV (July, August, September, 1897), 714.

[42]Fred C. Kelly, "The Great Bicycle Craze," *American Heritage,* VIII (December, 1956), 70.

[43]*Bicycling World,* XXX (November, 1894-May, 1895), 957; *Century Magazine,* XLIX (November, 1894-April, 1895), 306; *Scientific American,* LXXIII (July-December, 1895), 50.

[44]*Bicycling World,* XXXV (September 10, 1897), 13; *American Wheelman,* VIII (September 17, 1896), 41: *Scientific American,* LXXIV (January-June, 1896), 291; Theodore Roosevelt, *An Autobiography* (New York: Charles Scribner's Sons, 1925), pp. 182-83.

[45]*Bicycling World,* XXXIV (May 7, 1897), 17; *Scribner's Magazine,* XIX (January-June, 1896), 783: *Munsey's Magazine,* XV (April-September, 1896), 131.

[46]W.S. Beekman and C.W. Willis, *Cycle Gleanings* (Boston: Press of Skinner, Bartlett and Company, 1894), pp. 10-11; *Scientific American,* LXXX (January-June, 1899), 292.

[47]*McClure's Magazine,* II (December, 1893-May, 1894), 305; Schlesinger, *Rise of the City,* p. 433.

[48]Wells, *Recent Economic Changes,* p. 350; *Chicago Tribune,* quoted in *Current Literature,* XV (January-June, 1894), 521; *North American Review,* CLXIV (January-June, 1897), 559-60.

[49]George B. Bradley, M.D., *Why Should We Cycle?* (New York, 1895), p. 6; H.C. Clark, *Hygenic Bicycling* (Delaware City, Delaware, 1897), p. 12; *Wheel and Cycling Trade Review,* XI (June 9, 1893), 24; *Universal Medical Magazine,* quoted in *Bicycling World,* XXV (September, 1892-March, 1893), 256; *British Medical Journal,* quoted in *Literary Digest.* XII (December, 1895-April, 1896). 377.

[50]*Wheel and Cycling Trade Review,* XI (May 5, 1893), 30.

[51]*Harper's Weekly,* XXXIV (July-December, 1890), 686: Porter, *Cycling for Health and Pleasure,* p. 11; *Bicycling World,* XXX (June 26, 1896), II; *The Living Age,* CCXV (October, November, December, 1897), 470-72.

[52]Edmond Redmond, ed., *The Bards and the Bicycle* (New York: M.F. Mansfield, 1897), p. 33; *Scribner's Magazine,* XVII (January-June, 1895), 702; *Bicycling World,* XXXI (May-November, 1895), 53, 93.

[53]Redmond, ed., *Bards and Bicycle,* pp. 129-30.

[54]Columbia Bicycles (Pope Manufacturing Company, 1892), p. 38.

[55]While this account focuses on America, it should be recalled that during the 1890s the bicycle was also popular in Britain and on the continent — and for some of the same reasons. Nor is this surprising. The United States and the advanced Western nations shared many of the same values (such as utilitarianism), and were undergoing a similar process of urbanization and industrialization. Stressing this latter point, John Higham has argued that in both America and Europe during the 1890s a boom in sports and recreation, and a heightened interest in nature attest to a

common reaction to the constraints of urban-industrial life. See John Higham, "The Reorientation of American Culture in the 1890's," in John Weiss, ed., *The Origins of Modern Consciousness* (Wayne State University Press, 1956), pp. 27-29, 32-33.

Higham has also suggested, however, that this reaction expressed itself in a somewhat different fashion on this side of the Atlantic. He notes, for instance, the lead taken by the United States in sports as well as the unusual ferocity found in American sports. It seems likely, too, that the widespread fascination with speed was peculiar to the American scene. But until a full analysis is undertaken of the bicycle in a cross-cultural setting, any remarks on the vehicle's comparative attractions must necessarily remain tentative.

[56]Ray Ginger, *Age of Excess: The United States From 1877 to 1914* (New York: The Macmillan Company, 1965), p. 158.

[57]Blake McKelvey, *The Urbanization of America, 1860-1915* (Rutgers University Press, 1963), p. 187; Mark Sullivan, *Our Times: The United States, 1900-1925, 6 vols. (New York and London: Charles Scribner's Sons, 1925-35), I, 243.

[58]*Century Magazine*, XLIX (November, 1894-April, 1895), 306; *Bicycling World*, XXXII (May 15, 1896), 11; *Detroit Free Press*, quoted in *Literary Digest*, XIII (1896), 197; *Wheels and Cycling Trade Review*, XX (September 17, 1897), 36.

[59]*New York Times*, June 3, 1899, p.6.

[60]*Cosmopolitan*, XIX (May-October, 1895), 394; *American Athlete*, XII (December 29, 1893), 539; *Harper's Weekly*, XLVIII (January-June, 1904), 906; *Lippincott's Magazine*, XLIX (January-June, 1892), 605; Kelly, "Great Bicycle Craze," *loc. cit.*, p. 73; *Scribner's Magazine*, LXVII (January-June, 1920), 636.

[61]*Bicycling World*, XXXIV (February 5, 1897), 23; *Chicago Times Herald*, quoted in *ibid.*, XXX (September 18, 1896), 17; Merrill Deninson, *The Power To Go* (Garden City: Doubleday and Company, 1956), p. 61.

[62]*Scientific American*, LXXV (July-December, 1896), 69; *Bicycling World*, XXXVII (September 16, 1898), 20; XXXVI (April 8, 1898), 29; Kaempffert, ed., *Popular History of American Inventions*, I, 142.

[63]*Scientific American*, LXXXII (January-June, 1900), 5; *Thirteenth Census of the United States*, VIII (1910), 475; *Twelfth Census*, X, 328; Victor C. Clark, *History of Manufactures in the United States*, 3 vols. (New York: McGraw-Hill Book Company, Inc., 1929), III, 156; *The Bookman*, XIII (March-August, 1901), 425; *Fifty Years of Schwinn-Built Bicycles*, p. 55.

[64]Lewis Mumford, *Technics and Civilization* (New York: Harcourt, Brace and Company, 1934), pp. 309-10.

[65]Andrew W. Gillette, "The Bicycle Era in Colorado," *Colorado Magazine*, X (November, 1933), 213; *New York Evening Sun*, January 24, 1900.

[66]*The Horseless Age*, I (November, 1895), 8; Maxim, *Horseless Carriage Days*, pp. 4-5.

[67]*Outing*, XXXV (October, 1899-March 1900), 641. For a summary of the numerous mechanical connections between the bicycle and the automobile, see Allan Nevins, *Ford: The Times, The Man, The Company* (New York: Charles Scribner's Sons, 1954), pp. 186-90.

[68]Frederick W. Cozens and Florence Scovil Stumpf, *Sports in American Life* (Chicago: The University of Chicago Press, 1953), pp. 28-29, 215ff.

Suggestions For Further Reading.

Barney, Elizabeth C. "The American Sportswoman." *Fortnightly Review* LXII (August 1894): 263-77.

Betts, John R. "Sporting Journalism in Nineteenth Century America." *American Quarterly* 5 (Spring 1953): 39-56.

Bissell, Mary T. "Athletics for City Girls." *Popular Science Monthly* XLVI (December 1894): 145-53.

Carter, Greg Lee. "Baseball in Saint Louis, 1867-1875: An Historical Case Study in Civic Pride." *Missouri Historical Society Bulletin* 31 (July 1975): 253-63.

Davenport, Joanne. "The History and Interpretation of Amateurism in the United States Lawn Tennis Association, 1881-1966" (Ph.D. dissertation, Ohio State University, 1966).

De Martini, Joseph R. "Student Culture as a Change Agent in American Higher Education: An Illustration from the Nineteenth Century." *Journal of Social History* 9 (Summer 1976): 526-41.

Fielding, Lawrence W. "Sport: The Meter Stick of the Civil War Soldier," *Canadian Journal of History of Sport and Physical Education* 9 (May 1978): 1-18.

Fielding, Lawrence W. "War and Trifles: Sport in the Shadows of Civil War Army Life." *Journal of Sport History* 4 (Summer 1977): 151-68.

Freedman, Stephen. "The Baseball Fad in Chicago, 1865-1870: An Exploration of the Role of Sport in the Nineteenth Century City." *Journal of Sport History* 5 (Summer 1978): 42-64.

Hardy, Stephen. *How Boston Played: Sport, Recreation, and Community, 1865-1915* (Boston: Northeastern University Press, 1982).

Kadzielski, Mark A. "'As a Flower Needs Sunshine': The Origins of Organized Children's Recreation in Philadelphia, 1886-1911." *Journal of Sport History* 4 (Summer 1977): 169-88.

Kaye, Ivan N. *Good Clean Violence: A History of College Football* (Philadelphia: J.B. Lippincott, 1973).

Korsgaard, Robert. "A History of the Amateur Athletic Union of the United States." (Ph.D. dissertation, Columbia University, 1952).

Lewis, Guy. M. "The American Intercollegiate Football Spectacle, 1869-1917." (Ph. D. dissertation, University of Maryland, 1964).

Lucas, John A. "Pedestrianism and the Struggle for the Sir John Astley Belt, 1878-1879." *Research Quarterly* 39 (October 1968): 587-94.

Martin, John S. "Walter Camp and His Gridiron Game." *American Heritage* XII (October 1961): 50-55, 77-81.

Paxson, Frederick, L. "The Rise of Sport." *Mississippi Valley Historical Review* 4 (September 1917): 144-68.

Pesavento, Wilma J. "Sport and Recreation in the Pullman Experiment, 1880-1900." *Journal of Sport History* 9 (Summer 1982): 38-62.

Rader, Benjamin G., "Quest for Subcommunities and the Rise of American Sport." *American Quarterly* 29 (Fall 1977): 355-69.

Redmond, Gerald. *The Caledonian Games in Nineteenth Century America* (Rutherford, N.J.: Fairleigh Dickinson University Press, 1971).

Reiger, John F. *American Sportsmen and the Origins of Conservation* (N.Y.: Winchester Press, 1975).

Richardson, Sophia E. "Tendencies in Athletics for Women in Colleges and Universities." *Popular Science Monthly* 1 (February 1897): 517-26.

Riesman, David, and Reuel Denney. "Football in America: A Study of Cultural Diffusion." *American Quarterly* 3 (Winter 1951): 309-25.

Roberts, Gerald F. "The Strenuous Life: The Cult of Manliness in the Era of Theodore Roosevelt." (Ph.D. dissertation, Michigan State University, 1970.)

Rosenzweig, Roy. "Middle-Class Parks and Working Class Play: The Struggle Over Recreational Space in Worcester, Massachusetts, 1870-1910." *Radical History Review* 21 (Fall 1979): 31-46.

Sack, Alan, "Yale 29-Harvard 4: The Professionalization of College Football." *Quest* 19 (Winter 1973): 24-34.

Seymour, Harold. *Baseball:* Vol. I. *The Early Years* (N.Y.: Oxford University Press, 1960).

Smith, Robert. *Social History of the Bicycle* (N.Y.: American Heritage, 1972).

Somers, Dale A. *The Rise of Sports in New Orleans, 1850-1900* (Baton Rouge: Louisiana State University Press, 1972).

Spalding, Albert. *America's National Game.* (N.Y.: American Sports Publishing, 1911).

Taylor, Marshall W. *The Fastest Bicycle Rider in the World* (1928; reprinted, Battleboro, Vt.: Green-Stephen Press, 1972).

Tobin, Gary Allan. "The Bicycle Boom of the 1890s: The Development of Private Transportation and the Birth of the Modern Tourist." *Journal of Popular Culture* 7 (Spring 1974): 838-49.

Voigt, David Q. *American Baseball:* Vol. I. *From Gentleman's Sport to the Commissioner System* (Norman, Okla.: University of Oklahoma Press, 1966).

Walker, Francis A. "College Athletics." *Harvard Graduates' Magazine* II (September 1893): 1-18.

Westby, D.L., and Allan Sack. "Commercialization and Functional Rationalization of College Football: Its Origins." *Journal of Higher Education* 47 (November-December 1976): 625-47.

Willis, Joseph D., and Richard G. Wettan. "Social Stratification in New York City Athletic Clubs, 1865-1915." *Journal of Sports History* 3 (Spring 1976) 45-63.

The Golden Age of American Sport: The Early Twentieth Century

Introduction

One of the many neglected areas in American sport history is that of youth sports. In the nineteenth century, boys' sport was mainly spontaneous, unregulated and unstructured games, which in the eyes of the most contemporary observers did little to improve the boys and actually may have been harmful by teaching them bad habits and promoting the organization of gangs. During the Progressive Era, a variety of organizations were established which sought to use organized sports to indoctrinate urban youth into appropriate patterns of social behavior. Many of these reformers believed that the world they had grown up with was crumbling due to such forces as urbanization, industrialization and immigration. They wanted to maintain the traditional American values which they associated with a simpler rural life, and believed that sports could provide a vicarious means of inculcating those values in young boys. In particular, it would be through adult-managed team sports that high moral principles and manly qualities would be taught. The ideological impetus for this movement came first from muscular Christianity, but was supplanted in the early 1900s by a theory of play based on biological evolution. One of the most important of the voluntary sports groups was the Public School Athletic League (PSAL) of New York, organized in 1903 by New York sportsmen, philanthropists, and educators to help remedy the pathological conditions of slum life. The work of the PSAL has been carefully examined by J. Thomas Jable in his essay "The Public Schools Athletic League of New York City: Organized Athletics for City Schoolchildren, 1903-1914." Jable points out that the PSAL sought adult-managed sport for all children, not just the most athletically gifted. Through its badge tests, class athletics, and interscholastic competition, the PSAL hoped to acculturate immigrant children, exercise social control, improve character values, and raise standards of physical fitness. It became an important model for other cities to emulate.

The position of the American woman in sport in the nineteenth century reflected the dominant Victorian attitudes towards women's frailty. A middle class wife was put up on a pedestal and idealized for her virtue and moral strength. However, women were not expected to work or engage in any vigorous physical activity. Doctors asserted that that would create female "problems" and weaken their reproductive organs. A pale and stout wife clearly symbolized the economic success of her middle class husband.

Until the 1880s, women's sports were restricted to "social" sports like croquet, ice skating, or perhaps horse-back riding. In that decade a number of upper class women began participating in two socially elite sports, golf and tennis (introduced to the United States by Mary Ewing Outerbridge), which were played using minimum exertion, while wearing long dresses. The innovation of the safety bicycle, followed by sports clothes, increased women's limited participation in physical activities. At the turn of the century the main sites for women's sports were the elite seven sister colleges. In his essay "The Rise of Basketball for Women in Colleges," Ronald Smith, a leading expert on American college sports, examines the development of competitive intercollegiate women's sports. Smith asserts that basketball was the principal sport among college women. He examines the role of women physical educators in first promoting, and then subsequently discouraging competition in favor of sport for fun, friendship, and health. These physical educators rapidly came to the conclusion that women's needs from sports differed from men and decided to modify men's basketball to make it more amenable to their goals and values.

During the early 1900s, one of the principal criticisms made of women's sport was that it made girls more masculine. The implications of this issue are dealt with at length in a selection included below by Dr. Dudley Sargent, one of the leading proponents of vigorous physical activity for women. Sargent was one of the foremost figures in the history of physical education. A physician, like many of the other early physical educators, his career spanned three decades. He was appointed director of Harvard's new Hemenway Gymnasium in 1879, and two years later founded the Sargent School of Physical Activity where he trained future physical educators. By 1887 women were being admitted to the Hemenway's summer sessions. In an article published in 1912 in the influential *Ladies' Home Journal,* one of the most important middle class women's magazines, Sargent dealt with the proposition that athletics made girls more manly. He promoted sports for women in addition to gymnastic exercises. Unlike most nineteenth century physicians, Sargent believed that sport was not inherently harmful for women, but could be exhilarating and health giving. He felt that women were physiologically similar to men.

Both sexes needed exercise and both could become capable athletes. However, he was worried that participation in sport could make women more masculine, which was not socially desirable. As a consequence, Sargent recommended that women's sports be modified versions of men's sports in order to fit the requirements of contemporary women. Women's sports should be shorter, less strenous, and nonviolent.

By the turn of the century, baseball was, without doubt, the national pastime. It was the sport most Americans participated in regardless of where they lived. The best players were professionals, who sought high-paying careers in Organized Baseball, which had over forty leagues by 1912. The goal of these men was to become major leaguers and earn salaries which were much larger than most Americans were then earning. The only other important spectator sports were college football, restricted largely to the college set, horse racing, and boxing. Both of the latter two sports were severely restricted by most state governments because they were crooked and prize fighting was brutalizing. These sports were severely tainted by rumors of fixes and the sin of gambling.

Baseball, on the other hand, seemed to represent all that was the best in America, and its flaws were generally rather conveniently forgotten. Most journalists, especially sportswriters, eulogized baseball as one of the finest indigenous institutions which had many positive contributions to make to American society. In the selection included below, "Baseball and the National Life," we have one of the most typical of those essays which could be found in every major mass circulation periodical of the early 1900s. This selection appeared in *Outlook,* a popular sports magazine aimed at a middle class audience. The author, H. Addington Bruce, was not a sportswriter, but a professional writer who wrote on a wide variety of subjects, especially psychological topics. In this essay Bruce analyzed the role that professional baseball was playing in American life. The author presented a psychological interpretation to explain baseball's unchallenged preeminence during the Progressive Era. He claimed that baseball had such important functions as providing a safety-valve for the pent-up emotions of its fans, teaching basic American values to both participants and players, and promoting social democracy and public health.

Americans viewed their national pastime through rose-colored glasses. Journalist McCready Sykes wrote an article for *Everybody's Magazine* in 1911 which he titled "The Most Perfect Thing in America." The conventional wisdom was that the sport had originated in the American countryside, that crowds included people from all walks of life, that owners were civic-minded citizens who operated their clubs out of their concern for their local communities, that players were primarily rural in origin, and that anyone with talent and hard work could become a major league ballplayer. However, baseball historian Steven Riess has examined various aspects of these perceptions and his evidence calls into question these conclusions. In an article which appeared in the first issue of the *Journal of Sport History,* entitled, "The Baseball Magnate and Urban Politics in the Progressive Era: 1895-1920," Riess analyzed the type of men who became owners of professional baseball teams. He discovered that almost every major league baseball team, and many minor league teams, were owned by men with prominent political connections. In fact, many were themselves professional politicians, frequently closely connected to the urban political machine. Owners utilized political connections to counter potential interlopers and make their clubs more profitable. They received protection against costly assessments and cumbersome city regulations, secured preferential treatment in terms of city services, and obtained valuable inside information about such matters as real estate developments and transportation innovations.

One of the most important functions ascribed to baseball by contemporaries and even historians, was that the sport provided a valuable source of social mobility to young Americans who were unable to achieve success through more conventional routes. Indeed, sport in general has been regarded as an excellent alternate route to social success for the poor uneducated youths of America who possess outstanding athletic skills. This subject has not been extensively studied, but it does appear that the value of sports as a source of social mobility has generally been exaggerated. This issue has received considerable study in regards to professional baseball. In an essay prepared especially for this anthology, Steven Riess has summarized the data he and other colleagues have accumulated on the social origins of professional baseball players active between 1871 and 1920. Riess points out that ballplayers were rarely drawn from the bottom levels of society which were in greatest need of alternate routes of vertical mobility, but from families of white native-born Americans, Germans, or Irish, where the father was either white-collar, a farmer, or an artisan (skilled worker). Riess also studied the subsequent occupations of major leaguers and found that by the early 1900s they were seldom sliding out of the middle class, although retirees were hard pressed to maintain the income level of a big league ballplayer.

The bloody sport of prize fighting was probably the most brutal and violent American sport. It was illegal in virtually every state. Nevertheless, the drama of a man-to-man confrontation captured the public imagination, and the legal and illegal fights were well covered by the press. Matches were patronized by the "sporting fraternity," a male bachelor subculture world that included well-to-do gentlemen, politicians, and street toughs. The boxers were all drawn from the bottom rungs of society. Only men with no alternate means to success would choose an occupation where they would be brutalized. Recruitment was relatively democratic. For example, around the turn of the century, there were three black world champions in the lighter weight classifications. In 1908 Jack Johnson won the heavyweight championship, which was the most prestigious crown in boxing. Johnson immediately became a threat to white society and a hero to poor blacks. Throughout his reign as champion (1908-1915) there were repeated efforts to find a "Great White Hope" to dethrone him and reassert the superiority of the white race. Johnson's symbolic importance transcended his boxing prowess. He has been described by his biographer, Al-Tony Gilmore of the University of Maryland, as the "Bad Nigger." Johnson threatened white American society because he mocked conventional norms by courting and marrying white women, driving fast cars, and showing no respect for authority. He was a proud black man, the Ali of his day, who refused to kowtow before the power structure even when his career and personal safety were threatened. Gilmore examines the powerful symbolism of Johnson's career and personal life in his essay "Jack Johnson: A Magnificent Black Anachronism of the Early Twentieth Century."

Historians generally regard the 1920s as the Golden Age of Sports. Improvements in living standards and the weakening of Sunday blue laws provided more Americans with discretionary time and the money to enjoy that time as they pleased. Each sport seemed to have its own great hero, like Jack Dempsey in boxing, Bobby Jones in golf, Bill Tilden in Tennis, Red Grange in football, and Babe Ruth in baseball. These heroes seemed to certify that such traditional American values like hard work and rugged individualism were still relevant even though the country had become a predominantly urban nation. Babe Ruth was the most important sport hero of the decade, and he carried his heroics into the 1930s when he supposedly performed such superhuman feats as hitting home runs for invalid boys in hospitals or calling a home run shot off Charlie Root at Wrigley Field during the 1932 World Series. In a brief essay taken from the *American Scholar,* the late renowned Jeffersonian historian Marshall Smelser summarized his impressions of the Babe which he discussed more fully in his biography *The Life That Ruth Built* (1975). Smelser argued that Ruth was admired for his prowess and his money making ability, and that his hedonism was part of his mystique. Babe Ruth made baseball fun and enjoyable, unlike the sport's earlier hero, Ty Cobb, for whom playing baseball was serious work. Ruth is seen as a hero of epic proportions, who, like the heroes of mythology, stirred the imagination and captured the affection of their respective publics.

12

The Public Schools Athletic League of New York City: Organized Athletics For City Schoolchildren, 1903-1914*

by J. Thomas Jable

> I counted the other day the little ones, up to ten years or so, in a Bayard Street tenement [which] for a yard has a triangular space in the center with sides fourteen or fifteen feet long, just enough room for a row of ill-smelling closets at the base of the triangle and a hydrant at the apex. There was about as much light in this yard as in the average cellar. I gave up my self-imposed task in despair when I counted one hundred and twenty-eight [children] in forty families.[1]

> Given idleness and the street, and he [New York City's youth] will grow without other encouragement than an occasional "fanning" of a policeman's club. And the street has to do for a playground. There is not other . . . . Year by year the boys grow bolder

*The writer expresses gratitude to John C. Glading, assistant director of the Center for Health and Physical Education in charge of the Public Schools Athletic League of New York City, and to James MacKay, coordinator of the Center for Health and Physical Education, New York City Public Schools, for their assistance and cooperation in providing most of the materials for this paper.

Thomas Jable is Associate Professor, Department of Physical Education, William Patterson College.

From J. Thomas Jable, "The Public Schools Athletic League of New York City: Organized Athletics for City Schoolchildren, 1903-1914," in Wayne M. Ladd and Andrea Lumpkin,eds., Sport and American Education: History and Perspectives (Washington, D.C.: 1979), pp. ix, 1-18. Reprinted by permission of the American Alliance for Health, Physical Education, Recreation and Dance, 1900 Association Drive, Reston, VA, 22091.

in their raids on property . . . Stoops, wagons, and in one place a show-case containing property worth many hundreds of dollars, were fed to the flames. It has happened that an entire frame house has been carried off piecemeal, and burned up . . . . The germ of the gangs that terrorize whole sections of the city at intervals, and feed our courts and jails . . . may without much difficulty be discovered in these early and rather grotesque struggles of the boys with the police.[2] [emphasis supplied]

Jacob Riis, social critic and reformer, used the above passages to describe the plight of New York City's youth during the Progressive era.[3] Amid this unhealthy atmosphere in America's largest, and perhaps greatest, city emerged the Public Schools Athletic League. Its emergence was triggered by two main forces. One was the horrid living conditions created by the rapid and amorphous growth of the industrial city which packed millions of people into squalid and dreadful tenement buildings, so well publicized by Jacob Riis and other heralds of reform. The other was the new "scientific" developments occurring within the field of education.

Two avant-garde educators, William James and G. Stanley Hall, adopting principles of the "new psychology," advocated a revised curriculum with the child as its focus. In the child-centered curriculum, play, they contended, is a great facilitator of learning. Their ideas came to fruition in the Progressive education movement when John Dewey molded them with his own philosophy and applied them in educational settings. It was but a logical step for progressive physical educators to apply the principle of the "new psychology" to their discipline. When Thomas Wood, Clark Hetherington and Luther Halsey Gulick, the leading physical educators at the turn of the century, called for the replacement of formal gymnastics and calisthenics in the curriculum with play, sports and games, they ushered in the "new physical education."[4]

Taking their cues from these progressive educators and social critics, New York teachers and enlightened civic leaders pooled their efforts and resources to organize and conduct athletics on a grand scale under the aegis of the Public Schools Athletic League. Through athletics, these concerned educators and citizens hoped to provide enjoyable experiences for schoolchildren and at the same time keep them out of trouble.

The purpose of this study is to examine the origin, growth, influence and contributions of the Public Schools Athletic League of New York City (PSAL) from its inception in 1903 until 1914 when it became an official branch of the Board of Education. More specifically, this study will explore the motives and rationale of its founders, particularly those of Dr. Luther Halsey Gulick, the physical educator most involved in its formation.

Luther Halsey Gulick's Philosophy of Education and Athletics

Early in 1903 the New York City Public School appointed Dr. Luther Halsey Gulick as the director of physical training.[5] His philosophy of education and athletics contributed greatly to the formation of the PSAL, and his efforts, combined with those of other educators and prominent citizens, made it a reality in a city trying to cope with the numerous problems of the industrial age. Gulick was the catalyst whose actions fused the various popular ideas on school athletics, transforming them from utopian conversation pieces to authentic athletic experiences for the schoolchildren of New York City.

Long before Gulick came to New York City, he recognized America's urban problems. He described the industrial city as a "biological furnace . . . a breeding place of iniquities that blots civilization."[6] Despite the adversities associated with the city, Gulick hailed New York City as the greatest city in the greatest country in the world. He looked forward to meeting the challenges awaiting him there.[7]

Upon assuming his position in the New York City Public Schools, Dr. Gulick examined closely the conditions in which athletics took place. He found acceptable programs in operation during the summer months along with some effective recreation programs operating during the evening hours all year around. These programs, however, did not meet the needs of the city's older boys (early adolescents). Gulick also discovered, much to his dismay, many big semi-truant boys playing baseball for schools which they did not attend. Smaller boys looked up to these big semi-truants and idolized them as their heroes. The semi-truant, more often than not, resorted to unsportsmanlike tactics and dishonesty on the playing field. Gulick, having after-school programs under his jurisdiction, set out to devise a program that would eliminate the semi-truant and enable all the boys of the city, not just a few hundred, to benefit from the physical experiences and "moral and social lessons that are afforded by properly conducted games and sports."[8]

Elaborating on the moral and social lessons of athletics, Gulick extolled these benefits as the agent for developing loyalty. He reasoned that athletics involve intimate contact between individuals, causing one to subordinate himself to the loyalty of the team. These qualities were rapidly disappearing from society, particularly in the city where forces of industrialization and technological developments were pulling the family apart.[9] The gang, in some respects, had replaced the family, but it often engaged in adverse behavior. Cognizant of the gang phenomenon postulated by Jacob Riis, Gulick believed that gang members, in order to remain loyal to the group, often engage in activities which oppose the social order. Gulick argued that athletic competition, when conducted properly, will channel adverse behavior into constructive behavior.[10] Group loyalty becomes team loyalty, and team loyalty enhances school loyalty, for the spirit of loyalty and morality demonstrated publicly spreads to all the students, not just those who compete.[11] "In an institution where the athletic spirit is strong," maintained Gulick, "school spirit is strong and school spirit is likely to be of a high quality."[12]

Although the spirit of school athletics can have positive effects on the student body, Gulick believed strongly in mass participation and vigorous activities for adolescent boys. He promoted such vigorous activities as running, jumping, swimming, lacrosse, and basketball. At the same time he called for the deemphasis of fierce competition. He wanted the physically skilled boys to enjoy the benefits of closely supervised athletic competition, but he also wanted exercise programs that would interest students and, simultaneously, meet their physical needs. This could be accomplished best, he thought, through play, athletics and dance.[13] Gulick's philosophy of competitive athletic experiences for physically skilled boys and mass participation in physical activities by the entire student body provided the foundation upon which the Public Schools Athletic League was built.

Organization and Structure of the Public Schools Athletic League

Even though the PSAL was an expression of his philosophy, Dr. Gulick was not solely responsible for its genesis. Two other influential New Yorkers—General George W. Wingate, Civil War veteran currently serving on the New York City Board of Education, and James E. Sullivan, secretary of the Amateur Athletic Union—were involved. Both gentlemen had a keen interest in schoolboy athletics, and Gulick's ideas on education and athletics meshed well with theirs. Sullivan, at one point, asked Gulick to establish a branch of the AAU in the public schools.[14] Gulick responded with his plan for school athletics that would benefit everyone. General Wingate, a long-time advocate of physical training and athletics in the schools, welcomed Gulick's thoughts and supported them fully. With the encouragement and able assistance of Sullivan and Wingate, Gulick proposed an inclusive athletic program that involved extensive interschool competition and mass participation.

Although Dr. Gulick's proposal for school athletics was the most grandiose and far-reaching America had yet seen, his notion of interschool competition was not new to New York City public schools. High schools of the city and on Long Island had competed interscholastically in baseball, football and track and field during the 1890s.[15] Dr. C. Ward Crampton, physical director at Manhattan's High School of Commerce and later PSAL secretary, held a dual athletic meet between his school and Commercial High School of Brooklyn in February 1903. At this meet 50 boys from each school participated in four events—basketball, broad jump, shot put, and a relay race.[16] Public School 89 and several other schools conducted field day competitions before Gulick came to New York. Several years earlier General Wingate had introduced in the schools the American Guard, a schoolboy military organization. The boys engaged in calisthenics and military drill and practiced riflery. Shooting tournaments were held periodically.[17]

While inter-institutional competition had existed in various forms in the public schools of New York prior to Gulick's arrival, it was present also among Gulick's past experiences. As director of physical training at the Springfield YMCA College, Gulick was involved in the formation of the Athletic League of the YMCAs of North America in 1895 and was secretary of the League's Governing Committee. The League held athletic and gymnastic competitions among the Associations, subscribing to the principles of amateurism.[18] Gulick's experiences here undoubtedly helped to shape his philosophy on competitive athletics.

On the basis of his previous experiences, his assessment of athletics in the New York City schools, and the advice of Sullivan and Wingate, Luther Gulick devised the plan for the Public Schools Athletic League. In October 1903 he presented it to the superintendent of schools, William H. Maxwell, and several members of the board of education at a series of meetings. Superintendent Maxwell, a friend, controlled athletic competition, approved of the League concept to which the board of education concurred. James E. Sullivan, General Wingate and John Eustance Finlay, president of the City College of New York, also attended these meetings. Their allegiance to schoolboy athletics, combined with Superintendent Maxwell's bias for the same, influenced the board's decision.[19] Even though the board of education sanctioned the PSAL, the League remained a private corporation not eligible for public funding. The first order of business, then, for the League's founders was to attract financial and moral support for their new organization.

Seeking immediate backing for the new organization, the PSAL founders concentrated on New York City's business and merchant class. In early November 1903, James Sullivan and Luther Gulick drafted a letter, inviting carefully selected prominent citizens to serve on the PSAL's first board of directors. In the letter, they listed the objectives of the PSAL, justified its needs and outlined its structure. The League's primary objective was "to promote useful athletics among the boys and young men attending the public schools of the City of New York."[20] Justifying the need for athletic programs for boys, Sullivan and Gulick wrote: "What is wanted is something which can be done after school hours, which will tend to create a good physical development, teach the boys to "play fair" and to allow them to work off, in a natural way, the boyish energy which leads them to join the "gang" and get into mischief or worse."[21] Although the League founders' immediate concern was athletic programs for boys, they were well aware of the physical activity needs of girls, and planned to introduce athletic programs for them at a future date. Speaking on this subject, General Wingate remarked: "It is certainly just as essential that they [girls] be strong and robust, too, but our efforts in their behalf will come later on."[22]

With the emphasis on boy's athletics, the League founders, through their letter campaign, secured 17 men to serve on the PSAL's first board of directors. They served in this capacity until the first annual meeting when the general membership elected the directors. The League officers, in turn, were elected by the directors. General Wingate became the PSAL's first president and served in that capacity for more than 25 years. John E. Finley was elected vice-president, Solomon R. Guggenheim as treasurer, and Luther Halsey Gulick as secretary, a position he held until 1909.[23] In addition to recruiting individuals to serve on its board of directors, the League solicited general memberships on a subscription basis. Regular members paid $10 per year and life members paid $50. There were 328 memberships purchased during the League's first year.[24]

The League had to design an administrative structure that could provide exercise and athletic experiences for 600,000 students enrolled in New York City's 630 schools.[25] To accomplish this huge task, the PSAL organized the city into district athletic leagues on the basis of existing school districts. Each two adjacent school districts comprised one district league. The PSAL, thus, consisted initially of 22 district athletic leagues; by 1910 it had expanded to 25.[26] Each district league had its own board of directors which governed athletics and allocated funds. Forming the district boards of directors were members of local school boards, school principals, teachers and businessmen. While the district leagues administered athletic programs for elementary and high schools within its district, two PSAL committees—the Elementary Games Committee and the High School Games Committee— governed all general matters pertaining to athletics in the elementary and secondary school, respectively, throughout the 25 district leagues. One member from each district league served on the Elementary Games Committee, and one member from each high school sat on the High School Games Committee. Championships for each sport in the elementary and secondary schools were held at the district, borough and city levels.[27]

In order to obtain funds to initiate and sustain the work of the PSAL, Gulick, Wingate, Sullivan and other League officials appealed to New York City's most prominent entrepreneurs. The response was magnificent. Private citizens contributed $40,000 to the PSAL during the first four years. Among the private contributors were John D. Rockefeller; Andrew Carnegie; J. Pierpont Morgan; William K. Vanderbilt; Clarence H. Mackay, director of International Telegraph and Telephone; wealthy merchant Cleveland H. Dodge; banking and mining magnate Harry Payne Whitney; copper and tin baron Solomon Guggenheim; and the Pratt Brothers of Brooklyn's Pratt Institution.[28] In addition to money, several citizens donated expensive and seemingly lavish trophies to be awarded to the city champions of the various competitions. The most elegant trophies were provided by William Randolph Hearst of the *New York Journal,* former baseball pitcher and sporting goods manufacturer, Albert G. Spalding, Alfred G. Vanderbilt, Cleveland H. Dodge, and Harry Payne Whitney. Dr. R. Tait McKenzie, renowned physical educator, surgeon and sculptor, was commissioned to carve several of the trophies.[29]

Luther Gulick and League officials introduced the public to the PSAL when they held an athletic extravaganza at Madison Square Garden on December 26, 1903. As an attention getter for the schoolboy gala, Gulick proposed a pyrotechnic relay race from the board of education building to the Garden in which each runner would carry a flaming torch for two blocks. Superintendent William H. Maxwell and other school officials, however, objected to the relay spectacle, forcing Gulick to cancel it. The competition at Madison Square Garden, billed as the largest athletic meet in the world, attracted 1,040 boys, most of whom came from elementary schools. This number represented about one-fourth of the boys who had been training for this event during the past two months.[30]

This meet, consisting of track and field events and basketball contests, was extremely well organized. Because some boys participated in more than one event, meet officials had to handle 1,523 entries. At times there were as many as five events conducted simultaneously; for example, two basketball games, the relay race, high jump, and shot put. The enormous size of the meet was depicted in the 220-yard and 50-yard races. The former had 200 entries and took 38 heats to complete, while the latter had 338 boys entered and took 43 heats. Competition was spread over two sessions, one in the afternoon, the other in the evening. Cold weather kept the crowd down; nevertheless 4,000 spectators witnessed the afternoon events and 5,000 patronized the evening games.[31] PSAL officers and supporters, pleased with the success of the meet, proclaimed it the most important athletic event ever held in the United States. Luther Gulick reinforced this sentiment when he declared that "they are the greatest games held in any country in modern times, but it is nevertheless a fact that not since the days when gladiators entered Roman arenas in thousands have so many contestants decided the question of superiority with the same time limit we have brought."[32] Gulick, though praising the success of this athletic spectacle as the dawning of a new era in schoolboy athletics, emphasized that future meets would have fewer contestants.[33]

As League officials had hoped, New York newspapers enthusiastically endorsed the PSAL, giving it valuable publicity not only for this meet but for all of its future activities as well. The *Sunday World, Herald, Times, Globe, Evening Post, Tribune, Sun, Brooklyn Citizen, and Brooklyn Eagle* helped the most.[34]

While newspaper coverage was important, the Madison Square Garden meet and ultimately the PSAL itself could not have been successful without the voluntary help of numerous teachers. More than 400 of them donated their time to countless after-school practice sessions, helping the students acquire and perfect athletic skills. The teachers' assistance certainly enhanced teacher-pupil relations.[35]

The voluntary help of the teachers and newspaper publicity were doubtlessly crucial to the PSAL's operation and continued success. The new organization, however, received an immense boost in prestige and stature in 1905 when President Theodore Roosevelt accepted General Wingate's invitation to serve as the PSAL's honorary vice-president. Excited about the League's work, Roosevelt, in his letter of acceptance, commended public school officials and New York citizens for joining forces to form this organization. Of their altruistic effort, he wrote: "You are doing one of the greatest and most patriotic services that can be done, and you are entitled to the healthiest backing in every way from all who appreciate the vital need of having the rising generation of Americans sound in body, mind, and soul."[36]

Roosevelt praised athletics, viewing them as filling the breach created by the unpleasantries of urban life. Echoing the sentiments of Jacob Riis and Luther Gulick, the President believed that "wholesome exercise" and "vigorous play" would redirect the energies of young boys from the misdeeds of gangs to constructive behavior. Emphasizing the function of athletics in this behavioral transformation, he wrote, "every boy who knows how to play baseball or football, to box or wrestle, has by just so much fitted himself to be a better citizen."[37]

PSAL Activities and Events

The PSAL met one of its objectives by providing interschool athletic competition for boys through track and field meets, basketball and baseball contests, and other sporting events. To accomplish its ultimate goal of "sports for all," the League introduced two unique features—class athletics and the athletic badge test.[38]

Class Athletics

Class athletics encouraged the good student with mediocre or poor athletic ability to participate with the good athlete in physical activities. In class athletics students competed as a class; the average of the class, not individual performance, determined the victors. Because the League required 80 percent of the class to participate in this type of competition, the scores of the mediocre and poor performers were just as necessary as those of the highly skilled athletes. A second requirement for participation in class athletics was a "B" average in studies and deportment which had to be verified by the school principal. This stipulation induced poor students to make a greater effort with their studies and behavior so they, too, could compete with their class.[39]

Competition in class athletics was open to boys in the fifth, sixth, seventh and eighth grades. Classes at each grade level in every school interested in this competition performed the broad jump, pull-ups and a dash. Each school was responsible for testing its own classes. The three classes with the highest averages for each event in each of New York City's five boroughs were retested by League officials. On the retest, a class had to make an equal or higher score; if it failed to do so, it was disqualified, and the class with the next lower average in its borough took place. At each grade level, the class with the highest average score for each event received a revolving trophy which it kept for one year.[40] Participation in class athletics was massive. In 1914, for instance, 63,901 boys representing 2,248 classes took part in the broad jump, 43,345 boys from 1,609 classes performed pull-ups, and 34,377 boys from 1,192 classes ran the dash.[41]

Athletic Badge Tests

Just as class athletics stimulated athletic participation and enhanced scholarship, so, too, did the athletic badge tests. Any boy who attained the standards prescribed by the PSAL in running, jumping and chinning events qualified for the athletic badge—a bronze or bronze-silver medal in the elementary grades and a silver medal in high school. To be eligible for the badge test, however, an elementary school boy had to maintain a "B" average in effort, proficiency and deportment, while a high school boy had to perform "satisfactory work" in the classroom.[42] Athletic standards for the badge test were established according to age, with age 13 serving as the dividing line for elementary school pupils. To qualify for the athletic badge, boys under age 13 had to run the 60-yard dash in 8 3/5 seconds or less, do four or more pull-ups, and jump a distance of 5'5" or more from a standing position. The standards for boys over age 13 were 8 seconds in the 60-yard dash indoors or 14 seconds in the 100-yard dash outdoors, six pull-ups, and a standing broad jump of 6½'. For high school boys, the standards were 28 seconds in the 220-yard run, nine pull-ups, and a running high jump of 4'4". At the elementary school level, the athletic badge test was often held in conjunction with class athletics. Boys who reached the athletic badge standards in class competitions received the athletic badge.[43]

That mass athletic participation improved the strength of public schoolboys was evident from the results of the athletic badge tests during the League's first 12 years. In 1904 when the badge test was introduced, 1,162 boys or 2 percent of those taking the test won badges. Five years later 7,049 boys representing 59 percent of the boys taking the test won badges, and in 1915 the number of boys qualifying for athletic badges was 24,756. The school that qualified the highest percentage of boys for the athletic badge won the "Soldier or Marathon" trophy donated by Board of Education President Egerton L. Winthrop, Jr.[44]

Interschool Athletic Competition

For boys possessing unusual athletic skills who sought and needed greater challenges through athletics than either class contests or the badge tests could provide, the PSAL sponsored interschool athletic competition. To be eligible, a boy had to conform to the same scholastic standards established for class athletics and the badge test. Elementary school competition was conducted through the district leagues, and the high schools were all grouped into a single league. Initially the League emphasized sports with which the boys were already familiar. It held competition in basketball, baseball, rifle marksmanship, and the track and field events of running, jumping, relays, and the shot put. By 1907 competitions in soccer, cross-country, swimming, tennis, lacrosse, roller skating, ice skating, and rowing were added. The League dropped the latter two activities in 1908 because they were too expensive to operate.[45]

As a safety measure, the PSAL classified boys for athletic competition according to weight. There were two weight classes in basketball—95 and 125 pounds. Four weight brackets, 85, 95, and 115 pounds and the unlimited weight categories, constituted the divisions for track and field. Track and field events were different for each weight division. Smaller boys were not permitted to enter races and other competition that might place undue stress on their heart and lungs.[46]

Interschool competition in most individual and team sports culminated in city championships. The schools winning their district leagues competed for the championship of the borough where they were located. The borough champions then played each other for the city title. During the League's early years, the baseball tournaments were extremely popular. In 1907 a record 106 schools entered teams, making it the largest baseball tourney held up to that time.[47]

Unlike the team sports, individual sports such as track and field, swimming and cross-country permitted district winners to join borough champions at the city championship competitions. Perhaps the most dramatic city championships were the elementary track and field championships held at Madison Square Garden. At the 1914 city championships, 2,040 boys vied for the city championships. The meet began with the procession of athletes. Marching six abreast, the athletes, following the school band, passed in review. Then they formed two battalions in front of the reviewing stand with the band occupying the center position. When the color guard arrived and took its position, the athletes saluted the flag in unison and sang the national anthem. The 7,000 spectators joined them in this patriotic display. Following the opening ceremonies, the boys competed in their events. The meet directors ran the competition efficiently for it was completed in 2 hours and 20 minutes. At times they had as many as nine track and field events taking place at once.[48]

Hoping to induce large numbers of boys to run moderate distances at moderate paces, Luther Gulick introduced cross-country running. He brought in champion runners to instruct them in running techniques. He encouraged boys to run *en masse* each week for he believed running "tends to produce a steady vitality, and a will-power that does not flinch before fatigue—qualities which are peculiarly difficult to secure under present-day conditions of urban life."[49]

The most controversial activity sponsored by the PSAL was rifle marksmanship. The brainchild of General Wingate, riflery existed in the public schools prior to the League's inception. Considered educationally unsound by some citizens, they condemned it on the grounds that guns have no place in school. General Wingate retorted by claiming that rifle training produces marksmen which is the "greatest guarantee for national peace." He explained that "the way to insure peace is for the country to be prepared itself in case of war, and the only way this country will ever become prepared for war is to have the people as a mass trained in the use of the rifle, as their forefathers were at Lexington and Bunker Hill, so that as citizen soldiers they will be formidable to their opponents."[50]

Bolstering Wingate's stand on riflery in the schools came a strong endorsement from President Roosevelt. Reiterating Wingate's supposition that marksmanship deters aggressors, the President said that riflery lends itself to "increasing the military strength of the country and thus making for peace.[51] To foster the rifle program even more, Roosevelt announced he would send a personal letter to the student who made the highest average each year.[52]

Riflery, though, despite Wingate's and Roosevelt's support, would not have succeeded without the generosity of League treasurer, Solomon Guggenheim. He donated 12 sub-target gun machines which the League placed in various high schools through-out the city. The sub-target gun machine made it possible to teach marksmanship without ammunition. The shooter aimed the gun-machine at the target and this device, through simulation, recorded the position where an actual bullet would have struck the target. Marksmanship competitions were held among high schools having a gun machine. The winning school received the Wingate trophy, a rotating plaque which it kept for one year. Rifle tournaments with live ammunition were held at the rifle galleries of various National Guard armories in New York City during the winter months. In warm weather, the League held outdoor matches on the rifle ranges at Creedmoor and Peekskill, New York. Students who qualified as marksmen or sharpshooters received badges provided by the Brook-lyn Eagle.[53]

Special Events

In addition to organized athletic competition, the PSAL held special events. Several were sponsored by local newspapers, most notably the *Sunday World* which in 1906 inaugurated its annual field days for elementary schoolboys. The newspaper sponsored field days at the first 100 elementary schools that agreed to hold them. The victors at each meet were then brought together in one grand finale. The number of schools holding field days increased steadily each year, and the *Sunday World* increased its benevolence accordingly. In 1914 more than 100,000 boys at 176 schools participated in 181 field days; several schools, having more than 1,000 entries, had to con-duct two meets. At the 1914 finale, 1,200 boys classified into four weight divisions entered five track and field events.[54]

The *Sunday World,* along with financing the field days, spon-sored walking clubs. General Wingate drew up the rules for this activ-ity which involved boys and girls. When a group of eight pupils formed a squad, which was the basic unit of the walking club, they filed an entry list with the *Sunday World* and the PSAL. As soon as these two bodies approved their entry, the students began the competition, walking any of the various tours through the city designed by the League and the *Sunday World.* The majority of a squad had to walk at least two miles every time it began a tour and had to be accompanied by a teacher. There was no limit to the number of squads a school could have.[55] Medals were given to students covering predetermined distances. Bronze medals were awarded to boys who walked 50 miles per quarter (about two months) and to girls who walked 35 miles. Boys walking 100 miles in a quarter and girls walking 50 miles during the same time period won silver medals. In 1910 there were 512 squads with 4,000 members in 81 elementary schools; the girls' squads numbered 114. During the first quarter of the 1910 school year, the pupils won 1,300 medals.[56]

To show the public the results of the League's athletic programs and physical and hygenic training in the public schools, the PSAL occasionally put on public exhibitions. One of its most ambitious undertakings was the massive demonstration of 10,000 schoolboys held on the Central Park Green in June 1913. The boys, bedecked in white and arranged in teams of 45, marched three abreast onto the park green in mid-afternoon. Upon taking their position and responding to the sound of the bugle and the pistol, the ten thousand performed deep breathing, toe touching and knee bending in unison. Next came the shuttle relay race in which half of the group, or 100 teams, participated. Each team was divided so that half of its members was stationed at opposite ends of a 100-yard field: Each boy ran one length of the field, handing the baton to his teammate at the other end. The race continued until every member of each team had run. Following the shuttle relay, the other half of the group participated in the standing broad jump race. In this contest the second jumper began his jump where the first jumper's heels struck the ground, and the third where the second jumper hit, and so forth. When the jumpers finished, the borough champions of baseball, basketball and soccer played 10-minute exhibition games. The demonstration concluded with the boys passing in review and a patriotic closing ceremony. The ten thousand saluted the flag and sang the national anthem.[57]

Theodore Roosevelt, one of the guests of honor at the demonstration, congratulated the PSAL for its outstanding work with the schoolboys. In commending the League, he struck a patriotic note:

I feel the work of the league is the greatest force for good, not only in the city but in the Nation....Nothing could do more to show loyalty, enthusiasm, and democracy of the American people than those 10,000 boys of all races and creeds. It is indicative of the leveling force of athletics, where rich and poor are absolutely on an equality. No matter what dangers the Nation may have to face, boys of this kind becoming men will see to it that the Nation will live forever.[58]

Public demonstrations such as this highlighted the boys' athletic and exercise programs. The League, aware of the public schools' female population, though to a lesser degree, made provisions for their exercise needs through the Girls' Branch of the PSAL.

Girls' Branch of the PSAL

League officials and several wealthy New York women organized in 1905 the Girls' Branch of the Public Schools Athletic League to administer the exercise and activity program for girls. In addition to their financial contributions, several society women voluntarily served as officers of the Girls' Branch. Catharine Leverich was its first president and Mmes. Cleveland H. Dodge, S. R, Guggenheim and Richard Aldrich were the vice-presidents.[59]

For leadership and guidance, the Girl's Branch looked to Luther Gulick, whose philosophy of physical activity for women influenced the direction the Girls' Branch took. Gulick believed that girls were biologically inferior to boys from an evolutionary standpoint and therefore could not and should not engage in the same kind of strenuous activities that boys did.[60]

Equally influential as Gulick, if not more so, was Elizabeth Burchenal, physical educator and first secretary of the Girls' Branch. Subscribing to Gulick's philosophy of inherent biological differences between the sexes, Burchenal argued that girls and boys should not participate in the same types of athletic contests because athletics "evolved from the primitive pursuits and activities of men—not women." For boys, she continued, athletics served a "necessary outlet for their inherited fighting instinct" while for girls athletics are a "substitute for the natural wholesouled exhilarating activities which are necessary to health and happiness, and of which convention and dress and resulting unnatural habits have deprived her."[61]

Although Burchenal agreed with Gulick that separate physical activities should be provided for boys and girls, she insisted that women must determine for themselves what exercises are best suited for girls. She believed women were capable of prescribing exercises mechanically suited for the female body that would contribute to health and vitality. She opposed training girls to set records, fearing that such training would cause injury. She eliminated the combative elements from girls athletics by emphasizing relay races, dance and swimming. She wanted basketball and other team games to accentuate wit and agility, played for fun, rather than brute force and bodily contact.[62]

With the philosophies of Burchenal and Gulick molding the Girls' Branch, this arm of the PSAL promoted folk dance, certain games, and walking for elementary school girls and limited track and field activities for high school girls. In the latter, the pole vault, high jump, and broad jump were not permitted. The Girls' Branch stressed group participation and prohibited individual and interschool competition. Girls clubs could compete against one another but only if they were located at the same school. Formulating its policy, the Girls' Branch adopted the following precepts:

1. Sports for sport's sake—no gate money
2. Athletics for all girls
3. Athletics within the school and no inter-school competition
4. Athletic events in which teams (not individual girls) compete
5. Athletics chosen and practiced with regard to their suitability for girls and not merely in imitation of boys' athletics[63]

Adhering to these guidlines, the Girls' Branch stimulated folk dancing for girls in the school through free workshops for teachers. They, in turn, taught folk dancing in their own schools. This program was so successful that the in-service instructional program under the direction of Ms. Burchenal had to be expanded.[64]

To show the public the role of folk dancing in public schools, the Girls' Branch held park fetes in which thousands of girls from many different schools performed folk dances in the city's parks. There were 2,000 girls assembled in Central Park in 1908 for the first fete; in 1915, the Central Park demonstration attracted nearly 8,000 girls.[65]

The work of the Girls' Branch drew praise from PSAL officials. Dr. Gulick commended it not only for keeping young ladies out of trouble, but also for giving them opportunities to find happiness and joy through physical activity.[66] Dr. C Ward Crampton, Gulick's assistant and successor as League secretary, went a step further in lauding the work of the Girls' Branch. Crampton said, "It is eminently fitting that the greatest city in this hemisphere, with its huge responsibilities, should be the most advanced in the enlightened race and development of its children, and it is pleasing to note that the methods, materials and ideals of the Girls' Branch of the Public Schools Athletic League have been adopted all over the civilized world."[67]

PSAL's Effects and Influences

PSAL officials continuously spoke of the contributions of athletics to scholarship, morality, citizenship and health. League president, General George W. Wingate, a longtime believer that athletics improves scholarship, described this relationship in his 1914 Presidential address:

> With every year the standard of athletic ability in the schools becomes higher and records which were considered wonderful when made are surpassed. Accompanying this is a marked improvement in the carriage of the person, alertness of mind and body, and the general air of strength and health resulting from athletic experiences which the children have pursued.
>
> Gratifying as this is from the physical side, the improvement on the side of ethics, school discipline, and espirit de corps is even greater.[68]

General Wingate attributed these beneficial effects, in part, to the League's eligibility rule. Pupils had to have a "B" average in effort, proficiency and deportment during the previous month in order to participate in the League's athletics programs.

The impact of athletics on school discipline was observed at one upper East Side Manhattan school. At this school 50 incorrigible boys, known for their insolence, repeatedly disrupted classes. Ms. Hirtland, a basketball enthusiast, took over their class. With the principal's consent, she took these boys to the gym each day and played basketball with them for an hour. When she returned to the classroom with them, they were tired and ready to learn. From the time she began this practice, the boys did well in the classroom and caused her no further trouble.[69]

Not only did athletics improve discipline, League officers maintained, but it also motivated students to practice honesty. Public School 6 of Manhattan defeated Public School 77 by one point for the city track and field championship. Shortly after the contest, League officials discovered that Public School 6 unknowingly used an ineligible student in the relay race. When Public School 6 players heard this, they returned the championship trophy to the League office the very next day. General Wingate could not think of a greater example of honesty.[70]

Athletics, in addition to influencing morality, contributed to the boys' health. General Wingate, noting a 20 percent improvement in the boys' physiques during the PSAL's first three years, attributed the improvement to the League's athletic programs. He believed that the League's work also discouraged youth from smoking cigarettes. Wingate remarked that the PSAL "wages a persistent and highly successful war on cigarette smoking (that bane of youth) and other bad habits....This it does, not by preaching, but because in becoming interested in athletics, they are taught that they cannot excel unless they take care of their bodies, and to do this means keeping away from these things."[71]

Extending Wingate's ideas on the benefits of athletics to physical health, Dr. Crampton contended that athletics may well prevent tuberculosis. Exercising in the open air, he argued, makes the lungs strong and less susceptible to tuberculosis.[72] Both Wingate and Crampton proclaimed the PSAL's activities as an effective antidote to insidious city conditions—poor air, crowded living quarters and delinquent behaviour.[73]

Contributing to the city's problems and congestion were the hordes of immigrants who came to America's shores and settled in New York City during the late nineteenth and early twentieth centuries. PSAL activities helped to enculturate them. Concurring with Gulick's belief that athletics enhances school loyalty, Dr. Crampton viewed athletics as the agent which helped immigrants develop loyalties to their respective schools, which, in turn, Crampton reasoned, led to city loyalty and ultimately to national loyalty.[74]

Possibly the clearest statement on the League's influence, as seen through its founders' eyes, appeared in Dr. Crampton's 1910 report of the secretary to the PSAL:

The League is winning its way toward its great goal, the physical efficiency of its boys and girls and the inculcation of the great athletic ideals of courage, honesty, courtesy and strength. It has the support of the public and the city administration and will return large dividends in the form of able men and women trained in body and soul, for their own happiness and the welfare of the State.[75]

The PSAL's athletic programs not only affected the youth of New York City, but its influence extended also to millions of schoolchildren across America. By 1910, 17 other cities had formed athletic leagues modeled after the PSAL.[76] Nor was the League's popularity confined to America, for Chile, Argentina, India and Turkey inquired about its programs.[77]

Some school districts looked to the League for innovative athletic programs, while others sought its services for determining the amateur status of schoolboys. School districts in New Jersey and Connecticut repeatedly relied on the PSAL for interpreting the eligibility of their athletes.[78]

While the PSAL gained recognition from near and afar as the leader in public school athletics, the board of education elevated the League's status within the school district. The board, having previously sanctioned the League's work, formally approved it on December 30, 1914. The board made the League a part of it, so the PSAL could receive funds from the city budget to carry on its mission with schoolchildren.[79]

Summary and Conclusions

The Public Schools Athletic League, thus, was a progenitor of and leader in public school athletics. It organized athletics on the largest scale known up to that time and provided these programs to hundreds of thousands of children. As General Wingate often said, it was truly the world's greatest athletic organization. Its efforts attracted great support from the local citizenry as well as the respect and admiration of educators and school administrators throughout America. The Public Schools Athletic League succeeded in its mission to provide organized athletic experiences for city schoolchildren.

Footnotes

[1]Jacob Riis, *How the Other Half Lives* (Williamstown, MA: Corner House, 1890; reprint ed., New York: Hill & Wang, 1957), 134.

[2]Jacob Riis, *The Children of the Poor* (New York: Charles Scribner's Sons, 1892; reprint ed., New York: Arno Press and the New York Times, 1971), 74-75.

[3]The Progressive era is considered generally that period between 1900 and 1914 characterized by reform of society in general and of government, business and education in particular. For an interpretation of the Progressive movement, see Richard Hofstadter, The meaning of the progressive movement, in *The Progressive Movement, 1900-1915*, edited by Richard Hofstadter (Englewood Cliffs, NJ: Prentice-Hall, Spectrum Books, 1963), 1-15. While Hofstadter labeled this era a period of reform, Robert H. Wiebe in his *Search for Order, 1877-1920* (New York: Hill & Wang, 1967) contended that it was not so much reform, but order, that the Progressives wanted. They created order by applying bureaucratic techniques to America's unwieldy industrial and urban growth.

[4]Lawrence A. Cremin, *The Transformation of the School, Progressivism in American Education, 1876-1957* (New York: Knopf, 1962), 101-103; S. E. Frost, Jr., *Historical and Philosophical Foundations of Western Education* (Columbus, OH: Charles E. Merrill, 1966), 424-426, 491; Arthur Weston, *The Making of American Physical Education* (New York: Appleton-Century-Crofts, 1962), 51-53.

[5]Jessie Bancroft, Physical training in the public schools of New York City, *American Physical Education Review,* 8 (March 1903), 27.

[6]Bancroft, 28-29.

[7]Ibid.

[8]Luther H. Gulick, Athletics for school children, *Lippincott's Monthly Magazine* 88 (Aug. 1911), 205.

[9]Luther H. Gulick, Athletics for city children (advance copy), Report of Dr. Luther Halsey Gulick, Secretary of the Public Schools Athletic League of New York City, Dec. 1904, New York Public Library.

[10]Luther H. Gulick, Team games and civic loyalty, *School Review* 14 (Nov. 1966), 677.

[11]Gulick, Team games and civic loyalty, 676.

[12]Gulick, Athletics for school children, 210.

[13]Luther H. Gulick, Exercise must be interesting, *American Physical Education Review* 12 (March 1907), 63; Ethel Josephine Dorgan, *Luther Halsey Gulick* (College Park, MD: McGrath Publishing Co., 1972), 51.

[14]C. Ward Crampton and Emanual Haug, eds., *Official Handbook of the Public Schools Athletic League, 1909-10* (New York: American Sports Publishing Co., 1909), 111.

[15]"The public schools athletic league," Public Schools Athletic League Offices, New York; *New York Times,* Dec. 25, 1910, p. 7; Emmett A. Rice, John L. Hutchinson and Mabel Lee, *A Brief History of Physical Education,* 5th ed. (New York: Donald Press Co., 1969), 191.

[16]C. Ward Crampton, A group contest, *American Physical Education Review* 8 (June 1903), 82; Anthony Victor Patti, "C. Ward Crampton, M.D.: Pioneer in Health and Physical Education," Ph.D. dissertation, Columbia University, 1962, 62.

[17]*New York Times* Nov. 25, 1903, p. 10 and Nov. 29, 1903, p. 15.

[18]Luther H. Gulick, The athletic league of the YMCA of North America, *Physical Education* 4 (February 1896), 147-148.

[19]*New York Times,* Nov. 25, 1903, p. 10; George W. Wingate, The Public Schools Athletic League, *Outing Magazine* 52 (May 1908), 165.

[20]Letter from James E. Sullivan and Luther Halsey Gulick, Nov. 9, 1903, Public Schools Athletic League Offices, New York.

[21]Ibid.

[22]*New York Times,* Nov. 29, 1903, p. 15.

[23]Luther Halsey Gulick and Wm. C. J. Kelly, eds., *Official Handbook of the Public Schools Athletic League, 1904-1905* (New York: American Sports Publishing Co., 1905), 5, 21-23.

[24]Gulick and Kelly, 139.

[25]Wingate, Public Schools Athletic League, 166.

[26]Wingate, Public Schools Athletic League, 171; *Handbook of Public Schools Athletic League, 1909-1910*, 141-144; Arthur B. Reeve, The world's greatest athletic organization, *Outing Magazine 57* (Oct. 1910), 113.

[27]*Handbook of Public Schools Athletic League, 1904-1905*, 138-139; Gulick, Athletics for school children, 204-205; Wingate, Public Schools Athletic League, 171.

[28]George W. Wingate, President's Address, Fifth Annual Meeting of the Public Schools Athletic League, Dec. 1, 1908 in *Handbook of Public Schools Athletic League, 1909-1910*, 9; Gulick, Athletics for school children, 202, Wingate, Public Schools Athletic League, 167-168.

[29] *Handbook of Public Schools Athletic League, 1909-1910*, passim.

[30]New York *Times*, Dec. 9, 1903, p. 10 and Dec. 27, 1903, p. 80.

[31]New York *Times*, Dec. 27, 1903, p. 8.

[32]Ibid.

[33]Ibid.

[34]Dorgan, *Luth Halsey Gulick*, 80.

[35]Gulick, Athletics for school children, 202.

[36]Theodore Roosevelt to General George W. Wingate, Aug.1905, Public Schools Athletic League Offices, New York.

[37]Ibid.

[38]Wingate, Public Schools Athletic League, 168.

[39]Ibid.; George W. Wingate, Eleventh Annual Meeting of the Public Schools Athletic League, Jan. 26, 1915, in the *Offical Handbook of the Public Schools Athletic League, 1915-1916*, C. Ward Crampton, ed. (New York: American Sports Publishing Co., 1915), 15; Reeve, World's greatest athletic organization, 110.

[40]Athletic rules, *Public Schools Athletic League, Handbook,1915-1916*.

[41]Wingate, President's Address, Jan. 26, 1915, 15.

[42]*Handbook of Public Schools Athletic League, 1904-1905*, 144.

[43]Ibid.; *Handbook of Public Schools Athletic League, 1915-1916*, 106-107.

[44]*Handbook of Public Schools Athletic, 1915-1916*, 107; Lee F. Hamner, Athletics in public schools, *Bulletin No. 10* (New York: Department of Child Hygiene of Russell Sage Foundation, 1910), 5.

[45]Wingate, Public Schools Athletic League, 171; Gulick, Athletics for school children, 202.

[46]Gulick, Athletics for school children, 202-204; *Handbook of Public Schools Athletic League, 1915-1916*, 225, 229.

[47]C.Ward Crampton, Report of the Secretary, Public Schools Athletic League, June 30, 1915, *Handbook of Public Schools Athletic League, 1915-1916*, 27-29.

[48]Wingate, President's Address, Jan. 26, 1915, 31-35.

[49]Gulick, Athletics for school children, 203.

[50]Wingate, Public Schools Athletic League, 174.

[51]Wingate, President's Address, Dec. 1 1908, 13.

[52]Gulick, Athletics for school children, 203.

[53]Gulick, Athletics for school children, 202; Wingate, Public Schools Athletic League, 172; Reeves, World's greates athletic organization, 113; *Handbook of Public Schools Athletic League, 1915-1916,* 143-145.

[54]Wingate, President's Address, Jan. 26, 1915, 39-41; Crampton, Report of the Secretary, June 30, 1915, 161-163.

[55]Wingate, President's Address, Jan. 26, 1915, 43; Crampton, Report of the Secretary, June 30, 1915, 165.

[56]Wingate, President's Address, Seventh Annual Meeting of the Public Schools Athletic League, Dec. 22, 1910, New York Public Library, 5.

[57]*New York Times,* June 7, 1913 p. 2.

[58]Ibid.

[59]Burchenal, Elizabeth, ed. *Official Handbook of the Girl's Branch of the Public Schools Athletic of the City of New York, 1915-1916* (New York: American Sports Publishing Co., 1915), 18.

[60]Luther H.Gulick, Athletics from the biologic viewpoint,*American Physical Education Review* 11 (1906), 157-160.

[61]Elizabeth Burchenal, "Proceedings of the Third Annual Playground Congress," Pittsburgh, May 10-14, 1909, in *Handbook of Girl's Branch, 1915-1916,* 66.

[62]Burchenal, 72.

[63]*Handbook of Girls' Branch, 1915-1916,* 19.

[64]Catharine Leverich, Report of the President of the Girl's Branch of the PSAL, April 1, 1909, *Handbook of the Public Schools Athletic League, 1909-1910,* 19.

[65]Park fetes, *Handbook of Girls' Branch 1915-1916,* 45-47.

[66]Luther Halsey Gulick, Address, *Handbook of Girls' Branch, 1915-1916,* 61.

[67]C. Ward Crampton, Address, *Handbook of Girls' Branch, 1915-1916,* 55.

[68]Wingate, President's Address, Jan. 26, 1915, 47.

[69]Reeve, World's greatest athletic organization, 107.

[70]Ibid.

[71]Wingate, President's Address, Jan. 26, 1915, 47.

[72]C.Ward Crampton, Report of the Secretary of the PSAL, June 30, 1909, *Handbook of Public Schools Athletic League, 1909-1910,* 23.

[73]Ibid.

[74]Wingate, President's Address, Jan. 26, 1915, 11.

[75]Crampton, Report of Secretary, June 30, 1909, 33.

[76]The cities which organized athletic leagues modeled after New York's were: Baltimore; Birmingham, AL; Buffalo; Cincinnati; Cleveland; Fitchburg, MA; Kansas City, MO; Newark; New Orleans, Pittsburgh; Racine, WI; San Francisco; Schenctady, NY; Seattle; Springfield, MA; Tacoma, WA; and Troy, NY; Hamner, Athletics in public schools, 3.

[77]Reeve, World's greatest athletic organization, 109.

[78]New York *Times,* Nov. 15, 1914, pt. 4, p. 6.

[79] *Handbook of Public Schools Athletic League, 1915-1916,* 51.

13

The Rise of Basketball For Women in Colleges

by Ronald A. Smith

In January, 1892, the same month the first organized basketball game was played, a woman writer for the *Atlantic Monthly* claimed that "the part which athletics plays in college life for men has no answering equivalent in college life for women."[1] Two years later Senda Berenson, director of physical education at Smith College, was able to state that basketball is the game which has "helped to develop the athletic spirit in women more than any other, that has given us the best results, and aroused the greatest enthusiasm."[2] Basketball was one of a number of sports which had begun to change the feminine image in the nineteenth century from that of "taper-fingered, narrow-chested, lily-cheeked girls"[3] to that of a more vigorous outdoor-sporting type. If croquet introduced women to sporting activity in the 1860's and the bicycle made it fashionable for women to exercise by the 1890's, it was basketball within a decade of its origin that became the acclaimed game for women in colleges throughout America. In fact, women organized teams and began participating in intercollegiate basketball before men did in many colleges and universities.[4]

The history of basketball for women in colleges is more than a story of a man's sport which was adapted for women through various rule changes. It tells of the change in thinking concerning the amount and type of physical activity in which women should participate; it reflects the influence that men's intercollegiate athletics had on women's athletics; it shows to a great extent the direction taken by college women's physical education and sport; and it mirrors aspects of the larger social milieu out of which women attained greater rights and freedoms in the latter years of the nineteenth and into the twentieth century.

Ronald A. Smith is Associate Professor, Department of Physical Education, Penn State University. He is the co-author with John A. Lucas of The Saga of American Sport *(Philadelphia: 1978).*

From Ronald Smith, "The Rise of Basketball for Women in Colleges," Canadian Journal of History of Sport and Physical Education, *1 (December 1970): 18-36. Copyright © 1970, by* Canadian Journal of History of Sport and Physical Education. *Reprinted with permission.*

James Naismith, Luther Gulick, and the Origin of Basketball

The background for the development of basketball differs from the origin of most sports. Basketball was invented out of the natural physical education philosophy of Luther H. Gulick, director of the department at the Y.M.C.A. Training School in Springfield, Massachusetts, and the practical application of those principles by James Naismith, an instructor at the same institution.

Luther Gulick, who was to contribute much to the natural philosophy of physical education in the early twentieth century, saw the need for an athletic activity which might contribute to young men's physical well-being during the winter season between fall football and spring baseball. In his psychology seminar at the Springfield Y.M.C.A. Training School Gulick discussed the need for incorporating natural activities in the development of an indoor game. Naismith was a member of that class in which desirable rules for a new game were discussed.[5] Gulick later gave Naismith the assignment to develop an indoor game incorporating natural activities. Naismith experimented indoors with existing outdoor games and failed. He then listed those qualities which he believed would lead to a successful indoor game. Those attributes, he believed, should include: 1) the ability to hold the player's interest; 2) a game which would be easily learned; 3) the use of a large and light ball; 4) the elimination of roughness —thus no running with the ball; 5) the passing of the ball in any direction; and 6) a horizontal rather than a vertical goal.[6]

With a set of 13 original rules Naismith introduced his new game to a class of 18 in the Y.M.C.A. Training School. Despite some problems of roughness the game became an immediate success.[7] The rapid action combined with the challenge of throwing a soccer ball into a basket hung ten feet above the floor created enthusiasm for both player and spectator. Naismith recalled that word soon spread that students were having fun in his gym class and spectators began to visit the Springfield gymnasium.[8] Gulick and Naismith must have felt that their new game would spread to other regions. Shortly after its invention basketball was made the theme of an 1892 article printed in *Triangle,* the Springfield Y.M.C.A. Training School magazine. That same year *Physical Education,* a new publication edited by Naismith with Gulick as president, contained a full page advertisement. It said in part:

FOOT BALL MADE OVER!
BASKET BALL,
A New and Popular Game.
Instead of KICKING the ball, TOSS it.
Instead of KICKING a goal, THROW it.
Instead of "DOWNS," Keep the ball up.[9]

It was advertised, but it probably spread rapidly because Y.M.C.A.'s, schools and colleges found in basketball a game which filled a need as an indoor winter sport.

Basketball: A Feminine Approach

It was either the *Physical Education* advertisement or articles contained in the periodical that encouraged Senda Berenson to introduce the game to the Smith College girls in 1892.[10] Miss Berenson probably had more to do with the development of women's basketball than any other woman. She introduced the game to college women, was the chief modifier of rules for them, and was a long time committee woman and editor of the "official" women's basketball rules published by the Spalding Company.[11]

Many saw that basketball with or without rule changes could be played by women, but it was Miss Berenson who was most responsible for the major rule changes in women's basketball which influenced women's physical education for the next three-quarters of a century. Soon after it was introduced at Smith College she could see that the greatest tendency in the game was toward roughness.[12] The problem appeared to be the provision in men's rules which allowed the ball to be taken out of the opponent's hands, often resulting in physical confrontion. To remedy this Miss Berenson prohibited the snatching of the ball from the opponent. This led to the tendency for the girl to just stand with the ball knowing that no one could take it from her. She then introduced the rule which prohibited holding the ball for more than three seconds. Some innovative player later decided that the ball could be bounced every three seconds to prevent this violation of the three second rule. For this situation she ruled that the ball could be bounced no more than three times. This she believed would also encourage teamwork. The last major rule innovation by the Smith College instructor was an attempt to limit the best player from dominating play in all areas of the playing court. She devised a court divided into three areas with each player limited to one of the areas. The three areas (changed to two areas for small courts in 1914, but officially for all courts in 1938) were justified physiologically by limiting the amount of action by one player and thus reducing fatigue. All of these changes which with minor modifications existed in the mid-twentieth century were accomplished at Smith College within two years of the origin of the game.[13]

The fact that the Senda Berenson-Smith College women's rules were the basis for twentieth century women's basketball does not imply that these rules were quickly adopted. In 1899 a Woman's Basketball Committee of four was formed by representatives of Oberlin, Radcliffe, and Smith Colleges and the Boston Normal School of Gymnastics. Miss Berenson, the Smith representative, became editor of what the committee agreed upon as the official rules.[14] Even though the committee got the A.B. Spalding Company to publish the "Official Rules," as late as 1914 one authority believed that one-half to two-thirds of women were playing men's rules while the others were playing at least five different versions of women's basketball.[15] Even in 1921 the National Athletic Conference of American College Women heard a debate on the merits of women's rules vs. modified men's rules.[16]

The lack of uniform rules for women could probably be attributed primarily to the lack of a pervasive system of intercollegiate basketball contests for women. Though in many colleges co-eds played some intercollegiate games there seemed to be no women's leagues or championships in the first generation of the new sport. An example of an intercollegiate basketball game was that played between Smith College and Bryn Mawr in 1901. At what was called their annual intercollegiate match the Smith College "five" wore blouses and bloomers while covering their legs with long black stockings; Bryn Mawr was dressed in what was termed short skirts. Even organized cheering was heard before the game. It is difficult to imagine the excitement that was likely developed—especially when the scoring is recounted. Smith College scored a basket and a free throw in the first half of play. Bryn Mawr scored not a point. After a ten minute intermission Bryn Mawr scored three points, while the Smith College girls could only muster one foul shot. The game ended with Smith College victors, four to three.[17] Yet, even with games such as this the necessity for common rules was not as demanding as it was for men who early were playing basketball intercollegiately at a championship level. The men's National Collegiate Athletic Association had agreed to common college rules in 1908. The amateur Athletic Union and the N.C.A.A. agreed to common rules seven years later.[18] The women were not as anxious to join forces.

If the need for common rules was not as demanding for women as for men there was nevertheless continous support from many women leaders for standardized rules. But what should those rules be? Was it true that basketball was too rough a game under men's rules? Was roughness a result of the rule allowing the ball to be taken away by a defensive player? Was it physiologically unsound for women to play the entire court? Did a nondivided court in fact lead to the personal glorification of "star" performers rather than development of socially useful team play? Was acceptance of men's rules a symbol of male domination of women's basketball? These and other questions were discussed and debated by women leaders from the 1890's to the 1930's, indeed, even later.

Damn the Men's Commercialized Intercollegiate Athletics

Soon after its introduction basketball became the pervasive sport for college women.[19] With it developed the general belief that the negative aspects of men's intercollegiate athletics should not be imitated by the women. In coeducational colleges, girls colleges, and normal schools there were organized women's basketball teams throughout the United States by 1900. Intercollegiately Radclife was playing Mount Holyoke; Barnard was playing Syracuse; Ripon was playing Oshkosh Normal School; and Stanford was playing California within a few years of the turn of the century.[20] Said Senda Berenson in 1901: "The greatest element of evil in the spirit of athletics in this country is the idea that one must win at any cost—that defeat is an unspeakable disgrace."[21] At the same time she believed that women could "profit by the experience of our brothers and therefore save ourselves from allowing those objectionable features to creep into our athletics . . ."[22] The same thought was echoed by Lucille Eaton Hill, Director of Physical Training at Wellesley College: ". . . we must avoid the evils which are so apparent to thoughtful people in the conduct of athletics for men."[23] The next year, 1904, a female officer of the Wisconsin Physical Education society agreed with the Midwest Conference of Deans of Women who had passed a resolution opposing intercollegiate athletic contests for women.[24]

The problem of intercollegiate competition for women was first being faced as the twentieth century began. There was an early complaint that men acting as coaches for women were too harsh on the female performers; women coaches for women was advocated.[25] Another critic opposed interschool games because it was believed they were harmful psychologically as well as physiologically to the welfare of women.[26] Then, too, there was the utilitarian belief that "sport must be conducted for the good of the number, and not for the purpose of getting good material for championship teams." The writer of those words felt that the fun of playing should dominate women's sports, "not the grim determination to win at all costs."[27] Lucille Eaton Hill of Wellesley stated what many other women physical educators may have been thinking: that is, that women's sports should contribute the "greatest good to the greatest number; not the greatest good to the smallest number . . ."[28] She believed that highly competitive basketball was not womanly, tending to unsex the player.[29]

These and other problems associated with basketball were responsible for the organization of the Committee on Women's Athletics of the American Physical Education Association in 1917, forerunner of the Division for Girls and Women's Sports.[30] From the beginning of the D.G.W.S. there was a vocal group of women physical educators opposed to intercollegiate athletics for women. Elizabeth Burchenal, chairman of the American Physical Education Association Committe on Girls' Athletics, may have best summed up the feeling of those who thought that intercollegiate athletics for women was an anathema. An athletic program for girls, she proposed, should consist of no interschool competition; should be directed by a woman; and should not be an imitation of men's athletics. It was to be "sports for sport's sake," a statement later to become one of many cliches concerning women's athletics.[31]

By the 1920's leaders of women's physical education were in rather general agreement that the promotion of women's intercollegiate basketball (and other intercollegiate athletic activities) was an evil practice. In a 1923 survey of 50 colleges it was found that only 11 allowed intercollegiate competition while 93 percent of the physical educators were opposed to it.[32] Opinions expressed in the survey condemning intercollegiate athletics were often directed at what women believed to be negative results of men's intercollegiate athletics;that there would be excessive commercialism,that a win at all costs philosophy would be promoted, that betting on games would occur, that the many who needed exercise the most would get the lease and that a professional spirit would ensue if women conducted intercollegiate athletics. These beliefs were combined with the feeling held by 60 percent of those surveyed that intercollegiate athletics for women were harmful physically to the participants.[33] It was concluded by the surveyor that the "large majority" of women physical educators had been opposed to intercollegiate athletics "for years and are still opposed to it."[34]

Eight years later a similar survey of nearly 100 colleges was reported.[35] Only 12 percent of the colleges surveyed allowed intercollegiate athletics. Surveyor Mabel Lee, by then an established leader in women's physical education, concluded the 1931 report stating that statistics "prove how absolutely determined are the women of the physical education profession and . . . the women college students of today, not to permit women's athletics to follow in the footsteps of men's athletics."[36]

The direction that women's basketball would take in the colleges for the next generation had been set by the 1920's. The game was to differ from the men's in terms of rules and was not to be played intercollegiately, at least not with the approval of the women leaders of the physical education profession. There was never to be unanimity concerning the question of rules or that of intercollegiate play. There was always those women who believed what the men were doing was best. One was Helen Kirk, who in 1920 opposed the court division which she believed caused the players to run sideways rather than toward the goal, spoiling "the science of the game." She favored the men's game which she thought was "clean, open and skillful, and . . .

decidedly more interesting to play" and to watch.[37] But those who favored men's basketball for women were in the minority. Likewise there were few who favored intercollegiate basketball for women.[38]

A Generation of Social Play Days

If women were to emphasize "participation rather than competition," if they were to believe that "winning is not the important thing,"[39] and if women still desired some type of athletic relationship with other colleges, then some type of sporting activity other than intercollegiate competiton had to be found. The development of play days, later sports days, seemed to many to be the panacea. The play day is of uncertain origin, but it developed to its fruition during the 1920's following the formation of the Women's Division of the National Amateur Athletic Federation.[40] By the beginning of the 1930's it was reported that 80 percent of colleges had women's play days.[41] Mabel Lee appeared delighted that "the Play Day idea seems to have taken our colleges by storm . . . "[42]

The play day consisted of girls from a number of schools gathering together for a day of sport activities, ranging from basketball, tennis, baseball, and hockey to volleyball, swimming, archery and soccer.[43] Individual schools would not compete against one another, rather teams composed of players from a number of schools would play. Obviously victory would mean less in a basketball game in which none of the participants had previously played together than if a team had practiced as a unit for a number of weeks. Thus, play day activities, such as the most popular one—basketball—were the means by which girls from different institutions could socialize. The supposed social values derived from sport competition of this type fit nicely into the new philosophy of physical education made popular in the early twentieth century by Thomas Wood, Clark Hetherington, and Luther Gulick.[44] The social play day apparently was developed to keep "sports for sports sake," to stimulate social intercourse among various institutions, and to prevent what was believed to be gross malpractices of men's intercollegiate athletics. To be sure there were those like Ina Gittings who believed that the chief value of play days would be the re-introduction of intercollegiate competition. The play day, she believed, "will evolve into actual varsity competition or die from pure ennui."[45]

For a generation the play day was the pinnacle of athletic participation for college women. A survey in 1951 and another in 1954 revealed that the play day was still the most popular form of athletic competition for women in colleges.[46] Attitudes, however, were changing toward intercollegiate athletics for women. In 1931 it was reported that nearly three-fourths of college women's athletic associations were opposed to women's intercollegiate athletics; by 1955 half of the women physical educators favored intercollegiate team sports for women while 70 percent favored individual sports on an intercollegiate basis.[47] In this eastern area of the United States, where Women's intercollegiate competition has generally been most popular, about one-third of the colleges reported varsity competition in a 1945 survey. A quarter century later 84 percent had varsity competition of some type and over half of the schools had intercollegiate basketball. It was a startling change from that of the period dominated by play days.[48] Eleanor Metheny, an outspoken physical educator brought up during the generation of play days, explained why she thought a change in attitudes toward the play days occurred.

Speaking in 1964 she said:

In the days when there was a stigma attached to the concept of playing to win, the women who were responsible for our welfare devised the idea of a play day that would permit us to enjoy sports participation with girls from other schools . . . We had fun at these play days, and we enjoyed the tea and the sociability—but the better players among us felt frustrated by the lack of meaningful team play . . . These play days did little to satisfy our desire for all-out competition with worthy and honored opponents.[49]

Rule Changes and a Return to Intercollegiate Competition

The 1960's saw not only a change from the play day and sports day toward greater intercollegiate competition, but also rule changes in basketball which once again made the women's game resemble men's basketball. By then the Division for Girl's and Women's Sports was working closely with the influential AAU Basketball Committee on the standardization and modification of rules. Three rules for women had for years differentiated their game from that of men. In the first place the women's court was divided into three, later two, divisions with player movement prohibited from one section to another. Second, the girls had never allowed more than three (sometimes fewer) dribbles of the ball, while the men had the continuous dribble rule from the late 1890's. Third, the women had a long standing rule prohibiting the taking of the ball from an opponent which created a much less aggressive game.

The division of the basketball court into three divisions had been suggested by Senda Berenson in 1894. The idea was officially adopted by the rules committee in 1899 and it continued until the mid-1920's. At that time the mid-court line was generally used to divide the playing floor into two sections.[50] With the general acceptance of six players on a team, three players were primarily defense oriented and three were basically offensive players. A new rule was adopted in the fall of 1962 allowing two of the six players, a guard and forward rover, to enter or play in both sections of the floor.[51] This tended to create a faster game with more strategy involving more stamina for at least these two players. By 1969 the basketball rules committee was experimenting with a return to the original men's rule which allowed each player, now five, to move in any area of the playing floor.

If the elimination of court divisions tended to create a faster and more exciting game, so too did the rule change to allow a continuous dribble. The original three consecutive bounce rule introduced in the 1890's at Smith College was reduced to one bounce in 1914.[52] It remained until the post-World War II era when the D.G.W.S. experimented with two bounces, adopting it in 1949. In the early 1950's the continuous or unlimited dribble was experimented with and rejected. The limited dribble was expanded to three in 1961.Finally the continuous dribble was experimented with for two years before being accepted in 1966.[53] The acceptance of the continuous dribble, which early had been thought to be a deterrent to team play, added to offensive strategy and to the speed of the game. No longer could a good defensive player wait for the third dribble and then close in on the dribbler. The women had again returned to a feature of the game which men had legalized within a few years of the origin of the game.

The 1899 rule which had prevented the snatching or grabbing of the ball from an opponent remained unchanged for six decades. The innovation, intended to make the game less physically abusing, was being questioned by the 1950's by those who desired to play a more exciting and challenging game. The 1962 D.G.W.S. rules allowed a player to take or tape the ball away from an opponent.[54] Following a year of play under this rather radical rule change almost 90 percent of college players favored the new rule. The few who opposed it felt as Senda Berenson had seven decades before—that it made the game rougher and tended toward aggressiveness.[55]

The experimentation with the five player, full-court game as the decade of the 1960's began was probably the most far reaching change in women's basketball since the original 1899 rules committee modified the men's rules. There were various groups and forces which were bringing about a change from the six player game with a divided court to a five player, full-court game. First, but probably not most important, was the desire by skilled players to play in a game which called for greater mental as well as physical challenge. Second, there were at least six groups within the United States making women's basketball rules, some of whom allowed the five player, full-court game.[56] Third, and likely the most important, American women since 1950 had been participating in various international basketball events. Only American women were playing six player basketball in the 1960's; the other participating countries competed with five players on a team. Thus, there had been pressure in the 1960's to create a game in America that would produce qualified players to success-fully compete with international teams in the Pan American Games, the World Tournament, and the World University Games.[57]

Women physical educators had made strides especially in the 1960's toward creating intercollegiate basketball on a more per-vasive basis and in changing the rules to bring about a faster game demanding far more strategy that the previous game had demanded. Whether intended or not, the game became more and more like that the original developers of the game, Naismith and Gulick, had envisi-oned. If the D.G.W.S. would in the future accept the experimental, full-court basketball rules, the game in most important respects would return to a game resembling that played by men.

Women's Basketball in Retrospect With Queries for the Future

The invention and development of basketball has done much more than create the dominating American winter sport for men. The game was early adapted to what many women physical education leaders believed to be the best physical activity for developing positive social behavior among young women. It created for the first time a *raison d' être* for women leaders to join together to control physical education activity. Developments in women's basketball were the key to the origin and growth of the Division for Girls and Women's Sports.[58] But above and beyond that it was a game which girls enjoyed playing. Basketball, then, probably was the most potent force for creating a viable and effective women's physical education program in colleges.

From the first, many women leaders believed that only by adapt-ing the game to the needs of females could basketball positively con-tribute to the physical needs of college women. That adaptation occurred early, but the resulting rule changes were far from being accepted unanimously by the players, coaches, and those adminis-tering all levels of women's basketball. Like most aspects of Ameri-can society in the early 20th century the control of basketball on many levels of play was dominated by men or the thinking of men. Yet a group of women physical educators was arising at the college level who may have, like some women in other fields, believed "that they must declare their independence (from men) and prove their equality . . ."[59] College education for women was primarily a latter half of the nineteenth century phenomenon. The franchise for women was achieved nationally only after World War I. For many women leaders there was likely a crusade to break away from the world dominated by men; to promote a cause that they could control. In the control of col-lege basketball for women a "crusade" could be accomplished. First, a number of college educators in the late 1800's and early 1900's had written condemning various evils of men's intercollegiate sports. Many women leaders did not want to see basketball, the first inter-collegiate sport for women, became a highly commercial sport such as football had become for men. To prevent this a vocal group of dedicated women physical educators primarily at college level joined together to control and further the cause of women's athletics. Second, as there was a definite shortage of women leaders in physical education there was a tendency for men, where women were absent, to take charge of physical education and sports for women. Thus, where women were in the majority—the colleges—women controlled their own affairs, but at the high school level men often controlled activities such as basketball. Men, being used to interschool contests, tended to promote the same activities for girls, often using men's rules for the girl's games.[60] Such practice led college women physical educators to attempt to take control of women's athletics out of men's hands especially in the 1920's. It was Agnes Wayman in the early 1920's who spoke out for women's control of girls' athletics. "We are setting forth under our own sail," she emphasized, "with women at the helm and women manning the whole craft."[61] An extension of the policy of women controlling their own affairs led to the move to eliminate all intercollegiate and interschool athletics for girls. The same college women physical educators, people like Agnes Wayman, Rosalind Cassidy, and Mabel Lee, became the most vocal opponents of the exploitation of women athletes by men—even vociferously opposing women's participation in the Olympics.[62]

If men were dominating various aspects of women's basketball in the early 1900's, the same claim was being made six decades later. "The coaches and officials found in highly competitive programs are men," chided Mildred Barnes in 1966, "but until women prove themselves worthy of these responsibilities, there should be few complaints registered against those who undertake the job for us."[63] The desire to eliminate men from women's competitive basketball had not been entirely successful.

With greater control by women college physical educators, women's basketball took other directions away from men's basketball in the early part of the 20th century. Rule changes and the trend away from intercollegiate athletics were the major differences. But, the period following World War II saw the recurrence of rules similar to men's rules and a greater emphasis upon intercollegiate basketball. By returning to intercollegiate competition, away from the play day, certain questions were in need of being answered. Should intercollegiate competition be expanded to include organized conferences? Should an increase in paying spectators help pay for the expanded program? Probably of most importance to those who questioned men's intercollegiate programs was the question: should highly skilled performers be sought out by the colleges and be given financial aid for their physical prowess?

By the 1960's more colleges were beginning to offer women scholarships for athletic ability. Others were demanding equality with the men in allowing athletic scholarships. Though the D.G.W.S. had a policy disapproving of financial aid to girls solely for athletic prowess, there were those who felt the D.G.W.S. program was anachronistic. One small group of opponents of the D.G.W.S. policy clearly stated that they would not abide by its regulation. "Why," they asked, "should girls and women who are capable of benefiting from the chance to get a college education through their athletic ability, be denied the opportunity?"[64] Probably a more accepted view was that of Charlotte Lambert who cautioned her college colleagues concerning intercollegiate athletics: "We can plunge into this wholeheartedly, risking all the pitfalls of men's athletics," or "we can proceed cautiously, building and maintaining sound policies which protect and preserve the good qualities of competition." Forbidding athletic scholarships, she stated, is essential.[65] With the return to intercollegiate basketball many questions were yet to be answered.

College women's basketball had for the first seven decades of the 20th century been in many ways a dominating physical activity and sport. It had seen many transformations. Rules had been changed and later returned to almost their original form. The early examples of intercollegiate competition, which had nearly been given a death knell in the period between the two world wars, returned to thrive again. With the introduction of the first National Invitational Collegiate Women's Basketball Tournament in 1969[66] and the possibility of a D.G.W.S. sponsored national tournament, it is probable that basketball will continue to play an important role in the sporting activities of college women.

Footnotes

[1]Anne P. Call, "The Greatest Need of College Girls," *Atlantic Monthly,* LXIX (Jan. 1892), 102.

[2]Senda Berenson, "Basket Ball for Women," *Physical Education,* III (Sept. 1894), 106.

[3]"Our Sons," *Harper's Monthly,* XV (1858), 61.

[4]Walter Stemmons, *Connecticut Agricultural College—A History* (Storrs, Conn.: The Tuttle, Morehouse & Taylor Co., 1931), 86; Walter Paulison, *The Tale of the Wildcats: A Centennial History of Northwestern University Athletics* (Evanston: Published Privately, 1951), 89; James A. Woodburn, *History of Indiana University* (Bloomington: Indiana University, 1940), II, 395; J. Orin Oliphant, *The Rise of Bucknell University* (New York: Appleton-Century-Crofts, 1965), 236-237; Robert Ebert (ed.), *An Illini Century: One Hundred Years of Campus Life* (Urbana: University of Illinois Press, 1967), 64: Louis G. Geiger, *University of the Northern Plains History of the University of North Dakota 1818-1958* (Grand Forks, N.D.: University of North Dakota Press,

1958), 126. An account of the growth of basketball for both men and women in Wisconsin normal schools is found in Ronald A. Smith, "From Normal School to State University: A History of the Wisconsin State University Conference," Ph.D. dissertation, University of Wisconsin, 1969, pp. 62-65.

[5]Ethel J. Dorgan, *Luther Halsey Gulick, 1865-1918* (New York: Bureau of Publications, Teachers College, Columbia University, 1934), 34; and James Naismith, *Basketball: Its Origin and Development* (New York: Association Press, 1941), 33.

[6]Naismith, Ibid., 45-50.

[7]James Naismith, "Basketball," *American Physical Education Review, XIX (1914), 341.*

[8]*Naismith, Basketball: Its Origin and Development,* 57.

[9]*Physical Education,* I (1892), 143.

[10]Senda Berenson, "Basket Ball for Girls," *Physical Education* III (Sept. 1894), 106: and Edith N. Hill, "Senda Berenson," *Research Quarterly* (Oct. 1941, Suppl.), 661.

[11]By 1894, the monopolistic-like Spaulding Company had developed a new basket with a cord to release the ball from the netting, and within the women's rule book Spalding products were made the official equipment. See Senda Berenson (ed.), *Basket Ball for Women* (New York: American Sports Publishing Co., 1901), 29.

[12]Senda Berenson, "Basketball For Women," *Physical Education*, III (Sept. 1894), 107. On the center jump of the first college women's basketball game a Smith College player suffered a shoulder dislocation.

[13]*Ibid.,* 107-109.

[14]The other representatives were Alice F. Foster, Oberlin; Elizabeth Wright, Radcliffe; and Ethel Perrin, Boston Normal School of Gymnastics. See J. Parmly Paret, "Basket-Ball for Young Women," *Harper's Bazaar,* XXXIII (20 Oct. 1900), 1563-1567; and Senda Berenson (ed.), *Basket Ball for Women* (New York: American Sports Publishing Co., 1901), 6.

[15]Harry Stewart, "A Critical Study of the Rules and Present Day Conditions Of Basket Ball for Women," *American Physical Education Review,* XIX (Mar. 1914), 242.

[16]Margaret J. Swift, "Report of the National Athletic Conference of American College Women," *American Physical Education Review, XXVI (1921), 305-306.*

[17]*New York Times,* 29 Dec. 1902, p. 6.

[18]Naismith, *Basketball: Its Origin and Development,* 105.

[19]Patricia Bennett, "The History and Objectives of the National Section for Girls and Women's Sports," Ed.D. dissertation, Mills College, 1956, p. 19; Dorothy S. Ainsworth, *The History of Physical Education in Colleges for Women* (New York: A.S. Barnes and Co., 1930), 84-85; Ronald A. Smith, "From Normal School to State University: A History of the Wisconsin State University Conference," Ph.D. dissertation, University of Wisconsin, 1969, p. 63; Arthur C. Cole, *A Hundred Years of Mount Holyoke College* (New Haven, Conn.: Yale University Press, 1940), 295; James Naismith, *Basketball: Its Origin and Development,* 168.

[20]Senda Berenson (ed.), *Official Basketball and Officials Rating Guide for Women and Girls* (New York: A.S. Barnes and Co., 1905), 42; Ann H. Knipp and Thaddeus P. Thomas, *The History of Goucher College* (Baltimore: Goucher College, 1938), 475; Orison S. Marden (ed.), *The Consolidated Encyclopedic Library* (New York: The Emerson Press, 1903), 1859; Harriet I. Ballintine, "The Value of Athletics to College Girls," *American Physical Education Review,* VI (June 1901), 151: Elizabeth E.F. Reed, "Basketball at Smith College," *Outlook,* LIV (Sept. 1896), 557: Lavinia Hart,

"A Girl's College Life," *Cosmopolitan,* XXXI (June 1901), 193: Alice K. Fallows, "Undergraduate Life at Smith College," *Scribner's Magazine,* XXIV (July 1898), 46; Arthur C. Cole, *A Hundred Years of Mount Holyoke College* (New Haven: Yale University Press, 1940), 213: Mary C. Crawford, *The College Girl of America* (Boston: L.C. Page & Co., Publishers, 1904), *Passim:* "Festivals in American Colleges for Women: Bryn Mawr; Mount Holyoke; Smith; Vassar; Wellesley; Wells," *Century Magazine,* XLIX (Jan. 1895), 431.

21Senda Berenson, *Basket Ball for Women* (New York: American Sports Publishing Co., 1901), 20.

22*Ibid*

23Lucille Eaton Hill, "Introduction," in her *Athletic and Out-Door Sports for Women*

24"Wisconsin Physical Education Society-Report," *American Physical Education Review,* IX (1904), 57.

25Elma L. Warner, "Inter-School Athletics," *American Physical Education Review,* XI (1906), 182-186.

26William Orr, "Athletics in Secondary Schools," *American Physical Education Review,* XII (1906), 56-57.

27Frances A. Kellor, "Ethical Value of Sports for Women," *American Physical Education Review,* XI (1906), 161-162.

28Hill, "Introduction," in her *Athletic and Out-Door Sports for Women,* 5. In a 1903 speech to the New England Association of Colleges and Preparatory Schools, Lucille Hill suggested banning basketball for girls under college age and only gave it tentative approval to older women. See *New York Times,* 11 Oct. 1903, p. 11.

29*New York Times,* 11 Oct. 1903, p. 11.

30Patricia Bennett, "The History and Objectives of the National Section for Girls and Women's Sports," Ed.D dissertation, Mills College, 1956, pp. 33-39.

31Elizabeth Burchenal, "A Constructive Program of Athletics for School Girls," *American Physical Education Review,* XXIV (1919), 273. Other over used sayings were: "a game for every girl and every girl in a game," "participation not competition," "play for play's sake," and "the good of those who play."

32Mable Lee, "The Case For and Against Intercollegiate Athletics for Women and the Situation as it Stands Today," *Mind and Body,* XXX Nov. 1923), 251,255.

33*Ibid.,* 246-251.

34*Ibid.,* 255. For other statements opposing intercollegiate athletics at this time see Agnes R. Wayman, "Competition," *American Physical Education Review,* XXXIV (Oct. 1929), 469; Agnes Wayman, "Women's Division of the National Amateur Athletic Federation," *Journal of Health, Physical Education and Recreation,* III (Mar. 1932), 4: Rosalind Cassidy, "A Successful College Play Day," *American Physical Education Review,* XXXIII (Feb. 1928), 124; "Outstanding Problems of Girls' Athletics," *American Physical Education Review,* XXXI (May 1926), 846; Florence C. Burrell, "Intercollegiate for Women in Co-educational Institutions," *American Physical Education Review,* XXII (Jan. 1917), 19; Anne F. Hodgkins, "In Answer to 'Why Group Competition?'" *Journal of Health, Physical Education and Recreation,* II (Mar. 1931), 63: Linda G. Roth, "Are Sports Harmful to Women?" *Forum,* LXXXI (Mary 1929), 314.

35Mabel Lee, "The Case For and Against Intercollegiate Athletics and the Situation Since 1923," *Research Quarterly,* II (May 1931), 93-127.

36*Ibid.,* 127.

[37]Helen R. Kirk, "Discussion of Everyday Problems of Girl's Basketball," *American Physical Education Review*, XXV (Dec. 1920), 411-414.

[38]A leading physical educator, Frederick Rand Rogers, had an even more radical approach regarding women imitating men's athletics. Said Rogers in 1930: "'Games like basketball and baseball are combative sports. They develop ugly muscles— muscles ugly in girls—as well as scowling faces and the competitive spirit.'" He opposed all women's basketball. *New York Herald Tribune*, 11 Jan. 1930, p. 2.

[39]Agnes R. Wayman, "Competition," *American Physical Education Review*, XXIV (Oct. 1929), 471, 469.

[40]For a history of the Women's Division see Alice A. Sefton, *The Women's Division: National Amateur Athletic Federation* (Stanford: Stanford University Press, 1941), and Agnes Wayman, "Women's Division of the National Amateur Athletic Federation," *Journal of Health, Physical Education and Recreation*, III (Mar. 1931), 3-7.

[41]Mabel Lee, "The Case For and Against Intercollegiate Athletics for Women and the Situation since 1923," *Research Quarterly*, II (May 1931), 116.

[42]*Ibid.* 122. Editor E.D. Mitchell of the *Journal of Health, Physical Education and Recreation* agreed in 1931 that "the trend in girls' athletics today seems very decidedly toward the Play Day rather than toward varsity competition." Mitchell, "A Question for Play Day Administration," JOHPR, II (Mar. 1931), 22.

[43]The sports day was later used by many institutions. It was an extramural activity in which the participating teams were composed of players from the same school, but it was not considered the same as inter-collegiate play.

[44]See, for example, Thomas D. Wood, "Physical Education," *The Ninth Yearbook of the National Society for the Study of Education* (Part I), 1910, pp. 75-104: Clark W. Hetherington, "Fundamental Education," *American Physical Education Review*, XV (1910), 629-635; and Luther Gulick, "Interest in Relation to Muscular Exercise," *American Physical Education Review*, VII (1902) 57-62.

[45]Ina E. Gittings, "Why Cramp Competition?" *Journal of Health, Physical Education and Recreation*, II (Jan. 1931), 54.

[46]Naomi L. Leyhe, "Attention of Women Members of the American Association for Health, Physical Education, and Recreation Toward Competition in Sports for Girls and Women," D.P.E. dissertation, Indiana University, 1955, pp. 39,41.

[47]*Ibid.* p. 270. A 1945 survey of 227 colleges revealed that in 16 percent of the institutions women participated in intercollegiate athletics; 32 percent in the Eastern district. Only in the Eastern district did leaders feel that there was a trend toward intercollegiate competition. See M. Gladys Scott, "Competition for Women in American Colleges," *Research Quarterly*, SVI (Mar. 1945), p. 57, 67. See also N. M. Leavitt and N. M. Duncan, "Status of Intramural Programs for Women," *Research Quarterly*, VIII (Mar. 1937), 68-79.

[48]Scott, *Ibid,* 57; and Martha A. Adams, "Varsity Programs of Colleges Represented in EAPECW (Eastern Association of Physical Education of College Women, 1969)" monograph, in the writer's possession.

[49]Eleanor Metheny, "Where Will You Go From Here?" in her *Connotations of Movement in Sports and Dance* (Dubuque, Ia., 1965), 158.

[50]Alice W. Frymir, *Basket Ball for Women,* (New York: A.S. Barnes and Co., 1928), 10.

[51]Jan Sayre, "The Roving Player," *Division for Girls and Women's Sports Basketball Guide* (Wash. D.C., 1961), 40; and Shirley P. Martin, "The Roving Player Game," *Division for Girls and Women's Sports Basketball Guide* (Wash. D.C., 1962), 15.

[52]Helen B. Lawrence and Grace I. Fox, *Basketball for Girls and Women* (New York: McGraw-Hill Book Co., 1952) 211.

[53]J. Mildred Barnes, "Continuous Dribble-Why?" *Division for Girls and Women's Sports Basketball Guide* (Wash. D.C., American Association of Health, Physical Education and Recreation, 1966), 55.

[54]"Official Basketball Rules for Girls and Women," *Division for Girls and Women's Sports Basketball Guide, 1962-1963* (Wash. D.C.; American Association of Health, Physical Education and Recreation, 1962), 134.

[55]Shirley Winsberg, "Results of Opinion Survey: Allowing a Player to Take the Ball From an Opponent," *Division for Girls and Women's Sports Basketball Guide, 1962-1963* (Wash. D.C.; American Association of Health, Physical Education and Recreation, 1962), 54-57. Some individuals might see an association between the new rules which tended to bring about more competitive and aggressive play and the increasingly active role taken by women in American society.

[56]Mildred Barnes, "The Present and Future for Basketball for Girls: The National Scene," Fourth National Institute on Girls Sports *Proceedings,* 1966, p. 72.

[57]"Basketball Rules Experiment Announced," *Journal of Health, Physical Education and Recreation,* XL (May 1969), 70; and D.G.W.S.—A.A.U. Joint Basketball Rules Committee, "You decide!" *Division for Girls and Women's Sports Basketball Guide, 1969-1970* (Wash. D.C.: American Association of Health, Physical Education and Recreation, 1969), 34.

[58]Patricia Bennett, "The History and Objectives of the National Section for Girls and Women's Sports," Ed.D. dissertation, Mills College, 1956, p. 24.

[59]John M. McBryde, "Womanly Education for Women," *Swanee Review.* XV (Oct. 1907), 481. See also Margaret D. Greene, "The Growth of Physical Education for Women in the United States in the Early 19th Century," Ed.D. dissertation, University of California, Los Angeles, 1950. p. 75. Thomas Woody in his, *A History of Women's Education in the United States* (New York: The Science Press, 1929), Vol. II, 435, states that the motto for educated women of the 19th century might well have been: "education and agitate."

[60]H.S. Curtis, "Should Girls Play Interschool Basketball?" *Hygeia,* VI (Nov. 1928), 607-608.

[61]Agnes R. Wayman, "Women's Athletics—All Uses—No Abuses," *American Physical Education Review,* XXIX (1924), 517.

[62]See, for example, Patricia Bennett, "The History and Objectives of the National Section for Girls and Women's Sports," Ed.D. dissertation, Mills College, 1956, p. 74.

[63]Mildred Barnes, "The Present and Future of Basketball for Girls: The National Scene," Fourth National Institute on Girls Sports *Proceedings,* 1966, p. 76.

[64]Camille Dorman, Betty G. Blanton, and Bobbie L. Knowles, "Letters to the Editor," *Journal of Health, Physical Education and Recreation,* XL (Apr. 1969), 10.

[65]Charlotte Lambert, "The Pros and Cons of Inter-collegiate Athletic Competition for Women," *Journal of Health, Physical Education and Recreation,* XL (May 1969), 75. See also Katherine Ley, "Athletic Scholarships," *Journal of Health, Physical Education and Recreation,* XL (Sept. 1969), 76-77; and Patsy Neal, "Intercollegiate Competition," *Journal of Health, Physical Education and Recreation, XL* (Sept. 1969), 75-76.

[66]Nye, Robert, "National Basketball Tournament for Women Held at West Chester State," *Pennsylvania Journal of Health, Physical Education and Recreation,* XXXIX (June 1969), 8.

14

Are Athletics Making Girls Masculine? A Practical Answer to a Question Every Girl Asks

by Dudley A. Sargent, M.D.

That there is a change taking place in our American girls and women is unquestioned. And it is so elusive, so baffling of description that it is proving the most attractive of subjects for discussion in the newspaper and magazine. Every journalistic wind that blows either moans or shrieks, according to its source, of feminine activities, and we are forced to listen whether we will or not. Much of the reading matter put forth in certain somewhat sensational papers so utterly disregard truth and reason that we are in danger of half believing that womankind has already become a distorted Amazon creation, to be talked about and wondered at, but no longer to be loved and admired.

What It Is Believed Athletics Are Doing for Girls

There is really nothing in the present state of women's development, either mental or physical, which calls for the pen of a Jeremiah. As a nation we are probably deteriorating physically, and in enlarging upon this topic the alarmist might find much material to his liking. But this statement applies no more to women than to men, and perhaps not as much. Heretofore women have been more creatures of the kitchen and fireside than of the great outdoors, and the present generation of young women who will become the mothers of the next generation have more muscle and more lung capacity than their own mothers. The growth of athletics for girls is largely responsible for this. Colleges for women have more or less grudgingly made room in their curricula for gymnastics and athletics, and the non-collegiate world has followed suit and made athletic sports accessible to women.

From Dudley A. Sargent, "Are Athletics Making Girls Masculine? A Practical Answer to a Question Every Girl Asks," Ladies Home Journal 29 (March 1912): 11, 71 73.

Any one who practices gymnastics or engages in athletics with regularity must find a change in certain organs and muscles of the body: the waist-line is enlarged, the chest expansion is increased, the muscles of the back are strengthened. These are some of the results in both men and women. They are not regarded as alarming in men, but when we mention them in connection with our young women we are interpreted as claiming that our girls are becoming masculine.

Many persons honestly believe that athletics are making girls bold, masculine and overassertive; that they are destroying the beautiful lines and curves of her figure, and are robbing her of that charm and elusiveness that has so long characterized the female sex. Others, including many physicians, incline to the belief that athletics are injurious to the health. This double charge, of course, gives a serious aspect to the whole question, and it should be met.

What Athletics Really Are

Now, what are athletics and how are women affected by them? An athlete is one who contends against another for a victory; athletics are the events in which one contends. A gymnasium is a place for the performance of athletic exercises; a gymnast is a person who trains athletes, and gymnastics are the exercises practiced in the gymnasium for the purpose of putting one's self in proper condition for competing in the athletic contests. In our times the terms athletics, gymnastics and physical training are often used synonymously, while actually they are not alike and may bring about very different results.

If a schoolgirl practices jumping a bar with other girls, as one of the physical exercises prescribed for general development, she is engaging in gymnastics. If, however, the bar is jumped with the purpose of finding out which girl can clear the bar at the greatest height the performance becomes an athletic one. In the first instance the exercise would be undertaken as a means of physical improvement for its own sake. In the second instance, if the spirit of emulation ran high the girls would be engaging in a course of special physical training, not primarily to benefit themselves physically, but for the set purpose of improving their jumping powers so as to vanquish their nearest competitor.

This distinction, that gymnastics are pursued as a means to an end, and athletics as an end in themselves, would apply equally well to such forms of exercise as walking, running, vaulting, swimming and skating, which may be measured in time or space and thus be made competitive. The element of competition and "sport" must , therefore, enter into what we now term athletics.

Athletics for Men and Athletics for Women

All the highly specialized athletic sports and games have been developed to meet the requirements of men, but many of our girls and women have entered into them, and hence the query: "Are our women becoming masculine?" From the biologist's point of view, men and women, like the males and females of most animals, show by their organization that they have been evolved from a type in which both sexes were combined in the same individual. The separation of the sexes did not destroy this dual nature, as is demonstrated by the development of secondary male characteristics in women in extreme age and of feminine characteristics in aged men. This contention may also be supported by the structure of the body's tissue cells, the nuclei of which are made up of paternal and maternal parts.

It is in consequence of this dual structure that secondary sexual characters are latent in both males and females, which may make their appearance in abnormal individuals or under certain conditions of habit and surroundings. In the early history of mankind men and women led more nearly the same life, and were therefore more nearly alike physically and mentally than in the subsequent centuries of civilization. This divergence of the sexes is a marked characteristic among highly civilized races. Co-education and participation in occupations and recreations of certain kinds may have a tendency to make the ideals and habits of women approximate those of men in these highly civilized races. But such approximation would not belong to the progressive stages of the evolution of mankind.

Do Women Need as Much Exercise as Men?

Such changes would be convergences in structure and character, and while they might lead to what we should now consider an advancement this condition would not in any way alter the fact that the tendency would be for women to become virile and men to become effeminate, and both sexes would approximate each other, which would mean the retrogressive period of the evolution of the sexes. These biological theories, although usually considered in connection with the evils of co-education, are equally applicable to the consideration of the evils which have followed the entrance of women into commercial life, and must follow them into competitive athletics which are regulated according to men's rules and standards.

From a physiological point of view woman needs physical exercise as much as man. She has the same kind of brain, heart, lungs, stomach and tissues, and these organs in her are just as responsive to exercise as in men. Fundamentally both sexes have the same bones and muscles. They are much larger, however, in the average male than in the average female.

The average male weighs about one hundred and thirty-five pounds without clothes and is about five feet seven inches in height, while the female weighs about one hundred and fifteen pounds and is about five feet two inches in height. The male has broad, square shoulders, the female narrow, sloping ones. The male has a large, muscular chest, broad waist, narrow hips and long and muscular legs, while the female has little muscle in the chest, a constricted waist, broad hips, short legs and thighs frequently weighted with adipose tissue. The ankles, waist, feet and hands in the male are much larger than those in the female. In point of strength the female is only about one-half as strong as the male; and the average lung capacity of the male is two hundred and sixty cubic inches. To these average conditions there are, of course, many exceptions.

Acrobats Not Always What They Seem

In speaking of the mental or physical qualities of a man or woman we should bear in mind that each is the product of two factors, male and female. According to the law of chance a son may inherit from one-tenth to nine-tenths of his characteristics through his mother's side, and a daughter may inherit from one-tenth to nine-tenths of hers through her father's side, the inheritance from remote ancestry not being taken into consideration. Twenty-five percent of men and women, however, will inherit about equally from their fathers and mothers.

It is an interesting fact that most of the famous athletes whom I have examined attributed their great power largely to the fine physiques of their mothers. The mother of Louis Cyr, the strongest man in the world, could easily shoulder a barrel of flour and carry it up several flights of stairs. I have seen one of the scrubwomen who clean the Hemenway Gymnasium at Harvard University put a hundred-pound dumbbell above her head with each hand. Great feats of strength, skill and endurance are frequently performed by women at the circus and the vaudeville theater, and it is well known in the profession that some of the best gymnasts performing in public are women disguised as men. In justice to my sex I should mention the obvious corollary to this fact that many of the best acrobats are men attired as women.

No Athletic Sport Prohibitive to Women

I have no hesitation in saying that there is no athletic sport or game in which some women cannot enter, not only without fear of injury but also with great prospects of success. In nearly every instance, however, it will be found that the women who are able to excel in the rougher and more masculine sports have either inherited or acquired masculine characteristics. This must necessarily be so, since it is only by taking on masculine attributes that success in certain forms of athletics can be worn. For instance, a woman could not hope to be successful in practice of heavy gymnastics where she has to handle her own weight without reducing the girth of her hips and thighs and increasing the development of her arms, chest and upper back. She could not hope to succeed in rowing or in handling heavy weights without broadening the waist and shoulders and strengthening the muscles of the back and abdomen. Her relatively short legs and heavy hips and thighs would handicap her severely in all running, jumping and vaulting contests, and render it practically impossible for her to make records in these events comparable to those made by men.

These athletic limitations do not apply only to women as women, but also to men who have women's physical characteristics. Nor do the limitations which I have mentioned apply to young girls from ten to fifteen years of age, who, if properly trained, will often surpass boys of the same age in any kind of game or athletic performance. But it is at these ages that girls have neat, trim and boyish figures. If girls received the same kind of physical training as boys throughout their growing and developing period they could make a much more creditable showing as athletes when they become adult women. The interesting question is: Would such girls become more womanly women, and the boys more manly men?

The Best Sports for Girls

The athletics in which girls most frequently indulge are lawn tennis, running, jumping, hurdling, swimming, skating, field hockey, cricket, basket-ball, rowing, canoeing, fencing, archery, bowling, vaulting and certain forms of heavy gymnastics. Some girls also play ice hockey, lacrosse, baseball, polo and association football, while others box and wrestle and play Rugby footall just as their brothers do. There is really no such thing as sex in sport, any more than there is sex in education. All sports are indulged in by most men, and most sports are enjoyed by some women.

There are no sports that tend to make women masculine in an objectionable sense except boxing, baseball, wrestling, basket-ball, ice hockey, water polo and Rugby football. These sports are thought better adapted to men than to women, because they are so rough and strenuous. They afford opportunity for violent personal encounter, which is distasteful to many men as well as to most women. That is the real objection to all antagonistic sports, and that is the reason why it is so difficult for a lady or a gentleman to indulge in them. But we must bear in mind that all athletic sports are of the nature of a contest, and in this very fact lies much of their physical, mental and moral value.

These Make Women More Masculine

Physically all forms of athletic sports and most physical exercises tend to make women's figures more masculine, inasmuch as they tend to broaden the shoulders, deepen the chest, narrow the hips, and develop the muscles of the arms, back and legs, which are masculine characteristics. Some exercises, like bowling, tennis, fencing, hurdling and swimming, tend to broaden the hips, which is a feminine characteristic. But archery, skating and canoeing, which are thought to be especially adapted to women, tend to develop respectively broad shoulders, long feet and deep muscular chests, which are essentially masculine; while rowing, which is thought to be the most masculine of all exercises tends to broaden the hips, narrow the waist, develop the large front and back thighs and give many of the lines of the feminine figure.

Just how all-round athletics tend to modify woman's form may be judged by comparing the conventional with the athletic type of woman. The conventional woman has a narrow waist, broad and massive hips and large thighs. In the athletic type of woman sex characteristics are less accentuated, and there is a suggestion of reserve power in both trunk and limbs. Even the mental and moral qualities that accompany the development of such a figure are largely masculine, but this is because women have not yet had as many opportunities to exercise them.

Sports Should Be Adapted to Women

Some of the specific mental and physical qualities which are developed by athletics are increased powers of attention, will, concentration, accuracy, alertness, quickness of perception, perseverance, reason, judgment, forbearance, patience, obedience, self-control, loyalty to leaders, self-denial, submergence of self, grace, poise, suppleness, courage, strength and endurance. These qualities are as valuable to women as to men. While there is some danger that women who try to excel in men's sports may take on more marked masculine characteristics ... this danger is greatly lessened if the sports are modified so as to meet their peculiar qualifications as to strength, height, weight, etc. Inasmuch as the average woman is inferior to the average man in nearly all physical qualifications, all the apparatus used and the weights lifted, as well as the height and distance to be attained in running, jumping, etc., should be modified to meet her limitations. Considering also the peculiar constitution of her nervous system and the great emotional disturbances to which she is subject, changes should be made in many of the rules and regulations governing the sports and games for men, to adapt them to the requirements of women.

Modify Men's Athletics for Women

Any one who has had much experience in teaching or training women must have observed these facts in regard to them: Women as a class cannot stand a prolonged mental or physical strain as well as men. Exact it of them and they will try to do the work, but they will do it at a fearful cost to themselves and eventually to their children. Give women frequent intervals of rest and relaxation and they will often accomplish as much in twenty-four hours as men accomplish. So firmly have I become convinced of this fact that I have arranged the schedule of work at both the winter and summer Normal Schools at Cambridge so that periods of mental and physical activity follow each other alternately, and both are interspersed with frequent intervals of rest.

The modifications that I would suggest in men's athletics so as to adapt them to women are as follows: Reduce the time of playing in all games and lengthen the periods of rest between the halves. Reduce the heights of high and low hurdles and lessen the distance between them. Lessen the weight of the shot and hammer and all other heavy-weight appliances. In heavy gymnastics have bars, horses, swings, ladders, etc., adjustable so that they may be easily adapted to the requirements of women. In basket-ball, a favorite game with women and girls, divide the field of play into three equal parts by lines, and insist upon the players confining themselves to the space prescribed for them. This insures that every one shall be in the game, and prevents some players from exhausting themselves. If the field of play is large enough seven or nine players on a side are preferable to the five required by the men's rules. As the game is played today by men, with only five on a side and without lines, it brings a harder strain on the heart, lungs and nervous system than the game of football does.

I am often asked; "Are girls overdoing athletics at school and college?" I have no hesitation in saying that in many of the schools where basket-ball is being played according to rules for boys many girls are injuring themselves in playing this game. The numerous reports of these girls breaking down with heart trouble or a nervous collapse are mostly too well founded. Other instances are recorded where schoolgirls have broken down in training for tennis tournaments, or for running, jumping and swimming contests. These instances generally occur in schools or colleges where efforts are made to arouse interest in athletics by arranging matches between rival teams, clubs and institutions, and appealing to school pride, loyalty, etc., to furnish the driving power. Under the sway of these powerful impulses the individual is not only forced to do her best, but to do even better than her best, though she breaks down in her efforts to surpass her previous records.

There will be little honor or glory in winning a race, playing a game, or doing a "stunt" which every other girl could do. It is in the attempt to win distinction by doing something that others cannot do that the girl who is over-zealous or too ambitious is likely to do herself an injury. For this reason girls who are ambitious to enter athletic contests should be carefully examined and selected by a physician or trained woman expert, and the usual method of trying out unprepared candidates by actual contests in order to determine "the survival of the fittest" should not be allowed.

To Handle a Girl in Athletics

By slow and careful preparation a girl who is organically sound may be trained to participate safely in almost any form of athletics. But inasmuch as the heart, lungs and other important organs do not attain their full power and development until a girl is about eighteen to twenty years of age no girl should be pushed to her limit in physical or mental effort before that time, if ever.

It is during the youthful period of from ten to fifteen years of age that girls are most susceptible of improvement if judiciously looked after; it is during the same period that they are most likely to be injured if they are not wisely cared for. For this reason every girls' school where athletics are encouraged should have a special teacher to look after the physical condition of the girls, who should not be left to become victims of their own zeal and the unbridled enthusiasm of a partisan school community.

Parents should insist upon the supervision of the physical as well as the mental training of their girls, especially if the girls are encouraged, through school politics, to engage in athletic contests. Most of the colleges for women have directors of physical training and instructors in athletics and gymnastics whose duty it is to look after the physical condition of the girls and to supervise their athletic sports and games as well as their gymnastic exercises.

It is largely on account of the intelligent supervision of the physical work in the women's colleges that athletics are less likely to be overdone than in many of the schools for girls where there is little or no supervision, though it is much more necessary than in the colleges.

Cause of Good Health of College Girls

College girls as a class are more matured in judgment and discretion and know better what is best for them than other girls. Most of them have had gymnastics or athletics of some kind in the preparatory schools, which, in addition to vigorous mental and social training, have made habits of right living and obedience to the ordinary laws of hygiene quite necessary to enable the girls to withstand the test of fitting for college.

The good health of college girls as a class is not due so much to their studious life and regular habits of living, as has often been stated, as to their fine physique and good constitutional vigor. In a way they represent the natural correlation between a sound mind and a sound body, and they are the survival of a type from which the weaklings have been weeded out in the elementary and secondary schools. Sometimes these naturally strong and vigorous girls think they can go on working indefinitely with their brains without recreation or physical exercise. They make the fatal mistake of drawing too heavily on their inherited constitutional vigor, without doing anything to add to their capital stock. Sooner or later these girls break down and are out of the race for further honors and preferment. These are the girls whose vital resources the college should try to conserve, for they are going to do the work for which the college stands as soon as they have been graduated.

15

Baseball and the National Life

by H. Addington Bruce

On July 20, 1858, there was played the first recorded game of baseball to which an admission fee was charged. The opposing teams were made up of carefully selected players representing New York and Brooklyn; the scene of the game was the old Fashion Race Course on Long Island; and some fifteen hundred people paid $750 to see New York win by four runs.

October 16, 1912, or little more than fifty years later, another New York team, playing in Boston, lost by a single run the last of a series of inter-league games for the title of "World's Champions." The newspapers of the country reported the game in the most minute detail, and incidentally announced that the eight games of the series had been attended by more than 250,000 persons, whose admission fees aggregated $490,833, or an average in excess of 30,000 spectators and average receipts of about $60,000 per game. Nothing could exhibit more impressively than these contrasting figures the tremendous growth in popularity of baseball in the comparatively short interval between the earliest and latest championship game.

When, in the late summer of last year, the Boston "Red Sox" returned from a Western tour which virtually assured to them the championship of the American League, it has been estimated that nearly 100,000 people assembled in the streets of Boston to give them a welcome home. And later, when they played the New York "Giants" in the "World's Series," the course of every game was followed with the most eager attention not alone by the thousands in grand stand and "bleachers," but by many, many thousands more standing in compact masses before the bulletin boards of city newspapers, or in little groups at the telegraph offices of remote and isolated villages. So widespread, in fact, was the interest that the day

From H. Addington Bruce, "Baseball and the National Life," Outlook 104 (May 1913): 104-07.

after the deciding game the newspapers were able to print this astonishing item of news from Washington:

Unprecedented procedure was permitted today in the Supreme
Court of the United States, when the Justices, sitting on the bench
hearing the Government's argument in the "bath-tub trust" case,
received bulletins, inning by inning, of the "World's Championship"
baseball game in Boston. The progress of the playing was closely
watched by the members of the highest court in the land, especially by Associate Justice Day, who had requested the baseball
bulletins during the luncheon recess from 2 to 2:30 p.m. The little
slips giving the progress of the play went to him not only during the
luncheon recess, but when the Court resumed its sitting. They
were passed along the bench from Justice to Justice.

Veritably baseball is something more than the great American
game — it is an American institution having a significant place in the
life of the people, and consequently worthy of close and careful
analysis.

Fully to grasp its significance, however, it is necessary to study it,
in the first place, as merely a game, and seek to determine wherein lie
its peculiar qualities of fascination. As a game, as something that is
"playable," it of course must serve the ordinary ends of play. These,
according to the best authorities on the physiology and psychology of
play, are threefold: the expenditure of surplus nervous energy in a
way that will not be harmful to the organism, but, on the contrary, will
give needed exercise to growing muscles; the development of traits
and abilities that will afterwards aid the player in the serious business
of life; and the attainment of mental rest through pleasurable
occupation.

Until recently it has been customary to emphasize one or
another of these purposes and motives as affording the sole reason
for play. But scientists are beginning to appreciate that all of them
may be operant in determining the action of the play impulse, one
motive being influential in one instance, the second in another, the
third in yet another, or all three in combination. As between the three,
though, the preparation motive would seem to be uppermost, at all
events in the play of childhood and youth, children instinctively favor-
ing those games which, although they are completely unconscious of
the fact, tend most strongly to form and establish the characteristics
that will be most serviceable to them in later years. Or, as stated by
Professor Karl Groos, the first to dwell on this aspect of play:

Play is the agency employed to develop crude powers and
prepare them for life's uses, and from the biological standpoint we
can say: From the moment when the intellectual development of a
species becomes more useful in the "struggle for existence" than
the most perfect instinct, will natural selection favor those individuals in whom the less elaborated faculties have more chance of

being worked out by practice under the protection of parents—that is to say, those individuals that play.

Now, in all civilized countries of the modern world, and especially in countries of advanced economic development and of a form of government like that of the United States, success and progress depend chiefly on the presence of certain personal characteristics. Physical fitness, courage, honesty, patience, the spirit of initiative combined with due respect for lawful authority, soundness and quickness of judgment, self-confidence, self-control, cheeriness, fair-mindedness, and appreciation of the importance of social solidarity, of "team play" — these are traits requisite as never before for success in the life of an individual and of a nation. They are traits developed to some extent by all outdoor games played by groups of competitors. But it is safe to say that no other game — not even excepting football — develops them as does baseball.

One need attend only a few games, whether played by untrained school-boys or by the most expert professionals, to appreciate the great value of baseball as a developmental agent. Habits of sobriety and self-control are established in the players if only from the necessity of keeping in good condition in order to acquit one's self creditably and hold a place on the team. Patience, dogged persistence, the pluck that refuses to acknowledge either weariness or defeat, are essential to the mastery of the fine points of batting, fielding, or pitching — a mastery which in turn brings with it a feeling of self-confidence that eventually will go far in helping its possessor to achieve success off as well as on the "diamond." It takes courage of a high order to play infield positions, as, for example, they ought to be played when "stolen bases" are imminent; and, for that matter, it takes courage to "steal" them when the runner knows that he is likely to be "blocked off" by some courageous infielder of the type of the two Wagners of "Pirate" and "Red Sox" fame.

So, too, courage, and plenty of it, is needed at the bat — courage not simply to face the swiftly moving ball, but to "crowd" the "plate" so as to handicap the pitcher in his efforts to perform successfully and expeditiously the work of elimination. I well remember, in connection with the "World's Series" of 1911, the boldness in this respect displayed by the New York player Snodgrass, when batting against the pitching of the mighty Bender. Time after time Snodgrass stood so close to the "plate" as to draw vehement protests from his opponent, with whom, as an American League partisan, I heartily sympathized. But at the same time I could not withhold some slight measure of admiration for the courage of the batsman, typical of the spirit which, pervading the whole team, had no small share in winning for the "Giants" the National League honors in 1911 and again last year.

As an agent in the development of the "team spirit" baseball is no less notable. The term "sacrifice hit" eloquently expresses one phase of the game which must leave on all playing it an indelible impression of the importance in all affairs of life of unselfish co-operation. The extent, indeed, to which baseball tends to inculcate the lesson of subordination of self for the common good is well shown by a little story I heard not long ago regarding two professional base-ball players. One was the short-stop, the other the second baseman, of a "major" league team, and consequently they were required by the duties of their positions to work more closely together than any other members of the team except the pitcher and catcher. One day, the story goes, they had a quarrel so bitter that for the remainder of the season they did not address a word to each other when off the "diamond." But, once the umpire had cried "Play ball!" their antago-nism was temporarily dropped, and they fought the common foe in as complete accord as though they had been the best of friends. Surely a game that can develop such a social consciousness — and con-science — is a game of which any nation may be proud, and to which it may well feel indebted.

And, besides aiding powerfully in physical and moral develop-ment, baseball is also a splendid mind-builder. The ability to think, and to think quickly, is fostered by the duties of its every position as well as by the complicated problems that are constantly arising in its swiftly changing course of events. Time and again games have been won, or the way has been cleared to victory, by the quickness of a player or a manager in appreciating the possibilities of a critical situa-tion and planning a definite plan of campaign to meet the emergency. It was thus, to give a single illustration, with the final game of last year's "World's Series."

That game was won by the "Red Sox" by the score of three runs to two, an extra inning being necessary, as the score stood one to one in the ninth. The newspapers next day gave unenviable prominence to two New York fielders, to whose errors in the tenth inning the loss of the game was ascribed. Actually the turning-point came in the sev-enth inning, when New York led by one run to none for Boston.

From the start of the game Mathewson, the premier pitcher of the National League, had been disposing of the "Red Sox" batsmen with all his old-time skill. Bedient, his young rival, had been doing almost equally well, although New York had earned a run off him in the third inning. In Boston's half of the seventh, with two men out and a man on first base, the manager of the "Red Sox" — who also, as it happened, was the man then on first base — made the move that undoubtedly saved the game for his team. It was Bedient's turn to bat, but instead Manager Stahl sent to the "plate" a utility outfielder, Henriksen, who until that moment had not once been at bat in the series. Mathewson, utterly in the dark as to his weaknesses as a batsman, tried him with a variety of pitches. One proved so much to his liking that he drove it past third base for a hit that brought in the tying run. Stahl's judgment, plus Henriksen's ability to "make good," had turned impending defeat into possible victory.

So incessant and so varied are the demands made on the ball-player's intelligence that any one who really knows the game will be inclined to endorse unreservedly the published declaration of that most successful baseball-player and most successful business man, Mr. Albert G. Spalding:

"I never struck anything in business that did not seem a simple matter when compared with complications I have faced on the baseball field. A young man playing baseball gets into the habit of quick thinking in most adverse circumstances and under the most merciless criticism in the world — the criticism from the 'bleachers.' If that doesn't train him, nothing can. Baseball in youth has the effect in later years of making him think and act a little quicker than the other fellow."

To-day this is even more the case than in the days when Mr. Spalding led his Boston and Chicago teams to victory, for with the passage of time the technique of the game has been improved to an extent that makes it more of a developmental agent than it was even ten years ago. Lacking the strength, skill, and experience of the professional player, the schoolboy whose efforts are confined to the "diamond" of the vacant lot or public park plays the game under precisely the same rules as the professional, and with no less zest and earnestness, and profits correspondingly. To be sure, in playing it he does not dream for an instant that he is thereby helping to prepare himself for the important struggles of maturity. He plays it merely because he finds it "good fun" — merely because, in its variety and rapidity of action, in the comparative ease with which its fundamental principles may be learned, and in its essentially co-operative yet competitive character, it affords an intensely pleasurable occupation. It is, in truth, a game which makes an irresistible appeal to the instincts of youth precisely because it so admirably meets the principal objects of play — mental rest through enjoyment, exercise for the muscles, the healthy expenditure of surplus nervous energy, and practice and preparation for life's work.

This, of course, does not explain its popularity with the non-playing American public of mature years, a popularity which seems to many the more surprising and reprehensible in view of the fact that to-day, when baseball games are drawing larger crowds than in all the previous history of the sport, the Nation is burdened to an appalling extent by economic and social evils. But in reality this phenomenon is neither so unusual nor so ominous as alarmists would have us believe. "Give us games!" was the cry of the Roman populace in time of disaster many centuries ago, and it has since been unconsciously echoed by many another people under the stress of some great crisis.

Baseball itself, it is worth noting, was a product of the period of anti-slavery agitation that preceded the crisis of the Civil War, having been invented in 1839, two years after the murder of the abolitionist Elijah P. Lovejoy, and one year after the burning of Pennsylvania Hall, in Philadelphia, by a mob of pro-slavery sympathizers; and its first rise into favor as a public spectacle was but a year or so before North and South met in their epochal conflict.

What this means is simply an instinctive resort to sport as a method of gaining momentary relief from the strain of an intolerable burden, and at the same time finding a harmless outlet for pent-up emotions which, unless thus gaining expression, might discharge themselves in a dangerous way. It also means, there is reason to believe, a continuance of the play impulse as an aid in the rational and efficient conduct of life. It is no mere coincidence that the great sport-loving peoples of the world — the Americans, the English, the Canadians, and the Australians — have been pre-eminent in the art of achieving progress by peaceful and orderly reform. There have been times, as in the case of the Civil War, when the issues involved have been such as to make absolutely necessary the arbitrament of arms. But evolution, not revolution, has been the rule in the development of these nations — these nations which above all others respond to the impulse to play.

Baseball, then, from the spectator's standpoint, is to be regarded as a means of catharsis, or, perhaps better, as a safety-valve. And it performs this service the more readily because of the appeal it makes to the basic instincts, with resultant removal of the inhibitions that ordinarily cause tenseness and restraint. For exactly the same reason it has a democratizing value no less important to the welfare of society than is its value as a developmental and tension-relieving agent. The spectator at a ball game is no longer a statesman, lawyer, broker, doctor, merchant, or artisan, but just a plain every-day man, with a heart full of fraternity and good will to all his fellow-men — except perhaps the umpire. The oftener he sits in grand stand or "bleachers," the broader, kindlier, better man and citizen he must tend to become.

Finally, it is to be observed that the mere watching of a game of baseball, as of football, lacrosse, hockey, or any other game of swift action, has a certain beneficial physical effect. It is a psychological commonplace that pleasurable emotions, especially if they find expression in laughter, shouts, cheers, and other muscle-expanding noises, have a tonic value to the whole bodily system. So that it is quite possible to get exercise vicariously, as it were; and the more stimulating the spectacle that excites feelings of happiness and enjoyment, the greater will be the resultant good. Most decidedly baseball is a game well designed to render this excellent service.

Like every virile, vigorous game, it has its defects. But its qualities far outweigh its shortcomings, and it must be accounted a happy day for America when the first players met on the first "diamond" laid out on American soil. The little red school-house has long been extolled as a prime factor in the Republic's progress. I for one am firmly convinced that the lessons taught in it would have lacked much of their potency had it not been for the reinforcement they received from the lessons learned on the baseball field near by. Long may Uncle Sam play ball!

16

The Baseball Magnates and Urban Politics in the Progressive Era: 1895 - 1920

by Steven A. Riess

In the Progressive Era, club owners and sympathetic journalists created a self-serving ideology for baseball. They encouraged the public to believe that the game was one of the foremost indigenous American institutions and that it epitomized the finest qualities of a bygone rural age. Many sportswriters persuaded fans to regard the baseball magnates as benevolent, civic-minded individuals, dedicated to providing their fellow townsfolk with exciting and clean entertainment.[1] Professional baseball however was not really "dominated" by such men, but by individuals with extremely close ties to urban political leaders who were usually members of local political machines. Ironically, the national pastime which was said to exemplify the best characteristics of American society was operated by men who typified some of its worst aspects. In the period from 1901 to 1920, seventeen of the eighteen American and National League baseball teams were run by people with significant political connections. These club owners included political bosses, friends and relatives of men in what we could call high political places, and political allies like traction magnates and professional gamblers. In boss-riddled Cincinnati during the early 1900's for instance, the Cincinnati Reds baseball team was owned by a syndicate which at one time included the city's Republican boss, George B. Cox, his lieutenant, Water Works Commissioner August Herrmann, and the

Steven A. Riess is Associate Professor of History, Northeastern Illinois University. He is the author of Touching Base: Professional Baseball and American Culture in the Progressive Era *(Westport, Conn.: 1980).*

From Steven A. Riess, "Professional Baseball and Urban Politics, 1895-1920," Journal of Sport History, I:1 (May 1974): 41-62. Copyright © 1974 by the North American Society for Sport History. Reprinted with permission.

town's mayor, Julius Fleischmann. The Baltimore Orioles were run by such men as John Mahon, the leading Democrat in Maryland, Sidney Frank, brother of a prominent city councilman, and Judge Harry Goldman. And the Philadelphia Phillies owners included several traction magnates, state senators, and a former New York City police commissioner.[2]

The close alliance between professional baseball teams and urban politicians was not unique to cities of any particular size or geographic location. Politicos were nearly always involved in the operations of the local ball clubs. A study of the professional baseball teams in such regionally representative cities like Atlanta, Chicago, and New York, dramatically suggests the strong link between baseball and politics. New York and Chicago were the two largest American cities at the turn of the century, and after 1903 they had between them five of the sixteen major league clubs. New York's politics were dominated by the notorious Tammany organization, while in Chicago, political machines were very active on the ward level. The southern commercial center of Atlanta was a considerably smaller town, ranking forty-third among all U.S. cities in population with 89,872 inhabitants in 1900. It had just one minor league team which played in the Class B Southern League. There was apparently no important political machine in Atlanta.

By examining the ties between professional baseball and local politicians in these three cities, it becomes clear that the relationship was a mutually beneficial one. Ball clubs with political allies secured preferential treatment from city governments with regards to assessments and various municipal services; inside information about real estate and traction developments; and protection against competitors and community opposition. Politicians benefited because the ball clubs were fine investments which provided them with sources of honest and dishonest graft, patronage for their supporters, traffic for their traction routes, and favorable publicity.

The baseball franchise in Atlanta was nearly always in the hands of important politicians. In 1895 the team was controlled by a joint stock company which included Councilman Joseph E. Maddox and Alderman Joseph Hirsch, who was the team's president. These executives needed whatever political influence they could muster because the East Side residents near Jackson and Old Wheat where Athletic Park was located wanted the field shut down as a public nuisance.[3]

The club's enemies had failed in 1894 to secure a court order preventing the team from playing at Athletic Park, but a year later the issue was brought before the city council. The fight was led by Councilman William J. Campbell, who claimed that noise from the park would disturb the residential community, crowds attending the games were of a disagreeable character, and order could not be maintained there. Joseph Hirsch tried to counter these points by guaranteeing that disorder would not be tolerated, and promising that the park would get the best possible police protection. However the community's petition was adopted, and the Atlanta Baseball Association lost its license.[4]

There was considerable public disapproval of this move, led primarily by the daily newspapers which strongly deprecated the council's action. The city fathers were persuaded to reconsider their decision, and a compromise was reached whereby the team was given a trial period to prove that it could keep order at Athletic Park. There were no problems there that season, but in 1896 the owners moved their team to Brisbine Park, located on the South Side at Ira and Crumley, which was said to be better serviced by public transportation. The Atlanta Traction Company had a route near the site, and it offered the franchise certain inducements to get it to move there. People living in the vicinity protested loudly but to no avail and the club had no difficulty in renewing its license.[5]

Traction companies were always deeply tied into local politics because of their need to secure long term franchises and obtain the right of eminent domain. These firms often owned amusement parks and baseball fields since they felt that these were excellent attractions for riders, and they wanted to be sure that their routes serviced these entertainments. Transit companies were important supporters of professional baseball in all parts of the country, especially the South, and cities like Augusta, Birmingham, Charleston, Macon, Mobile, Montgomery, and New Orleans, all received substantial financial backing from the streetcar lines.[6]

The Atlanta baseball team failed to last out the 1896 season. One year later, a new team was organized by attorney W.T. Moyers, but it survived for just two months. In the winter of 1898, Moyers requested assistance from the local traction interests who were receiving large profits from the fares of fans without contributing to the upkeep of the sport. Moyers persuaded the Atlanta Street Railway Company to support him, and their superintendent, F.W. Zimmerman, purchased stock in the club and became its vice-president. The firm had made $600 on its ballpark route the year before, in spite of the abbreviated season, and Zimmerman was afraid that the streetcar line would lose money if the club failed again. He anticipated profiting by about $3,000 in 1898, but his hopes were crushed for the Southern League collapsed early that season.[7]

Professional baseball was not resumed in Atlanta until 1902 when the Selma club of the revived Southern League was moved there by its owners E.T. Peter and Abner Powell, a former baseball player and owner of the New Orleans franchise. Powell brought out his partner a year later, and developed the enterprise into a profitable venture. He invested about $10,500 in the club, and earned $40,000 by the end of 1904. His success aroused the ire of fans who watched with distaste as the proceeds from their tickets went to an outsider. As in the case of other American cities, the Atlanta fans had a great deal of pride in their hometown team. They preferred local control because they regarded the professional club as an important local institution which represented their city in inter-urban competition and vividly reflected the progressive character of their community.[8] A clique of powerful politicians decided to try to drive Powell out and replace him with Atlanta owners by raising his taxes and establishing a license fee at an inordinately high level. A bill was introduced in the city council in 1904 which proposed charging Powell a fee of fifty dollars plus a five percent tax on his gross receipts, at a time when no other baseball team was taxed outside of its license fee. Abner Powell's enemies were unable to push this drastic measure through the council, and instead it was decided to set the license fee at $200 plus another $100 for police protection. In the meanwhile, the county officials also established an annual $300 assessment against the ball club.[9]

Powell's difficulties were compounded that year because the municipality purchased the 189 acre Piedmont Park, which included the Piedmont Baseball Park where the Atlanta club had played since 1902, as well as other amusement attractions. Powell still had one year remaining on his lease, and had just signed an option to renew with the previous owner, but he was afraid that the city would make it difficult for him in the future. He also was being plagued by the traction interests, who not only did not give him any financial assistance, but actually charged Powell five dollars before every game to guarantee their service.[10] The owner was forced to accede to public pressure and sold his club for $20,000 to a local syndicate which included Fire Chief W.R. Joyner, the team's president in 1889, and Lowry Arnold, solicitor of the criminal court.[11]

Walthal R. Joyner had joined the fire company in 1870 when it was still a volunteer force, and remained after it became a municipal service, serving as fire chief from 1885 until 1906, when he resigned to become mayor. As fire chief, Joyner was the highest paid city official with a salary of $4,000.[12] Joyner's group received financial support from the Georgia Railway and Electric Company, which hoped that the sport would generate traffic along its lines. The team was moved in 1907 from Piedmont Park to a site owned by the transit company on Ponce De Leon Avenue, directly opposite its amusement park.[13] One year later, the streetcar line purchased complete control of the team, which it kept until 1915, when the company sold it for $37,500 to a group led by Councilman Frank H. Reynolds and J.W. Goldsmith, Jr. Goldsmith's father was a former Atlanta councilman, and his uncle was city comptroller. However, the traction firm continued to control the ballpark.[14]

In the midwestern metropolis of Chicago, the influence of politicians on the baseball teams was just as keen as in Atlanta. The Chicago National League club was owned by Albert G. Spalding, one of the first professional baseball players, who was also founder and head of a great sporting goods company. His partners included attorney Charles M. Sherman, Cook County Sheriff Edward Barrett, and Adrian Anson, a former star ballplayer and manager, who was elected city clerk in 1905. The baseball park was the property of the A.G. Spalding Land Association, whose officers included Spalding, James A. Hart, the president of the team, John A. Walsh, a prominent banker and politician, and Charles T. Trego, a Republican merchant and banker, and director of the Chicago Board of Trade from 1875 until 1879.[15]

The National League team enjoyed great success in Chicago during the late nineteenth century, and their good fortune encouraged the American League, which was founded in 1900, to place a team there. The franchise was awarded to Charles Comiskey, a native Chicagoan, who had been a ballplayer and manager before he purchased the St. Paul club of the Western League in 1895. Charles was the third son of John Comiskey, an Irish immigrant who arrived in Chicago in 1852. John Comiskey became a railroad executive and later entered local politics, serving a total of eleven years as alderman. He also held other high offices, including president of the city council, county clerk, and deputy United States internal revenue collector. This family background was immediately helpful for Charles Comiskey because a late winter had slowed down construction of his grandstand in 1900, but union artisans waived many of their rules proscribing night and Sunday labor so that John Comiskey's son would have his ballpark ready for Opening Day.[16]

In 1905 the Chicago Cubs were sold by Spalding's agent James A. Hart to Charles W. Murphy for $105,000. Murphy was a former sports editor of the *Cincinnati Enquirer,* assistant city editor of the *Cincinnati Times-Star,* and press agent for the New York Giants. Murphy had just been hired by the Cubs for a similar job when he discovered that the team was for sale. He immediately rushed to his former publisher Charles Phelps Taft, who loaned him $100,000 to complete the transaction.[17]

Charles P. Taft was the older half-brother, and political adviser of Secretary of War William Howard Taft. Charles was an important power in Ohio Republican politics, and had once served in the United State House of Representatives. He had strong aspirations for a Senate seat, but decided instead to devote most of his attention to helping his brother get elected president. Charles P. Taft had married a wealthy heiress, and they invested a considerable amount of their money in professional baseball.[18]

Charles Murphy's investment was a remarkable success and he quickly repaid the Taft loan, although Taft remained as a minority stockholder. In 1906, the Cubs made $165,000, or more than the price paid for the controlling shares one year before. Taft estimated that the franchise earned $1,260,000 for its stockholders between 1906 and 1915. During that decade the Cubs won four pennants (1906-08, 1910), two world championships (1907-08), and never finished worse than fourth in the league standings. Dividends on capital stock from 1907 to 1913 were an incredible 810 percent. However, competition from the Federal League and public resentment against Charles Murphy who fired his popular manager Frank Chance in 1912, and traded away several of the fans' favorite stars like Ed Reulbach and Joe Tinker in 1913, caused profits to plummet in the next two years to 20 percent and five percent, respectively.[19]

There was also considerable public displeasure over Murphy's mishandling of the ticket scalping problem. Speculators never seemed to have any trouble getting tickets and fans believed that politicians were supporting and protecting them.[20] The scalping of tickets probably received its greatest notoriety during the 1908 World Series between the Cubs and the Detroit Tigers when the Chicago fandom were unable to obtain tickets at the box office because the pasteboards had been secretly sold to speculators. Mayor Busse contemplated retaliating by forbidding the playing of the Series in Chicago on the grounds that the ballpark was unsafe, but the intercession of Corporation Counsel Edward Brundage on behalf of the Cubs owners deterred the mayor. The fans responded to the scalping scandal by boycotting the games played in Chicago.[21]

The combination of the ticket scalping scandals, the public alienation from Murphy by his trades of popular players, and his habit of making indiscreet comments to journalists which reflected poorly on baseball, persuaded the other National League owners to oust him before the start of the 1914 season. Charles P. Taft agreed to buy Murphy's controlling interest for about $500,000 but he simultaneously announced his intention to sell the franchise as soon as possible. Several syndicates were formed to purchase the club, and they all included prominent Chicago politicians. One group consisted of William Hale Thompson, a former alderman and future mayor, James A. Pugh, a promoter, who was Thompson's political ally, Charles A. McCulloch, a taxi cab executive and Republican politician, and John R. Thompson, a restauranteur and former county treasurer. Another combination included coal merchant John T. Connery, whose brothers were the city clerk and county recorder, his cousin Roger Sullivan, who was in his twenty-fifth year as a Cook County Democratic Committeeman, and was widely recognized as the dominant Democrat in the state, and Harry Gibbons, who had once run for county sheriff.[22]

Taft did not find any of their offers acceptable, and held on to the club for two more seasons until he sold it early in 1916 for $500,000 to Charles Weeghman, the owner of the Chicago Federal team, and his associates. Weeghman's partners were prominent Chicago businessmen and they included Albert D. Lasker, who was the principal stockholder, C.A. McCulloch, A.D. Plamondon, William Walker, and William K. Wrigley. They were important figures in local and national Republican politics who lunched together daily to plot strategy. Lasker was a member of the Republican National Committee, and he and William Wrigley were prominent supporters of California Governor Hiram Johnson for their party's presidential nomination in 1920. After the nominating convention, they rallied to the side of the Republican candidate, Senator Warren G. Harding of Ohio, and Lasker became his public relations director. Harding subsequently rewarded Lasker by making him head of the U.S. Shipping Board.[23]

In Chicago, as in Atlanta, the magnates' political influence helped the teams cope with such matters as the city's building codes and licensing policies. Municipal laws generally stipulated certain requirements for the baseball club to fulfill before they received their license so that the ballpark would be kept safe for spectators and the games would not disturb the surrounding communities. Strict new building codes were written in many large cities during the Progressive era and some of their sections had a direct impact on professional baseball. In Chicago, for instance, club owners had to obtain frontage consents for their site, and were prohibited from constructing a park within 200 feet of a hospital, church, or school. In addition, no new ballpark could be built within the city's fire limits unless it was built with fireproof materials. This condition benefited the older established franchises against potential interlopers just as other progressive regulatory legislation assisted the large firms in other industries, like meatpacking, discourage new competition and eliminate their weaker rivals.[24]

City inspectors were required to examine new baseball parks to make sure they were properly constructed, and then annually reexamine them to check for possible defects and safety violations. However magnates or their contractors could utilize their political influence to secure lax enforcement of the building codes. For example, when an addition was built to the grandstands at the Cubs' West Side Park in 1908, it was inadequately inspected because the contractor Michael F. Powers was a business partner of former Building Commissioner Joseph Downey.[25] These inspections were not intended to be punitive, unless the owners had foolishly incurred the wrath of some politico, but were aimed at discovering potentially dangerous violations which could then be rectified.[26]

The license fee varied widely from city to city, depending, at least partly, on the amount of political power the franchise could muster. In the early 1900's, New York's standard amusement fee was $500, but in Cincinnati, where the team was operated by members of the local Republican machine, the club paid just $100 until 1912 when Mayor Henry T. Hunt's reform administration raised the levy to $750.[27] Chicago's license fees were established on a sliding scale, which varied according to the ballpark's seating capacity. At first, the two professional clubs were assessed $300 each while the several semiprofessional clubs paid $100. Then in 1909 the amusement fees were substantially increased to a point where the Cubs were taxed $1,000 because their field seated more than 15,000 and the White Sox were assessed $700 since their smaller park seated fewer than 15,000.[28]

After World War I when the city was nearly bankrupt, various measures were taken to raise capital, including an increase in the license schedules for baseball parks. The license fee for fields with capacities in excess of 20,000 was set at $2,000, and the impost on grounds seating between 15,000 and 20,000 spectators was made $1,500. Comiskey Park fell under the higher rate since it seated well over 30,000 people, and the Cubs were assessed the lesser amount.[29] Then in 1921, Alderman Anton J. Cermak, the leader in the search for new sources of revenue, decided to raise previously established fees while also extending the licensing system to a variety of professions previously not covered. Cermak introduced a bill in the city council which called for a five percent tax on the gross receipts of the professional baseball teams. The local major league clubs were quite disturbed by the proposal, since if it had been operating one year before, the White Sox would have been taxed $30,000 and the Cubs, $20,000. Alfred Austrian, the attorney for both franchises, and a familiar figure to local politicians, met with the city council's Committee on Revenue, and tried to demonstrate the folly of Cermak's bill. Austrian convinced the aldermen not to adopt that legislation, and instead provided them with a compromise measure they later enacted, which doubled the established license fees for the major league teams.[30]

The baseball teams expected that as taxpayers, they were entitled to police protection, both inside and outside their fields. The danger of riot or some lesser disturbance always existed whenever thousands of people gathered in one place, and crowds at ball games tended to be particularly unruly. Fans jostled with each other as they lined up for tickets, and once inside the park they tended to make themselves obnoxious by shouting caustic comments at players, umpires and other spectators. Besides preserving peace, police officers were also needed to deter gambling inside the parks and ticket scalping outside. Chicago's municipal patrolmen were assigned to duty inside the ballparks even though it was private property. The teams were not charged for the service, which amounted to a daily savings of twenty to fifty dollars. Several bills were introduced in the city council to assess the magnates for the cost of this protection, but they were never passed.[31]

The single most important problem that faced Chicago baseball executives in the first twenty years of the century was not recruiting ballplayers, discovering a suitable location for their ballparks, keeping taxes low, or securing police protection. Rather the principal dilemma was the disclosure in 1920 that the previous year's World Series had been fixed by several White Sox players in the interest of certain professional gamblers. Despite the rhetoric of professional baseball which claimed the sport was free of that vice, baseball was strongly tainted by gambling. In fact, several baseball owners were professional gamblers, horsemen, heavy bettors, or friends of professional gamblers. The sport served as a nexus between politics and organized crime.[32]

While the main attraction of baseball was the action of the game, unlike horse racing for instance, the nature of the sport was highly conducive to betting, and people wagered on the outcome of ball games, the number of hits and runs, and even the probability of a batted ball being caught. Gambling on baseball was popular throughout the nation, especially in cities like Boston and Pittsburgh where there were no race tracks to interest the betting crowd. The baseball owners spoke out against pools and other betting systems because they were afraid that public gambling on the sport might harm its prestige and reputation for honesty, and thereby its appeal, by encouraging fans to believe that gamblers were fixing games.[33]

But in spite of their rhetoric, the baseball owners did little to curtail the gambling menace. Signs were posted inside the parks which declared that betting was forbidden there, and private police roamed the stands to discourage open wagering. Only on rare occasions were any bettors evicted from the premises. Professional gamblers were seldom arrested, and rarely convicted, since it was very difficult to prove a case against them and because they were protected by influential political allies. In addition, there was no great demand for strict enforcement of the anti-betting codes because the professional gamblers were dispensing a desired service for their clients and did not harm innocent bystanders.[34]

The gambling problem was climaxed by the revelation near the end of the 1920 season that the 1919 World Series between the Chicago White Sox and an apparently inferior Cincinnati Reds team had been fixed by eight White Sox players in the interest of the infamous Arnold Rothstein. When Charles Comiskey first became suspicious that the outcome of the Series had been prearranged, he visited with his friend, States' Attorney Maclay Hoyne, who promised to keep the matter out of the courts while Comiskey tried to clear up the affair by himself.[35] Hoyne cooperated fully with Comiskey and did not initiate an investigation of the rumored fix until after Chicago Cubs President

William Veeck, Sr., reported receiving a number of telegrams and telephone calls warning him that the Cubs game scheduled for August 31, 1920 was fixed. Hoyne then called for a special grand jury to investigate the entire matter of baseball gambling, responding both to the growing public demands for an inquiry, and his own need for a campaign issue for the forthcoming primary election.[36]

Hoyne lost his bid for reelection, but before leaving office, he stole the confessions made by several of the indicted ballplayers together with their waivers of immunity. The people behind this theft were Alfred Austrian, Comiskey's lawyer, and William Fallon, the attorney for Arnold Rothstein. The loss of that testimony severely hampered the prosecution's case, and the defendants were found not guilty. Nevertheless, Judge Kennesaw Mountain Landis, the newly appointed commissioner of baseball, refused to reinstate the athletes. In 1924, when Joe Jackson, one of the eight players involved in the scandal, sued to regain some back pay, the missing documents were conveniently produced by Comiskey to prove Jackson's complicity in fixing the World Series.[37]

The far reaching political ties of Chicago Baseball Clubs seem almost minor in comparison to the situation in New York City where the notorious Tammany Hall organization was intimately involved in the affairs of local baseball teams since the late 1860's. The New York Mutuals, for instance, a leading amateur club of the post-Civil War period, was controlled by the unscrupulous William Marcy Tweed, who got the city government to contribute $30,000 to its upkeep. The players were ostensible city employees, but they were really being subsidized to play baseball.[38]

Tammany had complete control of professional baseball in New York City until 1890 when several Republican politicians established a Brotherhood League team there. That association lasted just one year, but the competition bankrupted the Tammany owners of the New York Giants, who agreed to merge their club with the Brotherhood team. The Giants were operated for the next four years by Republicans Edward Talcott, a stockbroker, Cornelius Van Cott, postmaster of New York, and General Edward A. McAlpin, a tobacconist and realtor who had been active in elective politics before becoming a leader in the Republican club movement.[39]

The Democratic organization regained control of the franchise in January, 1895, when Andrew Freedman, a rising young realtor, purchased the controlling interest for $48,000. Freedman had joined Tammany in 1881 at the age of twenty-one, and he soon became an intimate friend of Richard Croker, the machine's future boss. Freedman was able to secure many choice business opportunities because of his close ties with Croker, and the two men cooperated in several ventures. Freedman never held any governmental position, but he did have enormous political influence through his alliance with

Boss Croker and as a member of Tammany's powerful finance committee, which was its central policy-making body. He also served as treasurer of the national Democratic party in 1897.[40]

Freedman ran his baseball team as if it were an adjunct of Tammany, fighting with the baseball players and the press, encouraging rowdy baseball playing, and bullying his fellow magnates into accepting many of his demands. For instance, the league awarded him an annual grant of $15,000 just so he would continue leasing Manhattan Field which was adjacent to the Polo Grounds and was the logical site for a competing league to use for a ballpark.[41]

Interlopers were afraid to invade New York as long as Andrew Freedman remained in baseball since he controlled most of the suitable locations for baseball fields through leases or options, and also because invaders knew that even if they did somehow secure a good lot, Freedman would use his political clout to get streets cut through their property or disrupt their transit facilities.[42] The American League hoped to establish a New York franchise, but they were deterred by Freedman's presence. The association proclaimed itself a major league in 1901, but a New York team was essential to certify that higher status and to obtain greater profits. Thus the American Leaguers were quite interested in the outcome of the 1901 mayoralty election because experts gave the Fusion ticket a good chance to beat the machine, and the baseball people anticipated that if the election went poorly for Tammany, Freedman would lose his power to prevent them from putting a team in the borough.[43]

Tammany was indeed soundly defeated in the elections as Seth Low was elected mayor, and William Travers Jerome was selected district attorney. Several newspapers predicted that the American League would soon establish a club in Gotham as a consequence. But in spite of the debacle, Freedman was still strong enough to forestall the efforts of the new league.[44] However the election did harm the Giants president's power within National League councils, by encouraging some of the other owners to finally stand up to him. An effort was actually made by the Spalding faction to ostracize him at the League's annual winter meeting in December of 1901 as a first move towards taking his franchise away from him. But enough magnates remained loyal to Freedman to prevent the move.[45]

Nine months later, Andrew Freedman sold his team to John T. Brush, the former owner of the Cincinnati Reds, for $200,000, keeping just a few shares of stock. Freedman said he was disappointed in his investment which had never reached its potential, and was tired of the abuse being heaped upon him from all quarters. Furthermore, he had more important business matters to attend to, principally the construction of the New York subway system. He was a director of the company that built the underground, and Freedman used his influence to block the Interborough Rapid Transit Construction Company from agreeing to subsidize an American League team early in 1903. He also prevented the Fourth Avenue Line from building a station close to the Brooklyn Dodgers' playing field.[46]

John T. Brush, the new Giants owner, was a highly successful Indianapolis clothing merchant, who first got into baseball when he acquired the Indianapolis team of the American Association in 1887 for a nominal sum. Three years later he purchased the Cincinnati Reds for $25,000, and then sold them in 1902 for $146,000.[47] A newspaper story was published several years later which asserted that Cincinnati's Republican political machine had apparently forced Brush to sell his club to them. The journalist alleged that a rumor had reached Brush that York Street was going to be extended through the ballpark as part of a series of municipal improvements. Brush was perturbed by the gossip and met with a local politician who advised him to sell the team to the Republican organization for a fraction of its real worth. Brush denied the story, but he did sell the franchise to a consortium comprised of Boss George B. Cox, Mayor Fleischmann, and August Herrmann.[48]

New York at this time had a second National League team, the Brooklyn Dodgers, as a result of the city's annexation of Brooklyn in 1898. The owner of that team was Charles Ebbets who had just purchased the club. He had been a printer until 1883 when he was hired by the Brooklyn franchise as a sort of general factotum, and his duties included printing scorecards and selling tickets.[49] In 1898 Ebbets moved his enterprise from its distant site in Brownsville to its original location near the Gowanus Canal in Red Hook where the team was much more accessible to its fans. He received considerable financial support in this venture from streetcar magnate Al Johnson, brother of Cleveland's future mayor, Tom Johnson. The traction executive had routes located near the old site which he expected would benefit from the traffic of fans attending games.[50] Fifteen years later, Ebbets moved his team to another spot in Flatbush, where he nearly went bankrupt building a modern fireproof stadium. Consequently he had to take in the McKeever brothers, who were prominent Brooklyn contractors, as partners. They were active in politics, and Steven McKeever had served a term in the city council.[51]

Charles Ebbets himself, was a notable political figure, having served several years as an alderman and a term in the state assembly. In 1904 he ran for the state senate but was defeated in the Roosevelt landslide.[52] Ebbets tried to put his political skills to practical use by campaigning for reform of the blue laws which proscribed Sunday baseball in New York. Sunday reform received substantial Tammany backing for it was a popular measure among its constituents. Ebbets hoped to secure Sunday baseball by staging Sabbath games in 1904, 1905, and in 1906, by circumventing the prohibitory laws. He did not sell tickets of admission to games, but admitted fans free if they purchased programs or magazines for fifty cents or seventy-five cents or if they volunteered a "donation. "He received cooperation from the police who rarely made arrests for violations, and from magistrates who rarely convicted anyone tried in their courts. However the vigorous Sabbatarian organizations prevailed because they secured redress in higher courts, and got a reform police commissioner to force Ebbets to cease his efforts at evading the law. Charles Ebbets and his allies then turned to the state legislature where they hoped to repeal the blue laws. Sunday reform bills had been introduced in Albany each year since 1897, but upstate rural Republicans controlled both chambers, and Democrats rarely even got their bills out of committee. Only after World War I, when a broad coalition of labor leaders, veterans organizations, reformers, and Tammanyites was established did the "repressive" Sabbath laws get amended to permit Sunday baseball. The results of this crusade indicated that the urban political machines were not omnipotent and could not do everything they wished.[53]

New York became the site of a third major league team in March, 1903, when the American League finally succeeded in placing a franchise there. American League President Ban Johnson had tried for some time to find a group of non-Tammanyites who had sufficient influence to counter Andrew Freedman and obtain a suitable site for a ballpark. But he was unsuccessful, and in desperation acceded to Tammany and granted the franchise to some politicos who found a location for a baseball field that Freedman did not control. The syndicate was ostensibly headed by Joseph Gordon, a former owner of the New York Giants, who had been an assistant district leader, state assemblyman, and city buildings superintendent. The real owners, though, were Frank J. Farrell, a leading gambler, and William Devery, a former police chief. Tom Foley, the leader of the Second District, and a future sheriff, was a minor stockholder. The lucrative construction contracts were awarded to Thomas McAvoy, the Tammany leader in Washington Heights where the new field was located.[54]

Frank Farrell was said to be the head of New York's gambling trust in 1901, which allegedly included Chief Devery, Police Commissioner Joseph Sexton, City Clerk J.F. Carroll, Mayor Van Wyck, and Tim Sullivan, the powerful leader of the Third District. Farrell had important interests in several local poolrooms, and he owned a luxurious casino, designed by the noted architect Stanford White, which was frequented by members of High Society. He also had substantial holdings at the Saratoga Springs resort, and was a partner with Julius Fleischmann in a major racing stable.[55]

Farrell's associate, William Devery, had joined the police force in 1878, and he advanced rapidly through the ranks, aided by his political friends, Richard Croker and Tim Sullivan. Devery was appointed police chief after a turbulent twenty-year career during which he was repeatedly castigated for taking bribes to permit gamblers and keep-ers of disorderly houses to operate. Throughout his flamboyant ten-ure, Devery could usually be found at the corner of Twenty-Eighth Street and Eighth Avenue, meeting with bailbondsmen, dive owners, and pool room operators. His regime was so blatantly corrupt that the state legislature decided in 1901 to abolish his position, and replace it with a commission system. However Tammany circumvented the intent of that reform by getting the new police commissioner to appoint Devery as his deputy, and then the commissioner left the department in his hands. When the Fusion mayor, Seth Low, took office on January 1, 1902, one of the first things he did was relieve Devery of his post.[56]

After the disastrous election in the fall of 1901, William Devery broke with the Croker wing of Tammany which had blamed him for their defeat. He ran for district leader of the Ninth Ward in 1902, and defeated the regular organization's hand-picked candidate. Tam-many's executive committee then issued him an unprecedented rebuff when they refused to accept his claim for admission to the central committee as the duly elected leader of the Ninth District. Miffed by this rebuke, he left the regular party and established his own district organization which was strong enough to elect an assembly-man. Buoyed by this success, Devery ran for mayor on an indepen-dent slate in 1903, but was soundly thrashed.[57]

The close relations between the owners of the New York base-ball clubs and Tammany Hall helped the teams obtain favored treat-ment from the police department, which not only maintained order outside the playing fields, but also patrolled the environs of the ball-parks. In 1907, however, this service was discontinued by the reform police commissioner, General Thomas A. Bingham, who decided to enforce the law which prohibited the use of municipal police within private property unless there was some manifest danger present. Bingham's decision was immediately tested by the New York Giants, who publicly announced that they would not engage any private police for the Opening Day game that year, and warned Bingham that he would be responsible for the consequences. The result was a riot when many of the 17,000 spectators swarmed over the field at the beginning of the ninth inning. After fifteen minutes of chaos, the man-agement appealed to police officers stationed outside for assistance, but the constables refused to go inside and help quell the disturbance.[58]

Bingham's action was supported by the *New York Times* which noted that the law was quite clear in its proscription of the use of city patrolmen to police private grounds. Bingham had previously com-plained of the way his staff was often weakened whenever officers were detailed to perform work that should have been done by special police at the expense of individuals running the particular event. He felt entrepreneurs should be made to realize that the cost of protection was a necessary and expected expense, and that people who assembled crowds for their own private financial gain should pay for the safeguarding of the affair out of their profits.[59]

After this confrontation, the Giants decided to hire a number of uniformed Pinkerton agents to keep order at the Polo Grounds. The New York Americans retained retired policemen for their field. As long as there was no disorder, these operatives were adequate. But on those occasions when the fans did get out of control, the special policemen were virtually useless because they did not have any legitimate authority or power, and spectators refused to listen to them. Besides, the guards were probably more frightened of the spectators than the fans were of them, and they were careful not to antagonize the crowds.[60] The owners continued for some time to try to reverse Bingham's decision and get uniformed policemen to patrol their events, but the city government only relented on rare occasions.[61] This was another of those rare instances when the political machine failed to assist the local ball clubs.

The police continued to work outside the ballparks, and as in Chicago, one of their biggest problems was ticket scalping. Extensive preparations were announced by the New York police to eliminate scalping at the 1912 World Series. Plainclothesmen and other officers were detailed to keep known speculators from obtaining extra tickets at the public sale, and an area was cordoned off for fans waiting in line for tickets. The first one hundred individuals in line were recognized as either plainclothesmen, uniformed officers, or speculators, and people with pull were seen going through the ticket offices several times. Instead of going to the end of the queue, these repeaters returned to the front where policemen helped them back into line. Scalpers also obtained additional paste boards by buying them from people who had waited in line or by bringing boys and women with them to purchase tickets. One leading sportswriter estimated that a quarter of the reserved seats were sold to speculators.[62]

In 1915 and 1919, respectively, the Yankees and Giants were sold to men with substantial influence in Tammany Hall. William Devery and Frank Farrell sold their club for $460,000 to Jacob Ruppert, Jr., the heir to the Ruppert Breweries fortune, and Tillinghast Huston, a civil engineer who made his fortune in Cuba after the Spanish-American War. The old owners had become estranged from each other as they bickered over the disappointing performance of their team on the field and at the box office, especially in comparison to their rivals, the Giants. Furthermore, they were both in dire need of funds.[63]

Jacob Ruppert, the principal figure in the new Yankee management, was an important Tammanyite. He joined the organization in 1888 at the age of twenty-one, in search of prestige, power, and protection for the family business. Ruppert eventually became a sachem of the association and served as a member of its finance committee. He was personally selected by Boss Croker in 1897 to run for the presidency of the city council in order to balance the ticket with a German candidate. However Croker had to withdraw the nomination because it failed to placate the German-Americans who had expected the mayoralty nomination, and since it aroused the jealousy of the other New York brewers. As a reward for his party loyalty, Ruppert was nominated for Congress from a Republican district in 1898. He was elected in an upset and served in that position until 1907.[64]

The New York Giants were sold by the Brush family in 1919 to Charles Stoneham for one million dollars. Stoneham was a member of Tammany Hall and counted Al Smith and Tom Foley among his political allies. He was a curb market broker of dubious integrity who had several brushes with the law because of his shady business transactions. Charles Stoneham had two minor partners in the baseball team, John J. McGraw, the Giants' manager, and Magistrate Francis X. McQuade, who was a leading figure in the movement for Sunday baseball. McQuade had handled several cases involving baseball playing on the Sabbath in his capacity as a judge, and he always released the defendants and urged reform of the antiquated codes. Stoneham's investment was quite profitable as the club made $296,803 in 1920, which was the most any National League club made that year. But the Yankees, who were Stoneham's tenants at the Polo Grounds did even better, earning $373,862.[65]

The close ties that existed between local politicians and the professional baseball teams in Atlanta, Chicago, and New York, were typical of the relationship that existed between most franchises and their communities in the Progressive Era. A ball club's political associations were often direct, in which case the team's executives were themselves party leaders or elected officials. In other instances, the political elite were friends of the owners or else they were closely tied to a traction company which supported the ball club. Political connections were useful for the baseball teams because they received preferential treatment from the city governments in matters relating to taxation and municipal services, their owners were privy to confidential information about real estate and traction developments, and they were protected against potential competitors and other enemies. In return, the politicos manipulated the local baseball for their benefit in several ways. They used the franchise as a source of honest graft and patronage, as an inducement to encourage people to travel on the traction routes they operated, and to improve their public image.

The domination of professional baseball by urban politicians reflected their ubiquitous presence in all aspects of city life. Businessmen and leaders of various public institutions had to come to terms with them if they wished to be successful. However even though the machines were extremely powerful, they were not omnipotent, as the New York magnates discovered when they attempted to play Sunday baseball or when they tried to prevent a reform police commissioner from withdrawing police protection inside their ballparks. The preeminence of politicos in the national pastime created an interesting paradox since contemporaries regarded baseball as an institution which epitomized the finest qualities of a bygone age, like individualism, honesty, competitiveness, courage, and fairmindedness, and which certified the relevancy of these values in an urbanized, industrialized, and bureaucratized era. Yet the sport was controlled by urban bosses, the enemy of the old-stock Americans who believed in these traditional American values. The machine politicians symbolized to them all that was evil in American society.

Footnotes

[1] Harold Seymour, *Baseball: The Golden Age* (New York: 1971), II, pp. 62-64; David Q. Voigt, *American Baseball: From the Commissioners to Continental Expansion* (Norman, Okla.: 1970), II, 107-108; For typical contemporary attitudes towards baseball, see e.g., H. Addington Bruce, "Baseball and the National Life." *Outlook,* 104 (May, 1913), 103-7; Hugh Fullerton, "Fans," *American Magazine,* 74, (Aug., 1912), 462-7; William A. Phelon, "The Great American Magnate," *Baseball Magazine,* 6 (Jan., 1913), 17-23; Allen Sangree, "Fans and Their Frenzies," *Everybody's,* 17 (Sept., 1907), 378-87: McCready Sykes, "The Most Perfect Thing in America," *Everybody's* 25, (October, 1911), 435-46.

[2] The exception was Milwaukee, which was in the majors just in 1901. See Steven A. Riess, "Professional Baseball and American Culture: Myths and Realities, 1892-1923, With Special Emphasis on Atlanta, Chicago, and New York," (Ph.D. diss., University of Chicago, 1974), chap. 3; Lee Allen, *The Cincinnati Reds* (New York, 1948), 73-75; Frederick G. Lieb, The Baltimore Orioles (New York, 1955), 24; *Philadelphia Inquirer,* 1 March, 1903; *Atlanta Constitution,* 25 Feb. 1909; *New York Tribune,* 23 Dec., 1912.

[3] *Atlanta Constitution,* 4 Feb., 1895, 10 March 1896, 13 July, 1896.

[4] *Ibid.,* 3 March, 1894, 3 April 1894, 19 March, 1895.

[5] *Ibid.,* 19 & 20 March, 1895; *Atlanta Journal,* 9 & 11 April 1896.

[6] Ben B. Seligman, *The Potentates: Business and Businessmen in American History* (New York: 1971), 159; W.E. Harrington, "Report of Committee on Promotion of Traffic," *Street Railway Journal,* 30 (Oct. 26, 1907), 864; *Atlanta Constitution,* 31 Jan. 1898, 30 Jan., 1903.

[7] *Ibid.,* 13 July, 1896, 6 Sept., 1897, 23 Jan., 1898, 16 Feb., 1898; *Atlanta Journal,* 20 Jan., 1898; *Sporting Life,* 5 March, 1898.

[8] *Atlanta Constitution,* 23 Dec., 1902, 16 Feb., 1904, 23 June, 1905; *Atlanta Journal,* 27 May, 1904, 24 & 27 Jan., 1905; Raymond B. Nixon, *Henry Grady: Spokesman for the New South (Atlanta, 1943),* p. 229.

[9] *Atlanta Journal,* 1, 27 May, 1904, 10 June, 1904; *Atlanta Constitution,* 8 May, 1904, 4 June, 1904, 27 Jan., 1905; *Atlanta Tax ordinance For 1904-5* (Atlanta, 1905), #33.

[10]*Atlanta Journal*, 27 Jan., 1905; *Atlanta Constitution*, 10 April, 1910.

[11]*Ibid.*, 27 Jan., 1905.

[12]*Prompt to Action — The Atlanta Fire Department 1860-1960* (Atlanta, 1961), 42-44.

[13]*Atlanta Journal*, 21 Oct. 1908; Wade Wright, *The Georgia Power and Electric Company, 1855-1956* (Atlanta, 1957), 88-89.

[14]*Atlanta Journal*, 27 Oct., 1908; 2 Nov., 1915; *Atlanta Constitution*, 3 Nov., 1915; *Atlanta Georgian*, 3 Nov., 1915.

[15]John W. Leonard, *The Book of Chicagoans, A Biographical Dictionary of Leading Living Men of the City of Chicago, 1905* (Chicago: 1905), I, 23, 44-5, 267, 540, 575; *Chicago Times*, 18 Dec., 1892; *Sporting News*, 24 Dec., 1892; *Chicago Daily News*, 18 July, 1919, Joel Tarr, "John R. Walsh of Chicago: A Case Study in Banking and Politics, 1881-1905," *Business History Review*, 40 (Winter, 1966), 451-66.

[16]Bessie Louise Pierce, *A History of Chicago* (New York, 1957), III, 478; Gustav Axelson, *"Commy", The Life Story of Charles Comiskey* (Chicago: 1919), 33-35, 39, 150.

[17]*New York Tribune*, 16 July, 1905; Edward Mott Woolley, "The Business of Baseball," *McClure's*, 39 (July, 1912), 245.

[18]*Ibid.*, 245; *Dictionary of American Biography*, s.v. "Taft, Charles P."

[19]Woolley, 245; *Chicago Tribune*, 18 March, 1916.

[20]*Chicago Daily News*, 23 Dec., 1911; *Sporting News*, 11 Jan., 1912.

[21]*Chicago Daily News*, 10 Oct., 1909; *Chicago Record-Herald*, 10 Oct., 1908; *Atlanta Constitution*, 19 Dec., 1908; *Albany Times-Union*, 14 March, 1914.

[22]Seymour, 34-36; *Chicago Tribune*, 7, 22, 24, 26 March, 1914; *New York Tribune*, 8 March, 1914; Albert Nelson Marquis, ed., *The Book of Chicagoans, A Biographical Dictionary of Leading Living Men and Women of the City of Chicago, 1917* (Chicago, 1917), III, 149, 455, 554, 661, 675.

[23]*Chicago Tribune*, 19 March 1914, 6, 16. 23 Jan., 1916; *Dictionary of American Biography, Supplement* (New York, 1944), I, 715; William Veeck, *The Hustler's Handbook* (New York, 1965), 267; John Gunther, *Taken at the Flood: The Story of Albert D. Lasker* (New York, 1960), esp. 98-125.

[24]Edgar B. Tolman, reviser, *The Revised Municipal Code of Chicago of 1905* (Chicago, 1905), #106, #109, #117; Edward J. Brundage, *The Chicago Code of 1911* (Chicago, 1911), #356-61

[25]*Chicago Record-Herald*, 24 April, 1909.

[26]*Ibid.*, 24, 26 April, 1909; *Brookly Daily Eagle*, 21 Mardh, 1903, 20 April, 1903.

[27]John C. Thompson, *The Greater New York Charter of 1901* (New York, 1901), #1483; Barney Dreyfuss to August Hermann, 15 June, 1912, August Herrmann Papers, The Baseball Hall of Fame, Cooperstown, N.Y.

[28]*Chicago Daily News*, 17 Dec., 1909; *Chicago Tribune*, 18 Dec., 1909.

[29]*Proceedings of the City Council of the City of Chicago*, 1918-1919 (April 2, 1919); 1947; *Ibid.*, 1919-1920 (Dec. 29, 1919), 1689, 1691; *Ibid.*, (April 7, 1920), 2534. The original bill had called for a maximum fee of $3,000. Parks seating 10,000-15,000 were assessed $1,000; 4,000-10,000 paid $350; and others paid $75.

[30]*Ibid.*, 1920-1921 (Feb. 4, 1921), 1746; The license fees for the smaller parks were not affected. *Chicago Daily News*, 26 Jan., 1921, 3 Feb., 1921; Alex Gottfried, "Anton J. Cermak, Chicago Politician: A Study in Political Leadership," (Ph.D. diss. University of Chicago, 1952), 275-6.

THE GOLDEN AGE OF AMERICAN SPORT **289**

[31]For examples of disorders, see *Chicago Record-Herald,* 15 Oct., 1906, 22 May, 1907; *New York Tribune,* 17 April, 1911; *New York Times,* 12 April, 1912, 16 Aug., 1920; *Brooklyn Daily Eagle,* 12 April, 1912; *Atlanta Constitution,* 31 Aug., 1919. In 1904 the Cincinnati management had to put a special officer near the players' bench to protect visiting athletes from the abuse of fans, and conversely, spectators from players. T.B. Collier to August Herrmann, 14 July, 1904, August Herrmann Papers, The Baseball Hall of Fame, Cooperstown, N.Y.; *Chicago Times,* 5 July, 1895; Ring Lardner, "The Cost of Baseball," *Collier's,* 48, (March 2, 1912), 30; *Proceedings of the Chicago City Council, April 10, 1899-April 4, 1900* (May 8, 1899), 281-2; *Ibid., 1919-1920* (Jan. 14, 1920), 1897; *Ibid., 1921-1922* (July 21, 1921), 903; *Ibid., 1928-1929* (Dec. 19, 1928), 4139; *1929-1930* (January 3, 1930), 1909; Bruce Smith, *Chicago Police Problems* (Chicago, 1931), 256.

[32]Charles Weeghman for instance was a personal friend of Mont Tennes, the head of the Chicago gambling ring. Seymour, 300. On gambling and organized crime, see Mark Haller, "Urban Crime and Criminal Justice: The Chicago Case," *Journal of American History,* 57 (Dec., 1970), 622-4; 631, 634, 635; *idem,* "Organized Crime in Urban Society: Chicago in the Twentieth Century," *Journal of Social History,* 5 (Winter, 1971-72), 221-7.

[33]Seymour, 274-6; Hugh Fullerton, "American Gambling and Gamblers," *American Magazine,* 77 (Feb., 1914), 37.

[34]See e.g. *Philadelphia Inquirer,* 11 Sept., 1903; *Atlanta Constitution,* 23 Jan., 1904, 5 May, 1912, 20 March, 1920; *New York Tribune,* 30 July, 1912, 27 June, 1914; *New York Times,* 17 June, 1913, 25 May, 1920.

[35]Elliot Asinof, *Eight Men Out* (New York: 1963), 130-1.

[36]*Ibid.,* 149-52; Seymour, 197-8.

[37]Seymour, 328, 331.

[38]Harold Seymour, "The Rise of Major League Baseball to 1891," (Ph.D. diss., Cornell University, 1956), 101.

[39]*New York Times,* 26 Oct., 1904, 13 April, 1917, 7 April, 1941; Mrs. Blanche McGraw, *The Real McGraw,* ed. by Arthur Mann (New York: 1953), 170.

[40]*New York Tribune,* 24, 25 Jan., 1895; *New York Times,* 3 Dec., 1897, 18 April, 1899, 5 Dec., 1915, 30 March, 1944; *Sporting Life,* 25 Dec., 1897; *Dictionary of American Biography* s.v. "Freedman, Andrew."

[41]*Sporting News,* 24 Aug., 1895; *New York Tribune,* 23 April, 1896, 4 June, 1898, 14 Dec., 1899.

[42]*Sporting Life,* 11 Nov., 1899, 26 Oct., 1901.

[43]*Chicago Daily News,* 15 June, 1901.

[44]*Sporting Life,* 16 Nov., 1901.

[45]"Annual Meeting of the National League and American Association of Professional Baseball Clubs, December 10 to 14, 1901" (1902), n.p.; *Sporting News,* 9 Nov., 1901, 28 Dec., 1901, Harold Seymour, *Baseball: The Early Years* (New York, 1960), I, 317-22.

[46]*New York Times,* 30 Sept., 1902, 5 Dec., 1915; *Sporting News,* 4 Oct., 1902; *Cincinnati Enquirer,* 8 Jan., 1903; "The Business Side of Baseball," *Current Literature,* 53 (Aug., 1912), 170; Mrs. McGraw, 176-77.

[47]Woolley, 243; Voigt, 108.

[48]Norman Rose to William Gray, 29 April, 1911, August Herrmann Papers, The Baseball Hall of Fame, Cooperstown, N.Y.

[49]*New York Times,* 19 April, 1925; Frank Graham, *The Brooklyn Dodgers: An Informal History* (New York, 1945), 7.

[50]*Brooklyn Daily Eagle,* 10 Jan., 1896, 15 March, 1898; *New York Tribune,* 16 March, 1898; *Sporting News,* 1 Dec., 1906.

[51]Graham, 35.

[52]*Ibid.,* 7.

[53]Steven A. Riess, "Professional Sunday Baseball: A Study in Social Reform, 1892-1934," *Maryland Historian,* IV. (Fall, 1973), 98-104.

[54]*Chicago Daily News,* 11 March, 1903; *New York World,* 13, 14 March, 1903; *New York Times,* 15 March, 1903; Woolley, 254; "Tammany Newspaper Clippings, 1913-34," in the Kilroe Collection, Columbia University; Al Fein, "New York Politics, 1897-1903: A Study in Political Party Leadership," (M.A. thesis, Columbia University, 1954), 81-91.

[55]*New York Times,* 20 Oct., 1901, 31 Aug., 1902, 2 Dec., 1902, 26 Feb., 1926; Maxwell F. Marcuse, *This was New York: A Nostalgic Picture of Gotham in the Gas Light Era,* revised and enlarged (New York, 1969), 170-1; Loyd Morris, *Incredible New York: High Life and Low Life in the Last 100 Years* (New York: 1951), 226.

[56]*New York Times,* 9 April, 1899, 21 June, 1919; *New York Sun,* 11 June, 1919.

[57]*New York Times,* 4 Nov., 1903; Morris R. Werner, *Tammany Hall* (New York: 1928), 487-91; Fein, 128-9, 142-3.

[58]*New York Times,* 12 April, 1907; Scrapbooks of Henry Chadwick, 5, (1907), A.G. Spalding Collection, New York Public Library.

[59]*New York Times,* 13 April, 1907; *Sporting Life,* 1 June, 1907.

[60]*New York Times,* 13, 1907; John J. Hickey, *Our Police Guardians* (New York: 1925), 152-53. For examples of disorders which the special police could not cope with, see the newspaper clipping for 30 May, 1907 in Diary of Henry Chadwick, A.G. Spalding Collection, New York Public Library; *New York Times,* 23 April, 1908.

[61]*New York Times,* and *Chicago Daily News,* 18, 19, 20, 21, 22, Sept. 1908; City police were assigned to patrol the Polo Grounds for the weekend series between the Giants and the Cubs which would decide the league champion. Charles Ebbets urged the municipality to allow him to use off-duty police to guard his park. See *Brooklyn Daily Eagle,* 3 April, 1912.

[62]*New York Times,* 8 Oct., 1912; Sid Mercer in the *New York Globe,* 8 Oct., 1912, cited in *Sporting News,* 17 Oct., 1912.

[63]Frank Graham, *The New York Yankees: An Informal History* (New York: 1951), 19-21.

[64]*Ibid.,* 21; *New York Times,* 1, 2, 10 Oct., 1897.

[65]*New York Tribune,* 17 Feb., 1919; Seymour, *Baseball;* II, 140, 390; For examples of Stoneham's low character, see *New York Times,* 12 Feb., 1908, 13 Nov., 1923; *Sporting News,* 25 Nov., 1923; Mrs. McGraw, 265; In McQuade's most notable Sunday case, he found McGraw and Christy Mathewson, then the manager of the Cincinnati Reds, innocent of desecrating the Sabbath by playing a Sunday game at the Polo Grounds. See *New York Times,* 20, 21, 22, Aug., 1917; U.S. Congress, House, Subcommittee on the Study of Monopoly Power, *Organized Baseball,* 82nd Congress, (1951), 1st session, serial 1, Part 6, 1599, 1600.

17

Professional Baseball as a Source of Social Mobility 1871-1919

by Steven A. Riess

One of the values which has most distinguished the United States from other societies is the strong emphasis placed on the idea of social mobility. Our country has always been regarded as a land of opportunity, and most immigrants came here to secure a better life for themselves and their families. The traditional route to social advancement for ambitious and motivated young men has generally required such conditions as education, capital, good connections, hard work, and the ability to take advantage of opportunities. Young men without these qualifications sought alternate routes to success in such areas as crime, entertainment, politics, and sports. In this paper I would like to examine the role that professional baseball played between 1871 and 1919 as a vehicle of social mobility. It was long believed by fans, sportswriters, and even historians, that the national pastime provided an excellent source of vertical mobility because it was a democratic occupation whose participants were hired solely on the basis of their athletic ability.[1]

The professionalization of baseball began in earnest after the Civil War as a natural response among the earliest amateur teams to secure victorious records. These clubs looked beyond their membership to recruit superior baseball players regardless of their social standing. These highly skilled athletes were encouraged to join up by offers of gifts, jobs, or even wages. The first team which acknowledged that all their men were on salaries was the Cincinnati Red Stockings which was organized in 1869 and went undefeated that year. The players earned from $600 to $2,000 that season.[2]

In 1871, representatives of ten professional clubs met in New York and organized the first professional baseball league, the National Association of Professional Baseball Players (BAPBBP), generally accepted as the first major league. During the league's five years in existence, at least 74.9 percent of its 311 players were American-born and 6.4 percent were foreign-born. The birthplace of

18.7 percent is unknown. The proportion of foreign-born is much higher than that of subsequent cohorts of major leaguers until the recent influx of Latin Americans. These men were mainly English or Irish, had no language barriers and could be rapidly assimilated into the core culture. Some were former cricket players or sons of cricket players and could utilize the skills used in that bat and ball game in baseball. In addition, baseball was a relatively new sport, and the native-born were scarcely more familiar with the game than the immigrants.[3]

The status of the ballplayers was low, partly attributable to their perceived lower class status, but also to their rowdy behavior off and on the field, and to repeated stories of cheating. Nevertheless, their pay was substantially higher than that of skilled workers, probably averaging from $1,300 to $1,600 a year. In 1876 the NAPBBP was superceded by the National League, a new organization which sought to bring sounder business standards to the running of the sport. One goal of the new magnates was to cut their costs, which were primarily wages. In 1879 owners introduced the reserve clause into their players' contracts. It required the athlete to play exclusively for the club which owned his contract, and prevented him from jumping to another club which promised a higher salary. Another method to keep down wages was by establishing a maximum salary scale. The major league owners agreed in 1885 to a $2,000 maximum. However, it was not always enforced since teams feared that their stars would jump to another club which chose to cheat on the agreement. For example, in 1889, player-manager Charles Comiskey was paid $6,000 by the St. Louis Browns. But the owners learned from their mistakes, and after the collapse of the Players League (1890), and the merger of the American Association with the National League (1891), a new $2,400 limit was set and adhered to. Wages at the end of the decade were lower than they had been in the mid-1880s. In 1899, the Baltimore Orioles, one of the best clubs of the era, averaged under $2,000 a man.[4]

Little is known about the social origins of the early professional ballplayers. They were recruited from amongst the finest amateurs of the day, men who had sufficient leisure time to develop proficiency in the sport. Stephen Freedman has found that after the Civil War 69.9 percent of Chicago's amateurs were white-collar and 30.1 percent were blue-collar. In the case of New York, Melvin Adelman has determined that 65.4 percent of a sample of 124 Brooklyn and New York amateurs active between 1866 and 1870 were white-collar and 34.6 percent were blue-collar. Futhermore, Adelman pointed out that nearly all the manual workers in his sample were skilled as just 1.6 percent of his cohorts were unskilled. The proletariat lacked the time, if not the energy and inclination, to participate in baseball. Particularly noteworthy in the context of this paper was Adelman's finding that

61.8 percent of the Brooklynites and New Yorkers who played in the NAPBBP were artisans, and the rest were white-collarites. Thus for most ballplayers, the occupation was a source of social mobility. However, the opportunity did not extend to men at the lowest levels of society.[5]

The early major leaguers were not very successful in maintaining their middle class status. Over one-third slid down into a blue-collar job (35.6 percent), which was a very high rate of skidding. Sixty-three percent secured white-collar employment, but usually in relatively low prestige occupations, and the remainder (1.4 percent) became farmers. The retired major leaguers did not fare well after retiring from baseball because they were not well educated, had saved little money for investment, had no marketable skills, and were poorly regarded by the respectable middle class who would not hire them for responsible positions.[6]

As one might expect, the retirees who became entrepreneurs were either involved in sports or recreational enterprises. Probably the most successful was Albert Spalding, who became the owner of the Chicago White Stockings and also established the A.G. Spalding & Bros. Sporting Goods Company, which eventually became a monopoly. However, most of the entrepreneurs were involved in small businesses where they hoped to utilize their fame to attract clientele. They were mainly involved in saloons, and secondarily in either bookmaking or billiard parlors. All told, one-eighth of the men in the NAPBBP were involved in these businesses which comprised an important focus of the Victorian bachelor subculture in which sportsmen played a principal role. In fact, nearly one-tenth of the retirees either ran or owned saloons, or worked as bartenders.[7]

The Major League Baseball Player, 1900-1919

The opportunities in professional baseball improved markedly after the turn of the century. The most important reason was the rise of the American League which proclaimed itself a major league in 1901. It competed vigorously for the services of established big leaguers by offering high salaries, and this in turn compelled the National League to raise its salaries. The result was that players' wages increased by about fifty percent in a decade. As early as 1904 stars like Christy Mathewson and his teammate Joe "Ironman" McGinnity of the New York Giants were paid over $5,000. By 1910 the top salary was $18,000 which was paid to the great Pittsburgh shortstop Honus Wagner. A rookie, on the other hand, usually started at $1,200, but if they stayed in the big leagues, their salaries would appreciate. For example, Ed Sweeney started as a catcher for the New York Highlanders (Yankees) in 1908 at $1,500, but by 1913 was earning $5,300, even though he had never hit above .270.[8]

The salaries underwent a dramatic increase in 1914 and 1915. The cause was the competition from a new self-proclaimed major league known as the Federal League. Like the American League in the early 1900s, the Feds sought to gain instant recognition by recruiting quality players, especially stars, from the established leagues. However, magnates in the American and National Leagues remembered that about one hundred men had jumped to the junior circuit in 1901 and 1902, and were determined to prevent this, and hopefully kill off the new competitor. Players took advantage of the situation to obtain substantial raises. For example, Ray Fischer, a pitcher for the Yankees had earned $3,000 in 1913, but in 1914 was granted a three-year contract worth $20,000. The greatest star of the era, Ty Cobb of the Detroit Tigers, got a raise to $20,000 a year. We don't have statistics for all the teams, but it is pretty certain that the typical major leaguer was earning over $3,000. One team for whom income data is available is the Philadelphia Phillies. The average player on the squad in 1914 earned about $3,400, and after they won the pennant in 1915, their salaries were increased to an average of $4,300. However, by 1920, when the club was in last place, most of the well-paid veterans had either been traded or had retired, and the average salary dropped to $3,300. By comparison, experts have estimated that the average major leaguer in 1923 was earning about $5,000. This was a very substantial income, and compared favorably with all occupations, including doctors and dentists.[9]

Major league players had many opportunities to supplement their income, if they chose to, during the long off-season. Nearly all would participate in some post-season baseball, such as the intra-city series in Chicago between the Cubs and White Sox, playing on weekends for semi-professional clubs until the weather got too cold, or barnstorming the country, to play exhibitions against local aggregates. The better known players had numerous opportunities to earn additional money because they were actively recruited by companies who wanted them to endorse various products or else work for them. Christy Mathewson, for instance, endorsed products, appeared in vaudeville, and received credit for ghostwritten newspaper articles and books.[10]

Most major leaguers were probably satisfied with their summer wages and did not hold a job during the off-season. There is really not a great deal of data on the off-season employment of the ballplayers, and the best we can do is establish general ranges. About one-twelfth of the employed players were professionals, mainly school teachers and engineers. About one-third owned their own business, but these companies generally had a high rate of failure which was not unusual for small businesses. These were usually billiard parlors, cafes, or taverns which catered to the sporting subculture. About one in ten were clerks, salesmen, or kindred workers hired because their employer expected their presence would attract customers. Opportunities were greatest with clothing stores, sporting goods shops, car dealerships, and insurance agencies. About one-sixth of the players farmed during the off-season, which reflected their social origins, since about one-fifth of the big leaguers had fathers who were farmers. The proportion of players who worked in a manual job is not altogether certain. At the very least, 9.2 percent worked at a blue-collar job, but it is not unlikely that as many as twenty-five percent were thus employed. For example, one-third of the Pittsburgh Pirates roster in 1908 held manual jobs, primarily as artisans, and they were largely a veteran team.[11]

At the same time that salaries rose, so did the prestige of the occupation. While there were still some rowdy and dissolute ballplayers, and teams were sometimes turned away from the finer hotels, the situation was definitely improving. The best example was probably Christy Mathewson, who became a hero to American youth. He was regarded as a paragon of virtue. A God-fearing college man, who almost never played on the Sabbath, he served his country overseas during World War I. In fact, a remarkable proportion, approximately twenty-five percent, were college men, at a time when only about five percent of the college age men were still in school. College men who were skilled athletes were for the first time becoming professional athletes in noticeable numbers. They were attracted by the new improved pay scale, the chance for fame, and the leisurely lifestyle of the paid athlete. Their presence greatly improved the prestige of the occupation.[12]

The social origins of the professional ballplayers was definitely not lower class, as the contemporary conventional wisdom had held. In reality, as baseball historian David Q. Voight has suggested, they were probably mainly lower middle class. I found that 44.6 percent had nonmanual fathers, 20.9 percent had farmer fathers, and 34.4 percent had manual fathers. In Table 1 the social origins of the ballplayers are compared to the occupational distribution of all American men in 1910, and it is obvious that their fathers were far more successful than most Americans. Twice as many players' fathers were nommanual compared to all males, and they were more likely to be high white-collar and less likely to be low white-collar. The number of fathers who owned their own farms (20.9 percent) was virtually identical to the national cohort (19.9 percent), but as far as I could tell, none were unskilled agricultural workers, compared to 14 percent of the national labor force. Merely one-third of the ballplayers' fathers were blue-collar workers, even though nearly one-half (45.9 percent) of all male American workers were non-agrarian manual laborers. Furthermore, the players' fathers were primarily skilled workers, while only one-third of all blue-collar American workers were skilled.[13]

The ethnicity of the major league ballplayers in the first decades of the twentieth century were overwhelmingly either native-born Americans or of Irish or German descent. The only change since the late nineteenth century was the increasing proportion of native white Americans entering the occupation as it became respectable and lucrative. Fewer than ten percent of the big leaguers came from other ethnic groups and hardly any of them came from the newest immigrant groups from Eastern or Southern Europe.

Baseball was a source of social mobility for Irishmen, who generally had a low rate of vertical mobility. Irish immigrants were not well prepared for life in the United States, although they did speak English. They were uneducated, unskilled, and impoverished. Most Irishmen had no alternative but to take a low paying job which required only a strong back. The problem was clearly pointed out in a recent study of social mobility in Boston by Stephen Thernstrom. Thernstrom found that in 1890 just ten percent of the Irish newcomers had a white-collar job, and also that subsequent generations of Irish-Americans did poorly when it came to getting a white-collar job in comparison to other white ethnic groups. However, there were certain avenues of

TABLE I

Father's Occupation of Major Leaguers, Active 1900-1919, Compared to All American Males

Occupation	U.S. Males, 1910(%)	Players' Fathers (%)
Professionals	3.1	10.2
Proprietary		
Farm	19.9	20.9
Others	7.9	27.0
Clerks	9.2	7.4
Skilled	14.5	23.7
Semiskilled	11.2	7.4
Unskilled		
Farm	14.0	0.0
Others	20.2	3.3
Total	100.0	99.9*

Source: Joseph Kahl, *The American Class Structure* (New York: Holt, Reinhart, and Winston, 1957), p. 265; weighted sample of 117 respondents to author's questionnaire sent to players active 1919 or before.

*Error due to rounding off.

social mobility open to ambitious Irishmen in such areas as construction, crime, politics, the Church, and various forms of entertainment, including sports. In boxing, for example, the Irish dominance in the nineteenth century was legion, and although their dominance slipped a bit after the turn of the century, eight of the twenty-six champions in the period 1900 to 1910 were Irish. They were also very successful in baseball. The professional clubs recruited most of their players from the northeastern and midwestern cities which often had large Irish communities. The presence of Irishmen in the majors encouraged others to follow in their footsteps, and these lads were often given positive support by their parents.[14]

Baseball was not a good source of social mobility for the sons of the new immigrants from Eastern and Southern Europe. In the years 1901 to 1906 there were just five Bohemian, two Jewish, and no Italian rookies. Their were no rookies from these groups in 1910, and in 1920 there was only one Bohemian and two Italians out of 133 first-year men. Those men of new immigrant stock who made the big leagues encountered discrimination from the veteran players who resented their presence and were worried about losing their jobs, seeing salary levels dropped, and having the prestige of their occupation destroyed.[15]

The new immigrants needed alternate sources of social mobility because most of them were not well prepared for life in America. The Jews, and perhaps the Czechs, were probably the best prepared. About one-fourth of Boston's Jewish immigrants in 1910 had white-collar jobs compared to 12 percent of the Italians. Jewish immigrants were more likely to have come from cities, and brought with them more skills, a tradition of entrepreneurship, and deep respect for education. Three-fourths of the second-generation Jews held white-collar jobs compared to only one-fourth of the Italians. Ambitious second-generation immigrants from Eastern and Southern Europe who were unskilled, poorly educated, lacked connections or the capital to start a small business might seek less respectable sources of social mobility in areas like crime, entertainment, or sports. Boxing was a natural occupation for ghetto youths to enter since it was very well suited to their daily experiences. These kids often got into fights with boys of other ethnic groups contesting for their "turf." Self-defense was a useful skill which could be learned at night after school or work at a local settlement house or gymnasium. Professional boxers became important heroes in the ghettoes and role models for youngsters to emulate. There was an Italian and Polish world champion boxer several years before a ballplayer from either ethnic group would win a major league batting title. In the 1910s there were as many Jewish champions as Irish or Germans, but only a handful of Jews played in the major leagues. Many of those Jews used pseudonyms to hide their ethnicity to protect themselves against discrimination. The lifestyle of these new immigrants did not prepare them for a baseball career. They usually lived in crowded ghettoes where there was very little space to play baseball; had few opportunities to get sound coaching; and had little free time during daylight hours.[16] Furthermore, there was generally strong opposition by their parents to baseball. A ball game played by men running around in short pants made no sense to their elders. As Eddie Cantor remembered, "To the pious people of the ghetto a baseball player was the king of loafers."[17] Thus it is not surprising that Jewish ballplayers did not come mainly from New York, the center of the Jewish population, but from places like Hamburg, Arkansas or Farmington, Missouri, where they were far from the ghetto.

Despite the underrepresentation of these ethnic groups, professional baseball maintained an image as a very democratic sport which recruited its players solely on the basis of their ability. There was, for example, a very noticeable native American presence on the diamond. About thirty Indians played in the big leagues during this period, including Jim Thorpe, the greatest American athlete of all time. Chief Bender, the outstanding pitcher for the Philadelphia Athletics was the finest Indian ball player. He left Dartmouth College to play baseball which "offered . . . the best opportunity both for money and advancement that I could see . . . There has been scarcely a trace of sentiment against me on account of birth. I have been treated the same as the other men."[18] There were also a handful of Cubans coming in by 1911. But here the matter of race was a big problem. Many of the star Cubans were black, but scouts could not sign them because of the racial barriers of American baseball.[19]

It was in the area of race that baseball's democratic claims fell flat. Blacks were excluded from Organzied Baseball because of prevailing social prejudice. Until 1898 there had been about fifty black professionals, but then the racial barriers shut them out. Two blacks, Moses Fleetwood Walker, and his brother Weldon, had actually played for a major league club, Toledo of the American Association, in 1884. In response to racism in professional baseball, blacks organzied their own semiprofessional teams and leagues. The finest players were really professionals who played year round. The Chicago Giants, for example, played up to 200 games a year. In the summer they toured the Midwest and in the winter either played in a California League or entertained guests at a Florida hotel. Wages were much lower than major leaguers received. Sol White, a leader in the development of black baseball, estimated in 1906 that the average black was paid around $466 for a season. In the 1910s, the typical black player got $40 to $75 a month and the stars got $105. The quality of play was very high among the best clubs. They often played exhibition games against all-star teams of major leaguers and were quite competitive. Their ability was generally recognized by white players, managers, and journalists. In 1920, Rube Foster, a former star pitcher who owned a semiprofessional club, organized the Negro National League with eight teams, all owned and operated by blacks.[20]

The Retired Major Leaguers

Professional athletes have relatively short careers. The athlete's skills quickly decline with advancing age, and he finds it hard to compete against younger and swifter rivals. It was rare to see a major leaguer active past his thirty-fifth birthday. Furthermore, an average player's tenure in fast company was usually short. If we discount men who lasted just a few games (for the proverbial "cup of coffee"), the average tenure was about eight years. As a consequence, ballplayers had to begin a second career at a relatively advanced age, at a time when most workers were well established in their jobs.[21]

To determine the post-retirement success of major league ballplayers, data was sought on the subsequent work experiences of a sample of 593 men who played in either Chicago or New York between 1900 and 1919 for at least one year (operationally defined as either fifty innings pitched or one hundred at bats). As summarized in Table II, nearly four-fifths (78.8 percent) secured a white-collar job, 3.4 percent became farmers, 13.4 percent skidded into the blue-collar world, and 4.4 percent never worked after retirement due to poor health or an early death. These results were far better than those achieved by players active between 1871 and 1882.

Nearly one-fourth of the retirees (23.8 percent) obtained high white-collar jobs. One in twenty (5.6 percent) had a profession which reflected the high proportion of players who had attended college. They were mainly engineers, doctors, and lawyers. Former players who held other important non-manual jobs were primarily baseball executives or governmental officials. Some time or other after retirement, thirty-one men either owned or helped operate a professional baseball team. Of course, some of them were actually just figureheads, like Casey Stengel who was the chief operating officer of the minor league club in Worcester in 1925, or Christy Mathewson who was the president of the Boston Braves in the early 1920s.[23] The success in government was interesting because of the sport's long standing ties to urban politicians, who were ardent fans and frequently owned the local franchise. The former players active in the nineteenth century frequently worked for the government, but mainly in service positions as policemen or firemen. But in the twentieth century, ex-players held more responsible jobs, such as Del Howard who was elected mayor of his hometown, or Nap Rucker, who served his community as water commissioner.

The majority of retirees (55.8 percent) held a lower white-collar job, usually in baseball. The primary job of 117 men in the sample (23.8 percent) worked as either managers, coaches, scouts or umpires. Furthermore, some time after retirement at least 246 of all the 593 men in the total sample (41.5 percent) were employed at these types of jobs. By comparison, only about 11 percent of the players active from 1871-1882 found such positions. This was a consequence of the enormous popularity of baseball which had reached a point where nearly every city had a minor league team. The most

TABLE II
Principal Occupation of Ex-Major Leaguers, Active 1900-1919

Occupation*	Number	Percentage
High White-Collar		
Professionals	28	5.6
Managers, high officials, and major proprietors	91	18.2
Low White-Collar		
Clerks, sales and kindred workers	48	9.6
Semiprofessionals	160	32.0
Petty proprietors, managers, and low officials	67	13.4
Total White-Collar	394	78.8
Farm		
Farmers	17	3.4
Blue-Collar		
Skilled	18	3.6
Semiskilled	42	8.4
Unskilled	7	1.4
Total Blue-Collar	67	13.4
Other		
Infirm or early death	22	4.4
Grand Total	500	100.0

SOURCE: Sample data of 593 men who played at least one year in New York between 1900 and 1919.[22]
*Categories from Stephan Thernstrom, *The Other Bostonians: Poverty and Progress in the American Metropolis, 1880-1970* (Cambridge, Mass., 1975), 290-292

common job was minor league manager, and over one-fourth of the total sample (150) worked at it some time after retirement. It was a job which required expertise in baseball, and having been a major league player demonstrated that. The typical manager in the sample was a better than average big leaguer because they averaged over nine years in the majors compared to the mean of eight. Managing was a popular job among retirees because it provided a means of maintaining a close connection to the sport they loved, and it also provided them with training for the job of major league manager. About one-third of the big league managers had prior experience in the minors. The pay in the high minors was good (Harry Wolverton earned $6,000 as manager of the Los Angeles club in 1917),[24] but there was a lot of traveling and living in second-rate hotels. In addition, there was very little security, and the average manager's tenure was quite short.

The men who were selected as major league managers came almost exclusively from the ranks of the stars. Fifty-nine men in my sample became big league managers, and they averaged about fourteen years in the majors. It was almost unheard of for a man to manage in the majors without prior experience, and extensive experience at that. Owners assumed that the star players would make the best managers because it was expected that they could readily instruct others in the techniques of the game, plot strategy, and gain the respect of their players by the force of their reputations. Eventually owners learned that this reasoning was inaccurate. An outstanding player like Ty Cobb or Rogers Hornsby did not necessarily have the temperament required for leadership, nor the patience needed to get the best possible performances out of their teams. By comparison, many of the finest managers in the 1960s and 1970s had limited or no major league experience, such as Walter Alston, Sparky Anderson, or Ralph Houk. Managing was a highly coveted position which paid well and was prestigious, although it was a very tenuous position. Managers were prominent individuals, constantly in the limelight, and could earn salaries in excess of $10,000. Players saw the position as a capstone to their careers, and it was the greatest disappointment of Babe Ruth's life that he never was asked to manage the Yankees.[25]

The ballplayers who ended up in blue-collar jobs suffered an enormous loss of income and prestige. The skilled men were found to be plumbers, electricians, machinists, printers, and tailors, trades which they had learned before becoming professional ballplayers. These were secure jobs which paid better than a clerk earned, however they provided fewer chances for continued upward mobility.[26] Nearly two-thirds of the blue-collarites were either semiskilled or service workers like policemen or firemen which both provided excellent security.

The new occupation of the retired big leaguer depended on a number of factors, including his fame, length of service, social background, and education. Tenure, which correlated highly with fame, was only an important factor in helping an individual obtain his initial job after baseball. But afterwards, certain other variables, including the first job, became more important in determining the principal job for the ex-player. The only exception was in the case of those men who remained in baseball since their tenure was two years longer than the mean.[27]

The most important variables for determining a player's principal occupation after his active days were over were education and social background. Over 93 percent of the college-educated respondents to my questionnaire had a white-collar job, and the rest were mainly farmers. By comparison, 67.5 percent of the non-college men got white-collar jobs, one-fourth ended up in manual positions, and the rest became farmers. Social background was almost as important a factor, even though the players were retiring in their mid-thirties. Eighty-five percent of the nonmanual fathers of major leaguers had ballplaying sons who ended up in a nonmanual job. By comparison, 77 percent of the farming fathers and 58 percent of the manual fathers had big league sons who ended up nonmanual. Furthermore, the major league son of a manual worker was three times as likely to become a manual worker compared to the son of a nonmanual worker, and six times as likely as the son of a farmer. The retiree's future occupational category could be better predicted by his education and social class than by either his batting average or won-loss percentage.[28]

Social background was important for several reasons. Middle class youngsters were more likely to have a decent education which would better prepare them for a higher paying and more prestigious jobs. They were encouraged by parents and school teachers to have high expectations and were taught traditional bourgeois values like thrift and deferral of immediate gratification for the future. Players coming from poor families were not as well educated and did not get the same kind of encouragement while growing up. They found themselves unprepared to handle their sudden wealth, and indulged in the worst practices of conspicuous consumption, spending their wages almost as soon as they were paid, if not before. They had grown up without developing a tradition of saving. They were also very insecure, and spent their money freely to prove their success to themselves and their teammates.

Conclusion

The evidence suggests that professional baseball was vastly over-rated as a source of vertical mobility. There were as few as twenty-one men on the sixteen major league rosters during the early 1900s, and their tenure was short in comparison to other careers. Most of the players were lower middle class descendants of Irishmen, Germans, or native white Americans. The high pay and prestige of baseball attracted the sons of respectable families who would never be attracted to a sport like boxing, which was dangerous and low in status. Opportunities were limited for lower class youth who needed alternate routes for success. They were unable to compete successfully with middle class boys who had better coaching, better equipment, and more time for practice. Few major leaguers came from the new immigrant groups who were at the bottom of the social ladder. Yet they at least had a theoretical chance for success. Blacks were completely excluded because of their race. Their acknowledged abilities meant nothing in a racist society.

Footnotes

[1]See, e.g, Leonard Dinnerstein and David M. Reimers *Ethnic Americans: A History of Immigration and Assimilation* (New York, 1975), 136-37.

[2] David Q. Voigt, *American Baseball,* vol. 1, *From Gentleman's Sport to the Commissioner's System* (Norman, Okla., 1966), 19; Harold Seymour, Baseball, vol. 2, *The Early Years* (New York, 1960), 56-61.

[3]Computed from *The Baseball Encyclopedia: The Complete and Official Record of Major League Baseball* (New York, 1969), 467-91.

[4]Harold Seymour, *Baseball,* 1: 104-20; Voigt, *American Baseball,* 1: 140-41.

[5]Stephen Freedman, "The Baseball Fad in Chicago, 1865-1870: An Exploration of the Role of Sport in the Nineteenth Century," *Journal of Sport History* 5 (Summer) 1978): 42-64; Melvin Adelman, "The Development of Modern Athletics: Sport in New York City, 1820-1870" (Ph.D. diss., University of Illinois, 1980), 443-46, 449-54.

[6]Compiled from raw data in Lee Allen, Notebooks Containing Statistical Data on Baseball Players, Office of the Historian, National Baseball Library, Baseball Hall of Fame, Cooperstown, New York; Sporting News, Oct. 4, 1886, Feb. 2, 1895; *Boston Evening Transcript,* Oct. 19, 1889; Atlanta Constitution, Sept. 2, 1907. On rates of skidding, see Stephan Thernstrom, *The Other Bostonians: Poverty and Progress in the American Metropolis,* 1880-1970, Cambridge, Mass., 1973), 234.

[7]Voigt, *American Baseball,* 1:281. For a more complete discussion of this subject, see Steven A. Riess, *Touching Base: Professional Baseball and American Culture in the Progressive Era* (Westport, Conn., 1980), 157-60.

[8]*Atlanta Constitution,* July 16, 1904; David Q. Voigt, *American Baseball,* vol. 2, *From the Commissioners to Continental Expansion* (Norman, Okla., 1970), 65-68; Hugh C. Weir, "Baseball: The Men and the Dollars Behind It," *World Today* 17 (July 1909): 759; New York Yankees Ledger Book, George Weiss Collection, National Baseball Library.

[9]New York Yankees Ledger Book; Voigt, *American Baseball,* 2: 66. Figures for the Phillies salaries were computed from the Philadelphia Phillies Ledger Book, 1913-1920, National Baseball Library.

[10]*Atlanta Constitution,* Dec. 31, 1908; New York Tribune, Oct. 13, 1910, Jan. 19, 1911, March 9, 1913; Seymour, *Baseball,* 1:333; Harold Seymour, *Baseball,* vol. 2, *The*

Golden Years (New York, 1971), 117-19; Frederick Lieb, *The Pittsburgh Pirates* (New York, 1947), 57-58.

[11]Riess, *Touching Base,* 168-170; Jake Daubert, "Why Business is Bad for a Ball Player, *Baseball Magazine* 29 (1922): 441-42; Frederick Lane, "Winter Occupations of Famous Baseball Celebrities," *Baseball Magazine* 24 *(March 1920): 575-78; Chicago Daily News,* March 31, 1908.

[12]Voigt, *American Baseball,* 2:68-71; "Editorial," *Commonweal* 2 (Oct. 21, 1925): 579; *Dictionary of American Biography,* s.v., "Mathewson, Christy." The raw data on education was drawn for a sample of 593 major leaguers who played at least one year (defined as either one hundred at bats or fifty innings pitched) in Chicago or New York between 1900 and 1919. Most of the information came from Allen, Notebooks. For the proportion of Americans in college at the turn of the century see Harold U. Faulkner, *The Quest for Social Justice* (New York, 1931), 196; and Laurence R. Veysey, *The Emergence of the American University* (Chicago, 1965), 2.

[13]For the methodology used to generate and weight the sample of 117 respondents to my questionnaire, see Riess, *Touching Base,* 237-38.

[14]Thernstrom, *Other Bostonians,* 131-32; Thomas J. Jenkins, "Changes in Ethnic and Racial Representation Among Professional Boxers: A Study in Ethnic Succession" (M.A. thesis, University of Chicago, 1955), 15. For comments on the Irish presence in baseball, see *Sporting News,* Oct. 8, 1892; *New York Tribune,* Feb. 24, 25, March 4, 8, 26, 1915; Fred Lieb, "Baseball—The Nation's Melting Pot," *Baseball Magazine* 21 (August 1923): 393-95; Lawrence Ritter, *The Glory of Their Times* (New York, 1966), 30.

[15]Computed from Allen, Notebooks.

[16]Thernstrom, *Other Bostonians,* 131, 135-37, 162-63, 168-73; Mark Haller, "Organized Crime in Urban Society: Chicago in the Twentieth Century, *Journal of Social History* 5 (Winter, 1971-72): 221-27; Daniel Bell, *The End of Ideology* (Glencoe, Ill., 1960), 127-50; Jenkins, "Ethnic Succession," 85-89; Frederick Lane, "Why Not More Jewish Ball Players?" *Baseball Magazine* 36 (January 1926): 341; idem, "He Can Talk Baseball in Ten Languages," ibid., (March 1928): 440; Joseph Gerstein, "Anti-Semitism in Baseball" *Jewish Life* (July 1952): 21-22.

[17]Quoted in Irving Howe, *World of Our Fathers* (New York, 1976), 182.

[18]"Indians Who Played in the Big Leagues," *Baseball Magazine* 27 (July 1921): 355; Seymour, *Baseball,* 2: 81-82; Chicago Daily News, Oct. 19, 1910.

[19]Semour, *Baseball,* 2:85-88; *Atlanta Constitution,* Jan. 10, 1909, Jan. 2, 1916; *New York Tribune,* Dec. 3, 1909, Dec. 26, 1911, April 15, 1917.

[20]Robert Peterson, *Only the Ball Was White* (Englewood Cliffs, N.J., 1970), 18-23, 57, 63, 67, 70, 77, 107; Voigt, *American Baseball,* 1:279.

[22]Data on tenure for the sample of 593 was taken from *The Baseball Encyclopedia.*

[23]Occupational data was culled from a wide variety of sources, including the Vertical Files, National Baseball Library, and obituaries in the *New York Times, Sporting News,* and home town newspapers of former major leaguers.

[23]*Dictionary of American Biography,* s.v., "Mathewson, Christy;" Joseph Durso, *Casey: The Life and Legend of Charles Dillon Stengel* (Englewood Cliffs, N.J., 1967), 82-83.

[24]*Los Angeles Times,* June 19, 1917.

[25]Marshall Smelser, *The Life that Ruth Built* (New York, 1975), 470, 473-74, 485-91, 512-14, 521-22.

[26]Thernstrom, *Other Bostonians,* 296-97.

[27]See Rudolf K. Haerle, Jr., "Education, Athletic Scholarships and the Occupational Career of the Professional Athlete," *Sociology of Work and Occupations* 2 (Nov. 1975): 373-403. This article modifies some of the conclusions he had previously presented in "Career Patterns and Career Contingencies of Professional Baseball Players: An Occupational Analysis," in *Sport and Social Order,* eds. Donald W. Ball and John W. Loy (Reading, Mass., 1975), 461-519.

[28]Computed for 117 respondents to questionnaire. On the correlation between education and class, Gamma = 0.66; on the father's status and the player's future status, Gamma = 0.48.

18

Jack Johnson: A Magnificent Black Anachronism of the Early Twentieth Century

by Al-Tony Gilmore

From 1908 to 1915, Jack Johnson, boxing's heavyweight champion, was public news item number one in the United States. He attracted more attention on a national level than any black man in this century's history to that time. One writer even goes as far as to say that his "impact on popular feeling was sharper than (President) William H. Taft's."[1] At one time or another during his reign as champion, almost every newspaper, governor, mayor and political aspirant in America voiced strong opinions on Johnson's life style, or on what he meant symbolically as the conqueror of white hopes. Much of the controversy and discussion surrounding the champion stemmed from the fact that he was unlike any publicized black man America had ever known.

Jack Johnson was his own man when it was not economically or physically advisable for blacks to be "men." He refused to allow anyone, white or black, or anything, including laws and customs, to dictate his place in society or the manner in which he should live. Born black in Galveston, Texas, in 1878—fifteen years after the Emancipation Proclamation and one year after the official ending of Reconstruction—he came to be the first of his race to fight for and to win boxing's heavyweight championship. However, in order to appreciate the impact on and the significance of this achievement to Americans, it is necessary to understand the man and the times in which he lived.

Al-Tony Gilmore was Chairperson, Department of Black Studies University of Maryland, and author of Bad Nigger! The National Impact of Jack Johnson *(Port Washington, N.Y.: Kennikta, 1977).*

From Al-Tony Gilmore, "Jack Johnson: A Magnificent Black Anachronism of the Early Twentieth Century,"Journal of Social and Behavioral Sciences, 19 (Winter 1973): 35-42.

In America, during Johnson's reign as world champion, there was a color bar, referred to as Jim Crow, that almost amounted to apartheid. The color bar received legal approval in the *Plessy vs. Ferguson* decision of 1896, when the Supreme Court upheld segregation in public transportation. In the following years the segregation principles were applied to nearly every facet of American life. There were unbelievably few places where blacks would be allowed in a hotel, theatre, church, educational institution, train or even a restroom occupied by white Americans without being restricted to the "Colored Section."[2] Even conservative black spokesman Booker T. Washington, who accepted segregation, was surprised when he drew the scorn of whites, in 1901, for dining at the same table with President Theodore Roosevelt in the White House.[3] By 1903, the racial situation was so despairing that militant black leader W.E.B. Du Bois was moved to say that, "the problem of the twentieth century is the problem of the color-line."[4]

Indeed the Jim Crow policies of the nation proved to be a formidable obstacle for blacks. What tended to complicate and make the situation more firmly rooted, however, was that this dehumanizing segregation was rationalized on the wide-spread assumption that blacks were inherently physiologically and mentally inferior to whites. Blacks were not believed to be "full-fledged" human beings. A vicious cycle operated here as the beliefs of the general white population were confirmed as "racial truths" by many white scientists. The basic purport of most of their pseudo-scientific studies was that the mental endowments of blacks were considerably less than whites, and the human intelligence increased in direct proportion to the amount of Caucasian blood. Such "findings" reinforced the beliefs of whites, and the cycle continued.[5]

Consequently, when Johnson won the title, alarm developed among many whites who felt that serious doubt was now cast over their highly revered notions of white supremacy. Seemingly, it should not have been a difficult task to explain away Jack Johnson. One need simply to accept the proposition that all races could produce men of superior physical endowments. But, as long as Americans found themselves under the spell of a racist ideology which declared that it was the Anglo-Saxon "manifest destiny" to rule over the darker, weaker peoples of the world, such an admission was difficult. Racist ideology, although stressing physiological and mental characteristics, did not ignore physical attributes. The Social Darwinian theory of evolution, with its physical implications, greatly influenced white social thought in the late nineteenth and early twentieth centuries.[6] The nature of society, nation, or race was presumed to be a product of natural evolutionary forces. "The evolutionary process was characterized by a struggle and conflict in which the stronger, more advanced . . . would naturally triumph over the inferior weaker

. . .peoples."[7] Thomas Gossett explains in his study, *Race: The History of an Idea:*

The idea of natural selection was translated to a struggle between individual members of a society; between members of classes of society, between different nations, and between different races. This conflict, far from being an evil thing, was nature's indispensable method of producing superior men, superior nations, and superior races[8]

Hence, many whites used the "natural laws" of Social Darwinism to justify policies and practices of white supremacy. What Johnson as champion implied was that non-whites could triumph in the "struggle between individual members of society." He was a notable contradiction to one of the fundamental tenets of white supremacy. Thus few stones were left unturned in search of ways to restore the heavyweight crown to the white race. Yet, it would be grossly inaccurate to assert that this was the only reason why whites overwhelmingly opposed Johnson. Equally important was the nature of the champion's character, personality and life style.

One scholar of Afro-American folklore has compared Johnson to sociologist Samuel Strong's definition of a "bad nigger." This personality type is one who adamantly refuses to accept the place given to blacks.[9] This idea and image of the "bad nigger" is the most important model to help us understand Johnson, the man, and his impact on both whites and blacks.

One characteristic of the life style of the "bad nigger" is an utter disregard of death and danger.[10] In this sense, Jack Johnson was truly a "bad nigger." Never once was his head bowed in mental acknowledgement of the superiority of a white man, for he feared no one. During his reign as champion, when the Ku Klux Klan and other anti-black organizations and individuals ranged the swamps, bayous, and mountaintops of "Dixie" as well as other places: when, at least 354 blacks were lynched, eighty-nine of whom were accused of insulting, assaulting, or raping white women; and when, in most states, it was illegal for black men to marry white women and strongly forbidden by social custom in others, Johnson married two white women and made no secret that he had had intimate relations with an entourage of others.[11] In fact, he conspicuously paraded all of his white women as if to flout the laws and customs of the nation.

Johnson undoubtedly took pleasure in aggravating whites. For example, upon entering his integrated night club, in Chicago—his city of residence—the Cafe de Champion, one was first met by a larger than life-size portrait of the champion embracing his white wife. And if that was not enough for openers, the champion would grace the bandstand with his bass violin and sing his favorite song, 'I Love My Wife.'[12] Such actions of Johnson are to be disassociated from the black males of the period who were less well known and who sometimes crossed the color line for marital happiness, because Johnson was the most publicized figure of his race with the heavyweight crown perched atop his black, cleanshaven head.

To intimidate Johnson was practically impossible, regardless of how trying the circumstances may have been. Shortly after his first white wife committed suicide in 1912, he was arrested on the charges of abducting a nineteen-year-old white woman. He was jailed until proper bond could be posted and disorder erupted among the white prisoners when they learned that Johnson had been locked up in the white, instead of the "Negro section" of cells. One white prisoner shouted, "Lynch him" and Johnson, in return, shouted back loudly, "I'll give fifty dollars just to slug that one."[13] After being transferred to the "Negro section," he displayed no signs of being frightened or concerned about the seriousness of the charges against him when he shouted to the guards, "I want a dozen candles so I can have more light, a box of cigars and a case of champagne."[14] Johnson's aides posted bond the following morning and the champion was released. By this time news had spread of the charges and angered whites made numerous threats and attempts at his life. One rumor was spread to the effect that Johnson had been shot and killed. The rumor reached Johnson's friends and they rushed excitedly to his home to find out if it was true. They found the champion unharmed and told him of the rumor, to which he replied, "Me shot? No such luck."[15] When the arraignment on the abduction charges was held, Johnson was, again, a "bad nigger" to the core as he showed no evidence of fear to the charges. The Chicago *Daily News* reported that, "Johnson appeared at the Criminal Court in a high powered automobile and with a bodyguard of two other Negroes and three white men . . . the Negro strolled into the courtroom half an hour late, carrying a long black cigar in his mouth and smiling every step."[16]

Perhaps nothing demonstrated Johnson's fearlessness clearer than his actions in the ring. Given the violence against blacks during the period, many feared that the angry white spectators would storm the ring; yet this strong possibility never seemed to worry Johnson. In fact, he took pride in exhibiting his bravery in the ring. According to one sports writer, he was so cocky in the ring "that during an average bout, he carried on more conversation with his opponent, ringsiders, handlers, and officials than a committee of neighborhood gossips."[17] And almost always his white wife or woman, depending on his marital status of the moment, was seated at ringside beautifully attired and wearing many diamonds.

Other aspects of Johnson's personality indicate that he was more than a "bad nigger." One historian has pointed out that in the North during slavery, next to the "bad nigger," the most despised black was the "uppity nigger." This personality type had achieved a degree of economic security and was relatively independent of whites.[18] It is doubtful that Northern white views of blacks changed by the time Johnson became champion. Writing of Southern attitudes toward blacks, a sociologist says that even without economic security, "The Negro male who dresses well consistently (ie., without overalls or work clothes on weekdays), or who in bearing or manner, does not suggest a certain deference or humility . . . is in danger of being labelled a 'smart nigger'."[19] Hence, Johnson, by his very life style was not only a "bad nigger" but an "uppity" and "smart nigger" as well. His financial holdings and his ostentatious manner of dress will attest to this fact.

With his ring earnings and the money that he made from theatrical tours through the black "belts" of the nation, Jack Johnson lived a life of luxury.[20] At a time when most blacks were barely carving out a living with their meager earnings, Johnson was busy purchasing expensive automobiles and clothing. Not one to be modest about his income, he told one black newspaper, while on vacation in New York, that he was "in town to pick up some diamonds and other souvenirs."[21] The Boston *Globe* was quite accurate in its description of him when it wrote:

> Good clothes and plenty of them; enough diamonds to illuminate his shirt front and hands to make him a conspicuous figure when he promenades the streets . . . Seldom does a day pass but what he will appear on the streets three or four times in changed attire from head to foot.[22]

The champion was well aware of the privilege that his money could afford. He knew that enough money would grant him and his family immunities from many of the racial policies of the period. For instance when it was announced that Johnson's mother and sister wanted to leave Chicago for a vacation in Galveston, railroads sent their representatives to his home. The Rock Island Railroad made the best offer by giving the Johnsons a written guarantee that it would "not only put them there but would give them first class passage all the way and that they may go to dinner at any call they choose and use the library or do anything that any of the other passengers are allowed."[23]

Another facet of Johnson the "bad nigger" was his insatiable love of having a good time.[24] Oldtimers still living in Chicago and New York, remember the 'good old days' when Johnson would frequent the night spots, "fingering an inevitable roll of gold-clipped thousand dollar bills." They recall that whenever he entered a club, it was a signal for champagne for everyone, and that he almost always had a "darling pink lady dangling on his bulging biceps."[25]

Money was never an object of consideration to the champion if enjoyment was to be had. After collecting more than $60,000 from one of his fights, he told reporters that he had reaped enough "spending money" to last a week.[26] On another occasion while vacationing and hunting in Maine, he missed his regularly scheduled train, and to the astonishment of all, rented an entire train to transport his wife, manager and himself to the big game country.[27]

Nothing in the way of circumstance or even personal tragedy stood much chance of deterring the champion from having a good time. On the day after the funeral of his first white wife, it was reported that "men and women of both races" were in the Cafe de Champion "having the time of their lives" and that Johnson "joined the band with his bass fiddle and played several lively and catchy selections."[28] One of the most obvious displays of Johnson's desire of having a good time came when he married his second white wife. Circumstances surrounding his personal life were tense. Not only had he recently been released of charges accusing him of having abducted a young white women, but he was also out on bond awaiting trial for charges of having violated the Mann Act with another white woman— the transportation of women across state lines for immoral purposes. Consequently, the wedding was expected to be a calm, solemn, non-boisterous affair. Johnson, however, was not to be denied the opportunity of having a good time. As soon as the nuptial vows were taken, he exhibited his showmanship by performing for the guests all of the latest dances, including the "Grizzly Bear" and the "Bunny Hug." After dancing Johnson went to one of his favorite pastimes—drinking champagne. He had brought twenty-four cases for the wedding, and boasted to reporters that he and his "henchmen" would drink it all before morning.[29]

Still another way in which Jack Johnson liked to have a good time was by racing at high speeds in his high powered automobiles. During his ring career, he was arrested and given scores of traffic citations for speeding.[30] He raced his automobiles so often the New York *Age* was moved to joke that his gasoline bill alone was "materially helping to increase the net earnings of the Standard Oil Company."[31]

While the "nigger" concept explains to a great extent why many whites deplored Johnson, it also aids significantly in an understanding of what he meant to many blacks. As Samuel Strong has pointed out, inarticulate and illiterate blacks admire the "bad nigger" even though they are "afraid to follow him."[32] Strong's contentions were well supported by one of Johnson's avid backers, the Richmond *Planet,* when it warned blacks that "a colored man who imagines himself Jack Johnson, will get an awful beating."[33] The Johnson image as a hero among many blacks also sounds very much like Roger D. Abraham's definition of the "hard hero" as being that hero who "is openly rebelling against the emasculating factors in his life."[34] Given the background of the repression of blacks, Johnson's personality elevated him to hero status, particularly among the more deprived of his race, because his exploits and publicized manner of living gave them the vicarious experience of leaving their inferior position.

Whenever Johnson visited black communities across the nation the excitement was stupendous. It was not uncommon for police officials to put extra officers on duty when the champion travelled to their cities.[35] So popular was he, that the black baseball leagues often requested Johnson to umpire their games, hoping that attendance would be increased.[36] One black writer described his return to Chicago after a victory.

Jack Johnson came to his own with the 'blare of trumpets.' The citizens clung to the wheels of his chariot; drew from there the horses and bore him on broad shoulders high above the shouting multitude. Not since the gladiator days of Rome has there been a scene enacted as that which greeted Johnson's return from Reno. His pathway was strewn with flowers; rich and poor alike lost distinction in the crushing throng to seize his hand.[37]

In that same crowd, it was observed that "gray-haired grandfathers" were carrying their grandsons, hoisting them high above the shoulders "that the little fellows might gaze upon Johnson." "Now watch close, dere, honey," one grandfather is supposed to have said, "cause you'se goin' to see the greatest cullard man dat ever lived."[38]

Although it is difficult to discern exactly how inarticulate and illiterate blacks reacted to Johnson at a specific moment or in a specific incident, black folklore helps to understand how they perceived him generally.[39] That perception was positive. Apparently what they liked best about Johnson was his ability to outwit whites. Much of the folklore on Johnson deals with this aspect of the man. One humorous story on his cleverness in the ring goes:

Man, Jack was too smart for them white fighters. He'd get them in a corner and pin their arms at the elbow joint between his thumb and index finger. Then he would smile sweetly and kiss them on the cheek. Man, this would make these fighters so mad they would forget about boxing and come out swinging wild. And that was all old Jack wanted. He'd step inside their leads and counter punch them to death.[40]

Another, dealing with the champion's ability to always "get the best" of whites, is about Johnson as a refused passenger of the ill-fated *Titanic.*

Look where and what has been done—1912, 12th day of May, when the Titanic sink in the sea. When they was getting on board (there) was no colored folks on. There was not no Negroes died on that ship. But Jack Johnson went to get on board. 'We are not hauling no coal' (they said). So Jack Johnson didn't like what the Big Boss said. He went and tried to do something about it, but it was so much Jim Crow he could have no go. And a few hours later Jack Johnson read the papers where the *Titanic* went down. Then the peoples began to holler about the mighty shock. You might have seen Jack Johnson doing the Eagle Rock so glad that was not on that ship.[41]

As should be expected, there is also folklore which involves Johnson in direct confrontation with Jim Crow restrictions. One story with a surprising and amusing ending follows:

Jack Johnson went to a Jim Crow Hotel and asked the desk clerk for a room. When the clerk raised and saw that the man was black he angrily responded, 'We don't serve your kind here'. Johnson again asked for a room and the clerk replied the same. The champion then laughed, pulled out a roll of money, and politely told the clerk, 'Oh you misunderstood me, I don't want it for myself, I want it for my wife—she's your kind'![42]

In addition to that folklore which dealt with the champion's ability to "put one over" on whites there are also items of folklore which glorify his fast life style. One story is concerned with Johnson and his automobile:

It was a hot day in Georgia when Jack Johnson drove into town. He was really flying: Zoooom! Behind his fine car was a cloud of red Georgia dust as far as the eye could see. The Sheriff flagged him down and said, 'Where do you think you're going, boy, speeding like that? That'll cost you $50,000'. Jack Johnson never looked up; he just reached in his pocket and handed the sheriff a $100,000 bill and started to gun the motor; ruuummmmmm, ruuummm. Just before Jack pulled off the sheriff shouted, 'Don't you want your change?' And Jack replied, 'Keep it, cause I'm coming back the same way I'm going'! Zoooooom.[43]

Other blacks, however, were not so fond of Johnson's antics or his life style. They, swayed by fear of white reprisals, condemned the man whose conduct in public tended to embarrass them. More often than not, these were articulate men, newspaper editors, preachers, teachers and race spokesmen.[44] Many black men of their category, however, were ardent supporters and followers of the champion. Thus, there was clearly no monolithic black view of Johnson. How one might judge Johnson at a given moment was highly dependent on the circumstances in which he was involved at the time.

This was Jack Johnson and the time in which he lived. Sports writer Dick Schaap aptly summarized Jack Johnson when he wrote, "think of the forces that shaped him, of the time in which he lived, and accept one conclusion: He must have been some man."[45]

Footnotes

[1] John Lardner, *White Hopes and Other Tigers* (Philadelphia: J.B. Lippincott, 1951). p. 13.

[2] One of the better accounts of segregation policies of the early twentieth century in

C. Vann Woodward's *The Strange Career of Jim Crow* (New York: Oxford University Press, 1966).

[3]Albon L. Holsey (ed.), *Booker T. Washington's Own Story of his Life and Work* (Naperville, Illinois, and Toronto: J.L. Nichols and Company, 1915), pp. 282-285.

[4]W.E.B. DuBois, *Souls of Black Folk* (New York; New American Library, 1969), p. 54.

[5]Rhett Jones, "Proving Black Inferior, 1870-1930," *Black World* (February, 1971), pp. 4-19

[6]Louis L. Knowles and Kenneth Prewitt (eds.), *Institutional Racism in America* (Englewood Cliffs, N.J.: Prentice Hall, 1969), p. 9.

[7]*Ibid.*

[8]Thomas Gosset, *Race: The History of an Idea,* (Dallas: SMU Press. 1963), p. 18.

[9]William H. Wiggins, Jr., "Jack Johnson as Bad Nigger: The Folklore of His Life," *Black Scholar* (January, 1971), p. 4-19.

[10]Samuel M. Strong, "Negro-White Relationships as Reflected in Social Types," *American Journal of Sociology, LXII,* 1946, p. 24.

[11]Lynching figures cover only the period from December 26, 1908 to April 5, 1915: the dates that Johnson won and list the title respectively. Excluded are black women. National Association for the Advancement of Colored People, *Thirty Years of Lynching in the United States, 1889-1918* (New York: Arno Press and the New York Times, 1969). For a detailed account of America's reaction to Johnson's affairs with white women see Al-Tony Gilmore's "Jack Johnson and White Women: The National Impact," scheduled for the January, 1973 edition of the *Journal of Negro History.*

[12]Chicago Broad Ax, September 26, 1912, p.2; Chicago *Defender,* July 13, p.1.

[13]Minneapolis *Tribune,* November 10, 1912, p.2.

[14]Indianapolis *Freeman,* November 23, 1912, p.7.

[15]Chicago *Daily News,* October 19, 1912, p.1.

[16]*Ibid.*

[17]A.S. Young, "Was Jack Johnson Boxing's Greatest Champion?" *Ebony* (January, 1963), p.67.

[18]Leon Litwack, *North of Slavery: The Negro in the Free State,* 1970-1860 (Chicago: University of Chicago Press, 1961), p.179.

[19]Hylan Lewis, *Blackways of Kent* (Chapel Hill: University of North Carolina Press, 1955), p.54.

[20]New York *Age,* July 7, 1910, p.6.

[21]Boston *Guardian,* January 6, 1912, p.7.

[22]*Globe,* December 27, 1908. p.10.

[23]*Defender,* February 18, 1911. p.1.

[24]Wiggins, "Bad Nigger," p.36.

[25]Pittsburgh *Courier,* March 5, 1960, p.M.2-3

[26]St. Louis *Post-Dispatch,* July 8, 1910, p.12.

[27]Baltimore *Afro-American Ledger,* November 26, 1910, p.2.

[28]*Broad Ax,* September 27, 1912, p.2.

[29]*Freeman,* December 14, 1912, p.7; New York *Herald,* December 4, 1912, p. 6.

[30]*Defender,* April 8, 1911, p.1; on June 10, 1946 Johnson was killed in an automobile accident.

[31]*Age,* January 10, 1910, p.6.

[32]Strong, "Negro-White Relationships", p.24.

[33]*Planet,* July 16, 1910, p.1.

[34]Roger D. Abrahams, "Some Varieties of Heroes in America," *Journal of the Folklore Institute, III,* 1966, p.35.

[35]*Defender,* March 23, 1912, p.5; *Galveston Daily News,* July 10, 1910, p.11.

[36]Robert Peterson, *Only the Ball Was White* (Englewood Cliffs, N.J.: Prentice Hall, 1970), p.61.

[37]*Freeman,* July 16, 1910, p.7.

[38]*Daily News,* July 7, 1910, p.1.

[39]In 1910, 30.4 percent of all blacks over age ten were defined as illiterate. Literacy was determined by the ability to write. U.S. Bureau of Census, *Negro Population in the United States, 1790-1915* (Washington: Government Printing Office, 1918). Consequently, the attempt to utilize folklore however humorous and "Anglo-Saxon unscholarly" it may appear to be is nothing less than a serious diligent, and painstaking effort to develop a revisionist methodology in researching, writing and undertaking Afro-American history; a history in which the masses of people left no written records. In the words of Roosevelt University historian Jesse Lemisch, a revisionist history seeks to write history "from the bottom up." Thus, the use of folklore along with other creative and innovative techniques such as the psychoanalytic approach of historian Earl Thorpe are extremely helpful when dealing with Afro-American history before the masses became literate. For excellent studies employing innovative approaches see Earl Thorpe's *The Central Theme of Black History* (Durham: Seeman Printery, 1969) and his *The Old South: A Psychohistory* (Durham: Seeman Printery, 1972).

[40]Wiggins, "Bad Nigger" p.43.

[41]Letter from Huddie Ledbetter to Moses Asch in Asch and Alan Lomax (eds), *The Leadbelly Songbook* (New York: Oak Publications. 1962), p.26.

[42]Folklore told to writer by humorist, folklorist, Rudy Ray Moore, Toledo, Ohio, April, 1972.

[43]Wiggins, "Bad Nigger," p.46.

[44]Because folklore does not usually deal with the negative images of its subjects, it is possible that, at a given time, many inarticulate blacks also condemned Johnson.

[45]Schaap Introduction in Jack Johnson, *Jack Johnson is a Dandy, An Autobiography* (New York: New American Library, 1969) p.16.

19

The Babe on Balance
by Marshall Smelser

Babe Ruth's success depended on his constitution and his temperament, but it also owed much to the accident of timing. If he had come
to New York before the First World War he would have played with a
weakly financed team much less able and popular than the Giants.
He came to New York when the Yankees had rich, ambitious owners
who were able to make the most of the interest he stirred. The result
was a rising zest for public spectacles, and Ruth rose with the flood, in
just the right place. From 1920 to 1932 there was a stormy excitement
over baseball unknown before or since. The only rival idols of baseball heroes were college football players and, occasionally, boxers. A
career like Ruth's is no longer possible. Today baseball has the lively
competition of professional football, hockey, golf, and basketball,
which split the popular interest. Imagine concentrating the popular
feeling for the darlings of basketball, hockey, and football entirely on
baseball heroes, and mostly on Babe Ruth. That's the way it was in
the 1920s. Where Ruth stood was the center of the world of games.
As the most cursory reading of the 1920 sports pages shows, his feat
of hitting fifty-four home runs in 1920 was deliriously exciting.

No one was more persistently popular, not even Lindbergh. The
press used hundreds of tons of extra newsprint to tell of Lindbergh,
but the story ran out in a few years. Babe Ruth's story went on and on.
He met an elemental need of the crowd. Every hero must have his
human flaw which he shares with his followers. In Ruth it was hedonism, as exaggerated in folklore and fable. If he had been nothing
more than an exceptional batter, he would have been respected, but

*Marshall Smelser was with the Department of History, University of
Notre Dame. He was a leading student of the Early Republic, and his
many books included* The Democratic Republic, 1801-1815 *(New
York, 1968), and* The Life that Ruth Built: A Biography *(New York,
1975).*

he attracted more than respect. The public love of Ruth approached idolatry, and his reputed carnality was necessary to the folk-hero pattern. As Waite Hoyt said, he was "the kind of bad boy it is easy to forgive." He fit the public image of what a highly paid ballplayer *ought* to be, and if he didn't really fit, the people wished to believe any legend that would shape the image. (They still do.) The combination of great skill on the field and a shared flaw off the field made him the most admired and theatrical man in the game.

He made money. Salaries, plus a bonus in the early twenties, and a percentage of club exhibition games paid him about a million dollars. World Series shares and barnstorming profits made him perhaps another half million. Many kinds of what we might call celebrity income also brought in about a half million. In real purchasing power, the only athletic heroes who have done better are a few heavyweight boxing champions and Pele, the Brazilian soccer player.

It is hard to think of him as doing anything else with his life. If he could have started earlier in golf, say as a caddie, he might have made as much as twenty-five thousand dollars a year, which was a high annual income for a golf professional in his time. With his nearly perfect physical coordination, he could no doubt have become a mechanically excellent pianist, but he showed no artistic tastes. Boxing had no money-ceiling at the time, but the company and the game itself were dangerous, and he did not have the kind of killer spirit necessary. Football was not then profitable. It had to be baseball.

People like to think he would have played even better if he were playing today, but the only advantage today's batters have is that American League fences, according to a calculation suggested by Cleveland Amory, are closer, on the average, by about twenty-four feet. This advantage is offset by all-night flying, less regular hours, the creation of the specialized relief pitcher, and the inferiority of the lighting for night games. Furthermore, Ruth didn't have to compete with blacks.

Ruth's last photographs have made him seem a freak carved out of blubber with no ability except to hit the ball a long way. Red Smith said what most expert witnesses felt: "The truth is that he was the complete ball player, certainly one of the greatest and maybe the one best of all time." Ruth seems almost to have been tailored to the game. We can list very few serious rivals for the adjective "best." Smith's word "complete" is the key word. Ruth could have been in the big leagues a long time at every position except second base, shortstop, and third base, positions in which left-handed throwers are handicapped. For example, only two pitchers in the Hall of Fame (Whitey Ford and Lefty Grove) have better won-lost percentages than Ruth's. His manysidedness was so dazzling that if it were supported only by oral tradition, apart from baseball's great heap of numbers called statistics, young people would snicker at the Ruth stories of their elders.

Every art form has its greatest practitioner. Every art form has able men who say there is *one* way to perform (the one way changes from time to time) and set down the rules. In each case the greatest practitioner first excelled according to the rules, then threw them away and soared higher. Ruth pitched conventionally, and as peer of the best, in 1915, 1916, and 1917, but found one position too confining. He went on to prove he could do almost everything else better than almost everybody else. The collaboration of Ed Barrow and Babe Ruth in converting a pitcher to a master of the whole game was the most influential single act in baseball history since the decision to pitch overhand instead of underhand.

To rate one player as the best is, of course, to place a high value on opinion. True, the pitching strategy of managers in Ruth's day differed from today's, and for the worse. But we can fairly contrast him with his contemporaries. After 1919, while in his prime, he was incomparable. There is no doubt at all that he was the best in his own time.

Ty Cobb's name naturally comes to mind, but Ruth could have done anything Cobb did, if he chose to do it, except steal as many bases. Branch Rickey, perhaps baseball's only true intellectual, saw Ruth as "a rational conservative in play as compared to Cobb." Cobb would often risk games in order to shine, but Ruth never. Ruth's risks were risks to snatch victory. We don't much dwell on Ruth as a man thinking, but thinking is not some kind of juggler's trick or a special exercise of the consciously literate. A man thinking is a man completely attending to something he is doing. In the ball game (although almost nowhere else) Ruth qualified as Homo sapiens.

He was, even more, an instinctive player. The leaping spirit of life that animated Ruth's play can solve many a game puzzle which reason is too slow to solve.

Hercules, the Greek patron of athletes, was usually pictured as a man carrying a club. Whether civilized man is man the tool-user, or man the time-keeper, or man the fuel-burner (as anthropologists debate), the oldest graphic symbol of civilization is said to be the club-carrying man. That is what Ruth was. Despite his pitching and fielding records, we remember him as the man with the club, primitive but successful, the fundamental man who was victor over everything. Like Hercules, he satisfied the feeling of the people of his time that there was practically nothing a man couldn't do if he was strong enough and had a big enough stick.

There is an old saw that says, "You can't win 'em all." Babe Ruth at bat seemed to be asking, "Why not?"

Ruth filled the parks by developing the home run into a hit of exciting elegance. For almost two decades he battered fences with such regularity that baseball's basic structure was eventually pounded into a different shape.

— Lee Allen

The explosive popularity of Babe Ruth in 1919 and 1920 marked the division between quite different styles of play. The characteristic elements of the earlier style were the bunt, the hit-and-run play, and the stolen base. In 1911 the total of stolen bases in both leagues was 3,394; in 1951 it was 863. The new idea was to clutter the bases with runners who waited for a long hit to bring them home in a group. But not only batting and running changed. Pitchers had to work more carefully, pitching to alleged weaknesses, preferring to walk batters rather than to chance the home run.

The earlier game was consciously dedicated to the nineteenth-century god Science. To bunt, to steal, to hit-and-run were explicitly called "scientific" baseball in the first decade of this century, by which time the religion of Science had trickled down to the popular culture. Babe Ruth, the iconoclast, showed the fans they need not believe in the old god — that baseball was for fun, not for a moral duty.

Ruth and those who tried to play as he played prompted changes in the rules, equipment, and strategy. If one Ruth could fill a park, wouldn't sixteen Ruths fill sixteen parks? The ball became livelier and the pitcher was forbidden to spit on it. Even welterweight infielders now had bats with heavy barrels and thin handles. The successors of those pitchers who were kings of diamonds from 1900 to 1920 faced the painful fact that slight .220 hitters could wreck winning games in late innings by swinging for the fences.

The change was not universally welcomed. For those who liked baseball as a game played with a sphere and a cylinder, blending the sport of gymnastics with geometry, it made the game much too dependent on strength. The new game has also somewhat lowered the standard of outfield play, since almost none of the annual three thousand home runs requires any response on the field. But the people, by buying tickets in greater proportion, showed they liked what had happened. It is still true that an advertised duel betwen two leading pitchers may sell an extra ten thousand tickets. Nevertheless, a 1-0 loss for the home team, pitched by a pair of journeymen, will please the crowd less than a 16-15 win.

You can't keep Ty Cobb's name out of this kind of discussion. It is only fair to the intelligent, flexible, and neurotic Cobb to say that if he had first appeared in 1925 instead of 1905, he would have been as great a player, but a different kind.

As it was, the earlier game was the Cobb game; the later was the Ruth game. Cobb hit roughly as many home runs as Ruth stole bases, which is the simple formula of the change. Their value to their teams, on the scoreboard, was about equal. Cobb was worth 170 runs per season, Ruth 167 (based on runs scored, plus runs batted in, minus home runs, divided by seasons of play). But Cobb did his work coldly and craftily while Ruth played loosely and joyously, and the happy big bang sold a lot more tickets than Cobb's foxiness did. Ruth was the first man who seemed capable of breaking up the ball game every day he played. "Did he hit one today?" became a national household question.

We often read that Babe Ruth "saved baseball" at the time of the 1919 Black Sox scandal (exposed in 1920) by reviving interest in the game. That is not quite accurate. His twenty-nine home runs of 1919 and his fifty-four of 1920 eclipsed the scandal, blocked it out of the mind of the *Volk,* so that the miscreants got about a tenth of the attention they would have had in, say, 1910. What he did for baseball was to enliven it so that the trend of attendance was reversed. From 1910 to 1918 baseball attendance did not increase as rapidly as the population. From 1919 to 1930 attendance increased at a much greater rate than did the population. Until we know some other cause we may credit the Ruth game with turning the figures around.

Despite his relatively high salaries, Ruth was a bargain for the Yankees. At his peak he was worth from a third of a million to half a million dollars to the franchise. To baseball as an industry, his value was simply incalculable. We can only say that every club benefited from the greater popularity of the game. His presence with the Yankees, according to their ablest scout, Paul Krichell, also had a good deal to do with the success of the Yankees in winning twenty-two pennants after Ruth left the team. In the days when the recruiting of beginners was an auction and not a kind of lottery, the Yankees found it easier to sign promising rookies because they all wanted to be Yankees. The American League profited in the same way. By outdrawing the National League, every American League club was better off, and therefore better able to outbid National League rivals for young talent. (This advantage lasted until the National League earned the gratitude of blacks by breaking down the skin-color barrier.)

Babe Ruth is better remembered than his contemporary presidents Harding, Coolidge, Hoover, better than his contemporary ethical hero Lindbergh, better than the foxy hero Cobb. He needs no rescue from oblivion. Proofs of his lasting fame are everywhere, as a few instances will show:

— An organized baseball program for boys too old for Little League and too young for American Legion junior baseball, called the Little Bigger League, changed its name in 1953 to the Babe Ruth League and, with Claire Ruth's help, has been flourishing ever since.

— As of this writing, the city of Baltimore is renovating Pius Shamberger's house, where George Ruth was born and lived for a few days, in order to make it a Babe Ruth shrine.

— The National Commemorative Society, which commissions

souvenir silver medals, polled its members in 1968, asking whose memory should be perpetuated on the 1969 medal. Babe Ruth won over Alexander Hamilton by a score of 760 to 724.

— *Der Sport Brockhaus; alles vom Sport von A-Z* (Wiesbaden, 1971) gave Ruth seven lines (with three errors of fact) and a portrait.

— In the part of Israel's "youth woodland" called the "freedom forest for Soviet Jewry," an ex-New Yorker named Jeff Shaya planted a tree in 1972 to memorialize Babe Ruth.

This list could be much longer.

Another kind of evidence is the interest of collectors. Dr. Helen Cripe of the American Antiquarian Society, studying the public sales of Americana, found in the catalogs of well-known dealers seventeen pieces of Ruthiana listed in the years 1963-1973, at prices from $6.50 to $250.00. Advertisements in the *Antique Trader* (Summer 1973) give us a relative evaluation: three Mickey Mouse watches of 1931, from $95 to $135, and one Babe Ruth watch at $110.

Babe Ruth's fame is grounded on firm achievement. A baseball player can't hide mistakes or clumsiness; he stands alone and naked. There is no way to build up an ordinary player artificially into a great player for very long. A few hot dogs become well known, but their days of true popularity are few. Ruth was even more than a great player, he was a folk hero. He didn't have all the qualities Thomas Carlyle insisted a hero must have (nor has Mickey Mouse), but he still gets from ordinary people most of the homage Carlyle said was due a hero.

His fame will last. Once a living legend persists from the first generation into the third generation, that legend is secure and durable. Captain John Smith made it; John Rolfe is rarely spoken of. Abraham Lincoln is remembered; Douglas is recalled, if ever, only as Lincoln's foil. Babe Ruth's name draws crowds of small boys to the Ruth exhibit at Cooperstown. Do many small boys beg to visit Lindbergh's trophies in St. Louis or Grant's tomb in New York?

Babe Ruth could not know the real world as obscure people know it. After living his formative years in a kind of monastery for boys, he leaped into a heroic place as a winner on winning teams. He never saw anything anonymously; it was all shown to him from where he stood on his pedestal. The ordinary person's world, how it worked, what it looked like, what it did to people, he couldn't know. Which may explain his fellow feeling for people institutionalized in artificial worlds — orphanages, hospitals, prisons.

He became a normal person by working to be normal. It was a hard struggle for him to become an acceptable member of society,

---

A man may be very imperfect and yet worth a good deal.
— Anthony Trollope, *Framley Parsonage*

partly because of his physical endowment. His appetites were strong, and his muscular urges even stronger. Driven by his make-up to satisfy his gut and to use his muscles more than he used his mental powers, he was initially out of balance. With effort he became what we call normal by the age of thirty. If he had had less human sympathy and even greater physical strength, he might have been in a state of permanent emotional disturbance. But his generosity and affections were as large as his hungers and his need to use his muscles.

It is rather sad that he never learned how typical a man he was. A reading of his memoirs and a study of his behavior raise the suspicion that he thought of himself as a kind of freak. Yet in every American cigar store, pool hall, barber shop, bar and grill, during his glory times, were specimens much like him — lacking only the ability to play baseball well.

Ruth had all of our faults, yet had the material success most Americans would like to have. Never did he try to be anything he was not; he never spoke on a subject he was unqualified to speak on, except in reply to interviewers' questions, and rarely even then. The ballplayer was larger than the man. His mind was empty of practically everything but baseball, and packed tight with baseball. He never said a banal thing about baseball except in situations contrived by press agents, where he echoed the puritan bosh about the uplifting gifts of sport — platitudes he had heard others use, *pro forma,* with apparent success. Except when cornered in that way, he was intellectually honest.

Did his manner of life hurt his play? The matter of keeping in shape for baseball has in it a deal of superstition. Inborn ability to make catlike movements is far more important than precise weight. Only in long games and double-headers does overweight take its price. He may have neglected to keep in condition, but that wasn't what killed him. Up to the age of thirty he tried hard to support the deathless belief of so many, that pleasure is happiness. Stories of the sins of popular heroes certainly grasp the attention of readers; so much has been written about Ruth's very ordinary and rather tiresome hedonism (but never with names, places, dates) that one is convinced there must be a real need to believe him a glutton who played best with a hangover. It reduces him to a smaller moral size so that some people can feel superior in some way to the otherwise titanic figure. And, as John McCabe well noted in his life of George M. Cohan, America sees itself as "Peck's Bad Boy," rough and hard to rule but instinctively doing good because it knows what is right. Ruth *had* to be a bad boy to be the paramount American. As Tristram Coffin said, "The hero must have a bit of the fool in him."

The record contradicts Ruth's reputation for self-destructive gluttony. As of 1972, only sixty-one out of ten thousand ballplayers had played twenty full seasons in the major leagues. Ruth was one who played twenty full seasons, and parts of two others. Whatever he did, it didn't destroy him as a player or a person.

Babe Ruth was driven by ambition and love. The ambition was to be the most successful baseball player, and the standard of success was the salary. Having money, he saw no reason not to enjoy it. He was driven by love in the sense of an urge to do good, which he saw in two ways — as being kind to the helpless and as not hurting people on purpose. He was good at both. The home runs and the dollars are famous, but we overlook the absence of permanent enemies and the number of people who knew him well and loved him.

With most professional athletes, play is work. With Ruth, play was play. And it was his life. Was his life trivial? Because the Greeks taught us that what is universally popular is literally vulgar and ignoble, we think the business leader, the statesman, and the soldier are really living, while the athlete is wasting his and our time. (Euripedes, for one, was very rough on athletes on this point; he had competing theaters to fill.) But there is a certain nobility in uniting mind and body in acts that need their perfect harmony. There is no need to apologize for athletes. The body has disorganized stimuli, gnawing hungers, and some unsystematic goals. The athlete makes it over into something controlled and directed toward its own excellence. If the mind merely lives in the body as a fish lives in a bowl, it would be folly to spend much time and effort to perfect the bowl. But man is mind and body in one, and the great athlete is a complete man who has found the limits of adventure within the bounds of the rules of his kind of play. That is not trivial.

Only in constant action was his constant certainty found. He will throw a longer shadow as time recedes.
— John Cornford, *A Memoir*

Babe Ruth lived only fifty-three years, but not all shortened lives are unfinished lives. Some are well rounded off, and end at a proper time. Since we have no reason to think he could have been a successful manager, and he had no other serious interest than baseball, we may say his was a finished, complete life. He was born at precisely the right time; it is hard to see how he could have been eminent if born earlier, or unique if born later. In the judgment of the people, no ballplayer has succeeded him. More than that, all others have diminished while he has grown. At the first election to the Hall of Fame in 1936, he ranked third. At mid-century, the Associated Press poll ranked him first over Cobb as the greatest ballplayer in the previous fifty years. In 1969, the centennial year of professional baseball, the Baseball Writers Association of America and the baseball broadcasters voted him the best player in the history of the game. They were nearly all strangers to him personally. Somehow that fact seems to add credibility to Babe Ruth's history; one feels like saying it really *did* happen.

A puzzled dramatic critic, in 1948, asked Babe Ruth's close friend, the sportswriter Dan Daniel, why Ruth should have a funeral unlike any before in New York (or one may add, since) and more obituary space than any New Yorker ever had, more memorializing than proposed for presidents, or scientists, or warriors. "Why all this? What did this man Ruth do? What did he have, to merit this?"

To answer, a generation later: he is our Hercules, our Samson, Beowulf, Siegfried. No other person outside public life so stirred our imaginations and captured our affections.

Suggestions For Further Reading.

Asinof, Eliot. *Eight Men Out: The Black Sox and the 1919 World Series* (N.Y.: Holt, Reinhart and Winston, 1963).

Cavallo, Dominick. "Social Reform and the Movement to Organize Children's Play During the Progressive Era." *History of Childhood Quarterly* 3 (Spring 1976): 509-22.

Creamer, Robert. *Babe* (N.Y.: Simon and Schuster, 1974).

Crepeau, Richard C. *Baseball: America's Diamond Mind, 1919-1941* (Gainesville: University of Central Florida Press, 1980).

Flath, Arnold, "A History of the Relations between the National Collegiate Athletic Association and the Amateur Athletic Union of the United States." (Ph.D. dissertation, University of Michigan, 1967).

Gerber, Ellen. "The Controlled Development of Collegiate Sport for Women, 1923-1936." *Journal of Sport History* 2 (Spring 1975): 1-28.

Gilmore, Al-Tony. *Bad Nigger! The National Impact of Jack Johnson* (Port Washington, N.Y.: Kennikat, 1975).

Johnson, Jack. *In the Ring and Out. The Classic Autobiography by the First Black Champion:* (1927: reprinted, Detroit: Gale, 1975).

Lawson, Hal A. and Alan G. Ingham. "Conflicting Ideologies Concerning the University and Intercollegiate Athletics: Harper and Hutchins at Chicago, 1892-1940." *Journal of Sport History* 7 (Winter 1980): 37-67.

Lester, Robin Dale, "The Rise, Fall and Decline of Football at the University of Chicago, 1892-1940." (Ph.D. dissertation, University of Chicago, 1974).

Lewis, Guy. "World War I and the Emergence of Sport for the Masses." *Maryland Historian* 4 (Fall 1973): 109-22.

Lucas, John A. "The Unholy Experiment—Professional Baseball's Struggle Against Pennsylvania Sunday Blue Laws, 1926-1934." *Pennsylvania History* 38 (April 1971): 163-75.

McArthur, Benjamin. "The Chicago Playground Movement." *Social Service Review* 49 (September 1975): 376-95.

Mormino, Gary Ross. "The Playing Fields of St. Louis: Italian Immigrants and Sports, 1925-1941." *Journal of Sport History* 9 (Summer 1982): 5-19.

Needham, Henry Beach. "The College Athlete." *McClure's* XXV (June, July, 1905): 115-28, 260-273.

Northam, Janet A., and Jack Berryman. "Sport and Urban Boosterism in the Pacific Northwest: Seattle's Alaska-Yukon-Pacific Exposition, 1909. *Journal of the West* 17 (July 1978): 53-59.

Riess, Steven. "Professional Baseball and Social Mobility." *Journal of Interdisciplinary History* 11 (Augumn 1980): 235-50.

Riess, Steven. "Sport and the American Dream: A Review Essay." *Journal of Social History* 14 (Winter 1980-81): 295-303.

Riess, Steven. *Touching Base: Professional Baseball and American Culture in the Progressive Era* (Westport, Conn.: Greenwood Press, 1980).

Ritter, Lawrence. *The Glory of Their Times* (N.Y.: Collier, 1966).

Roberts, Randy. *Jack Dempsey, The Manassa Mauler* (Baton Rouge: Louisiana State University Press, 1979).

Savage, Howard J. et al. *American College Athletics* (N.Y.: Carnegie Foundation for the Advancement of Teaching, 1929).

Schleppi, John R. "'It Pays': John H. Patterson and Industrial Recreation at the National Cash Register Company." *Journal of Sport History 6 (Winter 1979): 20-28.*

Seymour, Harold, *Baseball:* Vol. II *The Golden Years* (N.Y.: Oxford University Press, 1971).

Sorrell, Richard S. "Sports and Franco-Americans in Woonsocket, 1870–1930." *Rhode Island History* 31 (Fall 1972): 117-25.

Smelser, Marshall. *The Life that Ruth Built.* (N.Y.: Quadrangle/New York Times, 1975).

Smith, Leverett. *The American Dream and the National Game.* (Bowling Green: Bowling Green Press, 1970).

Spring, Joel H. "Mass Culture and School Sports." *History of Education Quarterly* 14 (Winter 1974): 483-98.

Twin, Stephanie L. "Introduction." In Stephanie L. Twin, ed. *Out of the Bleachers: Writings on Women and Sport* (Old Westbury, N.Y.: The Feminist Press, 1979), xv-xli.

Voigt, David Q. *American Baseball:* Vol II. *From the Commissioners to Continental Expansion* (Norman, Okla.: University of Oklahoma Press, 1970).

Wiggins, William H. Jr. "Jack Johnson as Bad Nigger: The Folklore of His Life." *The Black Scholar* 2 (January 1971): 34-46.

Sport in Contemporary America

Introduction

Professional boxing was one of the most prominent sports of the Depression era. Pugilism had gained a measure of respectability after World War I because it had been used to help train American soldiers, and in 1920 the sport was legalized in New York, the recognized center of the fight game. During the 1920s, interest in the sport grew considerably because of the use of radio to broadcast major fights and the presence of heroes like Jack Dempsey, the heavyweight champion from 1919 to 1926. Dempsey's fights attracted gates in excess of a million dollars. His 1927 rematch with Gene Tunney, the man who dethroned him, attracted over 100,000 to Chicago's Soldier Field and earned Tunney a $990,000 paycheck. During the Depression, many tough impoverished youths tried to fight their way out of poverty in the boxing ring. This theme was popularized in the 1930s and 1940s by movies like "Golden Boy," "Body and Soul," and "Champion." One of the first sociologists to study sports, Kirson Weinberg, focused his attention on prize fighting. In his well-known essay, "The Occupational Culture of the Boxer," written in collaboration with a former pugilist, Weinberg examined the subculture of the professional fighter. Weinberg pointed out how the prize fighter is dependent on his manager and trainer, who teach him pugilistic skills as well as values appropriate to the occupation, and also keep him in training. Weinberg focused on recruitment patterns, and found, as one would suspect, that boxers came from the lowest social classes, with one ethnic group replacing another as the main source of supply. Weinberg also followed the careers of the more successful boxers and discovered that after brief periods of fame, wealth, and adulation, they usually skidded into low status jobs.

Those problems which had plagued boxing in its illegal days, like fixes and close ties to organized crime, did not fade away once it was legalized. In 1960 a major investigation into the suspected links between prize fighting and the underworld was held by the Kefauver

Subcommittee on Antitrust and Monopoly of the Senate Judiciary Committee. The evidence presented during the hearings demonstrated the pervasive influence of organized crime on the fight game. The highlight of the investigation was the confession by former middleweight champion Jake LaMotta (1949-1951), that he had thrown a fight in 1947 against Billy Fox in order to get a crack at the world title. This fascinating story was made into a major motion picture in 1981 called "Raging Bull." The selection taken from the Kefauver hearings for this anthology highlights the testimony of former lightweight champion Ike Williams under interrogation by the subcommittee's chief counsel. The discussion focuses on Williams' relationship to his former manager Blinky Palermo, a man with known mobster connections. The dialogue points out how vulnerable the prize fighter was to his manager. Incidentally, in 1960 Palermo was the manager of one Charles "Sonny" Liston.

In the years immediately after World War II, major league baseball also underwent great turmoil. The principal crisis in baseball was the integration of the national pastime by Jackie Robinson. Robinson had been an outstanding football player and all-round athlete at UCLA, a ballplayer in the negro leagues, and an army officer during the Second World War. In 1946 he was given an opportunity by Branch Rickey of the Brooklyn Dodgers to break the color barrier which had kept baseball lily-white since 1898. Robinson joined the Montreal Royals, a Dodger farm team in the Class AAA International League, with the expectation of making into the major leagues. In a selection from his autobiography, *Jackie Robinson, His Own Story,* the author describes the trials and tribulations of his first spring training. The awesome challenge of breaking the color barrier was exacerbated that spring by Robinson's need to survive the racism of the South which had institutionalized segregation through various Jim Crow ordinances. He could not live with his white teammates or even dress with them. Despite all this, Robinson went on to have a banner year at Montreal and was promoted to the Dodgers just before the start of the 1947 campaign. He rewarded Branch Rickey's confidence with an outstanding season, capped by Rookie of the Year honors. Robinson's achievement in breaking the color line was an enormous symbolic victory. Baseball was regarded by most contemporaries as the most "American" of all our institutions, for it epitomized our values, beliefs and mores. Baseball represented teamwork, courage, rugged individualism and democracy. The integration of blacks into baseball represented a begrudging acceptance of their humanity by the core society and was a significant step in the fight against discrimination. Once the color line in baseball had been breached without any great calamity befalling the United States, it became easier to integrate other key American institutions like the military and education. Consequently, Jackie Robinson stands out as the most important black sportsman in American history and one of the most important blacks in our nation's experience.

The fourth article in this section deals with an important contemporary issue in sports. In "The Economics of 'Big-Time' Intercollegiate Athletics," economist James V. Koch analyzes the commercialization of college sports, a problem which dates back to before the turn of the century. He believes that the athletic market is dominated by those institutions in the NCAA which run the major athletic programs. This market is run like a cartel in which the NCAA establishes rules regarding the recruitment and use of student-athletes, seeks to regulate the behavior of its member institutions, and tries to maximize profits for them. The cartel is seen as most effective in dealing with student-athlete input, but there are, nevertheless, lots of opportunities for cheating. The cartel prefers promoting competition to pooling profits. However, everyone cannot win and victory is essential to fill up the expensive huge stadiums. Koch suggests that the future behavior of the cartel can be predicted to include cost-cutting in nonrevenue producing sports and the professionalization of student athletes in sports like football. He believes that revenue problems will compel the cartel to establish and enforce new rules to equalize competition, expenses, and revenues.

The final selection examines the impact of Title IX of the Education Amendments of 1972. Its purpose was to eliminate sex discrimination in scholastic and intercollegiate participation in American sports. Girls' sport was originally opposed by female physical educators as too dangerous and unwomanly. By the 1920s women's athletic programs were geared towards securing the greatest good for the greatest numbers, rather than training an elite corps of athletes who would engage in highly competitive athletics. "Feminine" sports like swimming, gymnastics, and tennis were regarded as acceptable, but not track or basketball which were "unladylike." However, by the 1960s, competitive athletics for girls and women were regarded by physical educators in a more favorable light, influenced in part by the feminist movement, and they organzied the Association for Intercollegiate Athletics for Women (AIAW) to provide a structure to facilitate high level sports competition. There has been growing participation in competitive athletics over the last twenty years, although sex stereotyping in sports remains a reality. There was discrimination in the allocation of facilities, equipment, practice time and budgets. An informal study in 1974 found that high school boys' sports received five times the amount for girls', while it was thirty times larger at the college level.

Title IX sought to promote equal opportunity for participation. No one could be excluded from participation on the basis of sex at any institute receiving federal financial assistance. Identical programs were not required, but a member of the opposite sex had to be permitted to try out for any noncontact sport, like golf, if opportunities for that sex had been limited in the past. The amendment did not require equal expenditures for each sex, but did hold institutions responsible for adequate equipment, practice time, travel allowances, medical and training facilities, housing, publicity, and coaching. Opportunities for athletic scholarships were to be proportionate to the sexual ratio among all student-athletes.

20

The Occupational Culture of the Boxer

by S. Kirson Weinberg and Henry Arond

Herein is described the culture of the professional boxer as discovered by personal experience, by reading of firsthand literature, and by interview with sixty-eight boxers and former boxers, seven trainers, and five managers.[1] The aspects covered are recruitment, practices and beliefs, and the social structure of the boxing world.

Recruitment

Professional boxers are adolescents and young men. Nearly all are of low socioeconomic background. Only two of our fighters might possibly have been of middle-class family. Most are immigrants to the city and are children of such. Their residences at the time of becoming boxers are distributed like the commoner forms of social disorganization, being almost all near the center of the city. Nearly all Chicago boxers lived on the Near South and Near West sides. There is an ethnic succession of boxers which corresponds to that of the ethnic groups in these areas. First Irish, then Jewish, then Italian, were most numerous among prominent boxers; now, Negroes (Table 1).

The traditions of an ethnic group, as well as its temporary location at the bottom of the scale, many affect the proportion of its boys who became boxers. Many Irish, but few Scandinavians, have become boxers in this country; many Filipinos, but very few Japanese and Chinese.

The juvenile and adolescent culture of the lower socioeconomic levels provides a base for the boxing culture. Individual and gang fights are encouraged. The best fighter is often the most admired, as well as the most feared, member of a gang. A boy who lacks status tries to get it and to restore his self-esteem by fighting.[2] Successful amateur and professional boxers furnish highly visible role-models to

S. Kirson Weinberg taught at Roosevelt and Loyola Universities, and is presently a consultant.

From S. Kirson Weinberg and Henry Arond, "The Occupational Culture of the Boxer," American Journal of Sociology 57 (March 1952): 460-69. Copyright © 1952 by the University of Chicago Press. Reprinted with permission.

the boys of the slum; this is especially so among urban Negroes at present. Since he has otherwise little hope of any but unskilled, disagreeable work, the boxing way to money and prestige may appear very attractive. As an old-time manager put it, "Where else can a poor kid get a stake as a fast as he can in boxing?"

Since the ability to fight is a matter of status among one's peers, is learned in play, and is the accepted means of expressing hostility and settling disputes, boys learn to fight early.

One fighter thought of becoming a boxer at the age of ten, because he could not participate in team game, as a child; his mother insisted that he had a "bad heart." He stated: "I tried to fight as soon as I got old enough, to be the roughest, toughest kid on the block." He fought so frequently and was arrested so often for fighting that one policeman told him that he might as well get paid for it. At the age of fourteen he participated in fights in vacant lots in the neighborhood. Because of his prowess as a fighter, the other boys in the neighborhood began to respect him more, and he began to associate status with fighting. When he was about seventeen, an amateur fighter told him about a gymnasium where he could learn to become a "ring fighter" instead of a "street fighter." He claimed: "I love fighting. I would rather fight than eat."

Most boxers seem to have been influenced to become "ring fighters" by a boxer in the neighborhood or by a member of the family.[3] One middleweight champion claimed that he "took after" his

TABLE 1
Rank Order of Number of Prominent Boxers
of Various Ethnic Groups for Certain Years*

Year	Rank		
	1	**2**	**3**
1909	Irish	German	English
1916	Irish	German	Italian
1928	Jewish	Italian	Irish
1936	Italian	Irish	Jewish
1948	Negro	Italian	Mexican

*Data tabulated from *World's Annual Sporting Record* (1910 and 1917); *Everlast Boxing Record* (1929); *Boxing News Record* (1938); and *Ring* (1948 and 1949). The numbers in the succeeding years are: 103, 118, 300, 201, and 149. There may be biases in the listings, but the predominance of two or three ethnic groups is marked in all the years. The Irish were very much above others in 1909 and 1916 (about 40 per cent of all boxers listed); in 1948 nearly half of all boxers listed were Negro. The Jews and Italians did not have so marked a predominance.

brother, followed him to the gymnasium, imitated him, and thus decided to be a boxer before he was fifteen years old. Another fighter was inspired by a neighbor and became his protégé. He continually followed his hero to the gymnasium and learned to fight himself. Eventually the neighbor induced his manager to take his protégé into the stable. A third fighter has stated:

> I was twelve when I went to the gym first. If there's a fighter in the neighborhood, the kids always look up to him because they think he's tough. There was an amateur in my neighborhood and he was a kind of hero to all us kids. It was him that took me to the gym the first time.

A former welterweight and middleweight champion who has been boxing since he was eleven years old has written in a similar vein:

> I didn't do any boxing before I left Detroit. I was too little. But I was already interested in it, partly because I idolized a big Golden Gloves heavyweight who lived on the same block with us. I used to hang around the Brewster Center Gym all the time watching him train. His name was Joe Louis. Whenever Joe was in the gym so was I. He was my idol then just like he is today. I've always wanted to be like him.[4]

Some managers and trainers of local gymnasiums directly seek out boys who like to fight and who take fighters as their models. One such manager says that he sought boys who were considered the "toughest in the block" or "natural fighters." He would get them to come to the gym and to become amateur boxers. He entered some in tournaments from which he received some "cut," then sifted out the most promising for professional work.

It is believed by many in boxing circles that those in the lower socioeconomic levels make the "best fighters":

> They say that too much education softens a man and that is why the college graduates are not good fighters. They fight emotionally on the gridiron and they fight bravely and well in our wars, but their contributions in our rings have been insignificant. The ring has been described as the refuge of the under-privileged. Out of the downtrodden have come our greatest fighters . . . An education is an escape, and that is what they are saying when they shake their heads — those who know the fight game — as you mention the name of a college fighter. Once the bell rings, they want their fighters to have no retreat, and a fighter with an education is a fighter who does not have to fight to live and he knows it . . . Only for the hungry fighter is it a decent gamble.[5]

It can be inferred tentatively that the social processes among juveniles and adolescents in the lower socioeconomic levels, such as individual and gang fights, the fantasies of "easy money," the lack of accessible vocational opportunities, and the general isolation from the middle-class culture, are similar for those who become professional boxers as for those who become delinquents. The difference resides in the role-model the boy picks, whether criminal or boxer. The presence of one or several successful boxers in an area stimulates boys of the same ethnic groups to follow in their footsteps. Boxing, as well as other sports and certain kinds of entertainment, offers slum boys the hope of quick success without deviant behavior (although, of course, some boxers have been juvenile delinquents).[6]

Within the neighborhood the professional boxer orients his behavior and routine around the role of boxer. Usually acquiring some measure of prestige in the neighorhood, he is no longer a factory hand or an unskilled laborer. He is admired, often has a small coterie of followers, and begins to dress smartly and loudly and to conceive of himself as a neighborhood celebrity, whether or not he has money at the time. Nurtured by the praise of the trainer or manager, he has hopes that eventually he will ascend to "big-time fights" and to "big money." The money that he does make in his amateur and early professional fights by comparison with his former earnings seems a lot to him.

Occupational Culture of the Boxer

The intrinsic occupational culture of the boxer is composed of techniques, illusions, aspirations, and structured roles which every boxer internalizes in some measure and which motivate him both inside and outside the ring. At the outset of his career the boxer becomes impressed with the need for training to improve his physical condition and to acquire the skills necessary to win fights and to avoid needless injury. When he has such status as to be sought out by promoters, he assigns a specified interval for training before the bout. But in the preliminary ranks he must keep himself in excellent physical shape most of the time, because he does not know when he will be summoned to fight. He may be booked as a substitute and cannot easily refuse the match. If he does, he may find it difficult to get another bout. The particular bout may be the chance he has been hoping for. The fighter is warned persistently by tales of the ritualistic necessity of "getting in shape" and of the dire consequences if he does not. "There is no more pitiable sight," stated one boxer, "than to see a fighter get into the ring out of of condition."

The boxer comes to regard his body, especially his hands, as his stock-in-trade. Boxers have varied formulas for preventing their hands from excess swelling, from excessive pain, or from being broken. This does not mean a hypochondriachal interest, because they emphasize virility and learn to slough off and to disdain punishment. But fighters continually seek nostrums and exercises for improving their bodies. One practiced yoga, another became a physical cultist, a third went on periodic fasts; others seek out lotions, vitamins, and other means of improving their endurance, alertness, and punching power.

"You have to live up to being a fighter." This phrase justifies their deprivations and regulated living. There is also a cult of a kind of per-severing courage, called a "fighting heart," which means "never admitting defeat." The fighter learns early that his exhibited courage—his ability, if necessary, to go down fighting—characterizes the respected, audience-pleasing boxer. He must cherish the lingering hope that he can win by a few more punches. One fighter was so severely beaten by another that the referee stopped the bout. The brother of the beaten fighter, a former fighter himself, became so outraged that he climbed into the ring and started to brawl with the referee. In another instance a boxer incurred a very severe eye injury, which would have meant the loss of his sight. But he insisted on continuing to fight, despite the warnings of his sec-onds. When the fight was stopped, he protested. This common atti-tude among boxers is reinforced by the demands cf the spectators who generally cheer a "game fighter." Thus the beaten fighter may become a "crowd-pleaser" and may get matches despite his defeat. On the other hand, some fighters who are influenced by friends, by wives, or by sheer experience recognize that sustained beatings may leave permanent injuries and voluntarily quit when they are beaten. But the spirit of the code is that the boxer continue to fight regardless of injuries. "If a man quits a fight, an honest fight," claimed one fighter, "he has no business there in the first place."

Fighters who remain in the sport are always hopeful of occupa-tional climbing. This attitude may initially be due to a definite self-centeredness, but it is intensified by the character of boxing. Boxing is done by single contestants, not by teams. Emphasis is on the boxer is a distinct individual. The mores among boxers are such that fight-ers seldom admit to others they are "punchy" or "washed-up." One fighter said: "you can tell another fighter to quit, but you can't call him punchy. If you do, he'll punch you to show you he still has a punch." He has to keep up his front.

Further, the boxer is involved in a scheme of relationships and traditions which focus upon building confidence. The boxing tradition is full of legends of feats of exceptional fighters. Most gymnasiums have pictures of past and present outstanding boxers on the wall, and identification with them comes easy for the incoming fighters. Past fights are revived in tales. Exceptional fighters of the past and present are compared and appraised. Second, the individual boxer is contin-ually assured and reassured that he is "great" and that he is "coming up." As a result, many fighters seem to overrate their ability and to feel that all they need are "lucky breaks" to become champions or lead-ing contenders. Many get self-important and carry scrapbooks of their newspaper write-ups and pictures.

The process of stimulating morale among fighters is an integral accompaniment of the acquisition of boxing skills and body conditioning. The exceptions are the part-time fighters who hold outside jobs and who are in the preliminary ranks. They tend to remain on the periphery of the boxing culture and thus have a somewhat different perspective on the mobility aspects of the sport.[8]

Since most bouts are unpredictable, boxers usually have superstitions which serve to create confidence and emotional security among them. Sometimes the manager or trainer uses these superstitions to control the fighter. One fighter believed that, if he ate certain foods, he was sure to win, because these foods gave him strength.[9] Others insist on wearing the same robe in which they won their first fight: one wore an Indian blanket when he entered the ring. Many have charm pieces or attribute added importance to entering the ring after the opponent. Joe Louis insisted on using a certain dressing-room at Madison Square Garden. Some insist that if a woman watches them train, it is bad luck. One fighter, to show he was not superstitious, would walk under a ladder before every fight, until this became a magical rite itself. Consistent with this attitude, many intensify their religious attitudes and keep Bibles in their lockers. One fighter kept a rosary in his glove. If he lost the rosary, he would spend the morning before the fight in church. Although this superstitious attitude may be imported from local or ethnic culture, it is intensified among the boxers themselves, whether they are white or Negro, preliminary fighters or champions.

When a fighter likes the style, punch, or movement of another fighter, he may wear the latter's trunks or one of his socks or rub him on the back. In training camps some fighters make a point of sleeping in the bed that a companion once occupied. For this reason, in part, some take the names of former fighters. All these practices focus toward the perspective of "filling the place" or taking the role of the other esteemed fighter. Moreover, many fighters deliberately copy the modes of training, the style and the general movements of role-models.

Since fighters, in the process of training, become keyed to a finely balanced physical and emotional condition and frequently are irritable, restless, and anxious, they also grow dependent and suggestible. The superstitions and the reassuring statements of the trainer and manager both unwittingly and wittingly serve to bolster their confidence.

Before and during the bout, self-confidence is esential. Fighters or their seconds try to unnerve the opponent. They may try to outstare him or may make some irritating or deflating remarks or gestures. In the ring, tactical self-confidence is expressed in the boxer's general physical condition and movements. His ability to outslug, to outspar, or to absorb punishment is part of his morale. The ability not to go down, to outmaneuver the other contestant, to change his style in whole or in part, to retrieve his strength quickly, or to place the opponent off-balance inevitably affect the latter's confidence. A fighter can *feel* whether he will win a bout during the early rounds, but he is always wary of the dreaded single punch or the unexpected rally.

Boxers become typed by their style and manner in the ring. A "puncher" or "mauler" differs from a "boxer" and certainly from a "cream puff," who is unable to hit hard. A "miller," or continual swinger, differs from one who saves his energy by fewer movements. A "butcher" is recognized by his tendency to hit hard and ruthlessly when another boxer is helpless, inflicting needless damage. A "tanker" is one who goes down easily, sometimes in a fixed fight or "set-up." The "mechanical" fighter differs from the "smart" fighter, for among the "smart" fighters are really the esteemed fighters, those who are capable of improvising and reformulating their style, of devising original punches and leg movements, of cunningly outmaneuvering their opponents, and of possessing the compensatory hostility, deadly impulsiveness, and quick reflexes to finish off their opponents in the vital split second.

Boxers have to contend with fouls and quasi-fouls in the ring. At present, these tactics seemingly are becoming more frequent. They may have to contend with "heeling," the maneuver by which the fighter, during clinches, shoves the laced part of his glove over the opponent's wound, particularly an "eye" wound, to open or exacerbate it, with "thumbing" in the eye, with "butting" by the head, with having their insteps stepped on hard during clinches, with punches in back of the head or in the kidneys, or with being tripped. These tactics, which technically are fouls, may be executed so quickly and so cleverly that the referee does not detect them. When detected, the fighter may be warned or, at worst, may lose the round. The boxers are thus placed in a situation fraught with tension, physical punishment, and eventual fatigue. They may be harassed by the spectators. Their protection consists of their physical condition and their acquired confidence. Moreover, the outcome of the fight is decisive for their status and self-esteem.[10]

The boxer's persistent display of aggression is an aspect of status. Thus his aggression becomes impersonal, although competition is intense. Thus two boxers may be friends outside the ring, but each will try to knock the other out in a bout, and after the bout they may be as friendly as competition permits. Furthermore, the injury done to an opponent, such as maiming or killing, is quickly rationalized away by an effective trainer or manager in order to prevent an access of intense guilt, which can ruin a fighter. The general reaction is that the opponent is out to do the same thing to him and that this is the purpose of boxing: namely, to beat the opponent into submission. The exception is the "grudge fight," in which personal hostility is clearly manifest.

In a succession of bouts, if the fighter is at all successful, he goes through a fluctuating routine in which tension mounts during training, is concentrated during the fight, and is discharged in the usual celebration, which most victorious fighters regard as their inevitable reward. Hence many boxers pursue a fast tempo of living and spend lavishly on clothes, women, gambling, and drink, practices seemingly tolerated by the manager and encouraged by the persons who are attracted to boxers. Many boxers experience intense conflict between the ordeals of training and the pursuit of pleasure.

Social Structure and Social Mobility

Boxers comprise a highly stratified occupation. Rank is determined by their rating in a weight division, by their position in a match, and by their status with stablemates who have the same manager. Annually, for each weight division, fighters are ranked. The champion and about twenty leading contenders are listed on top.[11] The other fighters are listed into "A," "B," and "C" categories. Many local preliminary fighters are not listed. Only the first twenty contenders and the "A" category seem to have any importance. Of 1,831 fighters listed for 1950, 8.8 per cent comprised the champion and leading contenders; 16.9 per cent were the "A" category; 74.3 per cent were in the "B" and "C" categories.

To determine the vertical mobility of fighters, the careers of 127 fighters were traced from 1938 onward.[12] Of these, 107, or 84.2 per cent, remained in the local preliminary or semiwindup category. Eleven boxers, or 8.7 per cent, became local headliners, which may be in the "A" category. They had been professional boxers for an average of almost eight years. Eight boxers, or 7.1 per cent, achieved national recognition, that is, among the first ten leading contenders. They also had been professionals for an average of almost eight years. One fighter became champion after twelve years in the ring.

The boxers who remain in the sport believe that they can ascend to the top because of the character of the boxing culture, in which the exceptional boxer is emphasized and with whom the aspiring boxer identifies. When the boxer ceases to aspire, he quits or becomes a part-time boxer. Yet the aspiring hopes of many boxers are not unfounded, because climbing in the sport does not depend upon ability only and also can be a result of a "lucky break."

Relationships of the Boxer

Boxers live in a wide social milieu of trainers, managers, and promoters. The boxer and trainer usually form the closest relationships in the boxing milieu. At one time, many managers were trainers, too; and a few owners of local gymnasiums still combine these roles, but their number has declined. Furthermore, the relationships between boxer and trainer are becoming increasingly impersonal. Consequently, the careful training and social intimacy which characterized the conditioning of many boxers by trainers in the past has also declined.[13]

Generally, the specialized trainer or trainer-manager represents the authority-figure to the boxer, transmits boxing skills to him, and becomes his anchor point of emotional security. The trainer's relationship with the boxer become crucial to his development. The effective trainer polishes his skills, compels him to train regularly, and distracts him from worrying about the fight, and he can control him by withdrawing praise or can restore his morale when he has lost. For example, a trainer reviewed a lost fight to his charge so skillfully that the boxer began to believe that his opponent had won by a few lucky punches. Had he averted these "lucky" punches, the fighter felt that he would have won. His confidence restored, he renewed his training with added vigor and determination.

The trainer may be of distinct help to the boxer during the bout. Frequently his "second," may advise him of his opponent's weaknesses and of his own faults. In addition, he can be a continuing source of confidence to the fighter. A fighter recalled that before a bout his trainer became ill. He felt alone and somewhat diffident when the fight began. He regained his confidence in the third round, when he felt that his opponent could not hurt him. Since the trainer can become so emotionally close to the fighter, he can help or hinder him, depending upon his insight and knowledge of boxing. Though very important to the fighter, the trainer is not a powerful figure in the boxing hierarchy, and some trainers are as exploited as are fighters by the managers.

One boxer has characterized managers as follows: "Some managers are interested in the money first and in the man second; other managers are interested in the man first." Our observations lead us to infer that the vast majority of managers at the present time are in the first category. They regard boxing as a business and the fighter as a commodity and are concerned mainly with making money. To do so, they are compelled to please the promoters and to sell their fighters' abilities to the promoters. Unless the manager is also a trainer, he is not concerned with the techniques of boxing, except to publicize his charge and to arrange matches which will bring the most revenue.

While the boxer devotes his aggressions to training and fighting, the manager slants his aggressions to machinations for better matches and for more money. Having few illusions about the fight business, acquainted with and often accepting its seamier side, he conforms to the standard managerial pattern of having the advantage over "his" boxers in every way. First, managers are organized into a guild, and, though some managers will try to steal boxers from one another, they usually bar fighters who run out on managers.[14] (One boxer, on the other hand, tried to organize fighters into a union.

His efforts were squelched quickly, and he was informally black-balled from fighting in New York City.) Second, many managers try to keep their fighters financially and, if possible, emotionally tied to them. Some managers will encourage fighters to borrow money from them and usually will not discourage them from squandering their earnings. One manager stated characteristically: "It's good to have a fighter 'in you' for a couple of bucks." By having fighters financially indebted to them, they have an easy expedient for controlling individuals who are unusually headstrong. Some fighters are in the continual process of regarding every fight as an essential means for clearing their debts.

Legally managers cannot receive more than one-third of the fighters' purses, but many do not conform to this rule. Frequently, they take one-half the purse, or they may put their fighters on a flat salary and get the rest. Some managers tell their preliminary fighters that the purse was less than it was actually and thus keep the rest for themselves.

Furthermore, many managers abuse their fighters so as to make money quickly. They may overmatch them with superior fighters, "rush" them into too many fights, force them to fight when they are out of condition, and hint that the fight is "fixed" and instruct them indirectly to lose. A few managers will match their fighters in another state when they are barred in one state because of injuries; they will obtain matches before the required sixty days have elapsed after their fighters have been knocked out. Fighters may be severely hurt, even ruined, by these tactics.

Some managers, however, are concerned mainly with building up their fighters and doing everything possible to develop their maximum ability; but these managers are in the minority. In short, managers have no informal standards to protect their boxers and are guided chiefly by their own personal considerations in these activities.

Since many ruthless individuals and petty racketeers who know little about boxing are increasingly drawn into this sport with the prime purpose of making money quickly, boxers tend to have little, if any, protection from managers except that provided by boxing commissions, whose rules can be evaded without difficulty. Moreover, it is extremely difficult for a boxer to climb or get important matches unless he has an effective manager.

The Boxer and the Promoter

The boxer's relationship with the promoter is usually indirect. Yet the promoter is the most influential person in the boxing hierarchy. He is primarily a showman and businessman, emotionally removed from the fighter and regards him chiefly as a commodity. His aim is to get the most from his investment. Thus the "show" comes first, regardless of the boxer's welfare. To insure his direct control over many boxers, the promoter, who legally cannot be a manager, may appoint one or a series of "managers" as "fronts" and thus get shares of many boxers' earnings, as well as controlling them. Furthermore, he can reduce the amount of the fighter's share because the nominal manager will not bargain for a larger share. In effect, most boxers are relatively helpless in dealing with promoters, especially at the present time, because of the monopolistic character of boxing.

When a potentially good fighter wants to meet leading contenders, the manager may have to "cut in" the promoter or "cut in" some other manager who has connections with the promoter. Thus the mobility of the fighter depends in large part upon the manager's relationship to the promoter. When the manager does not have this acceptable relationship and is unwilling to "cut in" a third party, he will not get the desired matches.[15]

Since the promoter is concerned primarily with attracting a large audience, he tries to select and develop fighters who will draw customers.[16] Thus the fighter must have "crowd-pleasing" qualifications in addition to ability. In this connection, the race and ethnic group play a part. A good white fighter is preferred to a good Negro fighter; and in large cities, such as New York and Chicago, a Jewish fighter is considered highly desirable because the majority of fight fans are Jewish and Italian. Despite the efforts of promoters to attract white fighters, especially Jewish fighters, few Jewish fighters have emerged because the role-models and practices in the local Jewish communities have changed. Even Negro fighters, despite their dominance of the sport in quality and quantity of fighters, are increasingly turning to other sports because the role-models are slowly shifting.[17]

The fighter whom a promoter does select for grooming can easily be made mobile once he has shown crowd-pleasing tendencies. He can be, as it were, "nursed" to the top by being matched with opponents who are easy to beat or by meeting "set-ups" who are instructed to lose. Thus he builds up an impressive record and is ready for big-time fights. Hence, it is difficult to tell how competent a fighter is on his early record alone, for his record may be designed for publicity purposes. When a fighter has won all or nearly all of his early matches and then loses repeatedly to leading contenders, he has been "nursed" to the top by the promoter, unless the fighter has incurred an injury in one of his later fights. In these ways the promoter can influence decisively the occupational career of the boxer.

Effect upon the Boxer

The punitive character of boxing, as well as the social relationships in the boxing milieu, effects the boxer-participants during and after their careers in the ring.

First, the physical effects of boxing, which are intrinsic to the sport, operate to the boxer's detriment. Although boxers may cultivate strong bodies, the direct and indirect injuries from this sport are very high. In addition to the deaths in the ring, one estimate is that 60 per cent of the boxers become mildly punch-drunk and 5 per cent become severely punch-drunk.[18] The severely punch-drunk fighter can be detected by an ambling gait, thickened or retarded speech, mental stereotypy, and general decline in efficiency. In addition, blindness and visual deficiency are so pervasive that eye injuries are considered virtually as occupational casualties, while misshaped noses and cauliflower ears are afflictions of most boxers who are in sport for five or more years. Despite these injuries, attempts to provide safeguards, such as headguards, have been opposed by the fans and by many boxers because such devices presumably did not "protect" and did not fit into their conceptions of virility and presumed contempt for punishment.[19]

Second, the boxing culture tends to work to the eventual detriment of the boxer. Many boxers tend to continue a particular fight when they are hopelessly beaten and when they can become severely injured. Many boxers persist in fighting when they have passed their prime and even when they have been injured. For example, one boxer, blind in one eye and barred from fighting in one state, was grateful to his manager for getting him matches in other states. Another old-time boxer had admitted characteristically: "It's hard to quit. Fighting gets into your blood, and you can't get it out." Many fighters try to make one comeback, at least, and some fight until they are definitely punch-drunk.

Boxers find further that, despite their success in the sport, their careers terminate at a relatively early age.[20] Since their physical condition is so decisive to their role, when they feel a decline in their physical prowess, they tend also to acquire the premature feeling of "being old." This attitude is reinforced by others in the sport who refer to them as "old men," meaning old in the occupation. Since boxing has been the vocational medium of status attainment and since they have no other skills to retain that status, many boxers experience a sharp decline in status in their postboxing careers. As an illustration, of ninety-five leading former boxers (i.e., champions and leading contenders), each of whom earned more than $100,000 during his ring career, eighteen were found to have remained in the sport as trainers or trainer-managers; two became wrestlers; twenty-six worked in, "fronted for," or owned taverns;[21] two were liquor salesmen; eighteen had unskilled jobs, most commonly in the steelmills; six worked in the movies; five were entertainers; two owned or worked in gas stations; three were cab-drivers; three had newsstands; two were janitors; three were bookies; three were associated with the race tracks (two in collecting bets and one as a starter); and two were in business, one of them as a custom tailor. In short, the successful boxers have a relatively quick economic ascent at a relatively young age in terms of earning power. But the punitive character of the sport, the boxers' dependence upon their managers, and their care-free spending during their boxing careers contribute to a quicker economic descent for many boxers. Their economic descent is accompanied by a drop in status and frequently by temporary or pro-longed emotional difficulties in readjusting to their new occupational roles.[22]

Footnotes

[1]One of us (Arond) has been a boxer, trainer, and manager. We first determined some common values, beliefs, and practices by a few unstructured interviews. We used the material thus gained to plan guided interviews which would help us sift out what is ethnic from what belongs properly to boxing culture. Mr. Leland White helped in the interviewing.

[2]Some juveniles who fought continually to retrieve their self-esteem and also in sheer self-defense later became boxers. One adolescent who was half-Negro and half-Indian was induced to become a boxer by a trainer who saw him beat two white opponents in a street fight. Another boxer admitted that he fought continually because other boys called him a "sissy." A third boxer fought continually because he was small and other boys picked on him. This compensatory drive among boxers is not unusual.

[3]For the last twenty-five years of boxers, we found the following brother combinations among boxers: 3 sets of five brothers, 5 sets of four brothers, 24 sets of three brothers, and 41 sets of two brothers. We also found sets of father-son com-binations. This number, very likely, is less than the actual figures, because some brothers fight as amateurs only and not as professional, and thus their records cannot be traced.

[4]"Sugar Ray" Robinson, "Fighting Is My Business," *Sport,* June, 1951, p. 18.

[5]*Ring,* July, 1950, p. 45.

[6]Merton has noted that, while our culture encourages the people of lower standing to orient their conduct toward wealth, it denies them opportunities to get money in the framework of accepted institutitons. This inconsistency results in a high rate of deviant behavior (Robrt K. Merton, *Social Theory and Social Structure* [Glenco, Ill.: Free Press, 1941] p.137).

[7]Because of the changing character of boxing at the present time, promoters or managers may sometimes tell fighters that they are "through"; but fighters, as we have indicated, seldom make these appraisals of other fighters.

[8]Since the number of local bouts have declined with the advent of television, many preliminary fighters and local club fighters are compelled to work at outside jobs in order to meet their daily expenses.

[9]According to boxing folklore, a former heavyweight champion, Max Baer, was stimulated into action by his trainer who gave him a mixture called "Go Fast," which presumably had the properties of making a "tiger" out of the one who drank it. The suggestive effects of this drink were so great that Baer knocked out his opponent. Thereafter, he demanded it in subsequent fights. This suggestive play also proved effective with a former middleweight champion, Ken Overlin. The drink itself was composed of distilled water and a little sugar.

[10]Some defeated boxers, as a result of physical fatigue and self-recrimination, lapse into a condition resembling combat exhaustion or anxiety. They react by

uncontrollable crying spells, tantrums, and random belligerency. The restoration of their confidence is crucial for subsequent fights, Some trainers and managers are quite skilled in accomplishing it.

[11]Data taken from *Ring*, February, 1951.

[12]These computations were made by following the fighters in every issue of *Ring* from 1938 on. This magazine lists all the fights for every month.

[13]"One of the troubles with boxing is what I call assembly line training. There are too few competent trainers and most of them have too many fighters to train. For the most part the boxers look upon training as a necessary evil . . . [In the past], hours were spent on perfecting a movement—a feint, the proper tossing of a punch, the art of slipping a blow successfully. [This] marked the difference between a skilled craftsman and a lumbering wild-swinging tyro" (Al Buck, "Incompetency the Cause," *Ring*, September, 1950, p. 22).

[14]The managers' guild also serves in part as a kind of collective protection against promoters.

[15]E.g., an outstanding light-heavyweight contender is unable to get a title match, although one whom he had defeated will get the match. He was slighted because his manager has not signed with the International Boxing Club. His manager has stated: "The I.B.C. dictates who fights who and when and where. They're big business. But I'll fight; I'm trying to keep the independents [boxers and managers] in business" (*Time*, July 9, 1951, pp. 58-59).

[16]The tastes of contemporary fight fans is directed mainly toward punchers rather than boxers. In the past, clever boxers were highly appreciated.

[17]"In 1937 when [Joe] Louis won the crown from Jimmy Braddock, every Negro boy in all corners of the country worshipped him. their thoughts centered on boxing and boxing gloves . . . The boys who once worshipped Louis as a boxer have gone daffy about a baseball hero, Jackie Robinson . . . The eyes of the boys who once looked upon Joe Louis with pride and envy and wanted to emulate him, now are focussed on Jackie Robinson and other top-notch ballplayers" (Nat Loubet, "Jackie Robinson's Rise Blow to Boxing," *Ring*, September, 1950, p.5).

[18]Arthur H. Steinhaus, "Boxing—Legalized Murder," *Look Magazine*, January 3, 1950, p.36.

[19]Some precautions have been innovated recently for the boxer's protection, such as the thickness of the padding on the floor of the ring or the absence of protrusions or sharp corners in the ring.

[20]Although the boxing myths emphasize the exceptions who fought past the age of forty—e.g., Bob Fitzsimmons fought until he was about fifty-two—the average fighter is considered "old" after he is thirty years of age. At present, some "old" fighters are still successfully active—e.g., Joe Louis and "Jersey Joe" Walcott, who are thirty-seven years old. In addition to being exceptions, their successful participation in the ring is also a result of the fact that few new heavyweights are entering boxing.

[21]Since successful boxers retain a reputation in their respective neighborhoods after they have quit the sport, some businessmen use their names as "fronts" for taverns or lounges. Hence it was difficult to find out whether the boxers themselves owned the taverns. In five cases they did not, although the taverns were in their names.

[22]One former champion said: "I like to hear of a boxer doing well after he leaves the ring.People think all boxers are punchy. We have a bad press.After I left the ring,I had a devil of a time telling people I wasn't punchy." The Veterans Boxing Association, an organization of former boxers, have protested occasionally against radio programs which present what they consider a false stereotype of the former boxer.

21

Corruption In Boxing:
The Ike Williams Testimony

MR. BONOMI. How much money, Mr. Williams, do you estimate that you made during your ring career?

MR. IKE WILLIAMS. Give or take a few thousand, I made a million dollars.

MR. BONOMI. You say your present take-home pay is about $35 or $40 a week, is that correct?

MR. IKE WILLIAMS. Yes.

MR. BONOMI. Who were your managers when you started out in your ring career?

MR. IKE WILLIAMS. Jesse Goss.

MR. BONOMI. How long was he your manager?

MR. IKE WILLIAMS. From 1940 until 1943.

MR. BONOMI. Then did Connie McCarthy and Joe Woodman become your managers?

MR. IKE WILLIAMS. That is correct, Mr. Bonomi.

MR. BONOMI. How long were they your managers?

MR. IKE WILLIAMS. From 1943 until 1946.

MR. BONOMI. About 1946, did Connie McCarthy cease or stop being your manager?

MR. IKE WILLIAMS. Well, he did not cease. I guess I left him. I saw to it that he ceased or stopped.

MR. BONOMI. Was there a period when you tried to manage yourself?

MR. IKE WILLIAMS. Yes, for several months, but I was unsuccessful in getting a fight. At the time I had 24 fights in Philadelphia, but for some reason or another, the guild was after me, and I couldn't get a fight anywhere in the country.

From U.S. Congress, Senate, Judiciary Committee, Professional Boxing: Hearings Before Subcommittee on Antitrust and Monopoly, *86th Cong., 2d. sess., Pursuant to S. Res. 238, December 5-14, 1960 (Washington, D.C.: Government Printing Office, 1961), pp. 664-77.*

MR. BONOMI. In other words, when you tried to manage yourself, you were boycotted?

MR. IKE WILLIAMS. That is right.

MR. BONOMI. Is that right?

MR. IKE WILLIAMS. I could not even get a sparring partner.

Senator KEFAUVER. Could not get a what?

MR. IKE WILLIAMS. Sparring partner.

Senator KEFAUVER. A training bout?

MR. BONOMI. Do you recall about that time—

Senator KEFAUVER. What is a sparring partner, Mr. Bonomi?

MR. BONOMI. Well, Ike, I am sure you are much more qualified. Will you tell us what a sparring partner is?

MR. IKE WILLIAMS. A sparring partner is someone to box with you to help you get into condition, instead of a real fight, you box with 14-ounce gloves on in a training camp to prepare yourself for the fight.

Senator KEFAUVER. You mean the organization controls the sparring partners, too, so that you could not even get one of them?

MR. IKE WILLIAMS. That is correct.

MR. BONOMI. In fact, when you tried to manage yourself, isn't it true that Jimmy White, who was a member of the managers guild, made a public statement saying that you would be boycotted unless you got a guild member to be your manager?

MR. IKE WILLIAMS. Yes; he said I was a wise guy and I was putting ideas into the other fighters' heads and he said they were going to show the people just how powerful they were.

MR. BONOMI. You were putting ideas into the other fighters' heads that they might become independent, too; isn't that right?

MR. IKE WILLIAMS. That is correct.

MR. BONOMI. Did there come a time when you came into contact with a man known as Frank "Blinky" Palermo?

MR. IKE WILLIAMS. During the interim, when I could not get a fight around 1946 and 1947, I was laying around training camp staying in condition, and Palermo at that time managed Billy Fox.

He approached me and said he would like to manage me and he would get me straightened out with the guild, so it sounded like a pretty good idea, because I could not get a fight, so I agreed to go with him.

MR. BONOMI. When he did become your manager, then you began to get fights again, isn't that right?

MR. IKE WILLIAMS. That is right.

MR. BONOMI. Let me ask you this, Mr. Williams:

Palermo continued as your manager, did he not, from about 1946 until the time you lost the championship?

MR. IKE WILLIAMS. From 1947—we signed a contract in January of 1947—and he continued managing me through 1952.

MR. BONOMI. When you lost the championship, you lost Palermo as your manager, isn't that right?

MR. IKE WILLIAMS. I lost the championship—actually, I was injured and after I lost the title, I had a couple of fights.

I lost those, so I retired for 6 or 7 months to get my shoulder back in shape and I had a couple of fights, and I did so-so, just so-so, and I guess he saw where my championship days were over so—

MR. BONOMI. He dumped you?

MR. IKE WILLIAMS. That is one way of putting it.

MR. BONOMI. That was shortly after 1952?

MR. IKE WILLIAMS. That is correct.

MR. BONOMI. When Palermo left you?

MR. IKE WILLIAMS. Yes.

MR. BONOMI. Is that right?

MR. IKE WILLIAMS. That is right.

MR. BONOMI. Do you recall that you fought Jesse Flores in Yankee Stadium, New York, on September 23, of 1948?

MR. IKE WILLIAMS. Yes, I do.

MR. BONOMI. That was a world's lightweight title bout, was it not?

MR. IKE WILLIAMS. Yes.

MR. BONOMI. What was the amount of your purse from that particular bout?

MR. IKE WILLIAMS. $32,500.

MR. BONOMI. $32,500?

MR. IKE WILLIAMS. Yes.

MR. BONOMI. And your manager at that time was this man, Frank "Blinky" Palermo, is that right?

MR. IKE WILLIAMS. That is right.

MR. BONOMI. Did you see one red cent of that $32,000?

MR. IKE WILLIAMS. No, I have not, not until today, I have not.

MR. BONOMI. The whole $32,500 disappeared, is that right?

MR. IKE WILLIAMS. The entire purse.

MR. BONOMI. Did you ever speak to Mr. Palermo about the location of the money or where it went?

MR. IKE WILLIAMS. Yes.

Well, he told me. Actually, I had left the money with the IBC because in 1948, that was my best year, and I made over $200,000 that year, so trying to ease the tax condition, I said I would collect the money in 1949, but I was buying some properties and I was buying an apartment house and I found I needed my end of the purse, so I told Palermo, I said, "I am going to"—you know—"collect my end of the purse."

So that is when he said, "Ike, I have been up against so and so," and so forth, and so forth.

He said, "That has been spent."

MR. BONOMI. Palermo said things were tough for him and he had gone out and spent your purse?

MR. IKE WILLIAMS. He said he collected and spent it.

Senator DIRKSEN. Mr. Bonomi, under what kind of an arrangement do the managers collect the purse? Is that entirely a contract between the manager and the performer or is there a provision in the boxing rules of the commission with respect to whom the purse is paid?

MR. BONOMI. Do you recall, Mr. Williams, whether the money was turned over to the manager at the time of the fight and then split with you, or whether you received the money?

MR. IKE WILLIAMS. The money was always turned over to the manager.

MR. BONOMI. In most cases, even though there may be a rule in the particular State that the money is to be turned over to the fighter, the manager is right there when the fighter cashes his check?

MR. IKE WILLIAMS. Only one State—

MR. BONOMI. And takes the money—

MR. IKE WILLIAMS. Only one State, Cleveland, which I think is a very good idea—I think it is very good idea—it is the only State that turns the money over to the fighter.

The Cleveland Athletic Commission gives the fighter his end of the purse and gives the manager his end.

MR. BONOMI. But in this particular case, in the Flores bout, you asked the promoter to hold on to the money, did you not?

MR. IKE WILLIAMS. Until 1949, that is right.

MR. BONOMI. Then when you went to Palermo and asked him where was your end of the purse, he said that he had run up against tough times and had spent your money, is that right?

MR. IKE WILLIAMS. That is right, Mr. Bonomi.

Senator KEFAUVER. I thought he was talking about the 1952 fight that Palermo kept his $32,000.

MR. BONOMI. This was the fight on September 23, 1948, with Jesse Flores at Yankee Stadium.

Senator KEFAUVER. You made $200,000?

MR. IKE WILLIAMS. A little better than $200,000, I made.

Senator KEFAUVER. You did not get any of it?

MR. IKE WILLIAMS. Positively, I did. I am speaking about this particular purse, the Flores fight. I did not get any of that purse, I did not get any of it.

Senator KEFAUVER. That was in 1952 or 1948?

MR. IKE WILLIAMS. 1948, Senator.

Senator KEFAUVER. I see.

MR. BONOMI. Mr. Williams, do you recall in that same year on July 12 of 1948, you fought Beau Jack in Shibe Park, Philadelphia?

MR. IKE WILLIAMS. Yes.

MR. BONOMI. That bout was also for the world's lightweight title?

MR. IKE WILLIAMS. That is correct, Mr. Bonomi.

MR. BONOMI. Was Frank Palermo your manager at that time?

MR. IKE WILLIAMS. Yes, he was.

MR. BONOMI. What was the amount of your purse in that particular bout?

MR. IKE WILLIAMS. For that fight, I received $32,400.

MR. BONOMI. That was the amount of your purse?

MR. IKE WILLIAMS. Yes.

MR. BONOMI. Did you receive any of that purse of $32,400?

MR. IKE WILLIAMS. No, not 5 cents.

MR. BONOMI. Not 5 cents.

Did you speak to Palermo about it?

MR. IKE WILLIAMS. Yes, I did.

MR. BONOMI. What did he say?

MR. IKE WILLIAMS. I got the same story. He was up against it, and he had spent the purse.

MR. BONOMI. So that in these two bouts during 1948, you received a total of about $65,000 in purses and you did not see 1 cent of that money, is that right?

MR. IKE WILLIAMS. That is right, Mr. Bonomi.

Senator KEFAUVER. Mr. Bonomi, will you clear this up? Was that $65,000 all supposed to be Mr. Williams' or was it supposed to be divided in some manner with Mr. Palermo?

MR. IKE WILLIAMS. Two-thirds was supposed to be mine.

MR. BONOMI. You were supposed to receive two-thirds of each of those purses?

MR. IKE WILLIAMS. Two-thirds, less expenses.

MR. BONOMI. After expenses?

MR. IKE WILLIAMS. That is right.

MR. BONOMI. And Mr. Palermo was to receive one-third of each of those purses, is that correct?

MR. IKE WILLIAMS. After the expenses, that is right.

MR. BONOMI. After the expenses.

So that your end in those two bouts amounted to about $65,000 and you did not see 1 red cent, is that right?

MR. IKE WILLIAMS. No, I did not.

Senator KEFAUVER. You mean that Mr. Palermo got his one-third in addition to the $65,000?

MR. IKE WILLIAMS. Pardon me, Senator?

Senator KEFAUVER. Palmer got his one-third in addition to the $65,000?

MR. IKE WILLIAMS. Yes.

Senator KEFAUVER. That you were supposed to get but he got?

MR. IKE WILLIAMS. He got his one-third and my two-thirds. He took the whole purse.

Senator KEFAUVER. Your two-thirds was the $65,000?

MR. BONOMI. That was your total purse; wasn't it, Ike?

MR. IKE WILLIAMS. Yes.

MR. BONOMI. Is that right?

MR. IKE WILLIAMS. He took the whole purse.

MR. BONOMI. He took the whole purse on both occasions?

MR. IKE WILLIAMS. Yes, sir.

MR. BONOMI. And when you went to him, he said, "Well, things are tough"; is that right?

MR. IKE WILLIAMS. Yes; that is right.

Mr. DIXON. Mr. Williams, who paid the taxes on that?

MR. IKE WILLIAMS. I paid the taxes, Mr. Dixon.

Mr. DIXON. You paid the taxes on money you never received?

MR. IKE WILLIAMS. Yes; I did.

Senator KEFAUVER. Did Palermo advise you to do that?

MR. IKE WILLIAMS. No; he did not.

Senator KEFAUVER. You just knew that the money was supposed to be yours and you paid taxes on it, thinking you would get it and never got it?

MR. IKE WILLIAMS. That is right, Senator.

Senator DIRKSEN. Mr. Williams, what is the customary procedure? Are you paid immediately after the fight, after you have gone to your dressing room, and showered and come back to the front office, are you paid then or are you paid at some subsequent day?

MR. IKE WILLIAMS. The following day, usually, you are paid.

Senator DIRKSEN. The following day?

MR. IKE WILLIAMS. Yes.

Senator DIRKSEN. Does anybody say anything about taxes at that time.

MR. IKE WILLIAMS. No; they don't.

Senator DIRKSEN. Neither the promoter nor your manager?

MR. IKE WILLIAMS. No; the taxes are the fighter's problem.

MR. BONOMI. Mr. Williams, do you recall that you fought Gil Turner on September 10 of 1951?

MR. IKE WILLIAMS. Yes; I did.

MR. BONOMI. In that bout, did you give Mr. Palermo some money for the training expenses that you had incurred?

MR. IKE WILLIAMS. Yes; I did.

MR. BONOMI. What happened with regard to the training expenses in that particular bout?

MR. IKE WILLIAMS. The training expenses, I don't remember the exact figures, but it was roughly around $750 or $800, and I gave him the money to pay for the training camp and 2 or 3 months later I received a lawsuit from his lawyer saying the bill had never been paid, so I had to pay that also again.

MR. BONOMI. In other words, you gave $750 or $800 to Mr. Palermo?

MR. IKE WILLIAMS. Yes.

MR. BONOMI. To pay the training camp?

MR. IKE WILLIAMS. Yes. Don't quote me on the figures, Mr. Bonomi, I am not sure, but it is approximately that.

MR. BONOMI. Approximately that amount to Mr. Palermo to pay the training camp expenses?

MR. IKE WILLIAMS. Yes.

MR. BONOMI. Then you had to pay those expenses once again because apparently Mr. Palermo did not pay them; is that right?

MR. IKE WILLIAMS. That is right.

MR. BONOMI. Did you speak to Mr. Palermo about that situation and ask him what had happened?

MR. IKE WILLIAMS. Yes; I did. I spoke to him.

MR. BONOMI. Did he tell you things were tough again?

MR. IKE WILLIAMS. I got no answer the second time, the third time.

MR. BONOMI. Got no answer?

MR. IKE WILLIAMS. No answer.

MR. BONOMI. Mr. Williams, you fought Freddy Dawson in a championship bout in Philadelphia on December 5 of 1949; did you not?

MR. IKE WILLIAMS. That is right, Mr. Bonomi.

MR. BONOMI. Will you relate what happened in connection with that particular bout?

MR. IKE WILLIAMS. Mr. Bonomi, would you go over that again, please?

MR. BONOMI. Yes.

You said you fought Freddy Dawson in a championship bout in Philadelphia on December 5 of 1949.

MR. IKE WILLIAMS. Yes.

MR. BONOMI. Let me ask you this with regard to that bout: Did you receive a $30,000 bribe offer in order to dump that bout or lose to Freddy Dawson?

MR. IKE WILLIAMS. It was put before me, Mr. Bonomi.

MR. BONOMI. It was put before you?

MR. IKE WILLIAMS. Yes.

MR. BONOMI. Will you relate to the subcommittee, Mr. Williams, under what circumstances you received that $30,000 bribe offer?

MR. IKE WILLIAMS. Mr. Bonomi, you and I have been over that before, I think.

MR. BONOMI. That is right.

Let me ask you this: Was that $30,000 bribe offer made to you through this man, Frank "Blinky" Palermo?

MR. IKE WILLIAMS. Yes; it was.

MR. BONOMI. Under what circumstances was that made? What happened at that time?

Senator KEFAUVER. Just tell us about it, Mr. Williams.

MR. IKE WILLIAMS. Well, Mr. Bonomi, I vetoed it like I did all the rest of them.

Senator KEFAUVER. You vetoed it like all the rest of them?

MR. IKE WILLIAMS. Yes; I did.

Senator KEFAUVER. There have been other offers from time to time?

MR. IKE WILLIAMS. Yes, Senator. I received several bribes. All fighters receive bribes. I will say even the biggest fighters that ever lived. I will say Joe Louis and Jack Dempsey, I will say some guy, some nut, would come to them, even with Dempsey.

Senator KEFAUVER. With bribe offers.

MR. IKE WILLIAMS. They were never considered, because I think—

Senator KEFAUVER. What to you mean, you and other fighters are always receiving bribe offers? You don't mean that they accept it?

MR. IKE WILLIAMS. No, positively not, but somebody always comes with some idea.

Even as big as baseball is, just a few years ago I read in the paper that someone had tried to bribe a baseball player, in Philadelphia I believe it was.

Senator KEFAUVER. But it happens to you fighters quite frequently?

MR. IKE WILLIAMS. That is right.

Senator KEFAUVER. Mr. Bonomi?

MR. BONOMI. When did Palermo make this $30,000 bribe offer in connection with your bout with Freddy Dawson?

MR. IKE WILLIAMS. It was some time, you can't quote me on the dates—

MR. BONOMI. As best you recall, Mr. Williams.

MR. IKE WILLIAMS. I imagine it was 3 or 4 weeks before the fight.

MR. BONOMI. What did Mr. Palermo say to you on that occasion?

MR. IKE WILLIAMS. That I have told you, Mr. Bonomi; that he told me that someone had offered him $30,000 for me to lose the fight to Dawson, but he said if it was me, he says, I would not take it.

I told you before that he said he told the guy to go and drop dead or something, or words to that effect.

MR. BONOMI. You say that Mr. Palermo said that you could make $30,000, if you lost the bout to Freddy Dawson, but then he told you, "Please don't take it"?

MR. IKE WILLIAMS. No, he says—Mr. Bonomi—

MR. BONOMI. Isn't it a fact, Mr. Williams, that Mr. Palermo made the $30,000 bribe offer, period, about 3 or 4 weeks before the bout?

MR. IKE WILLIAMS. Mr. Bonomi, quote me on this. I will tell you verbatim what the man said.

He said, "Ike, I was approached by a fellow." Whom the fellow was I do not know. But he said—he didn't call any names—he said: "A fellow offered me $30,000 for you to lose the fight." He said, "I told the fellow to go and drop dead." And he said, "If it is me," he said, "I wouldn't take it." He said, "Use your own judgment about it."

MR. BONOMI. But he went ahead and told you that you could make $30,000 if you lost the bout to Freddy Dawson; is that right?

MR. IKE WILLIAMS. He did not put it in those words. He said he was offered that.

MR. BONOMI. But he went ahead and informed you of this, did he not?

MR. IKE WILLIAMS. Yes. He told me about it. He also told me if it was him, he wouldn't take it.

MR. BONOMI. He said to use your own judgment?

MR. IKE WILLIAMS. That is right.

MR. BONOMI. What did you say in reply to him?

MR. IKE WILLIAMS. I said, "No."

MR. BONOMI. Was Mr. Palermo disappointed or did he express great joy at the fact that you refused his bribe offer?

MR. IKE WILLIAMS. No, he didn't seem to be disappointed to me, not at all, Mr. Bonomi.

MR. BONOMI. That was 3 or 4 weeks before the bout. What happened after that?

MR. IKE WILLIAMS. I went through my usual training procedure and subsequently—you said what happened after that. What do you mean, Mr. Bonomi?

MR. BONOMI. Do you recall an incident in your dressing room on the date of the title fight, December 5, 1949?

MR. IKE WILLIAMS. Yes, I do.

MR. BONOMI. What happened at that time?

MR. IKE WILLIAMS. I recall it vividly as if it happened this morning.

Approximately 10 minutes before the fight, I was going to defend the title against a very powerful contender, Freddy Dawson, of Chicago, whom I had fought twice before, and approximately 10 minutes, about 10 minutes to 10, a good friend of mine, Bill Keller, William Keller, of Trenton, he came in.

Well, he is an elderly man. He is 76 years of age now and he was in a high state of excitement and he said, "Ike," he said, "they are going to take the fight from you."

MR. BONOMI. He said, "They are going to take the fight from you"?

MR. IKE WILLIAMS. They were his exact words.

MR. BONOMI. What did you do at this point?

MR. IKE WILLIAMS. Well, Mr. Bonomi, in a condition like that, I called my trainer, Jesse Goss, who put the first pair of gloves on me, and Calvin Taylor.

I think you know Calvin Taylor. He is now in the schools, in the Jersey school system.

I called for a quick symposium and we talked it over, not having much time, and I was excited.

I was going to defend my title, the lightweight title, and I think it was the second biggest sports—I think it is the second biggest title in sports, exceeded only by the heavyweight title.

I told Calvin Taylor, I said, "Go down and get the sportswriters."

So in 2 or 3 minutes later he went down and he came back with Red Smith, John Webster, and Jack Sarnas, and all of the leading sportswriters at the fight, and I told the fellows, I said, "After I fight tonight, come back, I have a story for you."

This, you can check in the papers.

So after the fight—I won the fight, I received the decision—and they came back, they said, "Ike, what do you have to tell us?"

So I told them what the fellow told me, what Bill Keller told me.

He said if the fight went 15 rounds, I was going to lose it. But evidently the man had given me false information.

MR. BONOMI. In other words, a couple of weeks before this bout, you received the $30,000 bribe offer through Frank "Blinky" Palermo, is that right?

MR. IKE WILLIAMS. That is right.

MR. BONOMI. And you refused it, is that correct?

MR. IKE WILLIAMS. That is correct, Mr. Bonomi.

MR. BONOMI. Then on the night of the fight in your dressing room, a friend of yours came up and said that you were going to lose the bout anyway, is that right?

MR. IKE WILLIAMS. That is correct, Mr. Bonomi.

MR. BONOMI. He said, "They are going to take it away from you"?

MR. IKE WILLIAMS. That is correct.

MR. BONOMI. By "they," whom do you think he was referring to?

MR. IKE WILLIAMS. I had not given it a thought, but the only persons that he could have meant was the officials.

MR. BONOMI. The officials.

So that at that point you were quite frightened and apprehensive about the fact that even if you won the bout with Dawson, the officials would take it away from you, is that right?

MR. IKE WILLIAMS. That is right, Mr. Boomi.

MR. BONOMI. So at that point you called the newspapermen?

MR. IKE WILLIAMS. That is right.

MR. BONOMI. You told the newspapermen that if you lost this

bout, you would have a story for them, is that right?

MR. IKE WILLIAMS. That is right.

MR. BONOMI. You went out and won the bout, didn't you? Is that correct?

MR. IKE WILLIAMS. That is correct, Mr. Bonomi.

MR. BONOMI. You successfully defended your world's light-weight title?

MR. IKE WILLIAMS. That is right.

MR. BONOMI. You won by a decision, is that correct?

MR. IKE WILLIAMS. Decision. I won by decision, 15 rounds.

MR. BONOMI. Did you win by a large margin, do you recall?

MR. IKE WILLIAMS. I remember the New York Times, they gave me nine rounds and gave Dawson five—nine, five, and one even.

MR. BONOMI. So apparently if the officials had any idea of taking the bout away from you, they were scared by your conference with the newspapermen, is that right?

MR. IKE WILLIAMS. Probably so.

MR. BONOMI. After the bout, you had no story to tell the news-papermen, is that right?

MR. IKE WILLIAMS. That is correct, Mr. Bonomi.

MR. BONOMI. As a result of your conference before the bout with the newspapermen, were you called before the Pennsylvania State Athletic Commission?

MR. IKE WILLIAMS. I most certainly was.

MR. BONOMI. What happened on that occasion?

By the way, who was the chairman of the Pennsylvania State Athletic Commission?

MR. IKE WILLIAMS. The late Leon Raines.

MR. BONOMI. Let me ask you this: Did you know Mr. Raines as a friend and associate of Frank "Blinky" Palermo?

MR. IKE WILLIAMS. That, no, I did not.

MR. BONOMI. Isn't it a fact that on a number of occasions Mr. Raines and Mr. Palermo would travel together to the bouts in which you engaged?

MR. IKE WILLIAMS. Well, I have seen them, Mr. Bonomi. I believe I have seen them at maybe one or two fights.

MR. BONOMI. Those one or two fights were in California; weren't they?

MR. IKE WILLIAMS. I think the commissioner was out there at one of my fights.

MR. BONOMI. With Palermo; is that right?

MR. IKE WILLIAMS. That is right.

MR. BONOMI. Mr. Williams, tell us what happened before the State athletic commission the day after the Dawson bout?

MR. IKE WILLIAMS. I was called in and I was fined $500.

MR. BONOMI. You were fined $500?

MR. IKE WILLIAMS. That is right. Commissioner Raines said for inciting—I don't know—for stirring up, you know, accusing. I don't know, I don't remember verbatim what the man said, but words to that effect of accusing the officials of dishonesty or something. I mean it is going back 11 years now.

MR. BONOMI. You mean you were fined $500 because you reflected on the integrity of the boxing officials in the State of Pennsylvania; is that right?

MR. IKE WILLIAMS. That is right, Mr. Bonomi.

MR. BONOMI. Do you recall that you fought Kid Gavilan on January 28 of 1949 in Madison Square Garden?

MR. IKE WILLIAMS. That is right.

MR. BONOMI. At that time did you receive a $100,000 bribe offer to lose that about through Frank "Blinky" Palermo?

MR. IKE WILLIAMS. Yes; I do remember that.

MR. BONOMI. Will you state what happened on that occasion?

MR. IKE WILLIAMS. He said someone had offered him $100,000 for me to lose the fight, and he said—

MR. BONOMI. When you say "he," you mean this man "Blinky" Palermo?

MR. IKE WILLIAMS. Frank Palermo.

And he said, "You are doing all right, you don't need the money." So he said, "I wouldn't take it, if I was you."

And I didn't take it, although I thought I won the fight anyway. But they called it against me.

MR. BONOMI. Let me ask you this, Mr. Williams.

You received a $30,000 bribe offer through Frank "Blinky" Palermo in the Dawson bout; is that right.

MR. IKE WILLIAMS. That is right.

MR. BONOMI. The idea was for you to lose; is that correct?

MR. IKE WILLIAMS. That is right.

MR. BONOMI. You say that even though Mr. Palermo told you about this offer, he said, "Now, please, don't take it, Ike," or "Use your own judgment"; is that what you are saying?

MR. IKE WILLIAMS. That is what he said, Mr. Bonomi.

MR. BONOMI. You are sure that it was Mr. Palermo who told you about the $30,000 bribe offer in the Dawson bout?

MR. IKE WILLIAMS. It was Mr. Palermo.

MR. BONOMI. In the Kid Gavilan bout, are you saying that the same thing happened, you received a $100,000 bribe offer through this man Frank "Blinky" Palermo?

MR. IKE WILLIAMS. Yes; I did.

MR. BONOMI. There is no doubt about the fact that he made the offer to you; is there?

MR. IKE WILLIAMS. No, Mr. Bonomi. He did not make the offer, no, he did not make the offer.

MR. BONOMI. He told you about the offer; didn't he?

MR. IKE WILLIAMS. Yes; he told me about that.

MR. BONOMI. You say on this occasion, too, he said, "Use your own judgment"?

MR. IKE WILLIAMS. That is what he said, Mr. Bonomi. He said, "If it was me, I wouldn't take it."

He said, "You are doing all right. You don't need the money," but, of course, at the time I was behind with taxes, as we all are, and actually I am sorry I did not take it, Mr. Bonomi. I didn't, but I am sorry I didn't take it.

MR. BONOMI. You are sorry you didn't take the $100,000?

MR. IKE WILLIAMS. I am sorry I didn't take it.

MR. BONOMI. Why? You lost the fight anyway; is that it?

MR. IKE WILLIAMS. I lost the fight anyway, although I thought I won it. Most of the New York papers gave me the fight.

Dan Parker said he thought I won it, also Bill Corum. Well, most of the papers gave me the fight, but the officials, they called it against me, and that is their business, so I guess they know more about it than I do.

MR. BONOMI. Was Mr. Palermo disappointed when you rejected the bribe offer?

MR. IKE WILLIAMS. No; he didn't say anything about it. No more was mentioned of it.

MR. BONOMI. Did he seem delighted about the fact that you rejected the bribe offer?

MR. IKE WILLIAMS. Mr. Bonomi, Mr. Palermo said, I told you, he said, "You were offered $100,000," but he said, "You are doing all right."

He said, "You don't need the money that bad." He said, "If it was me, I wouldn't take it," and it was dropped right there, no more mention of it.

MR. BONOMI. By the way, there has been evidence before the subcommittee, Mr. Williams, that Kid Gavilan, your opponent in the bout, was controlled by Frankie Carbo. Do you know that as a fact at the time?

MR. IKE WILLIAMS. That is news to me, Mr. Bonomi.

MR. BONOMI. You knew Mr. Carbo at that time; did you not?

MR. IKE WILLIAMS. Yes; I knew Frank Carbo.

MR. BONOMI. Under what circumstances did you first meet Frank Carbo?

MR. IKE WILLIAMS. I first met Frank Carbo in Stillman's Gymnasium in New York.

MR. BONOMI. He was always around the places where fighters and managers congregated, even at that time?

MR. IKE WILLIAMS. I can't say always, Mr. Bonomi, I didn't see him that often.

MR. BONOMI. Did you meet Carbo through your manager, Frank "Blinky" Palermo?

MR. IKE WILLIAMS. No; I didn't.

MR. BONOMI. How did you meet him?

MR. IKE WILLIAMS. I was introduced to Frank Carbo by the late Chalky Wright, the former featherweight champion.

MR. BONOMI. Chalky Wright?

MR. IKE WILLIAMS. That is right.

MR. BONOMI. Had you ever heard that Frankie Carbo had an interest in Chalky Wright, the former featherweight champion?

MR. IKE WILLIAMS. I knew that.

MR. BONOMI. How did you know that as a fact?

MR. IKE WILLIAMS. Mr. Bonomi, being a fighter and being around the gymnasium and so forth, being at different fights, well, everyone, anyone would know that.

MR. BONOMI. Did Chalky Wright himself tell you that Frankie Carbo had "a piece" of him?

MR. IKE WILLIAMS. No, but I don't think it was any secret.

MR. BONOMI. It was an open secret, in other words?

MR. IKE WILLIAMS. An open secret? That is a new one on me, an open secret.

MR. BONOMI. An openly known secret, is that right?

MR. IKE WILLIAMS. That is one way of putting it.

MR. BONOMI. Do you recall that you lost the world's lightweight title in a bout with Jimmy Carter on May 25 of 1951?

MR. IKE WILLIAMS. Yes, I do.

MR. BONOMI. That bout was held in Madison Square Garden, New York, was it not?

MR. IKE WILLIAMS. That is right, Mr. Bonomi.

MR. BONOMI. The bout was promoted by the International Boxing Club?

MR. IKE WILLIAMS. That is right.

MR. BONOMI. By the way, the manager of Jimmy Carter at that time was Willie Ketchum?

MR. IKE WILLIAMS. That is right.

MR. BONOMI. There has been considerable testimony before ths subcommittee indicating that Mr. Ketchum was also Carbo-controlled.

MR. IKE WILLIAMS. That is news to me.

MR. BONOMI. In fact, the testimony before the subcommittee is that Mr. Ketchum was partners with Frank Carbo in the management of Jimmy Carter.

MR. IKE WILLIAMS. I read that in the papers.

MR. BONOMI. Did you receive a $50,000 bribe offer through Palermo in your championship bout with Jimmy Carter, which was promoted by the I.B.C.?

MR. IKE WILLIAMS. I did not receive a bribe offer from him, but I was told that he was approached. He told me someone approached him.

MR. BONOMI. Mr. Palermo said that somebody would put up $50,000 for you and Mr. Palermo, if you lost the bout?

MR. IKE WILLIAMS. That is right, Mr. Bonomi.

MR. BONOMI. What was the rest of the conversation you had with Mr. Palermo on that particular occasion?

MR. IKE WILLIAMS. As before, he told me, he said, "I'd pass it up. I wouldn't take it."

MR. BONOMI. So on three occasions you received substantial bribe offers, on one occasion $30,000, the next occasion $100,000 and on this occasion $50,000; is that correct?

MR. IKE WILLIAMS. That is correct, Mr. Bonomi.

MR. BONOMI. In all of those bouts the world's championship was at stake; is that right?

MR. IKE WILLIAMS. No, no, it wasn't.

MR. BONOMI. In the Dawson bout it was, was it not?

MR. IKE WILLIAMS. Yes, it was.

MR. BONOMI. The Gavilan bout, wasn't that a championship bout?

MR. IKE WILLIAMS. Gavilan outweighed me 10 or 12 pounds. I couldn't have fought him.

MR. BONOMI. That was an over-the-weight bout?

MR. IKE WILLIAMS. That is right, Mr. Bonomi.

MR. BONOMI. The third bout, however, with Jimmy Carter was a world's lightweight championship bout, is that right?

MR. IKE WILLIAMS. Yes, it was.

MR. BONOMI. In each case Mr. Palermo came to you and said that you and he could make $30,000 or $100,000 or so?

MR. IKE WILLIAMS. No, he did not say "he" or "we" can make that, no.

MR. BONOMI. He said "you" could make it, is that it?

MR. IKE WILLIAMS. He didn't use those words.

MR. BONOMI. What would he say, that he could make $30,000?

MR. IKE WILLIAMS. I'll repeat it, Mr. Bonomi, and this is verbatim what the man said.

He said, "I was offered that." He said, "I was offered that," but he said, "you are not pressed for money. You are doing all right. If it was me, I wouldn't take it." That was the end of the conversation.

MR. BONOMI. But in each case he informed you that there was money to be made, is that right?

MR. IKE WILLIAMS. That is right.

Senator DIRKSEN. Mr. Williams, were details ever discussed as to how this money was to be paid, how it was to be split up? Would it have been paid to the manager or were there any details?

MR. IKE WILLIAMS. The conversation never got that far, sir.

Senator DIRKSEN. I see.

MR. IKE WILLIAMS. It never got that far.

Senator KEFAUVER. All right, Mr. Bonomi.

MR. BONOMI. You lost the bout to Jimmy Carter, did you not?

MR. IKE WILLIAMS. Yes, I did.

MR. BONOMI. You lost your championship at that time?

MR. IKE WILLIAMS. I lost the championship.

MR. BONOMI. So that when you rejected the bribe offer of $50,000, you actually lost an awful lot of money anyway, didn't you?

MR. IKE WILLIAMS. I lost the greatest thing I ever had in my life when I lost the lightweight title, Mr. Bonomi.

MR. BONOMI. Did you feel the same way after the bout with Jimmy Carter as you felt after the Gavilan bout: That you lost the bout anyway; you should have taken the bribe?

MR. IKE WILLIAMS. No, I felt differently. I'll tell you, Mr. Bonomi, I was injured very seriously before the Carter fight, and, speaking for myself, I should have taken the money, but I didn't take it.

I should have taken it, because I said—I was due to fight, Art Aragon in Los Angeles 18 days after the Carter fight, and, speaking for myself, I said even if I beat Carter, I would not be able to beat Aragon in California. So I said actually I should take the money, you know. I should take it.

But I didn't, and I lost the fight anyway.

Senator KEFAUVER. I commend you for not taking it. Do you feel better that you didn't take it?

MR. IKE WILLIAMS. Pardon me?

Senator KEFAUVER. You feel better that you didn't take it, though, don't you?

MR. IKE WILLIAMS. I do not, Senator; believe me, I don't.

Senator KEFAUVER. You feel what?

MR. IKE WILLIAMS. I do not.

Mr. KITTRIE. Why didn't you take it?

MR. IKE WILLIAMS. Why? Because the lightweight title meant too much to me and I had a lot of people, loyal friends, that I would never let down.

They have bet their hard-earned money on me and I wouldn't doublecross them. But as things went on and things got tough, I found out how loyal they were.

Senator KEFAUVER. You mean they weren't very loyal?

MR. IKE WILLIAMS. That is right.

Mr. KITTRIE. You think you could have taken the money and it would have remained a secret or is the boxing business such a close-knit business that if you would have taken it, all the people concerned would have probably very soon found out that you took the money?

MR. IKE WILLIAMS. Not everyone would find out about it. Some would have found out about it, but not everyone. Boxing has its bad points, like there is some dishonesty in any profession on earth that you name.

Mr. KITTRIE. Palermo did not particularly make it easy for you to take the money, did he? Did he tell you, if you decide to take it, come and let me know; or if you decide to take it, call up so and so?

MR. IKE WILLIAMS. No, he didn't. When he finished the conversation, that was the end of it. It was never mentioned again, never mentioned again.

Mr. KITTRIE. But once he put it to you, "If I was you, I wouldn't have taken it," would you have felt bad to have gone back to him and said, "I still want it"?

MR. IKE WILLIAMS. I wouldn't have felt bad. Actually, I am sorry I didn't take it. I mean it is all over. My career is passé, but I am sorry I didn't take it.

22

Jackie Robinson's First Spring Training

My first year in organized baseball was probably the most crucial one in my life. It was the year I was sent to Montreal, and when it was over I was sure that I could make the grade in the Majors. I wasn't cocky, mind you, just confident; for in that year I learned a lot of things, the most important of which was that ball players—whether they came from the South or North—would accept me and play with me.

That was in 1946 and we were to train at Daytona Beach, Florida. With my wife I left Los Angeles late in February by plane. As we flew over the Western deserts, I wondered just how I would get along down in the deep South. Everyone knows that the Southern states have placed numerous restrictions upon the liberties of Negroes. It was going to be a comparatively new experience for me, and I wasn't sure what to expect.

We had a tough time getting to Daytona Beach. At one point we had to give up our seats because the Army still had priority on planes. So we took a train to Jacksonville, and when we got there we found we'd have to go the rest of the way by bus. We didn't like the bus, and we particularly didn't like the back seat when there were empty seats near the center. Florida law designates where Negroes are to ride in public conveyances. The law says: "Back seat." We rode there.

When we arrived in Daytona Beach we were met at the bus station by Wendell Smith, sports editor of *The Pittsburgh Courier,* and Billy Rowe, a photographer for the same paper. They had been there about four days and had arranged housing accommodations and other necessities. With them was Johnny Wright, a good friend of mine and a pitcher for the Homestead Grays of the Negro National League. Mr. Rickey had signed Johnny to a Montreal contract not long after he had signed me. Johnny had come up with a good record in the Negro

From Jack R. Robinson and Wendell Smith, Jackie Robinson: My Own Story *(New York: Greenberg, 1948), pp. 65-68, 70-75, 79-80. Copyright © 1976 by Chilton. Reprinted with permission.*

National League and had been a star pitcher for a Navy team in 1945.

They took us to the home of a prominent Negro family. The rest of the team usually stayed at a big hotel on the ocean front, but this particular time they were quartered at Sanford, Florida, where the Dodger organization was looking over at least two hundred players. As a result of our transportation difficulties, I was two days late. I learned from Smith and Rowe that Mr. Rickey was a bit upset about my late arrival; so we decided to get up early next morning and drive to Sanford, which is some twenty miles south of Daytona Beach.

We arrived in Sanford the next morning about ten o'clock, but instead of going to the ball park, we decided to go to the home of Mr. Brock, a well-to-do Negro citizen of the town, and call Mr. Rickey. We had to feel our way in this entire matter. We didn't want to cause a commotion or upset anything by walking into the park and surprising everyone. It was no secret that Johnny and I were going to be there, but we felt it best to remain as inconspicuous as possible.

Smith called Mr. Rickey at his hotel and he told us we should get over to the park as soon as possible. We took our shoes and gloves and hurried over. Clyde Sukeforth met us. We shook hands. "Go right into the dressing room and get your uniforms," he said. "Babe Hamburger, our clubhouse man, is in there. He'll see that you get fixed up."

I glanced at the players on the field. They had come from every section of the country-two hundred men out there, all hoping some day to become members of the Brooklyn Dodgers. Some were tossing balls to each other; others were hitting fungoes to the outfielders; still others were running around the field conditioning their legs. Suddenly I felt uncomfortably conspicuous standing there. Every single man on the field seemed to be staring at Johnny Wright and me. . .

We ducked into the clubhouse. It was empty save for one man, a big, fat fellow. I felt a bit tense and I'm sure Johnny did, too. We were ill at ease and didn't know exactly what to do next. The man saw us then and came right over and introduced himself. "Hiya, fellows," he said with a big, broad smile on his face. "I'm Babe Hamburger. . . . Robinson and Wright, eh? Well, that's swell. Which one is Robinson?"

I put out my hand and he gave it a hearty shake. "This is Johnny Wright" I said. Johnny shook Babe's big, soft mitt.

"Well fellows," he said, "I'm not exactly what you'd call a part of this great experiment, but I'm gonna give you some advice anyway. Just go out there and do your best. Don't get tense. Just be yourselves."

Be ourselves? Here in the heart of the race-conscious South? . . . Johnny and I both realized that this was hostile territory—that anything could happen any time to a Negro who thought he could play ball with white men on an equal basis. It was going to be difficult to relax and behave naturally. But we assured Babe we'd try . . . .

He was grand to us. I'll never forget that jolly disposition and winning smile.

We finally got dressed and headed for the field. Waiting for us was a group of reporters from New York, Pittsburgh, Baltimore, Montreal and Brooklyn. They surrounded us and started firing questions:

"What are you going to do if the pitchers start throwing at you?" one of them asked.

"The same thing everyone else does," I answered, smiling. "Duck!"

The next morning we were up bright and early. We went out to the park in a taxi and this time dressed with the rest of the players. Practice that day was a bit long, but not at all strenuous.

When we got back to Brock's, Johnny and I found Wendell Smith and Billy Rowe, our newspaper friends from Pittsburgh, waiting for us. Usually, they joked and kidded with us a lot; but that night they were both exceptionally quiet and sober. We all ate together. The conversation dragged until I began to feel uncomfortable. One or twice it seemed to me Smith and Rowe were exchanging significant glances, as though they had bad news they didn't want to announce in front of Johnny and me. I decided that maybe we had to put our foot in it somehow or other that they were angry at us. Why don't they say so, I thought. We're all friends, aren't we?

Rowe got up from the table suddenly and said to Smith, "I'm going to fill up with gas." He had a red Pontiac that he used to cover his assignments.

"We should be able to get out of here in fifteen or twenty minutes," Smith said. "Daytona isn't far, either."

"You guys leaving us?" I asked curiously.

"No," Smith said. "We're all going to Daytona."

Johnny and I looked at them in amazement. Were they losing their minds?

"Well." Smith said quickly, "don't just sit there. Pack your duds, fellows. We're blowin'."

"What about practice in the morning?" I asked. "After all, we came here to make the Montreal Club."

I was angry. What was this all about, anyway? No one had told us to move on to Daytona. Smith and Rowe didn't run the Brooklyn organization—nor did they run us, either. After all, things had been going beautifully. The first two days of practice had passed without a single incident. Surely we weren't being rejected after only a two-day trial! We were just beginning to loosen up a bit. The tenseness was going away. I was beginning to feel free and good inside.

As I sat there getting sorer by the minute, I heard Smith talking on the telephone: "Yes, Mr. Rickey" he said, I'm with them now. We're pulling out for Daytona in about twenty minutes. Just as soon as they get their bags packed." I heard Rowe's car pull up in the driveway. Smith continued talking on the phone. "No," he said, "everything is okay now. It's just one of those things."

Just one of those things? What in the world was he talking about? Maybe Rickey had decided he wasn't going to keep us. Maybe this was the end and we were being sent home. I was boiling over now. I went upstairs and packed my bag. Suddenly I hated everybody. I didn't care about the team or baseball or making good. All I wanted to do was get back home. I decided I would get my wife and head straight back to California. Rickey and Sukeforth had made a fool of me. "Damn 'em," I said under my breath.

We piled into the car and started for Daytona. Rowe was driving and Smith was sitting beside him. Johnny was in the back with me. None of us said a word. We stopped at the main intersection of the town for a traffic light. A group of men were standing on the street corner in their shirt sleeves. It looked like a typical small-town bull session.

I suddenly decided that Sanford wasn't a bad town at all. The people had been friendly to us. Apparently they liked ball players. The men on the corner turned to look at us. Easy-going guys, curious over where we were going — certainly not hostile, I thought. I smiled at them. I actually felt like waving.

Rowe broke the silence for the first time as the light changed and we picked up speed. "How can people like that call themselves Americans!" he said bitterly.

"They're as rotten as they come," Smith sneered.

"Now just a minute," I said. "They haven't done anything to us. They're nice people as far as I'm concerned."

"They sure are," Johnny agreed. "As far as I can tell, they liked us."

"Yeah," Smith said, swinging around and looking us in the face. His eyes were blazing with anger. "Sure, they liked you. They were in love with you . . . . That's why we're leaving."

"What do you mean?" I asked.

"I don't get it," chimed in Johnny.

"You will," Rowe said. "You will."

"Look," Smith said, "we didn't want to tell you guys because we didn't want to upset you. We want you to make this ball club. But . . . we're leaving this town because we've been told to get out. They won't stand for Negro ball players on the same field with whites!"

The expulsion from Sanford was a humiliating experience. I found myself wishing I had never gotten mixed up in the whole business. When the club moved into Daytona, our permanent training base, what hope was there that I would not be kicked out of town just as I had been in Sanford? I was sure that as soon as I walked out on the field, an objection would be raised. I didn't want to go through that all over again. What could I do? Quit? . . . I wanted to; but I just didn't have the nerve to walk out on all the people who were counting on me — my family and close friends, Mr Rickey, the fourteen million Negroes from coast to coast, the legion of understanding white people. Dejected as I was, I just had to stick it out. The rest of the team was quartered in a big hotel overlooking the Atlantic Ocean. I stayed in the home of a private family in the Negro section of the town. When we finished practice, I'd go home and play cards with Smith, Rowe, and my wife. Once in a while we'd go to a movie. There was only one Negro movie in town and the picture ran for three days. Consequently we'd see two pictures a week. Often there was absolutely nothing to do. Our life was so restricted and monotonous that sometimes we would go to see the same movie twice.

Now and then some of the local Negroes would invite us to dinner or for a game of cards. There was also a USO Club near-by and some evenings I'd go there to play table tennis or pinochle. But no matter how I tried I couldn't find a sufficient diversion to preoccupy me. I found myself stewing over the problems which I knew were bound to confront me sooner or later.

I had had no chance to know Clay Hopper, the manager of the Montreal team during my two-day stay in Sanford. When the club moved into Daytona Beach, I was anxious to find out just what kind of a guy he was. . . . Actually, I didn't want to know what kind of a guy *he* was — I wanted him to know what kind what kind of a guy *I* was.

There were about twenty-five or thirty fellows on the Montreal squad. Many of them had played on the championship team the previous year, and I knew I was going to have a difficult time breaking into the line-up. I was listed as a shortstop and had to beat out at least three other men, including a wonderful little fellow by the name of Stanley Breard.

Breard had been the first-string shortstop in 1945 and had done a fine job. Not only that, Stan was a French-Canadian, born and reared in Montreal and one of the few French-Canadians to make good in organized baseball. He was "box office" in Montreal and everyone knew it. "Breard isn't the best player on the club," I heard Hector Racine, President of the club, say two days after practice started, "but he's the most popular with the home-town fans." Futhermore, Breard had played under Hopper the previous season and the manager liked him. You could see it in the way he treated Stan. So it was pretty obvious I'd have to play spectacular ball to win the regular shortstop job.

When we started practice, Breard, naturally, was in the first-string line-up; I was on the second team. I set out to try to make a good impression on Hopper immediately. The very first day, I was racing all over the infield, trying to make "sensational" stops and throwing as hard and fast as I could. Clyde Sukeforth told me to slow down.

We were scheduled to play an exhibition game with the Jersey City Giants in Jacksonville. We made the trip by bus, and when we arrived at the park there was a big crowd waiting outside. We climbed out and went over to the players' gate leading onto the field. It was locked. We couldn't get in; nor, apparently, could the waiting fans.

"What's wrong here?" Hopper asked a man standing near-by.

"The game's been called off," the man said. "The Bureau of Recreation won't let the game be played because you've got colored guys on your club."

Mel Jones got hold of Charley Stoneham, the Jersey City business manager, and found that the man's report was correct. George Robinson, excutive secretary of the Bureau of Recreation, had informed the Jersey City club that he would not allow the game to be played. There was nothing for us to do but drive back to Daytona.

23

The Economics of "Big-Time" Intercollegiate Athletics

by James V. Koch

Organized intercollegiate athletics, long a fixture on the American scene, has developed into an economic phenomenon of considerable importance. The organization and operation of this market[1] is unique and interesting when viewed in the context of economic analysis. The task of this paper is to apply economic analysis to intercollegiate athletics and to highlight several of the most interesting features of that market such as the peculiar market for student-athlete inputs.

The contention of this writer is that the market approximates a cartelized arrangement and that considerable insight into intercollegiate athletics can be gained by taking this analytic viewpoint.

The Nature of the Market

The dominant force in intercollegiate athletics today is the National Collegiate Athletic Association. (NCAA).[2] All of the colleges and universities which operate expensive "big-time" athletic programs are members of the NCAA, and approximately 650 schools are members *in toto*. The NCAA currently conducts 27 national championship sporting events in 18 sports and engages in a host of other activities ranging from record keeping in negotiating television contracts for its members.

Until 1948, the NCAA did little except write playing rules for various sports and conduct occasional tournaments. Since that time, however, the NCAA has assumed great power and simultaneously exercises the legislative, executive and judicial functions necessary

James V. Koch is an economist who is presently Provost at Ball State University.

From James V. Koch, "The Economics of 'Big-Time' Intercollegiate Athletics," Social Science Quarterly 52 (September 1971): 248-60. Copyright © 1971 by the University of Texas Press. Reprinted with permission.

to the maintenance of an orderly, collusive intercollegiate athletic market. The structure of the NCAA and the sources of its power are specified in the Constitution of the NCAA, the Bylaws, including "Official Interpretations," the Executive Regulations, the Recommended Policies and Practices, and the Procedures Concerning Enforcement, all of which may be found in the NCAA Manual.[3] The members of the NCAA are bound by these documents and their adherence to such makes the intercollegiate athletic market openly imperfect and collusive in nature.

The effective control of the NCAA resides with the colleges and universities which maintain "big-time" athletic programs characterized by considerable scholarship aid to competing athletes, large coaching staffs, and athletic budgets which may exceed three million dollars annually. The annual conventions of the NCAA, where the rules of the intercollegiate athletic market are formulated, are dominated by the "big-time" schools, as are the committees which rule the NCAA between the annual conventions.[4] This is true despite the fact that considerably less than one-half of the total membership of the NCAA could reasonably be classified as maintaining a "big-time" athletic program. The attention of this paper is directed to the colleges and universities which maintain "big-time" programs.

The intercollegiate athletic market is appropriately viewed as being dominated by a national cartel which is frequently administered and modified on a regional or local basis. The national cartel, the NCAA, typifies the usual behavior of a cartel in that it: (1) sets input prices for student–athlete inputs; (2) regulates the duration and intensity of usage of those inputs and their subsequent mobility during their careers as collegiate athletes; (3) regulates the type and particularly the quantity of output of games; (4) seeks to pool and divide portions of the cartel's profits (for example, television receipts); (5) makes information available to cartel members, concerning transactions, market conditions, and business and accounting techniques; (6) attempts to police the behavior of the members of the cartel; and, (7) levies penalties against cartel members for infractions of the cartel's rules.[5]

Regional conferences of university-firms may modify the national cartel's rules and regulations. For example, a particular athletic conference may limit any university-firm to dispensing no more than 30 new football scholarships per year, or choose to ban spring football practice, or require home teams to share gate revenues with visiting teams.

We reserve until later a discussion of the success that has accrued to the cartel and its members as a result of their efforts and instead proceed to examine the production function of the university-firms.

The Production Function

The firm in the intercollegiate athletic market is the individual college or university (henceforth "university" for brevity). The production function of the firm is somewhat unusual in several respects. The unit of output of the firm is the competitive game between its own athletic team and that of a rival university-firm. Each unit of output (game) is differentiated in nature. The exact form and amount of this differentiation is never predictable *ex ante*, since the vagaries of the weather, the physical state of the players, and the tightness of the fight for the title of the league, etc., are not always predictable. Nevertheless, it is easily observed that the customer-fans who purchase one unit of output (for example, a Notre Dame versus Purdue football game), typically view it differently than they do another unit of the university-firm's output (for example, a Notre Dame versus Northwestern game).

It should be noted that the university-firm is a multiproduct firm. Football and basketball are essentially different products which may in fact compete with each other. Each of these outputs is capable of generating many different streams of utility which are consumed by many different individuals.

The university-firm's output exhibits a characteristic similar to that of many social goods, viz., the transference of utility to many individuals who do not purchase the output. Fans or even gamblers who follow the progress of the UCLA basketball game team by means of the public media need not purchase a ticket to attend a UCLA basketball game; nevertheless, they will still be possible recipients of one of the many different streams of utility emanating from the game. This phenomenon is hardly injurious to the actual purchaser of the ticket, however, since his own utility will not be decreased by the utility obtained by others, and may actually be increased if, for example, public enthusiasm is whipped up for the game for which he has a ticket or has attended. This interdependence of utilities illustrates yet another fact: the number of consumers of the same unit of output is virtually unlimited.

The university-firm's output and the streams of utility which emanate therefrom are strikingly similar to the circumstances of admittedly professional athletics. Indeed, there would be little reason to examine separately the intercollegiate athletic market if the emphasis were to be upon the output of that market. Penetrating analyses of professional athletics and the distinguishing features of its output have already been provided by Rottenberg, Neale, Jones and Davenport.[6] However, the distinctive and noteworthy features of the intercollegiate athletic market lie not on the output side of the market, but rather on the input side of the market and in the rules and regulations which govern the procurement and use of inputs.

The inputs in the production function include the student-athletes who compete, the stadiums, playing fields and facilities, the coaches, trainers, etc., the equipment and supplies (pep pills, steroids, and amphetamines, some would contend), and the indispensable element of competition personified by the other team. The last-mentioned input, the other team, is essential to the productive process. Without another university-firm with which to compete, there can be no meaningful output by the university in question. Indeed, a league or conference of competitors may be necessary if the university wishes to produce efficiently.[7]

It is interesting to note that when competition either is unequal or threatens to become so, the cartel steps in and attempts to lessen the imbalance. Such actions are usually taken, however, in the name of preserving the sanctity of amateurism, or in order to maintain the Panglossian relationship in which collegiate athletics are subservient to the overall academic life of the university.

Yet, such reasons for action are not convincing when one views the rules, regulations, and framework which remain to guide the body politic of the NCAA. The essential attributes of the cartel continue unaltered after each so-called "reform." Historically, the major reform movements in intercollegiate athletics (particularly those in the first and fifth decades of this century) have been preceded by or have coincided with great inequality of competition, brought about by the open exercise of various "abuses." Witness the crackdown in the late 1940's and early 1950's on the open bidding and payment for student-athletes.

It must be emphasized that the continued prosperity of the intercollegiate athletic program of a university-firm depends upon fielding winning teams. Consider the approximately 120 university-firms running "big-time" programs whose major revenues are gate receipts from attendance at home games. In the year 1969, the simple correlation between their average per game football attendance and their won-lost percentage was 40.[8] It is not surprising, therefore, that one football coach has reported that "The people you work for don't appreciate anything but winning."[9]

Since all teams cannot simultaneously have winning seasons, it is intelligent policy for the cartel either to require sharing of gate revenues among all university-firms (winners and losers alike), or to promote equality of competition. The NCAA has typically emphasized the latter approach.

The rules of the NCAA and of particular collusive groups of universities seldom specify how the universities may obtain, combine, or use the imputs in their production functions except in one case—the student-athlete input. The rules and regulations concerning permissible competition for the student-athlete inputs and the subsequent use of these inputs are voluminous and constitute the major restrictions placed upon the activities of the university-firm in the intercollegiate athletic market.

The market for student-athlete inputs may be characterized as one in which a seller (the student-athlete) with partial monopoly power due to unlimited supply and product differentiation faces potentially many buyers (universities) who are at least partial monopsonists. The university-firm can influence the price of the student-athlete input, but only up to a certain flexible maximum price. That flexible maximum price allows no payment to a student-athlete in excess of tuition, fees, room and board, books and necessary supplies, and $15 per month for laundry expenses. The maximum is indeed flexible in nature since the value of some of these items (for example, the tuition and fees allowing class attendance) will vary greatly from university to university. Lesser prices can be and are paid for the student-athlete input, particularly if the student-athlete is skilled in a so-called "minor" sport, such as tennis or gymnastics where spectator attendance does not generate great sales revenues.

Not every available Babe Ruth or Joe Namath who is walking the streets may be hired as an input, however. The university-firm must be able to predict at least a 1.60 grade point average (on a 4.00 scale) for its hireling based on experience tables provided by the NCAA. Since this predicted grade point average is based upon evidence such as previous academic performance, there is a great temptation for a coach to imitate the recent activities of a basketball coach at a major metropolitan university, namely, to enhance the previous academic performance of a prospective seven-foot center by altering his academic transcript. Needless to say, such activities are not tolerated by the cartel at large and are greeted with indignation and censure.

The university-firm also may not purchase or bid for student-athlete inputs who: (1) currently attend another university; (2) have already engaged in four seasons of athletic competition at the college level; (3) originally entered college more than five years previous;[10] (4) have ever played for pay (other than athletic teams of an academic institution).

Such rules are designed to prevent instances such as the proverbial halfback who at one time or another played in the backfield of every team in the Southern Conference. But the rules are most explicitly intended to prevent one well-heeled university-firm from raiding the ranks of another university-firm and hiring away its best student-athletes. It is interesting to note that the universities typically do not apply similar rules to the academic faculty market, nor do they seem to apply such restrictions to the coaching input in the athletic productive process. Witness the recent jumping of contract by the head football coach of one major southeastern university for the same position at another university in the same athletic conference.

The structural keystone of the market for the student-athlete inputs is the national letter of intent. Once a prospective student-athlete who otherwise qualifies for financial aid signs a letter of intent with a given university-firm he is bound to that university-firm for the space of one year and he may not sign with, not be signed by, any other university-firm. This provision effectively forecloses all other university-firms from competing for that student-athlete input. Should a student who signs a national letter of intent at State U. decide after his freshman year to transfer to Ivy U., he must sit on the sidelines without competing for one calendar year.[11] The national letter of intent is properly seen as a cartel contract which, if not fulfilled by either party to the contract, results in substantial penalties being levied by the NCAA.

National letters of intent may not be signed prior to a date late in spring of the year which is determined by the NCAA. It should be noted, however, that still another submarket exists in the overall student-athlete market which is not covered by the national letter of intent. There is no national letter of intent for student-athlete inputs transferring from senior colleges. The absence of such opens wide the floodgates for a strenuous competition in this submarket. Because of the previous mentioned quality restriction on prospective inputs which requires a predicted 1.60 grade point average, some student-athletes cannot be given financial aid for their athletic prowess at a four-year university. Hence, they and many others not in that identical circumstance enroll at a junior college.

The submarket for junior college transfers operates throughout the summer preceding the beginning of the academic year and has been known to terminate only a few seconds prior to the formal registration of a junior college transfer at the university of his choice. So competitive is this market for relatively experienced inputs that many university-firms grouped together in a collusive conference have imposed their own conference letter of intent to lessen the uncertainty and strife. The conference letter of intent is a widely used device to restrict competition for student-athlete inputs and is not limited to the market for junior college transfers.

As noted before, the formal price that may be paid for a student-athlete input is administered. Many conferences of colluding university-firms limit the number of student-athlete inputs that may be purchased during a year, both for any individual sport-product, and in an overall sense for all sport-products taken together. A Chamberlinian result emerges: barred from competing in terms of price, the university-firms instead compete primarily on a non-price basis for inputs. The coach who is a clever and skilled recruiter of student-athlete inputs will emphasize such things as the reputation of the coaching staff and the quality of the conference in which the university-firm competes, the high quality of the academic life at the university-firm, the probability of lucrative summer employment and enviable job placement after graduation. The coach may even seek to induce the prospective student-athlete to sign a national letter of intent by impressing him with the beauty of the coeds attending alma mater. (The female students who assist in athletic recruiting at the University of Florida are known as the "Gator Getters" because of their considerable success).

The ease of completing the requirements for a degree at Fudd U. may also be used to lure student-athletes. The world is full of uncertainty, however, and many a disappointed student-athlete input has departed the hall of ivy without his sheepskin. None of the starting five on a recent national championship basketball team of a southwestern university has ever received an earned degree from that institution.

The use of already hired student-athlete inputs in the production function is also regulated. Since the typical input can be used no more than four competitive seasons, but may be used over a time interval of five competitive seasons, a crafty coach may choose to withhold one or more inputs from competition in any given year. The student-athlete input continues to receive financial aid and is subject to all the usual restrictions placed upon the mobility of inputs. Although he continues to practice with the team, he does not compete in any games between the university-firm. This practice is known as "red-shirting" and can be used to toughen up the student-athlete input to give him additional experience. It may also be used by the university-firm to distribute its available student-athlete talent more propitiously over the five year interval.[12]

In general, the rules which regulate the use of the already hired student-athlete input are stacked heavily in favor of the university-firm at the expense of the student-athlete. The previously cited rule requiring transfer students to sit out one full season of competition seriously reduces the mobility of student-athletes as well as the negotiating power that they might have where fringe benefits are concerned. The university-firm is not required to grant assurance of financial aid to the student-athlete for more than one year. Further, the university-firm may wait until the July 1 preceding the academic year before it must notify any student-athlete input previously hired that it is or is not going to renew his financial aid.[13] The result has been likened to a mild form of involuntary servitude.

At going market prices for student-athlete inputs, there seems to be more than enough takers of scholarship offers, although the quality of these prospective inputs is far from uniform. Some student-athletes undoubtedly do not receive a wage equal to their marginal revenue products. The worth of O. J. Simpson to the USC football team of recent past was probably greater than the wage that the

NCAA rules allowed him to be paid. Unfortunately for "Orange Juice," the worth of his next best alternative was also visibly shrunk by the impact of an agreement between the NCAA and the professional football teams with forbids a professional team to sign a student-athlete until that student-athlete's regular college class would have graduated.

As a result, it is not unfair to speculate that a few student-athlete inputs earn positive rents inside the field of intercollegiate athletics. Their next best alternative, athletically, is usually not substantial in nature. Of course, when non-athletic alternatives are considered, then the rent probably disappears and may become negative. At any given point in time, the student-athlete must weight the capitalized worth of the training and education he is receiving against the primary cost of his education that he actually bears—the negative rent.

It is the availability of non-athletic alternatives that is the primary source of the student-athlete's negotiating power and which enables him to earn a positive rent, athletically speaking, even though he may be earning a negative rent with respects to all markets. This negotiating power is greatly reduced, however, by the considerable social pressure on prospective student-athletes to attend a university and to excel there. Many student-athletes may not seriously entertain the possibility of non-athletic, non-collegiate employment. This may be true for three reasons. First, due to the relative isolation of the inter-collegiate athletic market from other markets, the student-athlete may suffer from a lack of knowledge about his worth as an input in alternative productive processes. Second, the student-athlete may attach such great utility to his intercollegiate athletic activities that he is willing to earn the negative rent implied by the availability of more lucrative employment elsewhere. Third, the capitalized value of the training and education he is receiving may be more than enough to overcome that negative rent.

The Success and Profitability of the Cartel

The success of the cartelized arrangements, national and regional, is less than complete. Decisive evidence of a truly effective cartelized arrangement is usually the pooling and dividing of the profits of the cartel's members. The NCAA and the regional conferences have taken only minor steps in this direction. Instead, the NCAA has concentrated upon regulating the market for inputs and upon restricting output. These attempts have met with greater success.

The reasons why the NCAA and the regional conferences have been unable to perfect the cartelized arrangement are to be found primarily in the structure of the intercollegiate athletic market. The cost function of the university-firms are dissimilar and their revenue possibilities unequal. The outputs are differentiated. These factors cause a fundamental divergence of interest among cartel members and militate against continued joint action. Further, the number of university-firms is large and the transactions of the cartel, particularly on the input side, are not public knowledge. As a result, it will usually be profitable for at least one member of the cartel to violate the cartel's rules because the small risk of discovery increases the expected profits to be reaped from that violation. Whereas in the usual business cartel this often takes the form of secret price chiseling in order to increase sales, in the intercollegiate athletic market it takes the form of a violation of the cartel's rules concerning the procurement of student-athlete inputs in order to obtain the most talented of those inputs. Rumors of under the table payments and gifts to student-athlete inputs are legion, but few can match the documented case of a western university which paid a football star a weekly salary to see that the stadium was not stolen. Whatever the frequency of such episodes, it can be said that violations are a direct outgrowth of the cartelized market structure. While over 100 university-firms were penalized by the NCAA for rule violations during a recent 15 year period, most observers believe that only a small fraction of the actual violators is ever apprehended.[14]

Finally, the NCAA and the regional conferences have always upheld the principles of the " . . . amateur student-athlete . . . who engages in athletics for the physical, mental, social and educational benefits he derives therefrom, and to whom athletics is an avocation."[15] The NCAA asserts that it seeks to "develop educational leadership, physical fitness, sports participation as a recreational pursuit . . . "[16] Actions which might conceivably increase the joint profits or well-being of the cartel are not always taken if these actions might tend to tarnish the above self-images. To the extent that such statements are actually subscribed to by the NCAA and its members, deviations of the cartel from absolute profit-maximizing behavior might be explained by attributing the deviations to the maximization of utility and psychic income. Alternatively, the threats of governmental regulation, possible loss of privileged tax status, and antitrust suits may be sufficient to curb certain profit-maximizing tendencies of the cartel in favor of an outward devotion to the concepts of amateurism, physical fitness and the like.

Calculation of the accounting profits or losses earned by university-firms is hardly an exact science. Revenue figures reported by the university-firms are generally unrepresentative in that winning (losing) teams generate many side effects. It is alleged but not clearly demonstrated that alumni contributions soar when Tech caps a successful season by an appearance in the Prune Bowl. An appearance in a well-known and prestigious post-season bowl will, however, usually result in a direct payment of several hundred thousand dollars to each participating team.[17] Enrollment applications are said to climb when the university-firm's athletic teams win and community relations are undoubtedly smoother when State U. finds it possible to reward Senator Snort for his faithful legislative support by giving him a coveted 50-yard line seat.

Winning teams appear more often on the nationally televised series games sanctioned by the NCAA. In 1970, the NCAA split an estimated $12 million between university-firms and conferences whose teams appeared in televised games.[18]

In sum, the revenue figures reported to the national cartel by the individual university-firms are less than perfect. The cost figures reported to the NCAA are also deficient since debt service charges attributable to athletics and capital expenditures for buildings and stadia are not included. As a result, it is not proper to subtract reported costs from reported revenues and thereby obtain accounting profits.

There is reason to believe, however, that "big-time" collegiate athletics has not in general become the economic liability that many would have the public believe. Table 1 lists the recent revenues and costs of intercollegiate athletic programs reported to the NCAA by the universities operating a Class A ("big-time") program. Note that the ratio of revenues to costs has remained a favorable one and has not fluctuated greatly.

Why, then, do we hear the continual complaint that "big-time" intercollegiate athletics constitutes a drain upon the universities budget?[19] Several explanations have appeal. First, as previously indicated, the cost figures which the universities report to the NCAA are understated by virtue of not including some relevant expenses.

Second, the university-firm produces multiple outputs and some of these outputs do not generate sufficient revenues to cover the cost of producing those outputs. Typically, these outputs are minor sports such as gymnastics, tennis, or golf which do not attract revenues sufficient to defray the expense of maintaining a program which includes maximum allowable scholarship aid and lengthy spring warmup tours. Both the much ballyhooed devotion of the university-firms to a "rounded program" available to all students, and the prestige associated with fielding athletic teams in many sports, combine to prevent the university-firm from dropping an unprofitable sport.

Parenthetically, however, it should be made clear that major sports such as football are typically "profitable" in the sense of generating attributed revenues greater than attributed costs. Seventy-five percent of the universities maintaining an NCAA Class A athletic program reported revenues to be greater than costs for football in 1969.[20] It is of interest to note that this represents an increase of 7 per cent of the comparable 1960 figure.[21]

A third factor of some import has been the increase in the size of student bodies at many universities. Upon payment of a small activity fee, the students at most universities are entitled to a seat in the stadium or fieldhouse, with the end result that there are fewer seats available for sale to the public. Only at universities where students are charged a special fee destined for use in the intercollegiate athletic program can it be said that the growth of the student body is an unmixed blessing.

Finally, those who are impressed by the costs of maintaining a "big-time" intercollegiate athletic program frequently fail to recognize that the opportunity cost of these expenditures is not comparable to the opportunity cost of the typical expenditure by another area of a university such as a Department of Economics. Well over 90 percent of the revenues used for intercollegiate athletics are generated directly by that program so that these revenues would not be available except for the existence of the athletic program.[22] Hence, the foregone alternative of an expenditure on the intercollegiate athletic program is small when compared to an expenditure of the same magnitude by a Department of Economics.

Predicted Future Behavior

If the characterization of the intercollegiate athletic market as a loosely knit cartel is apt, and further, if the legal barriers to the cartel's

TABLE 1
The Relationship Between Average Revenues and Average Costs Per University Operating "Big-Time" Programs*

Year	Revenues (000's)	Costs (000's)	Revenue/Cost Ratio
1960	$ 672	$ 635	1.06
1961	723	685	1.06
1962	749	717	1.04
1963	804	769	1.05
1964	853	817	1.04
1965	945	887	1.07
1966	1,086	998	1.09
1967	1,176	1,094	1.07
1968	1,246	1,187	1.05
1969	1,397	1,322	1.06

*The revenues and costs are the arithmetic means of the figures reported to the NCAA. Source: An Analysis of Revenues, Expenses and Management Accounting Practices of Intercollegiate Athletic Programs (Kansas City, Missouri: National Collegiate Athletic Association, 1970).

actions remain minimal, then the cartel will probably react to its current problems in a predictable fashion. The members of the cartel currently suffer from rapidly rising expenses. Some of these expenses, such as those which derive from the hiring of student-athlete inputs, may be avoidable given certain actions by the cartel. A plausible way to reduce the expense of hiring student-athlete inputs is to impose a further restriction upon the quantity of student-athlete inputs that may be purchased by any university-firm. Alternatively, the members of the cartel could adopt as their own a version of the Ivy League model and progressively lower the permissible price that might be paid to a student-athlete input.

Either of the above solutions will inspire secret chiseling. Ultimately, therefore, one might expect the development of a draft system for inputs similar to that successfully employed by professional baseball. Such a system would give each university-firm the exclusive right to negotiate for the services of a given student-athlete input and will probably be initially constituted inside a given regional conference. One can envision, for example, the situation where (within the Big Eight Conference) only Nebraska has the right to negotiate with a given prospect. The draft system would greatly reduce recruiting costs and could lead to a uniform reduction by the cartel members in both the stated maximum price that can be paid to any student-athlete input and in the actual price that is paid for student-athlete inputs. The conference letter of intent may be viewed as a first step in this direction since it has the effect of insulating a given university-firm from competition for inputs by other university-firms in its conference.

Currently intercollegiate athletics serves as a training and proving ground for athletes who may later play for professional teams. The cartelized system maintained by the NCAA has developed into an inexpensive and riskless source of qualified inputs for professional teams. Cartels do not willingly assume the costs of other cartels without receiving compensation in some form.The NCAA has been slow to recognize the fact that professional teams have benefitted mightily from the cartelization of intercollegiate athletics although they have assumed only a very minor portion of the cost of that system. The NCAA as a monopolist may seek to impose costs upon the increasingly dependent professional teams by means of an agreement mutually acceptable to both parties. The prospects for such are not favorable.

It is more likely that in the long-run university-firms or the NCAA may sign student-athletes to long-term contracts for their services. These contracts will extend beyond the period of the student-athlete's eligibility with a given university-firm and will force the professional teams to buy the contract of that individual from the university-firm or the NCAA in order to obtain the individual's ser-

pants were girls; in 1974-75, 23.5 percent were girls; in 1976-77, 28.2 percent were girls; and in 1978-79, the most recent year for which data are available, 31.9 percent of all members of interscholastic teams were girls, approximately one out of every three participants. The proportion who are girls has quadrupled since 1970, and the number of female athletes has increased 570.5 percent. The number of male athletes increased during this period by 13.5 percent.

The dramatic growth in the number of girls in interscholastic athletics is illustrated by the increasing number of schools offering the two most widely available sports for boys and girls, basketball and outdoor track and field. Almost as many schools offered these two sports to girls as to boys in 1978-79. Basketball was available to boys in 19,647 schools in 1970-71 but available to girls in only 4,856 schools. By 1978-79 basketball was available to boys in 18,752 schools and to girls in 17,167 schools. Track was available to boys in 16,383 schools in 1970-71 and to girls in 2,992 schools; by 1978-79, 16,142 schools offered track to boys, and 13,935 schools offered it to girls.

Despite these impressive gains, large discrepancies remain in the boys' and girls' programs. Although basketball and track have become increasingly available to girls, and are now almost equally available to both boys and girls, the number of girls in interscholastic sports lags far behind the number of boys. This is largely due to the fact that girls do not participate at all in two of the five most popular sports—football and wrestling. Indeed, football with its comparatively large teams has more players nationwide than either basketball or track, even though it is offered in fewer schools. Although girls are quickly achieving parity in basketball and track, they have been offered no sport that compares with the nationwide popularity of football or wrestling.

Furthermore, large discrepancies also remain in the availability of less popular sports, which are offered to boys far more frequently than they are to girls. Some differences may be attributable to traditional sex stereotyping; for instance, 578 schools offer ice hockey to boys, but none offers it to girls. Other discrepancies, however, cannot be explained in this manner. Golf is offered to boys in over three times as many schools (9,437) as to girls (2,907). Water polo is offered to boys in 397 schools but to girls in only 28 schools. There are even differences in table tennis: 99 schools offer it to boys, but only 1 offers it to girls. Of the 29 sports available on the interscholastic level, 22 are more often available to boys than to girls.

Title IX requires recipient institutions to accommodate the interests and abilities of members of both sexes, but a comparison of the participation by girls on interscholastic teams with their participation in intramural sports suggests that the number of interscholastic teams may not be adequate at least insofar as their interests are concerned. Intramural teams are open to all interested players regardless of prior athletic training and skill, and the proportions of girls in intramural sports is far higher than in interscholastic sports. Analysis of data gathered in 1975-76 by the National Center for Education Statistics (NCES), shows that 43.9 percent of all intramural participants were girls. This is markedly higher than the percentage of interscholastic participants who were girls (28.7 percent).

Evidence that high school girls are indeed interested in competitive athletics is also available from their participation in Iowa, a State with a long history of athletic competitions for girls. Statewide girls' basketball tournaments in Iowa date back to 1920, and the Iowa Daily Press Association began selecting and publishing all-State teams as far back as 1946. Despite the fact that Iowa offers only the half-court game for girls (now abandoned by all other States except Oklahoma and Arkansas), basketball continues to be an enormously popular sport for spectators, as well as participants. Girls' softball, too, is very popular; in fact, gate receipts from girls' basketball and softball competitions generate sufficient revenue to help pay for the rest of the girls' athletic program, including seven other sports. The example of Iowa demonstrates that with the support of a dedicated athletic staff, girls will participate in interscholastic sports in large numbers.

Four-Year Colleges

Athletics are a dominant and integral feature of the Nation's 4-year, post-secondary educational institutions. Many colleges offer an extremely comprehensive sports program, and participation in college athletics is important both to the student who intends to continue in amateur athletics, including the Olympics, and to the student who plans a professional sports career following graduation. Colleges are also an important source of education, training, coaches, and facilities for future amateur and professional athletes. Colleges spend vast amounts of money on athletics; one study showed the total value of athletic facilities at the nation's college campuses to be well over $5 billion, and millions of dollars in grants-in-aid are given each year to students who participate in intercollegiate athletics.

Traditionally, the resources of college athletic departments have been directed towards men, and women's programs have enjoyed relatively limited support. Prior to the enactment of Title IX, few of the nation's intercollegiate athletic participants were women, and relatively few women participated in intramural sports programs. Since Title IX became effective, however, athletic departments have begun to recognize their responsibilities to female students, and athletic opportunities for women have been increasing.

Athletics in 4-year colleges are governed by two national organizations, one for women and one for men. The National Collegiate Athletic Association (NCAA) is the primary organization of men's athletics and represents the major athletic departments, including those with the most extensive and costly athletic programs. The NCAA establishes standardized rules for eligibility, competitions, grants-in-aid, and other aspects of athletics. In 1978, 726 colleges belonged to the NCAA.

Colleges that belong to the NCAA participate in athletic competitions in one of three divisions. Division I colleges have the most extensive and costly programs. Among them are the "big-time" sports schools with large stadiums; they may offer a maximum of 95 grants-in-aid to football athletes, 15 to basketball athletes, and 80 to athletes in other men's sports. Division III colleges, by contrast, offer no athletic grants-in-aid and have much smaller athletic programs overall. Division II colleges have programs intermediate in size and cost.

The Association for Intercollegiate Athletics for Women (AIAW) governs women's athletics. In the past, some regulations for female student athletes established by AIAW differed considerably from regulations for male athletes established by NCAA. Until recently, for instance, AIAW members institutions were not permitted to award grants-in-aid to female athletes that covered room and board, although the NCAA permitted its member institutions to award such scholarships to male athletes. Recent changes in AIAW regulations have led to the elimination of many of the differences in regulations.

Data on the numbers of men and women who participate in intercollegiate athletics are available from a 1977 survey conducted by the NCAA of its member institutions. In 1976-77, 170,384 men (72.6 percent of all athletes) and 64,375 women (27.4 percent) participated in intercollegiate sports. The number of female athletes has increased 102.1 percent since 1971-72, the time of the previous survey; moreover, the number of female athletes is four times the number 10 years ago.

The five intercollegiate sports with the largest number of participants at NCAA Institutions are football, baseball, basketball, track, and tennis. In some sports, the proportions of men and women are almost equal, but in others the proportions are far from equal. In tennis, for instance, women constitute 48.3 percent of all intercollegiate players, while men constitute 51.7 percent. In basketball, women constitute 42.5 percent of all athletes, and men are 57.5 percent. Although considerable numbers of women participate in track and softball, men in track outnumber women 4-to-1, and men playing baseball outnumber women playing softball 3-to-1. Football, the most expensive (in terms of aggregate expenditures) intercollegiate sport commonly offered by colleges, and the sport with the largest number of collegiate players nationwide, is the only major sport played solely by men. Women have no sport to compare with the nationwide popularity of football. In 1978-79 the typical college offered an average of 5.0 sports to women and 7.4 sports to men.

The number of sports offered by individual colleges varies widely. Some colleges have no sports at all for women; a few offer as many as 17 different sports to women in comparison with 22 sports to men. Generally, smaller colleges and colleges that do not offer football tend to have fewer sports for both women and men. For example, colleges with 1,000 or fewer students and without football offer an average of 2.7 sports to women and 4.0 sports to men; colleges with more than 10,000 students that have football offer an average of 6.4 sports to women and 8.9 sports to men.

The number of sports available for women has increased 100.0 percent since 1973-74, from an average of 2.5 per college to an average of 5.0 per college. Men's programs have increased very slightly (1.4 percent) during this time period, from an average of 7.3 per college to an average of 7.4 per college.

Although the number of sports offered to women has increased markedly since 1973-74, the number of sports available to men in 1978-79 was an average of 48.0 percent higher than the number of sports available to women. Differences in the number of sports for men and women were especially great at smaller colleges with football. Overall, colleges with football tended to have slightly fewer sports for women compared with the number of sports for men than did colleges without football.

Unlike the situation in high schools, the proportion of intramural participants who are women at 4-year colleges (21.8 percent) is smaller than the proportion in intercollegiate sports (27.4 percent). Nevertheless, the number of women on intramural teams has been increasing rapidly. In 1976-77, 576,648 women took part in intramural sports at NCAA institutions, compared with 2,067,107 men. The number of female participants has increased 108.8 percent since 1971-72, and the number of male participants has also increased somewhat, 23.3 percent. NCAA data show that these increases continue a trend that has been developing for a number of years; the number of women on intramural teams increased 67.3 percent between 1966-67 and 1971-72, and the number of men increased 31.6 percent in that time period.

An examination of the proportion of women on intramural teams reveals that these teams are far less sex stereotyped than intercollegiate teams. Touch football and soccer, for instance, are played by a total of 68,546 women on intramural teams, despite the fact that almost no women play either of these sports on intercollegiate teams. This relatively high level of intramural participation by women in touch football and soccer suggests that intercollegiate athletics may not be adequately serving the interests of female students and that women might enjoy competing in either of these sports on an intercollegiate basis.

Overall, these data on the status of women in college athletics show that the number of women athletes and the number of sports offered to women have increased markedly since the early 1970s. Nevertheless, the number of female athletes remains well below the number of male athletes, and women are still offered fewer sports than men at most colleges in the Nation.

Men's and Women's Intercollegiate Athletic Budgets

One important measure of the extent to which colleges treat men and women equally is the amount of money budgeted for men's and women's athletic programs. As the previous chapter demonstrated, the number of female athletes is larger than ever before, but there are considerably fewer female athletes than male athletes. Although there are many factors contributing to lower female participation rates, one factor that may limit the number of female athletes is relatively less money allocated to women's programs. Traditionally, women have received disproportionately less money for their programs then men. As recently as 1977-78, for instance, one major university was reported to have budgeted about $5 million for men's athletics but only $180,000 for women's athletics.

Information on college budgets for men and women has been collected by the Association for Intercollegiate Athletics for Women (AIAW). The typical college that belongs to AIAW has 102 female athletes (30.0 percent) and 238 male athletes (70.0 percent). The average athletic budget does not reflect these proportions, however. The typical budget in 1978-79 totaled $858,000; of this amount, 83.6 percent was for the men's program and 16.4 percent was for the women's program. On a per capita basis, the average AIAW college spent $1,382 for each female athlete and $3,013 for each male athlete, 117.9 percent more for men.

The differences are greater in colleges belonging to AIAW and to Division I of the NCAA. These colleges spend an average of 14.3 percent of their total athletic budgets on women's athletics, even though women constitute 28.9 percent of the athletes. The colleges spend an average of $2,156 on each female athlete and $5,257 on each male athlete, 143.8 percent more.

The disproportionately larger amount budgeted for men's athletics has frequently been explained by the fact that at least part of the men's program produces revenues. Gate receipts and broadcast fees from athletic competitions, particularly in mass spectator sports such as football and basketball, help defray the costs of men's sports and sometimes earn a profit. This is true especially in Division I. Data on men's athletic revenues and expenditures collected by the

National Collegiate Athletic Association (NCAA) show, however, that many men's athletic departments lose money. In 1976-77, 66 percent of all men's athletic programs failed to generate sufficient revenues to cover their expenses. In the popular—and expensive—spectator sports of football and basketball, the percentage of programs that lost money was even higher. About one-half of the colleges with Division I football lost money on that sport, and almost all Division II and III football programs lost money, as did 76 percent of basketball programs in all three divisions. Moreover, the revenues at 51 percent of NCAA colleges include mandatory admission fees collected from all students during registration. Without this source of funds, the proportion of programs that lost money would probably have been even greater.

In addition to losing money at many colleges that offer them, football and basketball are also the most expensive sports offered. The average college with Division I football spends $1,045,000 on that sport, or 47 percent of its men's athletic budget. The average Division I football squad is composed of 106 athletes: these colleges therefore spend an average of $9,858 on each football athlete. Men's Division I basketball costs an average of $245,000, or 11 percent of the typical Division I men's budget. The average Division I basketball team has 20 athletes, which is equal to an average expenditure of 231 athletes in all other sports, spend $332,000 on those sports, and thereby average $1,437 per male athlete for all sports excluding football and men's basketball.

The large amount of money budgeted for men's football and basketball is, to a great extent, attributable to the high cost of two items: grants-in-aid and travel and recruiting. These two items account for 36 percent of the Division I budget for football and men's basketball. NCAA regulations permit a maximum of 95 "full ride" grants-in-aid (tuition, room and board) for football athletes and 15 "full ride" grants-in-aid for basketball athletes. Almost all athletes in these two sports, in other words, are permitted to be on full scholarship. Recent efforts by Division I institutions to limit grants-in-aid to athletes with proven financial need have not been successful. In addition, NCAA regulations permit athletic departments to pay all recruiting expenses for prospective athletes, and football and male basketball athletes frequently receive first class travel and accommodations in intercollegiate competitions.

Although AIAW regulations also permit "full ride" grants-in-aid for female athletes, and for athletic departments to pay recruiting expenses, AIAW data show that women receive considerably less money for grants-in-aid than men. Moreover, women's travel budgets are often so restricted that women's teams are sometimes prohibited from participating in competitions beyond an arbitrary distance due to lack of funds, a restriction seldom placed on men's teams.

Despite the large differences in the money colleges typically budget for men's and women's athletic programs, the differences are not as great as they were 5 years ago. Data from AIAW show that the gap has narrowed considerably since 1973-74 (the earliest year for which data are available), although men continue to receive a disproportionately large share of the average college athletic budget. In that year, men's budgets were, on the average, more than 22 times larger than women's budgets; in 1978-79, men's budgets were five times larger. At AIAW colleges that also belong to NCAA Division I, men's budgets in 1973-74 were 44 times larger than women's budgets; 5 years later, in 1978-79, they were six times larger.

During the past 5 years, most of the decrease in the gap between men's budgets and women's budgets has occurred because of the tremendous growth in women's budgets, not because of a decline in men's budgets. At AIAW colleges, the average increase in the budget for women's athletics was over 400 percent, from an average of $26,000 in 1973-74 to $141,000 in 1978-79. At AIAW colleges that belong to NCAA Division I, the increase in women's budgets has been even greater. Budgets at these colleges are 10 times larger than they were 5 years ago, from an average of $27,000 to an average of $276,000. Men's budgets also increased during this period—by an average of more than 20 percent at all colleges belonging to AIAW and by more than 30 percent at those also belonging to NCAA Division I.

It is clear from these data that although women's budgets have increased, they continue to be considerably smaller than the men's budgets. Many men's athletic departments have expressed concern that funds to increase athletic opportunities for women would have to be taken from the men's program, adversely affecting other men's sports. The data presented in this and the previous chapters show, however, that men's budgets have increased substantially in the past 5 years and that men's programs continue to be considerably larger than women's programs.

The Current Status of Title IX Enforcement

Since 1972 the number of women and girls participating in competitive athletics in the Nation's secondary and postsecondary educational institutions has more than doubled, and budgets for women's athletic programs in the Nation's colleges are substantially larger than they were prior to enactment of Title IX. As the previous chapters have demonstrated, however, women and girls still lag far behind men and boys, and equality has not yet been achieved despite considerable progress.

Enforcement of Title IX is the responsibility of the Department of Health, Education, and Welfare (HEW). In November 1974 the Women's Equity Action League (WEAL) with several other groups filed suit in the U.S. District Court for the District of Columbia, charging the Department with failing to fulfill its responsibilities to women and girls by not enforcing Title IX. As a result of this suit, HEW was ordered by the court in December 1977 to enforce all Title IX issues according to a timetable and to close all complaints by September 1979. HEW also decided at that time to initiate its own compliance reviews rather than to rely on complaints as its sole enforcement procedure, as had been its policy in the past.

The Title IX implementing regulation, adopted on July 21, 1975, provided an adjustment period for athletic programs, and all educational institutions were to be in full compliance with Title IX by July 21, 1978. There is evidence, however, that by that date many institutions were not in compliance with all the requirements of Title IX. By November 1978, for instance, HEW had received 93 complaints alleging that 62 institutions of higher education were not providing equal opportunity for women. In an attempt to provide a policy framework within which athletic complaints against colleges could be resolved and to clarify what it meant by compliance, HEW issued a proposed policy interpretation on December 11, 1978. A year later, on December 11, 1979, HEW issued a final policy interpretation that incorporated some of the more than 700 comments it had received.

The purpose of the policy interpretation was to provide a framework for resolving complaints and to provide a definitive statement of the responsibilities under Title IX of institutions receiving Federal financial assistance. The policy interpretation applies specifically to intercollegiate athletic programs, but HEW notes that the "general principles will often apply to club, intramural, and interscholastic athletic programs, . . . "

The policy interpretation is in three parts. The first part requires recipient institutions that provide financial assistance to athletes to use a proportionate test in making athletic grants-in-aid, so that female athletes will receive financial assistance substantially in proportion to their percentage as athletes at the institution. For instance, if women constitute 30 percent of the athletes at a recipient institution, then HEW would expect that 30 percent of the financial assistance would be awarded to female athletes. HEW did not require a proportionate number of scholarships to men and women, or individual scholarships of equal dollar value, but said that it would measure compliance "by dividing the amounts of aid available for the members of each sex by the numbers of male or female participants in the athletic program. . . . "

Nondiscriminatory exceptions may make disproportionate amounts of financial aid permissible, however. For example, in some years public institutions may award more out-of-State scholarships to members of one sex, resulting in higher expenditures because of the tuition involved in out-of-State assistance. Or an institution "may make reasonable professional decisions" to postpone awarding some grants-in-aid until teams are better developed. HEW explains that institutions may need as much as a full generation of students (4 years) to develop high caliber teams, and that as a result less financial assistance than is proportionate may be granted to members of one sex during the initial years of this period of program development.

The policy interpretation sets forth four situations in which such differences may occur. First, certain sports played only by one sex (such as football) may require different facilities, equipment, and so forth, but such "sport-specific needs" should "be met equivalently" for men's and women's sports. Second, temporary circumstances not relating to sex (such as annual fluctuations in the need for new team members) may result in increased emphasis on the men's or women's programs (such as large disparities in recruitment activity), but these temporary circumstances must not "reduce the overall equality of opportunity." Third, the costs and resources devoted to event management for men's sports (especially football and basketball) are likely to be higher than for women's sports. This imbalance is allowed under Title IX, HEW says, only if the criteria used to justify expenditures (such as the size of the crowd) are truly sex-neutral, and if the potential for women's athletic events to rise in spectator appeal is not limited by the institution. Finally, affirmative efforts to increase the athletic opportunities to overcome past sex discrimination may result in a program that temporarily emphasizes athletics for one sex. Such disproportionate emphasis is allowed.

For each of the program components, the policy interpretation states specifically what is included and what is required. For example, "equipment and supplies" include "uniforms, other apparel, sport-specific equipment and supplies, general equipment and supplies, instructional devices, and conditioning and weight training equipment." The policy adds that compliance would be assessed by examining whether the following factors are equivalent for men and women:

(1) The quality of equipment and supplies;
(2) The amount of equipment and supplies;
(3) The suitability of equipment and supplies;
(4) The maintenance and replacement of equipment and supplies; and
(5) The availability of equipment and supplies.

To provide clear guidelines, the policy interpretation treats each of the components in a detailed manner. Further, it states that the overall determination of compliance will be based on whether the policies of an institution discriminate "in language or effect," or whether disparities of a "substantial and unjustified nature exist" in the program as a whole or in one component sufficient to "deny equality of athletic opportunity."

The third and final part of the policy interpretation concerns the requirement that institutions effectively accommodate the interests and abilities of members of both sexes. The policy interpretation states that in determining compliance HEW will examine the measurement of athletic interests and abilities, the selection of sports, and the level of competition available. The interests and abilities of students may be measured in any nondiscriminatory way, provided that the following factors have been considered:

a. The processes take into account the nationally increasing levels of women's interests and abilities;

b. The methods of determining interest and ability do not disadvantage the members of an underrepresented sex;

c. The methods of determining ability take into account team performance records; and

d. The methods are responsive to the expressed interests of students capable of intercollegiate competition who are members of an underrepresented sex.

HEW does not require that the same sport be offered for men and women, nor that teams be integrated. Where an institution sponsors a team in a particular sport for members of one sex, however, it may be required to permit the other sex to try out for the team or to sponsor a separate team for them. If a team is sponsored for members of one sex in a contact sport, one must also be sponsored for members of the other sex if opportunities for members of the excluded sex were limited in the past and if there is sufficient interest and ability to sustain a viable team with "reasonable expectation" that there will be opportunities for intercollegiate competition. The same rules apply to non-contact sports if, in addition, members of the excluded sex do not possess sufficient skill to be selected for a single integrated team or to compete actively on such a team. HEW does not require institutions to develop new teams or upgrade existing teams to the intercollegiate level if there is no "reasonable expectation" that there will be opportunities to compete. The interpretation notes, however, that institutions "may be required . . . to actively encourage the development of such competition . . . when overall athletic opportunities within that region have been historically limited for the members of one sex."

A recent Supreme Court ruling, *Cannon v. University of Chicago,* will probably provide added momentum for increased athletic opportunity for girls and women. In *Cannon* the court ruled that an individual has a right to sue a recipient of Federal funds for alleged violation of Title IX, and need not file a complaint with HEW (or in the future, the new Department of Education). In other words, women and girls who feel that they have not been offered equal athletic opportunity (as required by the 1975 implementing regulation and the new 1979 policy interpretation) may now sue the school or college directly. The *Cannon* case thus provides a second avenue in the pursuit of equality in athletic programs.

In addition, the Department of Justice has recently expressed its willingness to assist women and girls in Title IX athletic disputes by filing a motion to intervene in a lawsuit against the University of Alaska. The suit, *Pavey v. University of Alaska,* was filed in the U.S. District Court in Alaska on May 8, 1979 by three members of the 1978-79 basketball team who charged that the university was violating Title IX. The Department of Justice's complaint in intervention, filed November 20, 1979, charged that the university gave women disproportionately less coaching and funding, including grants-in-aid, than it gave men. The complaint also charged that women received less money for travel and publicity and had to make do with old, mismatched uniforms when men were given new uniforms. The intervention of the Department of Justice into this Title IX athletic suit indicates that this Department is concerned with sex discrimination, and its concern may provide a further incentive to voluntary compliance.

Since Title IX was enacted in 1972, women and girls have made considerable progress in participation rates and increased budget allocations, but they nevertheless have not achieved equal athletic opportunity. Increased attention to Title IX by concerned women's groups, the newly won right of individuals to sue directly over alleged Title IX violations, increased efforts of high schools and colleges to expand their women's programs, and vigorous administrative enforcement of Title IX will all help enhance women's athletic opportunities, so that the final hurdles in achieving equality may be cleared.

Suggestions for Further Reading.

Ali, Muhammed. *The Greatest: My Own Story* (N.Y.: Random House, 1975).

Axthelm, Pete. *The City Game* (N.Y.: Simon & Schuster, 1971).

Berryman, Jack. "From the Cradle to the Playing Field: America's Emphasis on Highly Organized Competitive Sports for Preadolescent Boys." *Journal of Sport History* (Fall 1975): 112-31.

Davis, Lance E. "Self Regulation in Baseball, 1909-1971." In Roger G. Noll, ed. *Government and the Sports Business* (Washington, D.C.: Brookings Institute, 1974), 349-86.

Durso, Joseph. *The All-American Dollar—The Big Business of Sports* (Boston: Houghton Mifflin Cp., 1971).

Edmonds, Anthony. *Joe Louis* (Grand Rapids: William B. Eerdmans, 1973).

Edwards, Harry. *The Revolt of the Black Athlete* (N.Y.: Free Press, 1973).

Flood, Curt. *The Way It Is* (N.Y.: Trident Press, 1970).

Gerber, Ellen W., et al. *The American Woman in Sport* (Reading, Mass.: Addison-Wesley, 1974).

Gilbert, Bill and Nancy Williamson. "Women in Sport." *Sports Illustrated* 38 (May 28, June 4, June 11, 1973), 41 (July 29, 1974).

Gottlieb, Moshe. "American Controversy Over the Olympic Games." *American Jewish Historical Quarterly* 61 (March 1972): 181-203.

Hare, Nathan. "A Study of the Black Fighter." *Black Scholar* 3 (November 1971): 2-8.

Horowitz, Ira. "Sports Broadcasting." In Roger G. Noll, ed. *Government and the Sports Business* (Washington, D.C.: Brookings Institute, 1974), 275-324.

Holway, John. *Voices From the Black Leagues* (N.Y.: Dodd, Mead, 1975.)

Honig, Donald. *Between the Lines: Baseball After World War II as Told by the Men Who Played It.* (N.Y.: Coward, McCann, and Geoghegan, 1976).

Huckle, Patricia. "Back to the Starting Line." *American Behavioral Scientist* 21 (January/Feburary 1978): 379-92.

Isaacs, Neil D. *All the Moves: A History of College Basketball.* (N.Y.: Lippincott, 1975).

Kahn, Roger, *The Boys of Summer* (N.Y.: Harper & Row, 1972).

Kennedy, Ray, and Nancy Williamson. "Money in Sports." *Sports Illustrated* 49 (July 17, 24, 31, 1978).

Koch, James V. "A Troubled Cartel: The NCAA." *Law and Contemporary Problems* 38 (Winter-Spring 1973): 135-50.

Kruger, Arnd. "'Fair Play for American Athletes': A Study in Anti-Semitism." *Canadian Journal of the History of Sport and Physical Education* 9 (May 1978) 42-57.

Lowenfish, Lee Elihu. "A Tale of Many Cities: The Westward Expansion of Major League Baseball in the 1950s." *Journal of the West* 17 (July 1978).

Meggysey, Dave. *Out of Their League* (Berkeley: Ramparts, 1970).

Olsen, Jack. *The Black Athlete: A Shameful Story* (N.Y.: Time-Life Books 1968).

Peterson, Robert. *Only the Ball Was White* (Englewood Cliffs, N.J.: Prentice-Hall, 1970).

Rosen, Charles. *Scandal of '51: How the Gamblers Almost Killed College Basketball* (N.Y.: Holt, Reinhart and Winston, 1978).

Rosentraub, Mark S., and Samuel R. Nunn. "Suburban City Investment in Professional Sport: Estimating the Fiscal Return of the Dallas Cowboys and Texas Rangers to Investing Communities." *American Behavioral Scientist* 21 (January/February 1978): 393-414.

Rottenberg, Simon. "The Baseball Players' Labor Market." *Journal of Political Economy* 64 (June 1956): 242-58.

Sack, Allen L., and Robert Thiel, "College Football and Social Mobility: A Case Study of Notre Dame Football Players." *Sociology of Education* 52 (January 1979): 60-66.

Scott, Jack. *The Athletic Revolution* (N.Y.: Free Press, 1971).

Scully, Gerald W. "Discrimination: The Case of Baseball." In Roger G. Noll, ed., *Government and the Sports Business* (Washington, D.C.: Brookings Institute, 1974) 222-73.

Shaw, Gary. *Meat on the Hoof: The Hidden World of Texas Football* (N.Y.: St. Martin's Press, 1972).

Spivey, Donald, and Thomas A. Jones. "Intercollegiate Athletic Servitude: A Case Study of the Black Illini Student-Athlete, 1931-1967." *Social Science Quarterly* 55 (March 1975): 939-47.

Wolf, David. *Foul! The Connie Hawkins Story* (N.Y.: Warner Books, 1972).